IRISH MEDICAL LAW

Irish Medical Law

David Tomkin

MPhil, PhD, Solr, of Dublin City University Business School

Patrick Hanafin

BA (UL), of Sussex University and Dublin City University Business School

THE ROUND HALL PRESS

First published in 1995 by
The Round Hall Press Ltd.
Reprinted by Round Hall Sweet & Maxwell
Brehon House, 4 Upper Ormond Quay,
Dublin 7.
Typeset in Ireland by
Gilbert Gough Typesetting, Dublin.
Printed in Ireland by Betaprint, Dublin.

© David Tomkin and Patrick Hanafin

ISBN 1-85800-041-3

A catalogue record for this book
is available from the British Library.

Round Hall Sweet & Maxwell
1995

PREFACE

This work endeavours to state the law in Ireland as it stands on 1 June 1994.

Since the initial preparation of the manuscript, the following developments have occurred:

1. The Health Insurance Act 1994 was passed on 30 June 1994. This Act allows for competition and for the regulation of the private health insurance market in accordance with the EC Third Directive on Non-Life Insurance. It requires all providers of health insurance to be registered. Providers of health insurance must comply with principles of community rating, open enrolment, and lifetime cover, subject to certain specific permitted exclusions. Such providers must also offer cover for in-patient services at a specified minimum level. The Minister for Health has powers to introduce a risk equilisation scheme, which may oblige providers to apportion risks amongst themselves. The Act empowers the Minister to set up a body called the Health Insurance Authority, which will be constituted either to supervise the sharing of risks among providers, or, otherwise, at such time as the Minister thinks appropriate in the light of market developments.

2. In *Farrell v Varian*,[1] a hand surgeon, prior to operating on a patient for Dupuytren's contracture, informed the patient that there was a significant risk of recurrence of this condition after surgery, that there was no guarantee of a full correction of the contracture, and that the main complication concerned loss of flexion of the fingers. The surgeon did not refer to the possibility of reflex systematic dystrophy which was less that 1%. The patient, who contracted sympathetic dystrophy, sued the surgeon, but O'Hanlon J held that the pre-operation warning was in the circumstances sufficient, and the surgeon consequently was held not liable.

3. In *O'Doherty v. Whelan*,[2] a general practitioner was held liable for failing to make a house call at the weekend, to a patient who was in the early stages of pregnancy, and whose husband, at least twice, spoke to the doctor

1. High Court, unreported, O'Hanlon J, 19 September 1994.
2. High Court, unreported, O'Hanlon J, 18 January 1993.

requesting a house call. The patient, who complained of nausea and vomiting, was ultimately hospitalised with a viral illness, which some two weeks later cleared up. The GP advised the husband that the patient should be brought to hospital. O'Hanlon J held that there was no general rule that a GP was obliged to make a house visit when requested; but in the instant circumstances, since the plaintiff and her husband needed reassurance, and the patient needed close monitoring, the doctor was liable. The patient was awarded £1,000 damages.

The authors would like to express their thanks to all those who assisted them in the preparation of this work. Dr Mary Redmond first suggested this project to the authors, and they are most appreciative of her scholarly interest. They acknowledge their respective debts to the DCU Research Fund, the Irish Legal Research and Educational Trust, Griffith College Dublin, Mr Diarmuid Hegarty, Dr R. Murphy, SC, and to all our colleagues and fellow-students. The authors thank all those who helped with advice and criticism and in particular, Mr Mark Cole, of Notre Dame Law School, Ms Aileen Kavanagh, Ms Derbhla Crotty, Dr James O'Neill, Dr W.D.H. Powell, Dr Derek Freedman, Professor J. Harbison, Mr Ray Murphy, BL, of UCG, Ms A. O'Connor, BL, Mr Eoin McCullogh, BL, Mr M. Cush, BL, Professor Blainpain, Professor Nys, and His Hon. Judge J.G. Buchanan. The authors gratefully acknowledge their debt to the libraries of the Incorporated Law Society (and Ms M. Byrne), Griffith College, Dublin City University, University College Dublin, the Royal College of Surgeons in Ireland, and Trinity College Dublin, to the Bodleian Library, Oxford and to the Institute for Advanced Legal Studies in London, and all of the members of staff at those institutions, who have been uniformly generous and helpful. David Tomkin would like to thank Ms Judy McCarthy and Ms A. Hegarty for advice and help, and Ms Maeve Mayberry for her assistance at every stage and at many levels of this project. The authors thank also Michael Adams and Eilis Maguire and all their colleagues at The Round Hall Press. Any errors and omissions are the responsibility of the authors alone. Each author has contributed to the entirety of the book, and none is solely responsible for part. The authors would be grateful for notification of any errors or omissions.

1 August 1994

TABLE OF CONTENTS

TABLE OF CASES

OTHER TABLES

TABLE OF UK STATUTES

TABLE OF AUSTRALIAN STATUTES

TABLE OF REGULATIONS & STATUTORY INSTRUMENTS

TABLE OF EC/EU LEGISLATION

INTRODUCTION

Medical law in Ireland[1] may be described as the application of the Constitution, legislation and case-law (and such international or supra-national laws[2] as apply in Ireland) to the creation, regulation and termination of the doctor-patient[3] relationship,[4] the regulation of the environment[5] in which this relation takes place, and all necessary incidences thereto.[6]

It embraces the regulation[7] not merely of therapeutic intervention and advice, but of health care provision generally.[8] It has both a civil and criminal dimension.

REGULATION OF THE IRISH HEALTH CARE SYSTEM

Primary legislation controls the structure of the Irish health care system. As in other parliamentary democracies overall control rests with the Government which is answerable to the legislature.[9] The Minister for Health, a

---

1 For a very brief discussion of the Irish legal system, readers with a non-law background may find Appendix A helpful.

2 This definition includes therefore aspects of public law governing the system of health care provision, such as constitutional and administrative law.

3 The existence of a therapeutic relationship is not always the critical factor, since a doctor-patient relationship may well be relevant after the death of the patient, as in the case of certification of cause of death. The importance of the doctor-patient relationship may indeed be marginal, as where the doctor is required to give an opinion pursuant to legislation about a person's mental or physical condition for the purposes of hospitalisation, or eligibility for benefit, or where the doctor is acting for an insurer and assessing the person's condition for the purposes of ascertaining risk of benefit.

4 It also includes, in the phrase 'doctor-patient' relationship, situations where medical care is provided to a patient for whom, by virtue of age or other incapacity, consent is impossible, and is obtained either from parent or guardian, or not obtained at all.

5 See Appendices B and E.

6 See Appendix C.

7 See Appendix B for a discussion of the outline in which the regulatory system operates.

8 See Appendix D.

9 Article 6, Constitution of Ireland 1937, discussed in G. Hogan and G. Whyte, *J.M. Kelly's The Irish Constitution*, 3rd ed. (Butterworth, Dublin, 1994), pp. 37-51.

member of Dáil Éireann and of the Cabinet, is accorded principal responsibility, but many of his functions must be carried out with the consent of
other ministers (principally, the Minister For Finance).[10] The Department
of Health is a division of the Civil Service, which is responsible to the
Minister, and which oversees policy and exercises ultimate control, in
conformity with specific legislative provisions.[11] However, it should be noted
that many of the detailed functions of the public health service have been
delegated to special advisory and executive bodies, which are generally under
the ultimate control of the Minister, who has power to appoint and remove
many of their directors. Some of these bodies were set up by statute, others
as companies under the Companies Acts; and many of the more recently
constituted bodies have been set up by ministerial order under the Health
(Corporate Bodies) Act 1961, which empowers the Minister to set up
corporate bodies to administer a health service.[12]

The present structure of the Irish health service has been comprehen-
sively described by Hensey.[13]

The Minister for Health has overall control over the Regional Health
Boards.

Ireland is currently divided into eight Regional Health Boards, namely:
Eastern, Midland, Mid-Western, North-Eastern, North-Western, South-
Eastern, Southern and Western. The Department of Health's strategy
document *Shaping a healthier future*, announces the Government's intention
to propose new legislation 'replac[ing] the Eastern Health Board and . . .
renam[ing]the Health Boards as health authorities'.[14] It may be that when
the changes are implemented by legislation, they will be so radical as to
make what follows redundant. However, we are fortified in continuing the
present exposition of the position by the strategy document's statement that
'it is not proposed to change the present structure'.[15]

Each of the Health Boards is managed by a Chief Executive Officer
assisted by a Finance Officer, a Personnel Officer and a Planning and
Evaluation Officer.[16]

The function of the Chief Executive Officer includes the day to day
management of the specific Health Board. This function includes the
provision and administration of the public health service and in particular
the running of the community care programme, general hospital services
and 'special' hospital services (principally covering mentally ill patients and

10 G. Hogan and G. Whyte, op. cit., p.
   265.
11 B. Hensey, *The Health Services of Ireland*, 4th ed. (IPA, Dublin, 1988; repr.
   1990), p. 137.
12 See Hensey, op. cit., p. 55.

13 See Hensey, op. cit., *passim*.
14 Department of Health, Dublin 1994,
   Pn. 0658, p. 30.
15 Ibid., p. 31.
16 See Hensey, op. cit., p. 145 and ff.

also the mentally handicapped.)[17] One of the most important functions of the Chief Executive Officer is the determination of individual cases of eligibility for health service benefits.[18]

The Community Care Division is responsible for the preventive health services, the general practitioner services and other domiciliary services, dental and public health nursing services and the community welfare programme.[19]

The Community Care Programme is administered by the programme manager in the preventive area. The Director of Community Care, whose task is to co-ordinate the services in the region, is responsible for control of infectious diseases, home nursing services, dental, ophthalmic and aural services, environmental services, maternity and infant services, school health examinations and social work services.[20]

The General Hospital Care Programme division[21] is responsible for planning of general hospital services for the population served by the Health Board. The programme manager for general hospital care has a small support staff. Each of the major hospitals has a hospital administrator; smaller hospitals may be grouped under one administrator. Health Boards may also establish executive committees for larger and more complex institutions.

The Special Hospital Programme division[22] manages psychiatric and mentally handicapped services. The psychiatric services are directed by chief psychiatrists and, in larger urban areas, clinical directors are appointed for subdivisions of the Health Board area in question.

The National Health Council[23] is the general statutory advisory body on the health services. Its function is to advise the Minister on general matters affecting or incidental to the operation of the health services. The Council is appointed by the Minister but half the members must be nominated by bodies representative of the medical and ancillary professions and of persons concerned with the management of voluntary hospitals. The Council appoints its own Chairman and regulates its own procedure but the Minister must consent to meetings in excess of the quarterly permitted meetings. The Minister is obliged to seek the Council's advice before he makes regulations under the Health Acts or the Mental Treatment Acts. This Council reports annually.

THE WELFARE MODEL IN IRELAND

The Irish health care system is described in Appendix B. It comprises a

17 Ibid., p. 146.
18 Ibid., p. 64.
19 Ibid., p. 147.
20 Ibid., p. 147-8.
21 Ibid., p. 116-29.
22 Ibid., p. 148.
23 Ibid., p. 406.

blend of public and private provision. A complex eligibility structure provides the foundation for entitlement to free and subsidised care. There are two sources of funding that are generally available: the first is eligibility under health and social welfare legislation, and the second is access to benefits under health insurance schemes. The General Medical Services (Payments) Board was established to reimburse general practitioners and pharmacists for their services to Category 1 patients.

GENERAL MEDICAL SERVICE

The objective of the GMS was to eliminate, as far as was realistic, the distinction between public and private patients. This development came about as a result of the 1970 Health Act. However, in practice, this objective was not achieved. Two-thirds of the population continued to pay privately for the services of a general practitioner. As Tormey has observed: '[p]ublic patients were often seen in a different setting and at different hours to private patients.'[24] Further changes were introduced in 1989, whereby the GP's contract was based on capitation with other benefits including illness payments, holiday locum cover, salary subsidy for practice staff and pension contributions.

In general, patients are divided into two categories of eligibility: full and limited.

Full eligibility covers those who are not able without undue hardship to arrange services for themselves and their dependents and are issued with medical cards by the Health Boards.

Limited eligibility covers those whose income is below a certain limit. They are entitled to free hospital treatment in public wards, or as out-patients. However, they are not eligible for free general practitioner services or for drugs other than under the special scheme, introduced by the Health Act 1970, whereby persons not entitled to GMS funds were assisted in meeting the cost of drugs. In some cases, the full cost of drugs is paid to those with certain long-term illnesses or conditions, such as diabetes (but, surprisingly, not asthma).

A third category existed until 1991. Persons in this category had similar benefits to those now covered by limited eligibility, but were liable for consultants' fees. This third category was abolished in 1991, under the *Programme for Economic & Social Progress*.[25] Those formerly in the third category are now covered by the limited eligibility scheme described above.

24 W.P. Tormey, 'Two-Speed Public and Private Medical Practice in the Republic of Ireland', *Administration* 40, No. 40 (Winter 1992-3), 371 at p. 374
25 Stationery Office, Dublin, 1991.

The entire population is entitled to free hospital and consultant care in the public wards of public hospitals.

At present, the financing of the general medical service is controlled by the General Medical Services (Payments) Board. This body is a corporate body, with a board of eleven members comprising one officer of each Health Board, and three other persons. The Board produces annual reports, which give information about the statistics of the operation of the scheme. The main function of the scheme is the payment of an annual capitation fee for each person registered on a doctor's panel, with other payments for out of hours panel care, emergency services, temporary resident services, EU patient services, and other special services. The system, in addition, provides a scheme of benefits for participating doctors, such as giving entitlement to sick leave, maternity leave, annual leave, contribution to superannuation funds, and other benefits associated with employment. The Board's overall structure comprehends scales of fees, medical indemnity provisions, a complaints officer and a GMS Tribunal.[26]

The operation of the payments system through the GMS has been judicially examined in *O'Connor v. Giblin & Ors.*[27] There, the facts were as follows. The plaintiff entered into an agreement with the Southern Health Board to provide services to persons eligible under s. 58 of the 1970 Act.[28] The agreement provided that the plaintiff should make available to persons for whom he was obliged to provide services 'all proper and necessary treatments of a kind usually undertaken by a general practitioner and not requiring special skills or experience of a degree or kind which general practitioners cannot reasonably be expected to possess'. The plaintiff was required to keep a record of attendances in a prescribed form, and to make the record available to officers of the Health Board and the Minister for Health. In consideration of the provision of services, the plaintiff was to receive remuneration in accordance with an approved scale of payments.

The agreement provided that where a claim for remuneration submitted by the plaintiff appeared to indicate an excessive rate of attendance by him, the circumstances should be investigated by a medical officer of the Health

---

26 *General Medical Services (Payments) Board Annual Report: 1992* (GMS (Payments) Board, Raven House, Finglas, Dublin), p. 53.

27 [1989] IR 583.

28 S. 58 of the Health Act 1970 provides that Health Boards shall make available without charge a general practitioner medical and surgical service for persons with full eligibility. By Article 5(1)(a) of the Health Services Regulations 1972, the service provided under s. 58 of the 1970 Act is made available through arrangements made by Health Boards by way of agreements with registered medical practitioners. Article 8(1)(b) of the Regulations provides for appeals to be made by practitioners to a committee apppointed by the Minister for Health.

Board. That officer could refer the matter for consideration to an investigating group consisting of three persons, which was entitled to decide that a deduction should be made in the remuneration due to the plaintiff. Such deduction could include disallowance of fees for past services. An appeal against the decision of the investigating group could be made to a committee appointed under Article 8 of the 1972 regulations.

In this case, the doctor's attendances were investigated by an officer of the Health Board and referred to an investigating group. The records of the most frequently visited patients were examined in detail, but no finding of excessive visiting was made in respect of any of these patients. The records of other patients were not examined. A statistical comparison was made with the average rate of attendance of other practitioners who provided services by agreement with the Minister, and it was found that the plaintiff's rate of attendance was much higher.

The investigating group decided to reduce the payments made. The plaintiff appealed the decision to an appeals committee. This committee, appointed under Article 8 of the Health Services Regulations of 1972, considered evidence relating to average rates of attendance of all practitioners in the area of the defendant Health Board, in the county in which the plaintiff carried on his practice, and in the town where his practice was situated. The statistical comparisons showed that the plaintiff's attendance rates were substantially in excess of each of the three average rates. The committee upheld the decision of the investigating group. The plaintiff appealed to the High Court.

The High Court held that a claim of excessive rate of attendance could be determined only by investigating the medical and other relevant circumstances of the patients on the plaintiff's patient panel. The use of such statistical samples as the Committee had taken, as the sole deciding factor was wrong. Failure to investigate whether in regard to any particular patient there had been an excessive rate of attendance, had vitiated the decision. Thus the committee had acted 'arbitrarily, unreasonably and ultra vires'.

A COMPARATIVE WELFARE MODEL: THE UK NHS

The National Health Service was created in 1948 with the aim of providing access to health care for all citizens without charge. The legislation which established the NHS, the National Health Service Act 1946, provided that the service would be under the overall control of the Government:

> It shall be the duty of the Minister of Health . . . to promote the establishment in England and Wales of a comprehensive health service

designed to secure improvement in the physical and mental health of the people of England and Wales and the prevention, diagnosis and treatment of illness, and for that purpose to provide or secure the effective provision of services in accordance with the following provisions of this Act.[29]

However, the system has not remained immune from change. In recent years, a wide ranging review of the NHS has taken place,[30] culminating in the National Health Service and Community Care Act 1990. This piece of legislation provides for a shift from the welfare model of health care provision to a more market-driven system.[31] The aim is to create an 'internal market' in health services, whereby the providers of care will compete for the provision of cost effective health care.

One of the key methods of bringing this system about is the notion of the NHS contract. The NHS contract is defined in s. 4(1) of the Act of 1990 as:

> an arrangement under which one health service body ('the acquirer') arranges for the provision to it by another health service body ('the provider') of goods or services which it reasonably requires for the purposes of its functions.

The way in which the Government envisaged these 'contracts' as operating was explained in the House of Lords by the then Parliamentary Under-Secretary of State for the Department of Health, Baroness Hooper, as follows:

> [c]ontracts are the mechanism which will give effect to districts' assessments of their residents' health care needs. I should emphasise . . . the impact of the new distinction between health care acquirers and providers. As acquirers, districts will be able to set out in more detail their service requirements. Having accepted those requirements in the terms of NHS contracts, providers of services will be held to them.[32]

---

29 National Health Service Act 1946, s. 1(1).
30 See R. Griffiths, *Report of the NHS Management Enquiry* (Department of Health and Social Security, London, 1983); R. Griffiths, *Community Care: Agenda for Action* (HMSO, London, 1988); the White Paper *Working for Patients* (HMSO, London, 1989); the White Paper, *Caring for People: Community Care in the Next Decade and Beyond* (HMSO, London, 1990).
31 For an analysis see D. Hughes and R. Dingwall, 'Sir Henry Maine, Joseph Stalin and the Reorganisation of the National Health Service', *Journal of Social Welfare Law* (1990), Vol. 5, pp. 296-309; and D. Hughes, 'Same Story: Different Words' *Health Service Journal* (1990), No. 5193, pp. 423-4.
32 *Hansard*, HL, Vol. 520, col. 1340.

Reference is made in s. 4(3) of the Act of 1990 to the legal status of such contracts:

> [w]hether or not an arrangement which constitutes an NHS contract would, apart from this section, be a contract in law, it shall not be regarded for any purpose as giving rise to contractual rights or liabilities, but if any dispute arises with respect to such an arrangement, either party may refer the matter to the Secretary of State. . . .

This does not conform to the traditional model of the contract as it is understood in English law. Where the parties to the NHS contract are unable to agree terms, they will be required to submit to a mandatory conciliation, and if this is unsuccessful, to binding arbitration. In relation to disputes over existing contracts s. 4(7) of the Act of 1990 empowers the Secretary of State for Health to vary its terms or to bring it to an end. The Secretary of State, in addition, has power to impose directions required to give effect to variation or termination of the arrangement. These directions are to be treated as if they were the result of agreement between the parties themselves. This is a departure from the traditional contract model in that while a judge in a contract case may imply terms, he does so by referring to the original intention of the parties, whereas the Secretary of State is not obliged to take the intention of the parties into account. Moreover, the traditional contractual model assumes that the parties to the contract have entered freely and voluntarily into the agreement. Under the NHS model the voluntariness of the health care bodies involved is not necessarily real, given the legislative imperative to enter such arrangements.

Another interesting legal hybrid created by the Act of 1990 is the concept of the NHS Trust. Though called a trust, this entity bears no resemblance to the trust concept as it is understood in the common law world.[33] Rather it is defined in the Act as a body corporate with a separate legal status from health authorities and from those who manage and are employed by such trusts.[34] Selected hospitals and health care providers who are seen to be cost-effective and well-managed are given the opportunity to apply for 'trust' status under the Act. On being granted 'trust' status, these bodies would be expected to compete within the internal health care market. To facilitate this the 'trusts' will have certain powers not vested in the District Health Authority or hospitals which continue to be managed by the NHS. These include the ability to acquire and dispose of assets, borrow, accumulate

---

33 See R. Keane, *Equity and The Law of Trusts in the Republic of Ireland* (Butterworth, Dublin, 1988).

34 S. 5(5).

surpluses and to decide the pay and conditions of staff. However, with such powers, also come responsibilities. The Secretary of State for Health may determine the membership of trust boards under s. 5(5) of the Act of 1990. The trusts must also comply with the Secretary of State's directions on the retention of assets and the appointment and employment of staff. It has been argued that the NHS trust is the first step on the road to a privatised medical service.[35] Indeed, the Secretary of State may dissolve a trust and transfer its assets to another body if he '. . . considers it appropriate in the interests of the health services'.[36]

It has been argued that these developments are but a step on the road to private health care on the American model.[37] It would appear from the language of the Act that health care is to become a product to be bought and sold like other commodities in the marketplace. This may result in areas of health care which are not as cost-effective as others being curtailed. Also, the less competitive health care providers may be forced out of the marketplace leading to an unequal geographical spread of health services.

PROPOSED HEALTH CARE REFORM IN IRELAND

The Department of Health's recent strategy document mentioned above – *Shaping a Healthier Future: A Strategy For Effective Health Care in the 1990s*,[38] proposes a reorientation of the existing system by reshaping the way that health services are planned and delivered, and it suggests that prevention, treatment and care services will be more clearly focussed on improving health status and the quality of life. In addition, more regional decision making, and greater sensitivity to the rights of the patient/consumer are proposed.

The strategy document contains some firm commitments. These include the implementation of the national policy on alcohol abuse, a statement of specific targets for the increase of the proportion of the population who exercise regularly, the reduction of dental diseases, the implementation of the national immunisation programme, reform of child care and adoption legislation, the expansion of residential and day places for people with physical or sensory handicap, a review of existing mental health legislation, and consideration of wider programmes of cancer testing.

35 Schedule 2, para. 6(2).
36 See Schedule 2, paras. 29-30.
37 See S. Harrison, et al., *Competing for Health: A Commentary on the HMS Review* (University of Leeds/Nuffield Institute for Health Services Research, Leeds, 1989).
38 Department of Health, Dublin, 1994, Pn. 0658.

2

MEDICAL EDUCATION AND LICENSING

When qualified, the practitioner is admitted into a professional association or body, and is thereby bound to observe certain standards of behaviour and conduct. In most cases, admission to a professional body is, practically speaking, a pre-requisite to providing professional services. These professional bodies are in the main self-regulating.

THE IDEA OF A PROFESSION

Fundamental to any discussion of the health care professions in Ireland, is the very concept or idea of a 'profession'.

According to Cotterell,* there are a number of sociological models of professions. One view sees the profession as a vocation based on universalism, disinterested service and affective neutrality. An adherent of this view is Talcott Parsons, who believed that professions hold collective values in that they look on the welfare of the client or patient as all important.[1]

A second approach views a profession as an occupational grouping that has developed certain self-perceptions and convinces outsiders to accept its self-image. This approach does not accept that professions are a distinct category of occupations. Thus Everett Hughes, a proponent of this position, states that all occupations have a licence to conduct certain activities with a view to obtaining a profit. If such a grouping has a sense of group identity, that grouping may define the terms on which they carry out this activity.[2]

A third approach sees a profession as a grouping which possesses a distinct set of traits and attributes. These would include theoretical knowledge as the basis of the particular skill; the development of specialised training and education; testing of the competence of members by formalised

---

*   See R. Cotterell, *The Sociology of Law—An Introduction*, 2nd ed. (Butterworth, London, 1992), chap. 6.
1   Talcott Parsons, 'The Professions and the Social Structure', *Social Forces* (1939), Vol. 17, pp. 458-67.
2   E.C. Hughes, *Men and Their Work* (Greenwood Press, London, 1958).

examinations; the development of a professional representative body or organization and the development of a professional code.[3]

A further approach is to be found in the writings of Eliot Friedson, who sought to define professions as being characterised by a more limited number of traits. Friedson[4] in his 1970 study of the medical profession saw the defining characteristics of a profession as autonomous control of occupational work and conditions. This autonomy was seen to be obtained through political power. Yet another approach sees professions as those occupational groupings which control the supply of specific services for their own benefit.[5] Other writers such as Maureen Cain see the concept of a profession as lacking all material grounding and such occupational groups exist only as part of the ideology justifying the privilege and practices of particular social groupings.[6]

Turner[7] has noted three systems by which the professional-client relationship has been structured. Firstly, he identifies the system of collegiate control where the professional or 'producer' defines the needs of the client or 'consumer' and the way in which these needs will be satisfied. The profession in this system controls itself through an internal or corporate system of regulation or surveillance. The second type of system which Turner notes is the patronage system where it is the client who defines his needs and determines the manner of their satisfaction.

Turner identifies two forms of patronage. Firstly, there is the oligarchic type which was exemplified by the royal court in the medieval period where artists were employed to provide services to the court. Secondly, there is corporate patronage where a particular occupation is regulated by a large enterprise which provides services internally. An example cited for this type of patronage is accountancy, which often functions as part of a larger corporate entity, for example, as the accounting service or department of a large corporation. As such the activities of such an occupational group are under the control of the corporation. A final model of the structure of the professional and client relationship is the structure of mediation. In this model, a third party, often the State, intervenes between the profession and the client to regulate professional activities. An example noted is that of

3   G. Millerson, *The Qualifying Associations* (Routledge & Kegan Paul, London, 1964); T.J. Johnson, *Professions and Power* (Macmillan, London, 1972).

4   E. Friedson, *Profession of Medicine: A Study of the Sociology of Applied Freedon* (Harper & Row, New York, 1970).

5   T.J. Johnson, *Professions and Power* (Macmillan, London, 1972).

6   M. Cain, 'The General Practice Lawyer and the Client: Towards a Radical Conception', in R. Dingwall and P. Lewis (eds.), *The Sociology of the Professions: Doctors, Lawyers and Others* (Macmillan, London, 1983).

7   B.S. Turner, *Medical Power and Social Knowledge* (Sage, London, 1987) at pp. 136-7.

social workers in a welfare state model where the function of the social worker is controlled through a system of mediation.

It is clear from this schema that the model into which the medical profession would most comfortably fit is the collegiate model.

This has two important ramifications. First, the professions to some degree control the education of 'new entrants'. Second, the professions themselves impose standards of behaviour and conduct on their members, and are, to a large degree 'self-regulating'. The Courts provide, as will be shown, a supervisory jurisdiction, which exists concomitantly with civil and criminal liability.

LICENSING: THE MEDICAL COUNCIL

The Medical Council, established under the Medical Practitioners Act 1978,[8] consists of twenty-five members, made up of five appointed by the authorities of the undergraduate medical schools, six appointed to represent medical and surgical specialities, psychiatry and general practice, ten registered medical practitioners elected by the profession and four other persons appointed by the Minister for Health (at least three of these being non-doctors representing the interests of the general public).[9] The members have a five-year term of office.

The principal functions of the Medical Council relate to the general registration of medical practitioners,[10] the maintenance of a register of medical practitioners,[11] control of standards of education and training at undergraduate and post-graduate levels,[12] determination of questions of professional misconduct or fitness to practise,[13] and the operation of EU directives relating to education and training in the practise of medicine.[14]

Though the 1978 Act provides for registration of medical practitioners[15] and medical specialists,[16] it appears as if, currently, all doctors on the register are registered as medical practitioners, and that therefore the medical specialist register is in fact not used. However, in early 1994 it was stated that the current Medical Council will make a start on a new register, which

---

8 This body now governs the medical profession in Ireland. For a review of those currently on the present Council, and for a discussion on the issues faced by the Membership of the previous Council (which has recently retired), see F. Bowers, 'Controversies Take Their Toll on Medical Council', *Irish Medical News* (1993), Vol. 10, No. 10 (15 March), p. 10.

9 Medical Practitioners Act 1978, s. 9(1).
10 Ibid., s. 26.
11 Ibid., s. 27.
12 Ibid., s. 35.
13 Ibid., s. 45.
14 Ibid., s. 36.
15 Ibid., s. 26(1).
16 Ibid., s. 30.

will include a specialist GP register, designed to ensure that only qualified and experienced doctors may practice in Ireland, and will complete the work already commenced on specialist registers.[17]

ADVISORY FUNCTIONS OF THE COUNCIL

S. 69 of the Medical Practitioners Act 1978, provides that the Council has a function to advise the Minister on all matters relating to the functions assigned to the Council. Furthermore, it is a function of the Council to give guidance to the medical profession generally on all matters relating to ethical conduct and behaviour, and to inform the public on all matters of general interest relating to the functions of the Council.

ETHICAL CONDUCT AND BEHAVIOUR

In the *Guide to Ethical Conduct and Behaviour and to Fitness to Practise*,[18] the Medical Council emphasises the 'long and honourable tradition of service and care within the Medical Profession, and the responsibility of each doctor to uphold this tradition and to maintain high standards'. In Ireland, the Medical Council does not consider it necessary to compile a catalogue of behaviour, of which non-observance would be regarded as professional negligence. Instead, the Guide articulates general principles of ethical conduct. It is 'only a means by which individual members of the profession may judge particular situations' and not a code. Although the Guide has no binding legal force, it is important to the internal regulation and setting of standards in the medical profession. It lays down what is considered to be 'ethical' in the practice of medicine in Ireland.

Furthermore, it is possible that the Code may be incorporated into law by another route, which has not yet been canvassed here. In the United Kingdom, the professional accountancy bodies have established a standard-making body, whose function is to issue standards in accounting practice. Formerly these standards were called 'Statements of Standard Accounting Practise' (SSAPs). They have been replaced by, *inter alia*, 'Financial Reporting Standards' (FRSs). Though in many cases far more detailed and technically specific than the Medical Council's Guide, the SSAPs nevertheless formed a body of professionally desirable standards for the various branches of the Accounting profession, very much as the Guide does for the Medical professions. In the case of the Accountancy profession, it was

17 'Specialist G.P. Register Now Planned for 1994' (1993), *Irish Medical News* (1993), Vol. 10, No. 27 (12 July), p. 3.
18 4th ed. (Medical Council, Dublin, 1994).

understood that it was both inappropriate, and perhaps professionally negligent, to diverge from the SSAPs unless there was a positive reason to do so. The status of SSAPs was considered by Woolf J (as he then was) in the English High Court, in *Lloyd Cheyham & Co. Ltd v. Littlejohn & Co.*[19] In particular, Woolf J questioned whether departure from the SSAPs would be tantamount to professional negligence. He said:

> [w]hile [SSAPs] are not conclusive, so that a departure from their terms necessarily involves a breach of the duty of care, and they are not as the explanatory foreword makes clear, rigid rules, they are very strong evidence as to what is the proper standard which should be adopted and unless there is some justification, a departure from this will be regarded as constituting a breach of duty.[20]

It would be open to an Irish court to make exactly the same point about the Medical Guide: that departures from it may constitute a breach of professional duty, unless justified in the circumstances of the particular case.[21]

In fairness, it should be noted that there is now a statutory obligation, in the United Kingdom, for limited companies to comply with all applicable accounting standards (including FRSs) except where non-compliance is specifically permitted.[22] At the time when Woolf J considered the status and effect of the SSAPs, the position in England was similar to that now obtaining in Ireland. Hence Woolf J's holding that departures from professional standards without good reason may constitute negligence, leaves it open to an Irish court to hold the same in respect of the principles in the Medical Council's Guide.

We stress that if some medical practice covered by the Guide were to be considered by a court in Ireland, that court might consider the Guide as no more than one factor that must be taken into consideration.[23]

19 [1987] BCLC 303.

20 Ibid. at 313.

21 *Dunne (Infant) v. National Maternity Hospital* [1989] IR 91.

22 S. 256 of the Companies Act 1985 as inserted by s. 19 of the Companies Act 1989.

23 There is another reason why the Medical Council's Guide may be important in the context of professional negligence actions. Where a plaintiff suffers damage as a result of a course of action taken by a doctor, and the gravamen of his claim is that the doctor departed with-

out reasonable grounds from the principles in the Guide, it might be open to him to argue that although the Guide is not part of the contract between patient and doctor, the plaintiff nevertheless has a 'legitimate expectation' that the doctor will follow the principles adhered to in the Guide. For a full review of the Irish cases on this topic, see R. Byrne and W. Binchy, *Annual Review of Irish Law* (The Round Hall Press, Dublin) (1988 volume at pp. 20-30, 1989 volume at pp. 9-12).

The Guide is updated from time to time. Some aspects of the most recent version of the Guide are discussed by G. Waters.[24]

The Guide contains an outline of the principles concerning the so-called continuity of care, the duty of confidentiality and the responsibility of the doctor to patients, colleagues and the community. It contains very broad outlines on reproductive medicine, human research, donor organ procurement, testing for HIV infection and a general statement on the legality of active euthanasia. It also deals with matters of etiquette and business practice; thus, for example, it contains a recommendation effectively precluding the practice of medicine through limited companies rather than by sole practitioners or practitioners in partnership.[25]

In the Guide, the Medical Council fully supports the document entitled 'Principles of Medical Ethics in Europe', which was prepared by the Conférence Internationale des Ordres et des Organismes d'Attributions Similaires, Paris.

REGISTRATION

One of the most important duties of the Council is to keep the General Register of Medical Practitioners and Medical Specialists.[26]

The Council's responsibility to maintain register(s) of properly qualified medical practitioners who are bound to the traditional standards of ethical conduct and behaviour is of course in the public interest. Registration is either of the two Medical Registers is important, since only those of the current register(s) are permitted by law to fulfil certain functions, such as the giving of medical certificates,[27] the recovery of fees for medical or surgical advice or attendance,[28] and the prescription of drugs.[29] It is a criminal offence to make either a false declaration or a misrepresentation, in order to be registered in either Medical Register,[30] and it is also a criminal offence to

---

24 G. Waters, 'A Threatening and Intimidatory Code', *Irish Medical Times* (1994), Vol. 28, No. 5 (4 February), p. 13.

25 See section D, 'The Council does not approve of doctor's forming companies which engage in the practice of medicine'. Although in general terms this sort of restriction is common to the professions of solicitor, barrister and accountant in Ireland, it is nevertheless common practice for solicitors and accountants to adopt tax-efficient structures for pratices whereby, for example, assets of the practice are owned by limited companies, even though the professional services are provided by the practitioner or staff. There is some discussion of this in A. McLoughlin, *Irish Medical Times* (1993), Vol. 27, No. 35 (27 August), p. 11.

26 'Specialist G.P. Register Now planned for 1994', *Irish Medical News* (1993), Vol. 10, No. 27 (12 July), p. 3.

27 Medical Practitioners Act 1978, s. 59.

28 Ibid., s. 60.

29 See Chapter 12, pp. 227-9.

30 Medical Practitioners Act 1978, s. 61(1)(a).

falsely represent oneself as a registered medical practitioner.[31] It would thus appear that there is nothing to prevent an unregistered person from diagnosis or from certain kinds of tratement, other than dentistry[32] or midwifery.[33]

The General Register of Medical Practitioners is published by the Council at intervals of not more than five years, with annual supplements in the intervening years.[34] It gives the address and qualifications of each doctor with the date of registration, indicating whether this is Full, Provisional or Temporary. Official Certificates of Registration are issued. This certificate must be displayed at the place where the practitioner conducts the practice of medicine at all times during which the registration continues and at no other time.[35]

Any person who is a national of a Member State of the European Union and has been awarded a qualification in medicine by a competent body or authority designated for that purpose by a Member State is entitled to be registered in the register.[36] Any person who satisfies the Council that he has undergone such courses of training and passed such examinations as are specified for the purposes of the Act may also be registered.[37] A person who has been awarded a primary qualification[38] is entitled to be provisionally registered[39] and then, after completing a year's hospital service in a residential medical capacity in one or more approved hospitals to become fully registered.[40]

S. 28 of the Medical Practitioners Act 1978 provides that a person qualified in medicine in a non-EU country is given temporary registration if the person intends to be in the State temporarily for the purpose of employment in the practice of medicine and such person holds sufficient qualification and experience. Temporary registration is limited to whatever period the council fixes in each case and lapses in any event when the foreign graduate is no longer employed in the hospital. The aggregate of periods of temporary registration which the Council is empowered to grant for any individual may not exceed five years. This section facilitates doctors from

31 Ibid., s. 61(1)(b).
32 S. 51 of the Dentists Act 1985 prohibits the practice of dentistry by person other than registered dentists, registered medical practitioners and certain supervised students and auxillary dental workers.
33 S. 58 of the Nurses Act 1985 prohibits any person attending a woman in childbirth, except a midwife, a registered medical practitioner, certain trainee professionals, and, exceptionally 'unless such attention is given, otherwise than

for regard, in any case of sudden or urgent necessity where neither a midwife nor a registered medical practitioner is immediately available'.
34 Medical Practitioners Act 1978, s. 61(1)(a).
35 Ibid., s. 26(4).
36 Ibid., s. 31(1)(c); ibid., s. 27(2)(c).
37 Ibid., s. 27(2)(b).
38 Schedule IV of ibid.
39 Ibid., s. 37(1)(g).
40 Ibid., s. 28.

a number of foreign states, who, after qualification, are employed in Irish hospitals to gain experience. Under s. 27(2)(d) of the Medical Practitioners Act, any person (including non-EU nationals) may be given full registration in Ireland if the Medical Council is satisfied as to the standard of his qualifications.

The above must now be considered in the light of current EU Law. Council Directive 93/16/EEC of 5 April 1993 provides for the free movement of doctors and the mutual recognition of their diplomas, certificates and other evidence of formal qualifications. This Directive consolidates previous legislation in this area, namely Council Directives 75/362/EEC of 16 June 1975 concerning the mutual recognition of diplomas, certificates and other evidence of formal qualifications in medicine, 75/363/EEC of 16 June 1975, concerning the co-ordination of provisions laid down by law, regulation or administrative action in respect of activities of doctors, and 86/457/EEC of 15 September 1986, on specific training in general medical practice.

Any registered medical practitioner may apply to the Council to have his name removed from any register maintained by the Council in which his name is registered provided no disciplinary or legal proceedings are pending.

It is an offence for any person falsely to represent himself or herself to be a registered medical practitioner, or to make any false representation for the purpose of obtaining registration.

Refusal to register a person who is entitled to be registered will give rise to compensation. This can be seen from the High Court decision in *Phillips v. Medical Council*,[41] where Costello J awarded £IR41,500 and costs to a plaintiff who successfully claimed that the Medical Council should have heard and determined his application for full registration under 1980 rules, rather than under rules made in 1989, under which he could not be registered.

The *Phillips* decision should be compared with *Bakht v. Medical Council*.[42] This case considers the rule-making functions of the Medical Council provided by s. 27(2)(d) of the Medical Practitioners Act 1978. It also discusses the powers of the Medical Council to register doctors, and the rules by which this is done.

The applicant was a doctor who qualified in 1973 in Bangladesh. He came to Ireland in 1977. He applied for and received a certificate of temporary registration from the Medical Registration Council, the prede-

---

41 See *Phillips v. Medical Council* [1991] 2 IR 115 discussed in 'Medical Council Forced to Compensate Doctor', *Irish Medical News* (1990), Vol. 25, No. 50 (14 December), p. 12.

42 [1990] 1 IR 515.

cessor to the current Medical Council. Further certificates of temporary registration were granted to him under s. 29 of the 1978 Act, between 1978 and 1984. During his period of work in Irish hospitals, he obtained further postgraduate qualifications. He became an Irish citizen in 1984. On 7 February 1984, he had written to the Medical Council applying for unlimited temporary registration. The registrar to the Council replied that the applicant's medical qualification did not entitle him to apply for full registration. From March 1984 the applicant worked in Saudi Arabia, and he returned in June 1987 to Ireland, whereupon he renewed his application to the Registrar of the medial council, stating that he was prepared to undergo or sit any examination required by the Council to satisfy itself that he was an appropriate person to be registered under s. 27.

The registrar informed the applicant's solicitor in September, October and November 1987 that his application was 'under active consideration'. Following notification, the applicant was unable to practice medicine in Ireland from 29 January 1988. The Council established a committee to draft rules for s. 27(2)(d) of the Act in October 1987. Certain draft rules were received by the Council and on 29 January 1988, the registrar wrote to the applicant's solicitors stating that the adopted rules would be sent to them 'early in February'. However, further amendments were directed by senior counsel and eventually, at the quarterly meeting of the Council in 1 June 1988, it was declared that the rule-making powers of s. 27(2)(d) were discretionary, and there was no obligation on it to make such rules. On 27 June 1988, the applicant on the High Court obtained leave to apply by way of judicial review for orders of mandamus directing the council to register him under s. 27(2)(d), and directing it to make and issue rules pursuant to the subsection.

A further subcommittee of the Council proceeded to make rules in September 1988, which were adopted by the Council on 20 March 1989, and came into force in October 1989.

At the hearing for the application for judicial review, Gannon CJ made orders declaring that the Council was in default in failing to inform the applicant of its requirements for registration and that he had thereby been prejudiced; that it should take up its application for registration without regard to the rules which it then proposed to bring into force; and that damages for loss sustained by him should be assessed by the Master of the High Court.

On appeal, the Supreme Court held that the rule-making functions of the Council provided by s. 27(2)(d) of the Medical Practitioners Act 1978 were mandatory and not discretionary. The Council, it held, had no power to register any doctor unless and until such rules specifying the requisite criteria were in place. The rules required by the subsection ought to be rules of general application and that the Council therefore had no power to consider the immediate application on an individual application in the absence of such rules as if it were an application for temporary registration under s. 29. In addition, the court held that the Council was entitled to a reasonable amount of time in order to frame rules of general application and that in the circumstances one year constituted a reasonable time.

PROFESSIONAL MISCONDUCT

The Medical Council is empowered through its Fitness to Practise Committee, to enquire into the conduct of a registered medical practitioner on the grounds of alleged professional misconduct or alleged unfitness to practise by reason of physical or mental disability.

Professional misconduct is defined by the Medical Council in the Guide as 'conduct which doctors of experience, competence and good repute consider disgraceful or dishonourable.'[43] The Council also states with specificity some types of behaviour which amount to professional misconduct, including: failure to accept the risk of treating patients with communicable diseases (para. 13.01), any sexual advance to a patient with whom there exists a professional relationship (para. 16.01), self-advertisement or publicity to enhance or promote reputation for the purpose of attracting patients (para. 19.01), failing to keep informed on developments which might bear on various aspects of patient care or failing to counsel and treat patients with understanding while simultaneously obeying the laws of the State, and being guided by the doctor's informed conscience (para. 39.02), failure to endeavour to maintain and preserve human life in situations where the life and/or health of a mother and/or the unborn are endangered (para. 39.03), withholding beneficial treatment of a pregnant woman by reason of her pregnancy (para. 39.04), and performing euthanasia, that is, deliberately causing the death of a patient (para. 43.01).

Of assistance in addressing the question 'what constitutes unprofessional conduct in Ireland?' is the decision of Kenny J in *In re Richard Lynch & Malachy Daly*.[44] The Department of Agriculture introduced a scheme for brucellosis eradication. Under this scheme, the department paid veterinary surgeons for vaccinations performed on heifers under six months old. The scheme did not cover payments on animals over that age, nor second vaccinations. The petitioner Daly employed Lynch as his assistant. Both Mr Lynch and Mr Daly did considerable numbers of these vaccinations. There was considerable paperwork to be done to support claims for payment. The

43 Para. 12.07, 4th ed. (Medical Council, Dublin, 1994).
44 [1970] IR 1.

petitioners did not deal correctly with this work, and as a result, claims for payment were made which could not be sustained. As a result, the Minister reported the petitioners to the Veterinary Council.

The then legislation was contained in s. 36 of the Veterinary Surgeons Act 1931 (as amended). It provided for a system of inquiry into alleged professional misconduct, and for disciplinary sanctions against 'a person guilty of conduct disgraceful to him in a professional respect'. The procedures were instigated and the petitioners here found guilty by the Veterinary Council. The petitioners appealed both on grounds of the procedures under which the inquiries into their alleged misconduct were held, and also on whether or not their conduct was 'disgraceful to [them]'. Kenny J, in the High Court, considered the meaning of the phrase 'a person guilty of conduct disgraceful to him in a professional respect'. He held that the words 'to him' emphasised the feature that the conduct must be of a kind which brings disgrace upon the person primarily in the eyes of the members of his profession but also in the eyes of the public.[45] He held that 'disgraceful' implies an element of conscious wrongdoing or the doing of something which a professional person by reason of his training must have realised would cause him to incur shame in the eyes of his professional colleagues.[46] Kenny J also pointed out that the conduct must relate to something which he does when carrying on his profession and in the course of the performance of the duties which it imposes.[47]

That the conduct must relate to conduct connected with professional activity is supported by the decisions in *Allinson v. General Council of Medical Education & Registration*,[48] and *Felix v. General Dental Council*,[49] both cases which suggest that there is a distinction between [disgraceful] conduct generally, and behaviour of such a type in the context of professional activity.

Kenny J pointed out that in *Felix v. General Dental Council*, the Privy Council held that some carelessness or inadvertence in dental record keeping was not necessarily 'infamous or disgraceful conduct'; and '[t]o make such a charge good there must, in their Lordships' opinion, (generally speaking) be some element of moral turpitude, or fraud or dishonesty in the conduct complained of, or such persistent and reckless disregard of the dentist's duty in regard to records as can be said to amount to dishonesty for this purpose. The question is to some extent one of degree'.[50]

Kenny J held that there was no element of moral turpitude or fraud or dishonesty in the acts charged against the petitioners. There was carelessness, delay, arrears, hurried attempts at completion, but not disgraceful conduct.

---

45 [1970] IR 1 at p. 11.
46 [1970] IR 1 at p. 11.
47 [1970] IR 1 at p. 11-12.

48 [1894] 1 QB 750 (CA).
49 [1960] AC 704 (PC).
50 [1970] IR 1 at p. 18.

Accordingly, Kenny J cancelled the two decisions of the Veterinary Council.

This case therefore is a useful guide to what constitutes disgraceful conduct in the context of professional activity. It is submitted that it may be applied in the context of medical professional misconduct, *mutatis mutandis*.

It stresses the difference between professional misconduct, and other sorts of misconduct, and suggests that the course of conduct adopted must be either unprincipled, or an extreme of carelessness or inadvertence amounting to persistent and reckless disregard of the professional person's duty.

It could be argued that where a doctor adopts a course of action from a principled position, that, under this case, he should not be held guilty of disgraceful professional conduct. However, it should be pointed out that 'professional misconduct' may well be judicially construed differently from 'disgraceful professional conduct'; and though the point appears not to have been decided directly in Ireland, 'professional misconduct' might be easier to prove, than 'disgraceful professional conduct', since the former might be taken to include a principled (but unjustified) departure from an accepted standard of professional behaviour.

In describing the English definition of professional misconduct, Kennedy & Grubb[51] list the types of conduct enumerated by the GMC's 'Blue Book' (Part II), including, but not limited to:[52]

(i) [n]eglect or disregard of personal responsibilities to patients for their care and treatment. (Including serious medical negligence and improper delegation of duties).

(ii) Abuse of professional privileges or skills. (Including unlawfully prescribing controlled drugs, issuing of medical certificates, and performing abortions; also including breaches of confidentiality, the exercise of undue influence on patients and sexual relationships with patients).

(iii) Personal behaviour which is derogatory to the reputation of the medical profession. (Including personal misuse or abuse of alcohol or drugs; dishonest, indecent or violent behaviour).

51 I. Kennedy & A. Grubb, *Medical Law: Text with Materials*, 2nd ed. (Butterworth, London, 1994).
52 Para. 65 of 'The Blue Book' states: '[i]t must be emphasised that the categories of misconduct described . . . cannot be regarded as exhaustive. Any abuse by doctors of any of the privileges and the opportunities afforded to them, or any grave dereliction of professional duty or serious breach of medical ethics, may give rise to a charge of serious professional misconduct' (quoted in Kennedy & Grubb, p. 580).

(iv) Self-promotion advertising and canvassing.[53]

In England, in his decision in *Doughty v. General Dental Council*[54] Lord MacKay proposes a two-part test to determine whether something is professional misconduct:

1. Did the doctor's conduct fall short, by act or omission, of the standard of conduct expected among doctors? If yes, then:

2. Was this falling short 'serious'?[55]

In *Doughty*, Lord Mackay refused to disturb the decision of the Professional Conduct Committee of the General Dental Council that the following constituted serious professional misconduct. Failing to retain radiographs of patients for a reasonable period of time, failing to submit the radiographs to the Dental Estimates Board when required to do so; failing to exercise a proper degree of skill and attention to a second group of patients; and failing to satisfactorily complete the treatment required by a third group of patients.[56]

The authors suggest that the English approach from these cases is is different to that of Kenny J's in *In re Lynch & Daly's Petition*.

The difference is less marked in the English decision of *McEniff v. General Dental Council*.[57] There the decision to remove a dentist's name from the register was upheld, after it was proven that the dentist had allowed unqualified members of the staff to fill the teeth of the patients after he had drilled them. The argument of the defendant-dentist was that while his conduct was negligent, it was not disgraceful or infamous. Lord Edmund Davies refused to make such a distinction, and allowed the decision of the General Dental Council to stand. It is unlikely that a judge following the approach of Kenny J would disagree with Lord Edmund Davies about such conduct.

In *O'Donoghue v. Veterinary Council*,[58] a veterinary surgeon appealed a decision by the Council that he had been guilty of professional misconduct when he allegedly duplicated blood tests for brucellosis, which he was performing for the Minister for Agriculture. While the decision of the

---

53 I. Kennedy & A. Grubb, Medical Law: Text with Materials, 2nd ed. (Butterworth, London 1994), pp. 579-80.
54 [1988] AC 164; [1987] 3 All ER 843 (PC) in Kennedy & Grubb, op. cit., p. 575-7.
55 Kennedy & Grubb, op. cit., p. 577.
56 Kennedy & Grubb, op. cit., p. 575.
57 [1980] 1 All ER 461; [1980] 1 WLR 328 (PC), in Kennedy & Grubb, p. 577-8.
58 [1975] IR 398.

council was cancelled by the High Court because a member of the council allowed his name to be used as a complainant at the original inquiry,[59] perhaps it can be inferred from the Kenny J judgment in *In re Lynch & Daly* that even if the procedure had gone smoothly, the alleged duplication might not have amounted to disgraceful professional misconduct.

In the context of criminal acts, such as alleged misappropriation of funds, the recent case of *McAllister v. General Medical Council*,[60] provides useful guidance as to the extent to which an analogy may be presumed between professional conduct committees and criminal trials. There the House of Lords provided some interesting observations on the rules of evidence applicable in medical disciplinary proceedings. They observed that where the events leading to the charges could also result in serious criminal charges, it may be appropriate to apply the criminal standard of proof. In cases of a less serious nature, the House believed that it would be undesirable to impose upon the disciplinary committee the restrictions applicable to jury trials. Rather, the primary consideration in all cases is that the conduct of the proceedings be fair to the doctor subject to the charge.

PROFESSIONAL MISCONDUCT: PROCEDURE

Since professional misconduct is defined in terms of the accepted and approved practice within the Medical Profession, the Guide is an important formulation of this practice which is necessary in order to ascertain not only the ethical but the legal obligations of doctors. The Council considers that the circumstances of any individual case may be so complex and varied that the question of a doctor's fitness to practise must be considered on the merits of the case. Traditionally, in Ireland, cases of alleged professional misconduct are examined by the peers of the practitioner concerned, with due regard to his or her constitutional rights.

Under s. 45 of the Medical Practitioners Act 1978, either the Medical Council or any person may seek from the Fitness to Practise Committee an enquiry into the conduct of a registered medical practitioner on the grounds of his alleged professional misconduct. On receiving such an application, the Committee may decide that there is not a *prima facie* case and so report to the Council. In that event, the Council may not continue with its investigation, or, alternatively, may direct the holding of an enquiry. If the Committee decides that there is a prima facie case or if they have been so

---

59 See G. Hogan & D. Morgan, *Administrative Law*, (Sweet and Maxwell, London, 1986), p. 253-4.
60 [1993] 1 All ER 982 and see P. Fennell's discussion in *The All England Reports Annual Review 1993* (Butterworth, London, 1994), pp. 216, 307.

directed by the Council, they then proceed to hold an enquiry after giving due notice to the medical practitioner in question.

In conducting the enquiry, the Committee has the same privileges as those vested in the High Court in respect of the enforcement of the attendance of witnesses and the compelling of production of documents, and witnesses appearing before them have the same immunities and privileges as witnesses before the High Court.[61]

On completion of the enquiry, the Committee reports to the Council. The Council then considers the report. If the Committee in its report has concluded that the medical practitioner in question is guilty of misconduct, the Council may then choose between a number of alternative courses of action. It may decide either that the name of the practitioner be erased from the register, that during a specified period 'the registration of the practitioner's name in the register shall have no effect' (s. 46), or to attach such conditions as it thinks fit to the retention in any register of a person whose name is entered there (s. 47). In addition to, or in substitution for, any other powers, the Council may 'advise, admonish or censure the practitioner in relation to his professional conduct' (s. 47).

If the Council decides to erase the practitioner's name or suspend it from the register under s. 46, or if it decides under s. 47 to attach conditions to the retention of the practitioner's name in the register, the practitioner has the right to apply within twenty-one days from the date of the decision to the High Court for cancellation of the decision. Upon the hearing of such application, the High Court, in the case of a decision by the Council under s. 46, may make one of three orders:

(i) cancelling the decision;

(ii) confirming it, and directing the erasure of the name from the register, or,

(iii) confirming the decision and suspending the registration of the practitioner.

---

61 The constitutionality of this provision has been questioned. It is thought that legislative attempts to invest quasi-judicial bodies with powers equivalent to contempt of court are unconstitutional and ineffective. In *In re Haughey* [1971] IR 217 the Supreme Court held unconstitutional a provision which enabled a Dáil Committee to certify that a person who had refused to give information to the Committee and purported to empower the High Court, on foot of the certificate, to punish the person 'as if he had been guilty of contempt of court'. A fuller discussion of this point in the context of the powers of inspectors appointed under the Companies Act 1963 (as amended) may be found in R. Keane, *Company Law in Ireland* (Butterworth, Dublin, 1991), pp. 406-7. The general issue is fully considered in J. Casey, *Constitutional Law in Ireland* (Sweet & Maxwell, London, 1992), pp. 211-15.

In the case of a decision made by the Council under s. 47, the High Court may either:

(i) cancel the decision;

(ii) attach the same conditions as those imposed by the Council to the retention of the registration, or,

(iii) attach to the retention of the name in the register any other conditions it may see fit.

In the event of a decision made under ss. 46 and 47, and if the medical practitioner does not apply for cancellation within twenty-one days of the decision, the Council may apply *ex parte* to the High Court for confirmation of the decision and the High Court shall, unless it sees good reason to the contrary, confirm the decision.

A problem arises under Irish law with disciplinary tribunals. Health professionals and others whose ability to practice their profession is dependent on their being on a professional register, are particularly vulnerable if they are removed or suspended. Even where legislation provides for a disciplinary tribunal whose powers may involve the consequent erasure or suspension of a health professional from a register, it is now doubtful whether in all but uncontested cases, such erasure or suspension is effective. The reason lies in *CK v. An Bord Altrainis*.[62] There professional misconduct was alleged against the applicant, and an inquiry was convened by the Fitness to Practice Committee, constituted under s. 38 of the Nurses Act 1985. At the inquiry, the thrust of the applicant's defence was that the allegations were untrue and motivated by ill-will. However, acting on the report of the Fitness to Practise Committee An Bord Altrainis decided that the allegations had been made out in part, and that the applicant's name should be erased from the register. Subsequently, the applicant appealed this finding to the High Court pursuant to s. 30(3) of the 1985 Act.

In the High Court, an order was refused. It was held by Costello J that the applicant did not have a right of re-hearing in the High Court. This was based on Costello J's view that, the role of the court was a *supervisory* one to 'ensure that the decision had been taken in accordance with fair and proper procedures'. He added that the court should neither hear fresh evidence, nor re-hear evidence in the inquiry. In addition, it was held that the procedures set out in the 1985 Act had been operated in a fair, reasonable and constitutional way, and the applicant had been afforded the right to representation and to make submissions to the Board.

This decision was appealed to the Supreme Court, which allowed the

62 [1990] 2 IR 396.

appeal and made the orders sought by the applicant. This was to the effect that the contested issues of fact be tried on oral evidence before the High Court.

The Supreme Court held that the essence of the statutory procedure was that it was in the High Court that the effective decision relating to an erasure or suspension of the operation of registration was to be made. To allow the decision to be made by a body not a court established by the Constitution would be impermissible.

The Supreme Court further held that in order to fulfil this role, any essential decisions in a particular case must be made by the High Court. In a case such as the one before the court, where the decision depended on the truth or falsity of evidence as to conduct and not on any question of standards rules or principles of professional conduct, it was essential that the High Court must reach its own conclusions as to the truth or falsity of the allegations.

SAFEGUARDS FOR THE PRACTITIONER

The Council does not proceed directly to erasure or suspension. The practitioner must be informed of the Council's decision[63] and may apply to the High Court within twenty-one days for its cancellation.[64] There are procedures set out to ensure that there will be no undue delay in such an application.[65] Alternatively, if no application has been made to the High Court by the practitioner the Council may itself apply for confirmation of the decision.[66] The court may cancel the decision or confirm it. If it is confirmed, the court may order the Council to erase the name of the practitioner or to suspend effective registration.[67] Similarly, when the Council, instead of erasure or suspension, decides to attach 'conditions as it thinks fit', an application to the High Court is also available.[68]

In all instances involving erasure or suspension the matter is considered by the High Court on an application either of the practitioner or of the Council, and that the Council does not erase or suspend the name until directed to do so by the High Court.[69] If professional misconduct is under consideration at the hearing the Court may also admit evidence from 'any person of standing in the medical profession as to what is professional misconduct' – a further safeguard for the practitioner.[70]

---

63 Medical Practitioners Act 1978, s. 46(2).
64 Ibid., s. 46(3).
65 Ibid., s. 46(3)(b).
66 Ibid., s. 46(4).
67 Ibid., s. 46(4).
68 Ibid., s. 47(4).
69 Ibid., s. 46(3) and s. 47(4).
70 Ibid., s. 46(9).

3

CONSENT

The law requires that a doctor can only treat a patient if (i) the patient has properly consented to treatment or (ii) where the patient by age or incapacity is unable to give consent but proper consent has been obtained from some person entitled to give consent on the patient's behalf, or (iii) in exceptional cases, when the situation is so grave that the doctor's duty is to treat the patient and dispense with consent.

THE NOTION OF INFORMED CONSENT

The idea of consent appears to express the law's respect for the autonomy of the individual. In the words of Cardozo J in *Schloendorff v. Society of New York Hospital*,[1] '[e]very human being of adult years and sound mind has a right to determine what shall be done with his own body; and a surgeon who performs an operation without the patient's consent commits an assault.'

The idea of individual autonomy is grounded in the theories of philosophers such as Immanuel Kant (1724-1804) and John Locke (1632-1704). According to Kant, the autonomous person is capable of 'pure reason' and is thus to be considered a self-determining agent worthy of respect,[2] but, in order to be an autonomous person, one must be capable of pure reason. The rational being is thus the only one who may be capable of self-determination. However, as Alderson[3] notes:

> [t]his model may apply when patients are confidently able to state their needs. Yet it ignores complications in doctor-patient relationships such as discrepancies in knowledge, power, and status, as well as patients' dependency, anxiety, weakness, vulnerability and other handicapping states. . . . The relation of rational beings as a prototype for doctor-patient relationships fails when patients are too young or senile, too ill, or frightened to state their needs. Communication with these

---

1 105 NE 92 at 95 (1914).

2 See I. Kant, *Groundwork of the Metaphysics of Morals*, trans. H.J. Paton (New York, 1964).

3 P. Alderson, 'Consent to Children's Surgery and Intensive Medical Treatment', *Journal of Law and Society* (1990), vol. 17, no. 1, p. 52.

patients can only be through more than purely rational means. However, Kantian autonomy tends to be confined to 'pure' reason.[4]

It is also interesting to note that Kant's conception of the ideal society excluded from the franchise women, children and workers.[5] These groups were not included in the class which enjoyed autonomy. Similarly in the philosophy of John Locke, the rational being is seen as possessed of rights due to his ability to recognise the natural laws which define those rights.[6] Thus, those whose reason is not fully developed, such as the mentally incompetent, are not possessed of autonomy in the Lockean sense:

> [b]ut if, through Defects that may happen out of the ordinary Course of Nature, any one comes not to such a Degree of Reason, wherein he might be supposed capable of knowing the Law, and so living within the Rules of it, he is never capable of being a Freeman, he is never let loose to the Disposure of his own Will, (because he knows no Bounds to it, has not Understanding, its proper Guide) but is continued under the tuition and Government of others, all the Time his own Understanding is incapable of that Charge. . . . :
>
> The Freedom then of Man, and Liberty of acting according to his own Will, is grounded on his having Reason, which is able to instruct him in that Law he is to govern himself by, and make him know how far he is left to the Freedom of his own Will.[7]

This interpretation of autonomy may result in the interests of certain groups being discounted.*

Another interpretation of autonomy was put forward by John Stuart Mill (1806–73).** In Mill's view, the individual was free to act in an autonomous manner unless he interfered with another's interests:

4   Ibid., p. 54.
5   See generally J.M. Kelly, *A Short History of Western Legal Theory* (Clarendon Press, Oxford, 1992).
6   See J. Locke, *Two Treatises of Government* (New English Library, London, 1965).
7   Ibid., VI p. 54-7.
*   See D.A. Richards, 'Constitutional Privacy, the Right to Die and the Meaning of Life: A Moral Analysis', *William and Mary Law Review*, (1981), vol. 22, no. 3 (Spring), 327, who views the following as the attributes of the autonomous agent (at p. 340): 'The cluster of capacities constitutive of autonomy include human capacities for language and self-consciousness, memory, logical relations, empirical reasoning about beliefs and their validity (human intelligence), and the capacity to use normative principles, including, *inter alia*, principles of rational choice in terms of which ends may be more effectively and coherently realized'. One may then ask the question how does one fit the mentally handicapped patient or anencephalic neonate into this model of autonomy?
** See, for example, R. Cotterell, *The Politics of Jurisprudence: A Critical In-*

the only purpose for which power can be rightfully exercised over any member of a civilised community, against his will, is to prevent harm to others. His own good, either physical or moral, is not a sufficient warrant. He cannot rightfully be compelled to do or forbear because it will be better for him to do so, because it will make him happier, because, in the opinions of others, to do so would be wise, or even right. These are good reasons for remonstrating with him, or reasoning with him or persuading him, or entreating him, but not for compelling him, or visiting him with any evil in case he do otherwise. . . . The only part of the conduct of any one, for which he is amenable to society, is that which concerns others. In the part which merely concerns himself, his independence is, of right, absolute. Over himself, over his own body and mind, the individual is sovereign.[8]

This view of autonomy perhaps underpins Cardozo J's statement on self-determination in the medical context in *Schloendorff*. In that case Cardozo J considered unauthorised medical treatment as a species of battery. In later American cases the term 'informed consent' came to be employed by the judiciary in cases involving medical treatment. The case in which the term was first employed was *Salgo v. Leland Stanford, Jr, University Board of Trustees*,[9] where the court recognised the need for adequate details of the treatment, its risks and the alternatives to be supplied to the patient so that he may make a rational, intelligent or 'informed' choice on whether to submit to the proposed treatment. However, as Teff[10] has observed:

> *Salgo*, in its equivocal language, set a pattern which has characterised the informed consent doctrine in the United States ever since. While proclaiming the rhetoric of self-determination and 'patients' rights' it contrived to leave substantial scope in practice for medical paternalism.[11]

This is based on the dictum in *Salgo* that it was for the medical professional to judge the amount of information it was necessary to disclose. What will determine the amount of information to be released to the patient in such a situation is to be based on the amount of information which the 'reasonable practitioner' would disclose in such circumstances. This position

troduction (Butterworth, London, 1989) chap. 3; C.L. Ten, *Mill on Liberty* (Clarendon Press, Oxford, 1980).

8 J.S. Mill, *On Liberty*, introduction in *Utilitarianism, Liberty and Representative Government* (J.M. Dent, London, 1960).

9 154 Cal App 2d 560, 317 P 2d 170 (1957).

10 H. Teff, 'Consent To Medical Procedures: Paternalism, Self-determination Or Therapeutic Alliance?', *Law Quarterly Review* (1985), Vol. 101, p. 432.

11 Ibid. at 438.

was to change after the decision in *Canterbury v. Spence*[12] where the court held that:

> respect for the patient's right of self-determination on particular therapy demands a standard set by law for physicians rather than one which physicians may or may not impose upon themselves.[13]

The focus thus shifted from the reasonable practitioner to the reasonable patient. Under the *Canterbury* test practitioners were required to disclose such information in relation to the proposed treatment as would be deemed material by a reasonable person in the patient's position. The perceived result is that *Canterbury* widened the scope of patient autonomy. However, the emphasis in the test is on the disclosure of information; the ability of the patient to comprehend such information is not dealt with. In addition, the court added a qualification to the effect that in the area of medical judgment 'prevailing medical practice must be given its due.'[14] Thus, the practitioner continued to have a discretion where prevailing medical standards hold that disclosure of certain facts would have a detrimental effect on the patient. This led to a situation where:

> the *Canterbury* formula has been largely nullified by the therapeutic privilege exception, while still prompting a misplaced preoccupation – excessive even from a legal standpoint – with the sheer quantity of information disclosed and the mechanics of obtaining signatures to elaborate and abstruse consent forms. . . .
> . . . Self-determination has not been perceptibly advanced, prompting the cynical but supportable assertion that the main purpose of the *Canterbury* doctrine was to provide added scope for successful personal injury litigation under the guise of advancing individual autonomy.[15]

A general statement of the obligation to inform a patient is contained in the Canadian case of *Kenny v. Lockwood*.[16] Hodgins JA there stated that a doctor should deal honestly with his patient 'as to the necessity, character and importance of the operation and its probable consequences and whether success might reasonably be expected to ameliorate or remove the trouble'.

'CONSENT' IN IRELAND

Though the term 'informed consent' is used widely in Irish medical and

12 464 F 2d 772 (1972).
13 Ibid., p. 784.
14 Ibid., p. 785.
15 H. Teff (1985), op. cit. at p. 442. For a practitioner's critique of the doctrine of consent, see S. Westmacott, 'Cutting the Truth', *The Guardian*, 8 December 1993.
16 (1932) 1 DLR 507 at 525.

legal circles, there is no Irish judicial or statutory definition of this term. There has been no Irish judicial approbation of the principles laid down by courts in other jurisdictions who have favoured the use of the term. It is perhaps a misleading phrase, since information comprises only one aspect of comprehensive or enlightened consent.

In Ireland, the doctor must give the patient or the patient's guardian or parent (where the consent is obtained from the patient's guardian or parent) information about the patient's condition, the effects (including side effects) of treatment, including, where appropriate, alternative forms of treatment. It is usually said that this is to enable the patient (or his surrogate) to give consent to treatment.

Therefore the question, in Ireland, is, what constitutes appropriate information prior to treatment? This depends on several factors.

Patient's capacity to comprehend and decide The greater the patient's capacity to comprehend the issues involved and come to a decision about them, the greater will be the extent of the duty to disclose relevant information. Conversely, the more restricted his capacity, the less may be the extent of any duty to inform.

This factor was discussed in *Daniels v. Heskin*.[17] It should be said at the outset that this case does not discuss what constitutes appropriate information prior to treatment, but rather, what information must be given after treatment has commenced and does not go according to plan. In this case, the patient gave birth at home, where she was attended by the local midwife. The next day, she was attended by a doctor for the purpose of inserting stitches in her perineum. While the doctor was inserting the stitches, the needle broke. The doctor failed to find the broken portion of the needle, but completed the stitching. Subsequently, the patient became ill, and had to undergo a procedure for the removal of the remnants of the needle. In this case, the doctor was not held to have been negligent in deciding to complete the stitching and to defer the operation for the removal of the broken part, and the non-disclosure was reasonable in the circumstances. Kingsmill Moore J held:

> I cannot admit any abstract duty to tell patients what is the matter with them, or, in particular, to say that a needle has been left in their tissue. All depends on the circumstances – the character of the patient, her health, her social position, her intelligence, the nature of the tissue in which the needle is embedded. . . . In the present case the patient was passing through a *post-partum* period in which the possibility of nervous or mental disturbance is notorious. . . .

17 [1954] IR 73.

In *Walsh v. Family Planning Services Ltd*[18] where a vasectomy patient contracted orchalgia, a very rare testicular condition, Finlay CJ examined the Kingsmill Moore criteria, but found them 'difficult to understand as relevant'.[19] He stated that:

> [i]n determining whether or not to have an operation in which sexual capacity is concerned, it seems to me to supply the patient with the material facts is so obviously necessary to an informed choice on the part of the patient that no reasonably prudent doctor would fail to make it.[20]

Nevertheless any court in assessing whether or a not a doctor has made sufficient disclosure, will be bound to take into account two aspects. First, the court will consider the doctor's appreciation of the likely effect of disclosure on the particular patient. Second, it will take into account what accepted medical practice is in the particular circumstances, and whether any particular factors in the instant case require departure from accepted medical practice or not.

Risks involved In the absence of other considerations, the greater the risks to the patient which the doctor knows or ought to know, but which the patient cannot be expected to know, the greater will be the duty to disclose information about them. Conversely, where the risks are particularly remote, or of little consequence, or ones which the patient can be presumed to know, the duty to disclose will be correspondingly less.

Clearly, a doctor must warn about likely or probable effects. The question is how far must a doctor warn the patient about a statistically remote possibility, and how clearly must this remote possibility be explained to the patient? In *Walsh v. Family Planning Services Ltd*[21] it was alleged, but not accepted, that the doctor had failed to warn the vasectomy patient about the statistically insignificant chance of contracting orchalgia. In fact, the trial judge accepted that the patient was warned. However, the Supreme Court stated that in elective surgery in particular, such as a vasectomy, there was a duty to warn the patient of all relevant likely consequences. There are, however, no Irish cases where a patient has successfully sued a doctor for detailing possible side-effects, adverse sequelae and so on, with alleged disadvantageous results. No accepted definition or formula for what constitutes appropriate explanation in the context of treatment has yet been accepted by the Irish courts.

18 [1992] 1 IR 496.   20 Ibid., p. 521.
19 Ibid., p. 520.   21 [1992] 1 IR 496.

Patient's wishes to be informed   Many patients will indicate that they wish to leave all decisions to the doctor, and in these cases the obligation to inform will generally be very different from that in which a patient asks for information about the proposed procedure, or any alternatives. In *A Guide to Ethical Conduct and Behaviour and to Fitness to Practise*,[22] the Medical Council stresses that a request for information by a patient always requires a positive response.

In general, the more a patient asks, the more the doctor should tell him, since such questioning implies a wish to be fully informed.

Nature of the procedure   Where the proposed procedure is thought to be essential for the patient's health, the obligation to disclose information about, for example, the risks involved, will generally be much less than it is where the procedure in question is not essential. It was held in the case of *Walsh v. Family Planning Services Ltd*[23] that there may be instances where as a matter of medical knowledge, notwithstanding substantial risks of harmful consequence, the carrying out of a particular surgical procedure is so necessary to maintain the life or health of the patient, and the consequences of failing to carry it out are so clearly disadvantageous, that limited discussion or warning concerning possible harmful side-effects may be appropriate and proper. The obligation to give warning of the possible harmful consequences of a surgical procedure which is elective (not necessary for the maintenance of life or health of the patient, for example, a vasectomy) is more stringent and more onerous.

However, if one of the aspects of 'harmful consequences' is a risk of failure of an elective procedure, then the doctor might not be negligent for failing to warn, so long as a substantial number of those in the medical community would likewise not warn about the risk of failure. In *Gold v. Haringey Health Authority*,[24] the plaintiff became pregnant after an unsuccessful sterilisation operation. The plaintiff sued and was awarded damages in the lower court, partly based on the legal theory that where medical advice is given by a doctor in a non-therapeutic context (a contraceptive context), the *Bolam* test (a principle which limits the duty of care, and thus liability)[25] does not apply; that is, a higher standard might be required.

22   The Medical Council, *A Guide to Ethical Conduct and Behaviour and to Fitness to Practice*, 4th ed. (Medical Council, Dublin, 1994).

23   [1992] 1 IR 496.

24   [1987] 2 All ER 888.

25   The *Bolam* test states: A health carer 'is not guilty of negligence if he has acted in accordance with a practice accepted as proper by a responsible body of medical men skilled in that particular art . . . merely because there is a body of opinion that takes a contrary view.' [1957] 2 All ER 118 at 122; [1957] 1 WLR 582 at 587, quoted in *Gold v. Haringey Health Authority* [1987] 2 All ER 888 at 891.

The Court of Appeal, *per* Lloyd LJ, refused to accept this argument, holding that where medical advice is given, the standard of care required of the doctor does not depend on the context (whether therapeutic or non-therapeutic) of the advice given, but on whether there was a substantial body of doctors who would have given the same advice. Thus, the limiting principles of *Bolam* do apply to a contraceptive context. Since a substantial body of doctors would not have given the warning which was not given by the defendant, and since the defendant acted in accordance with a practice accepted as reasonable in the medical community, then the defendant could not be guilty of negligence.[26]

Effect of information on patient   In those rare cases where prior to medical or surgical intervention, information is likely to have a directly detrimental effect on the patient's health, a doctor will not normally be in breach of his duty of care if he does not disclose this information. It is less clear whether a doctor is legally permitted to shield patients from information in cases where it would not have directly detrimental effects but where it would cause anxiety. Whether the anxiety or worry of the patient would justify non-disclosure would depend on the circumstances of the case. Since this is an exception to the general duty to disclose, based on the rights of patients to make autonomous decisions about their own health, it would be interpreted strictly.[27] It should be stressed that different considerations apply after medical and/or surgical interventions.[28]

FAILURE TO OBTAIN CONSENT

Capacity to give a legally effective consent depends upon capacity to

26   *Gold v. Haringey Health Authority* [1987] 2 All ER 888 at 891. In summary, Lloyd LJ writes: '[a] distinction between advice given in a therapeutic context and non-therapeutic context would be a departure from the principle on which the *Bolam* test is itself grounded. The principle does not depend on the context in which any act is performed, or any advice given. It depends on a man professing skill or competence in a field. . . . If the giving of contraceptive advice required no special skill, then I could see an argument that the *Bolam* test should not apply. But that was not, and could not have been suggested. The fact (if it be the fact) that giving contraceptive advice involves a different sort of skill and competence from carrying out a surgical operation does not mean that the *Bolam* test ceases to be applicable.' Ibid. at 894.

27   *Lee v. South West Thames Regional Health Authority* [1985] 2 All ER 385; *Naylor v. Preston Area Health Authority* [1987] 2 All ER 353.

28   Thus, insofar as *Daniels v. Heskin* [1954] IR 73 appears to suggest that a doctor has wide discretion not to inform the patient, post-operatively, of any complications, this decision appears to have been superseded by other decisions, e.g., *Helvin v. Graham* (1973) DRS 659 (Ont. HC); *Cryderman v. Ringrose* (1978) 3 WWR 481 (Alta CA); *Kueper v. McMullin* (1986) 37 CCLT 318 (NBCA).

understand and come to a decision on what is involved, and the capacity to communicate that decision. In the absence of special statutory provisions, the common law does not designate any categories of persons to be automatically incapable of giving consent. It always depends on the ability to comprehend the nature of the procedure involved in each individual case. Nevertheless, the Medical Council urges special caution whenever minors or the mentally ill are involved.[29] Failure to obtain appropriate patient consent will in general constitute breach of contract. It may also ground an action for negligence and (maybe) battery, as we explain further in chapter 5.

IMPLIED CONSENT

Consent will often be specific but will sometimes be given in general terms.[30] Courts will not be hasty to find that a patient has given a general consent but they should not prevent a patient who so desires from giving an effective consent to whatever is necessary for the treatment of his illness.[31]

Consent may be implied by conduct. Thus if a patient holds out his arm to receive an injection this may be taken to be an implied consent.[32] However, a doctor cannot assume that merely because a patient has consulted him about a medical complaint, the patient has impliedly consented to treatment of it.[33]

EXCEPTIONS TO CONSENT RULE

Emergency In certain instances it may not be possible to obtain the consent of the patient to a particular medical intervention. This situation

---

29 Specific aspects of the problem of informed consent, and its absence are dealt with in: R. Pearce & D. Tomkin, 'Medical Negligence: The Damoclean Sword', *Irish Medical Times* (1981), Vol. 15, No. 23, p. 16-17; 'Outlining the Legal Implications of Consent to an Operation', *Irish Medical Times* (1981), Vol. 15, No. 28, pp. 18-19; G.H. Tomkin & D. Tomkin, 'Information about Medical Treatment – The General Rules', *Irish Medical Times* (1986), Vol. 20, No. 14, p. 20 and Vol. 20, No. 15, pp. 20-23; D. Tomkin & R. Pearce, 'Patient Claims for Damages for the Failure to Obtain Consent', *Irish Medical Times* (1986), Vol. 20, No. 36, pp. 18-19; D. Tomkin & R. Pearce, 'The Fiction of Implied Consent to Medical Examination', *Irish Medical Times* (1986), Vol. 20, No. 37, pp. 18-19; D. Tomkin & R. Pearce, 'Deliberate Disregard of A Patient's Wishes', *Irish Medical Times* (1986), Vol. 20, No. 39, pp. 20-1; D. Tomkin & R. Pearce, 'Think Before You Go To Rescue', *Irish Medical Times* (1982), Vol. 16, No. 9, p. 28.
30 *Pridham v. Nash* (1986) 33 DLR (4th) 304 (Ont. HC).
31 *In re T. (adult: refusal of medical treatment)* [1992] 4 All ER 649, 653d *per* Lord Donaldson MR.
32 *O'Brien v. Cunard SS Co.* (1891) 28 NE 266.
33 *Mohr v. Williams* (1905) 104 NW 12; *Pridham v. Nash* (1986) 33 DLR (4th) 304 (Ont. HC).

may arise in cases where the patient is in urgent need of medical attention
but due to unconsciousness, for example, is unable to consent to such
treatment. For guidance, one must look to a number of Canadian cases in
which this particular issue was addressed. In *Marshall v. Curry*[34] the
Supreme Court of Nova Scotia was presented with a case in which during
the course of an operation for a hernia, the surgeon in question noticed that
the patient had a diseased left testicle. Rather than wait until the patient
awoke from the anaesthetic, the surgeon decided that he would remove the
diseased testicle during the course of the instant operation. The patient sued
the surgeon in trespass. In dismissing the patient's claim, the court stated
that in the case of an emergency a doctor would be justified in so acting if
it was required to save the life or preserve the health of the patient.[35] In
the instant case Chisholm CJ stated that in removing the testicle, the surgeon
had acted with the aim of protecting the health of the patient, and, as such,
his actions were justified.[36] In the subsequent case of *Parmley v. Parmley
and Yule*[37] the Canadian Supreme Court stated that, in principle, in cases
of emergency, great latitude may be given to the doctor. In the particular
case, however, it was added that the fact that the plaintiff was anaesthetised
provided a 'convenient, but not necessary, opportunity'[38] for proceeding
without consent.

In *Murray v. McMurchy*[39] the patient was the subject of a Caesarean
section procedure. During the procedure, the surgeon who was conducting
the operation, discovered a number of tumours in the patient's uterus.
Without waiting until such time as the patient could consent, he decided
after consultation with the doctor who was assisting him to tie the patient's
Fallopian tubes. The patient subsequently sued the surgeon in trespass. In
holding that it would not have been unreasonable for the surgeon to wait
until the patient's consent to the second procedure could be obtained the
Supreme Court of British Columbia made the distinction between the
situation where the operation:

> was necessary in the sense that it would be, in the circumstances,
> unreasonable to postpone the operation to a later date[40]

and the situation where as in *Parmley* it was merely convenient to proceed
without consent.

---

34 (1933) 3 DLR 260.
35 Ibid. at 175.
36 Ibid. at 275-6.
37 (1945) 4 DLR 81.
38 Ibid. at 89.
39 (1949) 2 DLR 442.
40 Ibid. at 444.

This issue has also arisen in the United States. In *Mohr v. Williams*[41] the plaintiff had consented to an operation on her right ear. However, during the operation, the surgeon decided that the condition of the right ear did not warrant an operation. He found instead that the condition of the left ear was more serious and warranted an operation. He thereupon operated on the left ear without asking the patient's consent for that intervention. The operation was successful but the patient consequently sued in trespass. In holding for the patient, the Supreme Court of Minnesota outlined the approach to be taken in such situations:

> [r]easonable latitude must, however, be allowed to the physician in a particular case; and we would not lay down any rule which would unreasonably interfere with the exercise of his discretion, or prevent him from taking such measures as his judgment dictated for the welfare of a patient in the case of emergency. If a person should be injured to the extent of rendering him unconscious, and his injuries were of such a nature as to require prompt surgical attention, a physician called to attend to him would be justified in applying such medical or surgical treatment as might reasonably be necessary for the preservation of his life or limb, and consent on the part of the injured person would be implied.
>
> And again, if, in the course of an operation to which the patient consented, the physician should discover conditions not anticipated before the operation was commenced, and, which, if not removed, would endanger the life or health of the patient, he would, though no express consent was obtained or given, be justified in extending the operation to remove and overcome them.[42]

Minors Legally effective consent may be given by a parent, where the procedure is in the best interests of the minor and the minor is incapable of consenting on its own behalf. The best interests of the minor's health may include procedures for the purposes of assessment and prevention, as well as those for the treatment of an existing condition. Thus, in the case of younger children, the consent of parents to treatment will be legally effective in relation to treatment of a beneficial nature. Thus, as one writer, put it 'no battery is committed by a doctor who, with parental consent, vaccinates a protesting 4-year-old against measles'.[43]

There are cases where the benefit to the child is, at best, indirect. An

---

41 (1905) 104 NW 12.
42 Ibid.
43 Margaret Brazier, *Street On Torts*, 8th ed. (Butterworth, London, 1988), p. 77.

example is where there is benefit gained from a non-therapeutic experimental procedure. It is likely that the Irish courts would adopt the principle enunciated by the House of Lords, that a parent can give a legally effective consent to any procedure to which a 'reasonable parent' would consent: see *S v. McC; W v. W*.[44] Concerning the taking of blood samples for forensic purposes, Lord Reid[45] stated that a reasonable parent would consent to his child taking a blood test unless he thought that such a test would not be in the child's interests.

As Skegg points out:[46]

> it is not suggested that this case provides binding authority on the issue under consideration; simply that it provides an indication of the attitude of some leading members of the judiciary, and that statements in the case can be used as the basis of a helpful test in relation to the capacity of parents to consent to medical procedures on minors.

A reasonable parent would not normally put a child's interests in jeopardy, whether for the benefit of any other individual or of the public generally.

S. 2(1) of the Age of Majority Act 1985 provides that the age of majority is eighteen years. At common law the rule is that a contract entered into by a person under the age of majority is voidable at his/her election. In other words, the courts recognise that contracts in which a minor was capable of being subjected to a series of recurring obligations were valid unless the infant repudiated the contract within a reasonable period of time. Such contracts would include *inter alia*, insurance contracts, contracts to take shares and leases. There are other kinds of contract which are voidable in the sense that unless the minor affirms them they are not binding. An example of a contract valid at common law is a beneficial contract for services, of which a contract for medical treatment is one.[47] Therefore, the consent of the child should be obtained where such consent is meaningful.[48] Otherwise, the consent should be obtained from the child's parent or guardian.

44 *S v. McC; W v. W* [1972] AC 24.
45 [1972] AC 24 at p. 45.
46 P.D.G. Skegg, *Law, Ethics and Medicine: Studies in Medical Law* (Clarendon Press, Oxford, 1990), p. 66.
47 For a general discussion of the contractual capacity of minors in Ireland, see R. Clark, *Contract Law in Ireland*, 3rd ed. (Sweet & Maxwell, London, 1992).
48 This is particularly important, if the argument of I. Kennedy & A. Grubb, *Medical Law: Text with Materials*, 2nd ed. (Butterworth, London, 1992) at p. 392–3 is accepted. They state that there is a strong argument that the courts should stay their hand when the decision-maker is a competent child.

The common law does not fix a specific age above which a minor's consent to medical treatment is valid. However, in England it has been held that minors may give valid consent if they fully comprehend the nature and consequences of the proposed medical treatment, without requiring parental consent.[49] Where the child is incapable of giving consent, and where the procedure is in the 'best interests' of the child, then legally effective consent may be given by a parent. In Ireland, this issue has not yet been addressed by the courts. It is therefore necessary to examine the situation in a jurisdiction where the judiciary has analysed the issue. In England, the important factor in this area is whether the child has sufficient understanding and intelligence to appreciate what is entailed in the particular treatment. A case in which the topic of consent was discussed in the context of contraceptive advice, was *Gillick v. West Norfolk and Wisbech Area Health Authority*.[50] The case arose as a result of the issuing by the then Department of Health and Social Security of a circular which stated that a doctor consulted at a family planning clinic by a girl under the age of sixteen would not be acting unlawfully if he prescribed contraceptives for the girl, as long as he was acting in good faith to protect her against the harmful effects of sexual intercourse. The plaintiff, a mother of five daughters under the age of sixteen, sought an assurance from her area health authority that her daughters would not receive contraceptive advice without her consent. The health authority refused such an assurance, whereupon the plaintiff brought an action against the health authority and the DHSS seeking a declaration that the advice contained in the circular was unlawful as it amounted to advice to doctors to commit the offence of causing or encouraging unlawful sexual intercourse with a girl under sixteen, contrary to s. 28(1) of the Sexual Offences Act 1956, or the offence of being an accessory to unlawful sexual intercourse with a girl under sixteen, contrary to s. 6(1) of the 1956 Act. The plaintiff also sought a declaration against the health authority that a doctor or other professional person employed by it in its family planning service could not give advice and treatment on contraception to any child of the plaintiff below the age of sixteen without the plaintiff's consent.

In its decision in the case, the House of Lords recognised the right of the minor to autonomy in this area. Thus, the fact that a girl was under the age of sixteen did not imply that she was incapable of consenting to such treatment and advice. The relevant factor was not the age of the individual but rather her ability to understand fully what was proposed. This would be a question of fact based on the particular capacity of the individual in question. As a result, a doctor could engage in such treatment, once he was

49 See *Gillick v. West Norfolk and Wisbech Area Health Authority* [1985] 3 All ER 402.
50 [1985] 3 All ER 402.

satisfied that the minor was of sufficient understanding and intelligence to appreciate the particular treatment, without incurring the sanction of the criminal law, or infringing the rights of the parents. Thus, in the words of Lord Scarman:

> as a matter of law, the parental right to determine whether or not their minor child below the age of sixteen will have medical treatment terminates if and when the child achieves a sufficient understanding and intelligence to enable him or her to understand fully what is proposed. It will be a question of fact whether a child seeking advice has sufficient understanding of what is involved to give a consent valid in law. Until the child achieves the capacity to consent, the parental right to make the decision continues save only in exceptional circumstances. Emergency, parental neglect, abandonment of the child or inability to find the parent are examples of exceptional situations justifying the doctor proceeding to treat the child without parental knowledge and consent.[51]

However, in the subsequent case of *In re R. (a minor) (Wardship: Consent to Treatment)*,[52] Lord Donaldson MR dealt a serious blow to the autonomy of minors in relation to medical treatment when he stated that the failure or refusal of the '*Gillick* competent child to consent is a very important factor in the doctor's decision, whether or not to treat, but does not prevent the necessary consent being obtained from another competent source.[53] The other 'competent source' would be a parent or someone acting *in loco parentis*.

In Ireland the issue has not, as yet, come before the courts for decision. However, the presence in the Constitution of Articles 41 and 42 may constitute a barrier to a decision similar to that in the *Gillick* case being arrived at. Article 41 sets out to give explicit constitutional protection to the family and the institution of marriage. The family is seen under Article 41.1.2 as 'the necessary basis of social order'. Article 42.1 holds that the family is 'the primary and natural educator of the child'. Gavan Duffy J in *In re Tilson*[54] left no doubt as to the provenance of these articles:

> Articles 41 and 42, redolent as they are of the great Papal encyclical *In Pari Materia*, formulate first principles with conspicuous power and clarity . . . which exalt the family by proclaiming and adopting in . . . the Constitution . . . the Christian conception of the place of the family in society and in the State.[55]

51 [1985] 3 All ER 402 at 423-4.   54 [1951] IR 1.
52 [1991] 4 All ER 177.   55 Ibid. at 14.
53 Ibid. at p. 186.

The Constitution's view of the child owes something to either Kant's or Locke's view of him or her as a being who has not yet attained 'reason', and as such is not capable of self-determination.[56] Locke's view that children are not born in the full state of equality that the rational adult possesses and as such:

> all Parents [are] by the Law of Nature, under an obligation to preserve, nourish, and educate the children they [have] begotten, not as their own Workmanship, but the Workmanship of their own Maker the Almighty, to whom they were to be accountable for them.[57]

appears to be echoed in Article 41.1.1 of the Constitution, which states:

> [t]he State recognises the Family as the natural primary and funda-mental unit group of Society, and as a moral institution possessing inalienable and imprescriptible rights, antecedent and superior to all positive law.

and in Article 42.1 which provides that:

> [t]he State acknowledges that the primary and natural educator of the child is the Family and guarantees to respect the inalienable right and duty of parents to provide, according to their means, for the religious and moral, intellectual, physical and social education of their children.

Professor Kelly[58] has noted the Thomistic Natural law ethos of these articles when he states:

> [t]hese Articles are wholly inspired by Christian (or, more specifically, by Catholic) orthodoxy, in particular by well-known Encyclicals of modern Popes, [ie Pope Pius XI's] *Divini Illius Magistri* (1929) and *Casti Connubii* (1930)].[59]

These articles have been interpreted by the courts in a number of important

---

56 I. Kant, *The Critique of Pure Reason*, trans. N. Kemp-Smith (New York, 1956) and J. Locke, *Two Treatises of Government*, New English Library (London, 1956).

57 Ibid., VI 54.

58 J.M. Kelly, *Fundamental Rights in the Irish Law and Constitution* (Allen Figgis & Co., Dublin, 1967).

59 Kelly, ibid., pp. 57-8. In addition, D. Keogh, *The Vatican, The Bishops and Irish Politics 1919-1939* (Cambridge University Press, Cambridge, 1986); J.H. Whyte, *Church and State in Modern Ireland 1923-1970*, 2nd ed. (Gill & Macmillan, Dublin, 1980).

cases. In the case of *Ryan v. Attorney General*[60] the plaintiff alleged that the Health (Fluoridation of Water Supplies) Act 1960 was unconstitutional, claiming that it violated the constitutional rights of the family. In the course of his decision in the High Court, Kenny J referred to the meaning of the word 'education' in the context of Article 42 stating:

> [i]n the *Shorter Oxford* [English] *Dictionary* issued in 1933 the meanings given for the word 'education: are '(1) the process of nourishing or rearing' (this is marked with a sign to show that this meaning was obsolete in 1933), '(2) the process of bringing up young persons (3) the systematic instruction, schooling or training given to the young (and, by extension, to adults) in preparation for the work of life. Also the whole course of scholastic instruction which a person has received.' In other dictionaries the meaning which [counsel for the plaintiff] contends is also described as obsolete. Moreover, it seems to me that the terms of the Article show that the word education was not used in this wide sense in the Constitution. S. 1 of the Article recognises 'the right and duty of parents to provide according to their means, for the religious and moral, intellectual, physical and social education of their children', but in subs. 2 it is provided that the parents are free to provide this education in their homes or in schools recognised or established by the State. The education referred to in s. 1 must, therefore, be one of a scholastic nature. It seems to me, therefore, that the fluoridation of the public water supply (even if it be harmful) does not interfere with or violate the rights given to the family and to the parents by Article 42 of the Constitution.[61]

The Supreme Court upheld the decision of the High Court stating:

> [e]ducation essentially is the teaching and training of a child to make the best possible use of his inherent and potential capacities, physical, mental and moral. To teach a child to minimise the dangers of dental caries by adequate brushing of his teeth is physical education for it induces him to use his own resources. To give him water of a nature calculated to minimise the danger of dental caries is in no way to educate him, physically or otherwise, for it does not develop his resources.[62]

In the case of *G v. An Bord Uchtála*[63] the Supreme Court outlined in

---

60 [1965] IR 294.
61 Ibid., pp. 339-10.

62 Ibid., p. 350.
63 [1980] IR 32.

detail the personal rights of the child. In his judgment in this case, O'Higgins CJ stated that:

> [t]he child also has natural rights. Normally, these will be safe under the care and protection of its mother. Having been born, the child has the right to be fed and to live, to be reared and educated, to have the opportunity of working and of realising his or her full personality and dignity as a human being. These rights of the child (and others which I have not enumerated) must equally be protected by the State.[64]

On this analysis, one could argue that the child is not entitled to complete autonomy until he or she attains the age of majority or 'reason'. Thus, in the medical context the 'Gillick' conception of child competence as originally conceived in England may not be in accordance with this conception of the autonomy of the child.

Special questions arise with regard to minors and organ transplantation. May a child validly consent to the donation of an organ? In the absence of Irish or English judicial authority on this subject, one must look to the United States for judicial guidance. In the case of *Strunk v. Strunk*[65] the donor in question, while not a minor, was incapable of giving consent on his own behalf as he was a mentally handicapped adult with a mental age of six. The procedure under review was the donation of a kidney by the donor to his brother. The court allowed the transplant to proceed stating that it would be in the 'best interests' of the donor due to the close relationship between the donor and his brother. However other common law jurisdictions are not as willing to allow minors who cannot consent to such procedures to donate organs. Thus, in the state of Western Australia, the Human Tissue and Transplant Act 1982 prohibits the removal of non-regenerative material (for example, kidneys, livers and lungs) from living children.[66] This approach is perhaps preferable in that it respects the autonomy of the individual minor and protects them from undergoing a non-consensual organ extraction. Nonetheless, one could argue that if the donation was required to save the life of a sibling, then, it would appear to be in the minor's best interests to allow the donation to proceed. In France, a compromise solution has been reached in respect of this aspect of organ donation. The Loi Cavaillet du 22 Decembre 1976 governs organ donation in France. Under this statute, a living minor may only donate to his brother or sister. In addition, consent to this donation must be given by the donor's legal representative. As an added safeguard, the transplant procedure must

64 Ibid., pp. 55-6.
65 445 SW 2d 145 (Ky, 1969).
66 Ss. 12 and 13.

be authorised by a panel of three relevant experts, two of whom must be medical practitioners. However, reform of the law in this area is imminent. At present, three bills covering the entire bioethics area are being examined by the legislature.[67] The Bill relevant to organ donation and transplantation is the *projet de loi no.2600* relatif au don et a l'utilisation des elements et produits du corps humain et a la procreation medicalement assistée. This Bill, recently adopted by the French Parliament,[68] no longer allows the transplant of organs by living minors in any circumstances. The only exception allowed is the transplant of bone marrow by a minor to a sibling who requires it in order to save that sibling's life.

The pregnant woman and the foetus A special problem may arise where a pregnant mother does not wish to avail of treatment for example on conscientious grounds, but medical opinion is that such treatment is necessary for the health of the foetus she is carrying.

In England, the Court of Appeal rejected the argument that an unborn child could be made a ward of court, in the case of *In re F (in utero)*.[69] There the mother in question was a 36-year-old sufferer from mental illness, and a drug addict. In the later stages of her pregnancy, she 'went missing'. Her local authority was concerned about the welfare of the foetus. As a result, the local authority attempted to make the foetus a ward of court in order that the mother could be found and ordered to reside in a certain place and that she should be compelled to attend a named hospital. Balcombe LJ, in his judgment, stated that:

> since an unborn child has *ex hypothesi* no existence independent of his mother, the only purpose of extending the jursidiction to include a foetus is to enable the mother's actions to be controlled.[70]

He then went on to explain the role of the judiciary in such a case. He stated that it would be intolerable to place a judge in the position of having to make such a decision without any guidance as to the principles upon which his decision should be based. If the law were to be extended in this manner so as to impose control over the mother of an unborn child, then it was for parliament to decide whether such controls should be imposed, and if so, subject to what limitations and conditions.

---

67 See J.C. Honlet, 'De la bioethique au biodroit', *Regards sur l'actualite* (1993), No. 183, p. 3 (Fevrier).
68 J-Y. Nau, 'Bioethics Laws in France', *The Lancet* (1994), Vol. 344, p. 48 (2 July).
69 [1988] 2 All ER 193.
70 Ibid., 200.

In such a sensitive field, affecting as it does the liberty of the individual, it is not for the judiciary to extend the law.[71]

This case followed the previous English cases of *C v. S*,[72] and *Paton v. British Pregnancy Advisory Service Trustees*,[73] which held that the foetus had no legal status until it was capable if sustaining life independently from its mother.

It is however submitted that in Ireland a refusal of treatment by the mother in these circumstances, and, more particularly, where the mother requires blood or similar transfusions in order to safeguard the viability of the foetus, may well be challengeable. This is as a result of the Constitutional provision which specifically accords rights to 'the unborn' in Article 40.3.3 (as amended). We deal with this subject in our discussion of the *X* case, in chapter 9.

The Mentally Incompetent Medical treatment of the mentally incompetent forms naturally into two divisions. First, questions rise about the psychiatric diagnosis, treatment and care of the mentally ill. Second, and this is in one way a more extensive problem, questions rise about how a doctor should deal with a mentally incompetent patient who requires diagnosis and treatment for an illness or condition unrelated to the amelioration of his mental state.

We deal in chapter 7 with the specific problem of diagnosis, care and treatment of the mentally incompetent for psychiatric conditions. Here, the question is, what sort of understanding and information must be given to those whose mental condition precludes their giving appropriate consent to medical treatment generally, and in particular, non-psychiatric treatment?

The question of consent to medical treatment in the case of the mentally incompetent adult patient was discussed by the House of Lords in *In re F (Mental Patient: Sterilisation)*.[74] The case concerned a thirty-six year old mentally handicapped woman who had formed a sexual relationship with a male patient, also mentally handicapped, in the hospital in which they were both patients. The hospital authorities felt that she would be unable to cope with the demands of pregnancy and motherhood, and that as they considered all other methods of contraception unsuitable, she should undergo a sterilisation procedure. In its judgment, the House of Lords took the opportunity to discuss the issue of consent in relation to the mentally incompetent patient.

While basing the decision on the common law principle of necessity,

---

71 Ibid., 200-1.
72 [1987] 1 All ER 1230.

73 [1978] 2 All ER 987.
74 [1989] 2 All ER 545.

Lord Goff then went on to state the test to be applied in this particular case as the 'best interests' test.

> But where the state of affairs is permament or semi-permament, as may be so in the case of a mentally disordered person, there is no point in waiting to obtain the patient's consent. The need to care for him is obvious; and the doctor must then act in the best interests of his patient just as if he had received his patient's consent so to do. Were this not so, much useful treatment and care could, in theory at least, be denied to the unfortunate. . . . In the case of routine treatment of mentally disordered persons, there should be little difficulty in applying this principle. In the case of more serious treatment, I recognise that its application may create problems for the medical profession; however, in making decisions about treatment, the doctor must act in accordance with a responsible and competent body of relevant professional opinion, on the principles set down in *Bolam v. Friern Hospital Management Committee* [1957] 2 All ER 118.[75]

A distinction must be drawn between those who are mentally handicapped, and those who are mentally ill. In general, the problems of treating patients in the former category are satisfactorily resolved by proceeding along the lines suggested in *In re F* above. However, in relation to the mentally ill, a problem arises. Some may be permamently unable to give consent, but others may be only temporarily incapacitated, and in such circumstances, in is submitted that it would be inappropriate to proceed to treatment. This issue was discussed briefly by McCullough J in *R v Hallstrom, ex p. W*, when he stated that . . . 'unless clear statutory authority exists, no one is to be detained in hospital or to undergo medical treatment or even to submit himself to a medical examination without his consent. This is true of a mentally disordered person as of anyone else'.[76] Skegg, commenting on this dilemma, states:

> the fact that a person is suffering from a mental disorder . . . does not of itself preclude that person from giving a legally effective consent. Whether the person is capable of doing so depends on whether that person can understand and come to a decision upon what is involved. Most patients in mental hospitals are capable of giving a legally effective consent, including many who are compulsorily detained. Doctors are sometimes free to proceed without consent, but even then a patient will sometimes have the capacity to give a legally effective consent

---

75 Ibid., p. 567.   76 [1986] QB 1090 at p. 1104.

which would, of itself, prevent the doctor's conduct from amounting to the tort or crime of battery.[77]

This view seems to have been confirmed in the recent case of *In Re C Adult: Refusal of Treatment*.[78] There the patient was suffering from chronic paranoid schizophrenia, and was detained at Broadmoor. He had been diagnosed as suffering from gangrene of the foot and was transferred to Heatherwood Hospital. At this hospital, the consultant who was responsible for C's care was of the opinion that unless his leg was amputated below the knee, C would die quite shortly. C refused to consent to the amputation. However, the surgeon persisted, knowing the seriousness of C's condition, and eventually he succeeded in obtaining C's consent to less radical treatment. After this treatment, C's condition improved and his life was no longer in danger. C nonetheless applied for an injunction to prevent any future attempt to amputate his leg without consent. The court was satisfied that C, though suffering from schizophrenia, understood and retained the relevant treatment, and that in his own way, he believed it, and in the same fashion he arrived at a clear choice. Thorpe J stated that the relevant question in such cases is whether it has been established that the patient's capacity is so reduced by his mental illness, that he does not sufficiently understand the nature, purpose and effects of the treatment.

This case was decided aginst the background of the (English) Mental Health Act 1983. Nevertheless, this case was decided on common law principles, and, as such, could be followed in Ireland. In a recent English case,[79] the High Court ruled that the Mental Health Act 1983 allowed doctors to feed a 24-year-old psychiatric patient by naso-gastric tube, against her will. The Court made the ruling, depite accepting that the patient was capable of deciding to refuse treatment, and that force feeding would reduce the chances of success for psychotherapy. Thorpe J stated that feeding agaist her will would not be in her best interests 'unless and until her physical state was so debilitated as to threaten her survival'. However, Thorpe J felt that it was disquieting that the 1983 Act legalised what common law would not permit, that is, the treatment of a competent patient against her will.[80]

However, if the (Irish) Mental Treatment Act 1945 is, as has been promised, amended,[81] specific provisions ought to be introduced to provide

77 P.D.G. Skegg, *Law Ethics and Medicine* (Clarendon Press, Oxford, 1984), p. 56-7.
78 [1994] 1 WLR 29; see pp. 163-4 *infra*.
79 *In re B, The Guardian*, 26 July 1994.
80 S. 63 of the 1983 Act states that the consent of a patient held under the Act is not required for any treatment for mental disorder. This was interpreted to include tube feeding in this case.
81 As we note in chapter 5, proposals were made to amend the 1945 Act in the late seventies

that a person suffering from mental disorder may nonetheless be capable of giving legally effective consent to treatment, or to refuse it, where that patient is capable of understanding, and to provide special safeguards where the patient is incapable of understanding.

Compulsory treatment   It is often presumed that prisoners, members of the defence forces and those suffering from certain forms of disease (tuberculosis, notifiable diseases) can be compulsorily treated, but this may not be accurate.

First, a prisoner may well fall to be treated medically in the sort of emergency where the exigency of the circumstance outweighs the requirement to obtain consent, for example where a prisoner is injured and is unconscious while at work. Presumably there would not be any problem if the reason for dispensing with the patient's consent is that he was unconscious. However, where there is no exigency, there is no general rule of Irish law which allows the doctor to dispense with the required consent. Indeed, both the Medical Council, in its *Guide to Ethical Conduct* and the World Medical Association's *Declaration of Tokyo* as adopted by 29th World Medical Assembly in October 1975, though considering different circumstances, both lay stress on the doctor's duty to treat prisoners as far as possible no differently from all other patients.[82]

Second, members of the Defence Forces likewise must be treated in nearly every case just as civilian patients. It may be, however, that a commanding officer could legitimately order his subordinate to obtain medical treatment. Such an order is presumably like any other, and disobedience is punishable under s. 131 of the Defence Act 1954. It is suggested that this is so, even though the act of disobedience is the refusal or withholding of consent.

In the case of venereal disease, it should be noted that a specific regulation (Regulation A, para 39) requires members of the defence forces who have

and early eighties. To this end, the Health (Mental Servies) Act 1981 was passed by the Oireachtas, and signed by the President, but it was never brought into force. C. Keane, *Mental Health in Ireland* (Gill & Macmillan/Radio Telefis Éireann, 1991), pp. 120-1 mentions the 1981 Bill, and states that 'the Department of Health is now actively reviewing the whole topic'. This comment is supported by the statement in the Department of Health's *Shaping a healthier future: A strategy for effective healthcare in the 1990* (Department of Health, Dublin, 1994) (Pn. 0685), p. 70, where one of the priorities is stated as '[t]o introduce a new Mental Health Act to give greater protection to the civil rights of the small number of people with mental illness who have to be detained for treatment and to bring out legislation into conformity with the European Convention in Human Rights'.

82 4th ed. (Medical Council, Dublin, 1994). See para 31.03 (p. 30) and the text of the *Tokyo Declaration*, p. 69.

exposed themselves to risk to obtain prophylactic treatment; and it is submitted that any refusal to do so (whether by the withholding of consent or for any other reason) is a breach of regulations, irrespective of whether or not a commanding officer has issued specific orders.

In chapter 12, we explain that the requirement to consent to treatment is different in cases where the treatment is immunisation or protection against certain specified diseases. There the position seems to be that in such cases the patient must submit himself to medical examination (including the taking of blood and other specimens for tests), and must submit to specified measures in relation to the protection or immunisation against such disease. It should be noted that these requirements apply in cases where the patient is not suffering from any of the specified diseases, but rather may be at risk from the disease, if not treated. In terms of consent, the position seems to be that if the patient is at risk, his consent to immunisation or protection must be forthcoming.

There are different regulations for those suffering with extremely serious infectious diseases, dealt with in chapter 12. These regulations permit the detention of patients suffering from the defined diseases; however, they do not provide any clear basis for assuming that the patient's consent to treatment is not necessary. It is submitted, though the point is very much undecided, that a doctor would not be justified in treating a conscious patient who is being lawfully detained under these regulations, if that patient has refused consent, and no other exceptional circumstance would justify treatment. The appropriate action would be to seek guidance from the courts, by emergency application if necessary.

4

PRIVACY AND CONFIDENTIALITY

The right to privacy, though not expressly guaranteed by the Constitution of Ireland, has been recognised by the courts as one of the unenumerated personal rights guaranteed by Article 40 of the Constitution. However this right is not of general application. Rather, certain realms of human activity are deemed to be worthy of constitutional privacy protection. In the case of *McGee v. Attorney General*,[1] the Supreme Court established a right to privacy in the context of marriage. Yet in *Norris v. Attorney General*,[2] it was held that the right to privacy was not absolute; because the State has an interest in the moral character of society. Thus, homosexual acts between consenting adult males were not to be included within the scope of constitutional privacy protection. Therefore, while a right to privacy *per se* has been derived from Article 40 of the Constitution, such a right is not to be considered absolute and can be overridden by competing interests. From the *McGee* and *Norris* decisions, one can see privacy in the form of individual freedom to act. However, privacy also embraces the right to be let alone. McCarthy J in *Norris* recognised this aspect of privacy.[3] Thus, as well as encompassing freedom to act, such a right can include a right to non-interference with a person's private affairs.

This aspect of privacy (the right to be let alone) was examined in *Kennedy & Arnold v. Ireland*[4] which involved the clandestine intercepting of telephone conversations of two journalists by order of the Minister for Justice. Hamilton P recognised the general right of privacy, in holding that the plaintiffs' constitutional rights had been interfered with; he added that such a right was not absolute, and that exceptions to it did exist. There were, he stated, a number of circumstances in which such a privacy right could justifiably be restricted. These circumstances included the exigencies of the common good, public order and morality, and when privacy came into conflict with the Constitutional rights of others.

---

1 [1974] IR 284.
2 [1984] IR 36.
3 Ibid., p. 101.
4 [1987] IR 587.

DATA PROTECTION

The right of privacy gives rise to concerns about the protection of data privacy. Following Lindop,[5] Clark defines data privacy as an individual's right to control the dissemination of and access to data about himself.[6] When personal data one wishes to keep private, that is, credit details or perhaps medical records, is held on an automated system, data control becomes vital and more difficult. Data on an automated system can be processed quickly, it can be accessed easily by many persons, even unauthorised persons, it is easy to corrupt, and it can be exported across national boundaries instantaneously.[7] In these circumstances, data distribution and access must be regulated if privacy rights are to exist in a modern technological society.

Clark quotes the then Minister for Justice, Mr G. Collins TD, who gave the rationale behind the Data Protection Act 1988 in its introduction:

> In the early seventies large information systems had become computerised to such an extent that fears began to be expressed on an increasing scale about the threat to privacy that they could pose. The fears were not based primarily on the amount of the information stored in the systems. The real basis for the concern was the ease and speed with which computerised information could be collected, rearranged, transferred and retrieved, and the fact that this information could include sensitive personal information and could be used for all kinds of purposes without the knowledge of the individuals to whom it related. Moreover, the ability to link computerised information systems gave rise to apprehension that the state would be in a position to have virtually instant access to all the information it held separately on each individual and, through file matching, to build up a comprehensive profile on every member of society. There were fears, too, that computerised personal information could more easily be stolen or copied or otherwise obtained improperly by those to whom it should not be disclosed.[8]

The Data Protection Act 1988 protects and validates this right of privacy against these hazards.[9] This Act is designed to afford protection to

---

5   Sir Norman Lindop, *Report of the Data Protection Committee*, HMSO, London, 1976 (Cmnd. 7391).

6   R. Clark, *Data Protection in Ireland* (The Round Hall Press, Dublin, 1990), p. 14.

7   Ibid., p. 15.

8   375 *Dáil Debates*, cols. 2846-7, quoted by Clark, p. 15-16.

9   With the Irish legislation in 1988, Ireland has followed other countries who have strengthened domestic privacy laws to include data protection: Sweden (1973), Austria

individuals in relation to personal data kept on computer about them. As to whether medical records constitute 'data', this depends on how the information is stored. The Act only extends to certain data, so for example, patient's notes recorded in handwriting or in typescript are not covered.

It is worth noting that the existence of the Data Protection Act 1988 does not preclude an action at common law. At common law, the abuse or mishandling of data can give rise, in specific contexts, to an array of grounds of civil liability: interference with the right of privacy in communications, defamation, negligence, deceit and the infliction of emotional suffering. The data controller owes a (tortious) duty of care in civil law not to injure any person by his acts or omissions, consonant with the general duty of care not to injure any person by his acts or omissions in the context of the general duty of care in negligence. Such a person is now under an extended duty of care to the subject as regards the collection by him of personal data or information intended for inclusion of such data or his dealing with such data.

The present position in Ireland is as follows; and is deduced from Kennedy & Grubb, who describe the common law position in England. A patient's right of access to medical records under common law is a question of ownership, which is decided by reference to the contract between the patient and the health care provider. If the patient's contract is with the doctor, and if the contract between the doctor and the clinic does not specify that the clinic gives up ownership of medical records, then the clinic owns the records. If the doctor is made the owner of the records, then whether or not the doctor gives the patient access to the records depends upon the relationship between the doctor and the patient. Access in this case would depend upon the express or implied terms of the contract between the doctor and the patient. In the absence of an express term, a court would probably imply that the doctor maintains ownership, but a patient has a right of access or possession, should the patient need the records for further health care, for example, to change doctors.[10]

If the patient's contract is with the hospital or clinic, then the agreement between the patient and the clinic will govern ownership of the medical records. Again, in the absence of an express term of ownership, a court would be likely to imply a term that ownership of the medical records

(1978), France (1978), Federal Republic of Germany (1977, implemented 1979), Luxembourg (1979), Norway (1978, implemented 1980), Iceland (1981, implemented 1982), Israel (1981), the United Kingdom (1984, implemented 1987), the Netherlands (1988, implemented 1989): see Clarke, p. 17.

10 I. Kennedy & A. Grubb, *Medical Law: Text with Materials*, 2nd ed. (Butterworth, London, 1994), pp. 610-11.

remains with the clinic. However, the patient might be entitled to possession, if this were necessary for the continued health care of that patient.[11]

If a patient does not own the documents, and can make no claim for possession and access, the common law, in general, has not recognised a right of general access of a patient to his or her medical records.[12]

Rights of the patient as data subject   S. 4 of the Data Protection Act 1988 guarantees a right of access to personal data. Subject to some quite substantial limitations set out in the Act, an individual who so requests a data controller, in writing, shall be informed whether the data kept by the data controller includes personal data relating to that individual and further, the applicant shall be supplied with a copy of the information constituting the data. S. 4 provides that if the information given by the data controller is provided in a form which is not intelligible to the average person without explanation, the information should be accompanied by an explanation of those terms. This is particularly useful for those seeking medical records. A data controller is not obliged to disclose to a data subject personal data relating to another individual unless that other individual consents to the disclosure.

An individual has certain rights in respect of erroneous data. These include rectification or where appropriate erasure. The data controller is deemed to have satisfied the rights of the individual concerned if he 'supplements the statement with a statement (to the terms of which the individual has assented)' and provides that the data is no longer inaccurate.

Duties of hospital/doctor as data controller   A data controller is defined as 'a person who, either alone or with others controls the contents and use of personal data.' S. 2(1)(a) of the Data Protection Act 1988 requires him to ensure that as regards personal data, the data or the information constituting the data shall have been obtained, and the data shall be processed

---

11   See *McInerney v. MacDonald* [1991] 2 Med LR 267 (NB CA), cited by Kennedy & Grubb, p. 611.

12   There are exceptions of limited applicability. First, a party who seeks to obtain the identity of an alleged wrongdoer from a third party who has relevant information may compel the third party to release it. In the context of medical records, this might be relevant if a patient wishes to obtain the identity of a doctor whom the patient wishes to sue, but whom the patient cannot identify without access to medical records. *Secretary of State for Defence v. Guardian Newspapers Ltd* [1985] AC 339; [1984] 3 All ER 601, cited by Kennedy & Grubb, p. 612. Second, a doctor may not refuse to give information normally held in medical records, if asked by the patient, to 'assist in the course of justice', that is, to resolve litigation. (In the case, the information was regarding the patient's venereal disease, the patient was a litigant in the suit, and the opposing litigant agreed that the information should be released.) *C v. C* [1946] 1 All ER 562 (Birmingham Assizes), cited by and quoted in Kennedy & Grubb, p. 612-13.

fairly. The Act further requires that the data be accurate, not excessive, up to date and that it shall be kept only for lawful purposes. Under s. 2(6) of the Act the Minister of Health may amend subs. (1) for the purpose of providing additional safeguards in relation to personal data as to physical or mental health. This provision ensures that there are specific guarantees in respect of the processing of particularly sensitive personal data such as that relating to health.

We turn now to the question of modification of the data subject's rights by the Minister. The 1988 Act generally presupposes that it is in the best interests of the data subject that personal data held by others is readily available to that individual. The subject access right is, however, not unqualified. Article 4(1) of the Data Protection (Access Modification) (Health) Regulations 1989 provides that information constituting health data shall not be supplied by or on behalf of a data controller to the data subject in response to a subject access request, if it would be likely to cause serious harm to the physical health of the data subject. Health data is defined as 'personal data relating to physical or mental health'. If the data is held by a health professional (physician, dentist, optician, nurse etc.) he can make up his mind about whether the personal data can be released. Where the data controller is not a health professional, then the disclosure of health data to the data subject, or a decision to keep back health data cannot be taken without reference to the appropriate health professional.

In the light of the general emphasis in the Act on the right of the individual to obtain information about himself, the health modification regulations would be narrowly interpreted. Even if the data controller forms the view that the release of personal data would be likely to cause serious harm to the physical or mental health of the data subject, the data controller is obliged to edit the data in such a way as to release that part of the data that would not cause harm.

CONFIDENTIALITY

Duty of confidence – the general principle   Confidentiality may be an express or implied term in any contract: its breach may therefore constitute breach of contract. It is not however an incidence of contract only. Even where there is no contractual relationship, the courts may give a remedy where there has been breach of confidence.[13]

13 The earliest relevant case is *Prince Albert v. Strange* (1849) 2 De G & SN 652. There Queen Victoria and Prince Albert, keen amateur artists, obtained an injunction against a person who published a catalogue of pictures, from selling it as it contained details of drawings and etchings done by them, presented to friends and relations, but somehow

One of the most important legal obligations owed by the doctor to the patient is the protection of confidences revealed by the patient to the doctor. The general principle is that a duty of confidence is breached when:

> a defendant is proved to have used confidential information, directly or indirectly obtained from a plaintiff, without the consent, express or implied, of the plaintiff, he will be guilty of an infringement of the plaintiff's rights.[14]

In the Irish case of *Cook v. Carroll*,[15] the test as to where a relationship of confidence exists was stated as follows:

> . . . four fundamental conditions may be predicated as necessary to the establishment of a privilege against the disclosure of communications between persons standing in a given relation:
> (1) [t]he communications must originate in a confidence that they will not be disclosed.
> (2) This element of confidentiality must be essential to the full and satisfactory maintenance of the relation.
> (3) The relation must be one which in the opinion of the community ought to be sedulously fostered; and
> (4) The injury which would enure to the relation by the disclosure of the communication must be greater than the benefit thereby gained for the correct disposal of litigation.[16]

In Ireland, the law of confidence was authoritatively reviewed by Costello J in *House of Spring Gardens v. Point Blank Ltd*,[17] where it was said that the court is being asked to enforce:

> what is essentially a moral obligation. In so doing it must firstly decide whether there exists from the relationship between the parties an obligation of confidence regarding the information which had been imparted and it must then decide whether the information which was communicated could properly be regarded as confidential. Once it is established that an obligation of confidence exists and that the information is confidential then the person to whom it is given has the

---

purloined by the defendant. The injunction was grounded (a) on copyright and (b) on breach of confidence.

14 *Per* Lord Greene MR in *Saltman Engineering Co. Ltd v. Campbell Engineering*

Co. Ltd (1948) 65 RPC 203.
15 [1945] IR 515.
16 *Per* Gavan Duffy J at p. 520.
17 [1984] IR 611.

duty to act in good faith and this means that he must use the information for the purpose for which it was imparted to him and cannot use it to the detriment of the informant.

There are exceptions. An example is the overriding public interest, as occurred in *Lion Laboratories Ltd v. Evans*,[18] and, most notoriously, in the Spycatcher legislation, *Attorney General v. Guardian (No. 2)*.[19]

The limits of confidentiality in the doctor-patient relationship depend to some degree on the special nature of the relationship. Thus in *Faccenda Chicken Ltd v Fowler*,[20] the nature of the confidentiality relationship was defined by the employment relationship in the course of which confidential information was given and received.

Duty of confidence – doctor-patient relationship   There is no specific legislative provision governing the duty of confidence in the doctor-patient relationship. The duty of confidence in the medical context is more in the line of a moral duty. It is therefore governed by codes of professional conduct as well as by the general common law duty of confidence. Thus, in the Hippocratic Oath the physician is obliged to adhere to the following duty of confidence:

> [w]hatever, in connection with my professional practice, or not in connection with it, I see or hear, in the life of men, which ought not to be spoken of abroad, I will not divulge, as reckoning that all such should be kept secret.[21]

18 [1984] 2 All ER 47. There two ex-employees of the manufacturer of the 'intoximeter' contacted a newspaper with details of the misfunctioning capacity of an apparatus designed by their ex-employees. They were held not to have breached either copyright or confidentiality, in revealing the details of the design fault of the machine in question (a mechanical breathalyser) as a defence in respect of overriding public interest would be allowed. This is a much criticised decision.

19 [1988] 3 All ER 545, which appears to hold (a) that members of the security services are under a lifelong duty not to publish details of their work activities but (b) where publication has taken place, and the matters are generally known, no injunction will be granted in respect of further publication of such matters. This case left open the question of whether and how the breacher of confidence should or could account to the Crown for the profits of his wrongdoing.

20 [1987] Ch 117. The defendant was a former employee of the plaintiff, and when he went into business for himself he allegedly 'stole' some of the plaintiff's clients. The court distinguished between different types of information and stressed that the obligations of an employee are determined by his contract of employment. In deciding whether information is confidential the court held that regard must be had to the nature of the information and the nature of the employment.

21 J. Walton, P.B. Beeson and R.B. Scott, *The Oxford Companion to Medicine*, 2 vols. (Oxford University Press, Oxford, 1986), Vol. 1, p. 545.

In the Declaration of Geneva[22] the doctor pledges 'to respect the secrets which are confided in me, even after the patient has died'. The physician's duty of non-disclosure applies not only to information obtained directly from the patient, but also to information concerning the patient which the doctor learns from other sources in his capacity as the patient's doctor. Thus the obligation extends to reports received by a doctor about a patient from medical specialists or from para-medical services.

There is no absolute right to confidentiality as between doctor and patient. Thus doctors must weigh the duty of confidentiality against conflicting interests. The Medical Council has suggested[23] that where a patient is suffering from AIDS, the need to disclose this fact to spouses or other partners who are at risk, may outweigh the physician's duty of confidentiality. The Medical Council stresses that the physician must urgently seek the patient's consent to disclosure. If this is refused, the doctor may, in all the circumstances of the case, consider it a duty to inform the spouse or other partner.

Indeed, in the US in the case of *Tarasoff v. The Regents of the University of California*[24] the parents of a student who was killed by her ex-boyfriend sued the killer's doctors for failing to warn the victim of their patient's homicidal tendencies and threats towards her. The doctors were held liable in negligence to the victim's family. In such cases the risk of harm must be proved to be real.

Subsequently, the California Supreme Court limited this duty to warn, explaining that it would be damaging to the therapeutic relationship if a patient were inhibited from voicing threats. Furthermore, the inexact nature of psychiatry, the possibility of the public becoming complacent if every threat were reported, and the general burden of an expansive duty require a limit on the duty to warn.[25]

Following the California court, the Sixth Circuit of the United States Court of Appeals announced this rule, likewise a limitation on the potentially broad duty in *Tarasoff*: 'when a psychiatrist determines or, pursuant to the standard of care of his profession, should determine that his patient poses

---

22 See Declaration of Geneva, 1947, cited in British Medical Association, *Handbook of Medical Ethics* (BMA, London, 1984), pp. 70ff.

23 *A Guide to Ethical Conduct and Behaviour and to Fitness to Practise*, 4th ed. (Medical Council, Dublin, 1994), p. 39.

24 551 P 2d 334 (1976). See L.R. Wilson and Ors., 'Unexpected Features of the Tarasoff Decision: The Therapist and the Duty to Warn',. *American Journal of Psychiatry* (1983), Vol. 140, p. 601-3; E.J. Kermani & Ors., 'Tarasoff Decision: A Decade Later Dilemma Still Faces Psychotherapists', *American Journal of Psychotherapy* (1987), Vol. 41, p. 2, pp. 271-85.

25 See *Thompson v. County of Alameda* [1980] 27 Cal 3d 741 at 752, 614 P 2d 728 at 734.

a serious danger of violence to a readily identifiable person, the psychiatrist has as a duty to use reasonable care to protect against such danger'.[26] So, while a duty to warn may still exist, it only becomes a duty when the threat is a serious one, and when a potential victim is a readily identifiable person. If a duty to warn is imposed, then the psychiatrist must use reasonable, not extraordinary, care to protect the potential victim, and some deference to the standards of the profession will be allowed to determine if a doctor has acted reasonably.

In Ireland, there have been no cases on breach of confidence in the context of the HIV/AIDS patient. However in England, in the case of *X v. Y & Others*,[27] the need for confidentiality with regard to HIV/AIDS patients was stressed by the court. In that case, employees of a Health Authority supplied a national newspaper with confidential information pertaining to two doctors who were carrying on general practice, despite having contracted the HIV virus. The newspaper published an article under the headline 'Scandal of Docs With Aids', which implied that there were doctors in England who were practising despite having contracted AIDS, and that the then Department of Health and Social Security wished to suppress this fact. The defendants had intended to publish a further article which would identify the doctors concerned. The plaintiffs sought an injunction restraining the defendants from publishing this article. In holding that the plaintiffs were entitled to a permament injunction restraining the defendants from publishing the identity of the doctors, the court held that the public interest in preserving the confidentiality of hospital records identifying actual or potential AIDS sufferers outweighed the public interest in the freedom of the press to publish such information.

The rationale for this decision was that those with AIDS ought not to be inhibited by fear of discovery from seeking medical treatment for their condition, and free and informed public debate about AIDS could take place without publication of the confidential information acquired by the defendants.

Another situation where the duty of confidentiality between patient and doctor may be over-ridden is found in the case of *W v. Egdell & Ors*.[28] The defendant, Dr Egdell, a consultant psychiatrist, was asked by a firm of solicitors to prepare a report on a prisoner, who was their client. The prisoner had been convicted of a series of murders, and two assaults. The purpose of the report was to assist a Parole Board to form an estimate of the prisoner's capacity to be paroled. In the event, the psychiatrist, though in fact retained

---

26 *Sellers v. United States* (1989) 870 F 2d   27 [1988] 2 All ER 648.
     1098 at 1101, quoting *Davis v. Lhim*   28 [1990] 1 All ER 835.
     (1983) 335 NW 2d 481 at 489.

by the prisoner's solicitor, formed the view that the prisoner, if released, would be a serious danger to others. The solicitors did not proceed with the application for parole. Dr Egdell's views were not communicated by anyone to the hospital which had clinical responsibility for the prisoner's medical management. When Dr Egdell discovered this, he contacted the medical director of the hospital, and furnished him with a copy of his report on the prisoner. The hospital, at the prompting of Dr Egdell, sent a copy of his report to the Secretary of State. When this was discovered, the prisoner sued both the doctor and the recipients of the report, seeking an injunction prohibiting the use of the report, and other ancillary remedies. The President of the Family Division, Sir Stephen Brown, held that though there was a duty of confidentiality between Dr Egdell and the prisoner, this competed with questions of public interest, and the balance came down decisively in favour of disclosure of the report to the Authorities, and thus Dr Egdell had acted quite properly.

In Ireland, the 4th edition of the Medical Council's *Guide to Ethical Conduct and Behaviour and to Fitness to Practise*[29] deals with confidentiality. It provides that:

> confidentiality is a time honoured principle of medical ethics. There are four circumstances where exception may be made:
>
> - When required by a judge in a court of law.
> - When necessary to protect the interests of the patient.
> - When necessary to protect the welfare of society.
> - When necessary to safeguard the welfare of another individual or patient.

The *Guide* specifically endorses the safeguarding of medical records, whether held in hospitals or by doctors. In particular, the Council endorses the statement on confidentiality in the use of computers and electronic processing in the field of health service administration, passed by the 27th World Medical Assembly.[30]

The Guide specifies that doctors belonging to certain disciplines may experience problems in relation to the conduct of medical examinations, and when reporting to a third party. The doctors in this category are medical officers of health, occupational physicians, doctors employed by and/or acting for the police, defence forces, prison medical officers and civil service [doctors].

The *Guide* further states that 'the following points should be borne in mind':

29 1994, p. 29.
30 See the text quoted in *A Guide to Ethical Conduct and Behaviour and to Fitness to Practise*, 4th ed. (Medical Council, Dublin, 1994), pp. 58-9.

- the doctor–patient relationship should be respected at all times.

- Where circumstances permit, the examinee's own personal doctor should be informed.

- The significance, rather than the precise details, of medical findings should be conveyed to any third party with the patient's consent only.

- Documents containing medical details should always be transmitted under confidential cover.

- Medical information obtained by a doctor in the process of patient examination should always be used for the betterment of that patient.

The *Guide* states that when a doctor reports to a patient's employer, the doctor must 'interpret the medical findings'. An employer does not have the right to be informed of the clinical details of illness or injury without the consent of the patient; though the *Guide* does permit (with the consent of the patient) an employer to have access to a patient's medical record where an occupational physician is presenting to an employer the significant aspects of a medical condition.

Exceptions arise where there is a statutory duty to report notifiable communicable diseases, and/or there is a real or potential risk to public health.

Duty of confidence: insurance reports   Requests from insurance companies to complete a medical report on the patient pose ethical problems. The Guide stresses that the doctor is 'advised to ensure that the patient fully understands what may be involved in furnishing a medical report, and that the contents may change [the patient's] insurance [position]'. With that knowledge, the patient has to give full consent to the issuing of such a report. The Guide stresses that a report on a deceased patient can only be released to an insurance company 'with the full consent of the next of kin'. The Guide continues to state that '[e]ven though the patient is deceased, the medical records still remain confidential. Death of a patient does not absolve a doctor from this obligation'.

In this context, it should be noted that although an insurance contract is a contract *uberrimae fidei*, and that this formerly allowed insurers to disclaim liability where an insured person failed to disclose all material facts the position is not longer as clear. In *Keating v. New Ireland Assurance Co. plc*[31] the plaintiff and her late husband took out a life insurance policy with the company. A medical examination was carried out on behalf of the

31 [1990] 2 IR 383.

defendant, at which the plaintiff's husband disclosed that some months previously, he had undergone examination and treatment for what he believed to be epi-gastric discomfort. However, this examination had revealed a condition of angina, but there was no evidence that his doctors had informed him of this. The insurer made no further inquiries as to the state of the plaintiff's husband's health. The policy granted the plaintiff provided that:

> the Policy is conditional upon full and true disclosure having been made in the proposal, and medical statement, if any, of all material facts of which the company ought to have been informed for the purpose of the contract of assurance (and that the contract of assurance expressed on this policy is based on the proposal made in that regard . . . by the assured and on the medical statements . . . in connection with the proposal.

At a medical examination arranged by the insurer, the deceased had answered a specific question as to whether he now or ever had any 'affection of the heart' in the negative.

The plaintiff's husband died. The plaintiff made a claim on foot of the insurance policy.

The insurance company sought to repudiate liability, on the basis that the policy was expressed to be conditional upon full and true disclosure having been made in the proposal and medical statement of all material facts of which the insurer ought to have been made aware for the purposes of the assurance contract, and that therefore the failure to inform them of the proposer's angina rendered the policy void. It was also contended that the statements made by the proposer constituted an absolute warranty as to the state of his health. In both the High Court and the Supreme Court, it was held that on the evidence the deceased had not known of his condition at the time of the execution of the policy and that the policy could not be avoided by a failure to disclose facts of which the proposer was not aware at the relevant time. A life insurance policy, like any other contract, must be given 'a reasonable interpretation', and it was demonstrably irrational to construe the requirement of disclosure as a warranty that the proposer accepted the contract on the basis that he had disclosed facts of whose existence he was wholly ignorant.

In a similar case, *Kelleher v. Irish Life Assurance Co. Ltd*,[32] pursuant to a special offer made to members of the Irish Medical Organization, Irish Life issued a policy of insurance whereby they agreed to insure the life of

32 [1993] ILRM 643.

the plaintiff's husband for £80,000. As part of this special offer, questions on the proposal form concerning the health of the plaintiff's husband had been crossed out. Instead it merely required that the life to be assured should be a member of the IMO under sixty years of age who had not been absent from work through illness or injury for more than two weeks in the three months prior to the date of the policy, nor have undergone medical treatment during the six months prior to that date.

The policy was issued on 10 October 1985. The plaintiff's husband died on 30 November 1985, following which the plaintiff claimed under the policy. It transpired that the deceased had failed to disclose that he had suffered from cancer in 1981, and although the treatment had been successful it caused radiation damage. The insurance company repudiated liability on the grounds of the alleged suicide of the deceased and his alleged failure to disclose all material facts prior to the issue of the policy.

In the High Court, Costello J held that the defendant had failed to prove that the deceased had committed suicide, but the defendant was allowed to repudiate liability because of the non-disclosure of material facts. The plaintiff appealed to the Supreme Court. In allowing the appeal, the Supreme Court held that in such circumstances, the appropriate test was whether a reasonable person reading the proposal form would conclude that information over and above that sought in the form was not required. In applying this test to the special proposal form in this case, the Supreme Court held that a reasonable person would assume that if he could truthfully answer the two questions, namely as to their absence from work through illness for not more than two weeks in the previous three months and as to their not having undergone medical treatment within six months prior to the date of the policy, he would be entitled to the insurance having fulfilled the other qualifications of being a member of the IMO and under the age of sixty. The court went on to hold that the insurance company had significantly limited the disclosure required from the proposers and the non-disclosure by them did not entitle the defendant to repudiate liability.

The holdings of these two cases seem to suggest that an insurer must express the terms of the agreement in unequivocal language and any ambiguity must be construed against the insurer.

From the list of principles articulated by the Supreme Court, it would appear as if the traditional *uberrimae fidei* interpretation of insurance contracts is giving ground slowly to suggestions that essentially an insurance contract is just like any commercial contract.

It is submitted that the changing view of the law of insurance contracts poses difficulties to doctors in Ireland who deal professionally with insurers and policy holders alike.

ACCESS TO MEDICAL RECORDS

The doctor must keep records of his attendance on the patient. Though there is no statutory basis for this, it would appear from *Toal v. Duignan (No. 1)*[33] which dealt with the problem of patient records, and access by the patient to these records, that there is a duty to keep proper medical records.

However, *Toal v. Duignan (No. 1)* does not state for how long medical records should be kept, nor whether a hospital which moves premises and thereby fails to keep all records of a patient who attended there, is *ipso facto* negligent or otherwise in breach of some duty.

The case does highlight a practical problem: if, as was the case in *Toal*, a hospital failed to keep the plaintiffs' medical records and was unable to produce them some twenty-six years after the patient's last attendance there, then an action against the hospital or its doctors will not succeed. The reason is that *Toal* states that where the records are so incomplete, it would be impossible for the hospital or the consultants to defend themselves. However, whereas this approach is quite understandable in cases of delay on the part of the patient, it appears from *Toal* that the plaintiff there did not make unreasonable delay in bringing his action.

This case has suggested to one commentator[34] who reviews the alternatives (storage of records until death, microfiche, summaries of notes) that hospitals should have a policy of destroying records after a minimum period. If adopted, this practice would need to be communicated to the patient at the time of his or her initial attendance.

33 [1991] ILRM 135.
34 E. Maguire, 'Should Medical Records be Kept by Patients', *Irish Medical News* (1993), Vol. 10, No. 38 (18 October), p. 10.

5

CLAIMS AGAINST DOCTORS: THE CIVIL LAW

The doctor-patient relationship is governed by principles of contract law. Claims are however rarely if ever taken solely in contract. Tort actions tended to attract higher damages than contract actions, either because most tort actions in the past were heard by juries who were sympathetic to plaintiffs,[1] or because the technical rules governing breach of contract were different from those compensating an injured party in a tort case.[2]

CONTRACT

In interpreting the doctor-patient 'contract' Irish law is slow to imply a warranty that the physician will achieve a specified result, but rather an implication that the doctor will use reasonable care and skill in the diagnosis and treatment of the patient.

Theoretically, however, a patient and doctor could by express contract agree on the performance of a specific procedure, service, or result. Liability would be incurred in the event of a failure to achieve what was promised. Such an approach is not generally taken.[3]

Perhaps because of the pervasive influence of the traditional voluntarist contract model,[4] the courts have placed great emphasis on the necessity of information, consent, and agreement about courses of action and the consequences thereof.

In certain instances, patients may take an action for breach of contract

---

1 B. McMahon & W. Binchy, *Irish Law of Torts*, 2nd ed. (Butterworth, Dublin, 1990), ch. 1.

2 R.A. Percy, *Charlesworth & Percy on Negligence*, 8th ed. (Sweet & Maxwell, London, 1990), ch. 4.

3 Except to non-medically qualified practitioners: see *Brogan v. Bennett* [1954] IR 119 discussed below.

4 See P.S. Atiyah, *The Rise and Fall of Freedom of Contract* (Clarendon Press, Oxford, 1979); H. Collins, *The Law of Contract* (Weidenfeld & Nicolson, London, 1986); D.N. Tomkin, 'Judicial Approaches to the Interpretation of Commercial Contracts', unpublished PhD thesis (Essex University, England, 1986).

where an operation proves unsuccessful. In the English case of *Eyre v. Measday*[5] it was held that where a doctor contracted to carry out a particular operation on a patient and a particular result was expected, the court would imply into the contract between the doctor and the patient a term that the operation would be carried out with reasonable care and skill, but would be slow to imply a term that the expected result would actually be achieved, since it was probable that no responsible medical man would be prepared to give such a warranty. In the case of *Thake v. Maurice*[6] the defendant surgeon performed a vasectomy on the plaintiff, Mr Thake. However, Mrs Thake became pregnant after Mr Thake underwent the vasectomy. As she did not suspect that she was pregnant, she did not even consider having an abortion until it was too late to have one safely. It was agreed that it was an implied term of the contract between the surgeon and the patient that the vasectomy would be carried out with reasonable professional care and skill and that, in fact, reasonable professional care and skill had been exercised. It was argued on behalf of the Thakes that the defendant had undertaken not only to use reasonable care and skill, but had guaranteed the ultimate success of the operation. This claim was based on what the Thakes understood the surgeon to have said at the pre-operative consultation. It was accepted that the surgeon had emphasised the irreversible nature of the procedure at the consultation. However, the Thakes understood this conversation to mean that there was no possibility of the operation failing to make Mr Thake sterile, if it was carried out with reasonable care and skill. It was established that the surgeon knew that there was a possibility of recanalization, which, as occurred in this case, would make Mr Thake fertile once more, without his knowing it. The majority of the Court of Appeal held that objectively construed, the conversation did not have the effect placed upon it by the plaintiffs, since:

> [m]edicine, though a highly skilled profession, is not, and is not generally regarded as being, an exact science. The reasonable man would have expected the defendant to exercise all the proper care and skill of a surgeon in that speciality; he would not in my view have expected the defendant to give a guarantee of 100% success.[7]

The court did, however, hold that the surgeon was liable in negligence for his failure to warn of the possibility of recanalization occurring.

Actions based on breach of contract taken by patients against doctors in respect of professional services contracts are singularly rare in contemporary

5   [1986] 1 All ER 488.
6   [1986] 1 All ER 497.
7   [1986] 1 All ER 497 at 510 *per* Neill LJ.

circumstances. However, as A.P. Bell points out, such actions are possible,[8] and, in Ireland, may be covered by the Sale of Goods and Supply of Services Act 1980.[9]

It is probable that most such contracts will be 'work and materials contracts', rather than contracts for the supply of goods, *simpliciter*. If this is so, then a question will arise as to whether the doctor would be liable for deficiencies in the goods supplied. The problem which can be demonstrated by quoting *Perlmutter v. Beth Davis Hospital*,[10] concerned a hospital which gave a patient a blood transfusion using blood contaminated with jaundice viruses. The New York Court of Appeals held that the hospital was not liable, for its only duty was to exercise reasonable care, and that had been complied with.

Turning to the 1980 Act, this provides that the supplier of goods and services warrants (a) that he has the necessary skill to render the service,[11] (b) that he will supply the service with due skill, care and diligence,[12] (c) that any goods will be sound and reasonably fit for the purpose for which they are required,[13] and (d) that any goods supplied will be of merchantable quality.[14]

S. 39 may be modified by s. 40, with the result that a doctor could exclude liability to a patient (always assuming that the patient was a 'consumer') for defective goods by an exclusion clause, if the exclusion clause was 'fair and reasonable and specifically brought to the attention' of the patient/consumer.

Furthermore, s. 40 permits the supplier of goods and services to avail of exclusion by course of dealing and usage, so that if the goods supplied were unsatisfactory, and the doctor were able to show that either a course of dealing existed between the doctor and patient, or could exclude liability by usage, then the patient would have no redress.

TORT

Battery   In chapter 3, we dealt with the conditions in which consent can be vitiated, and we discussed the consequences of such vitiation. As will be recollected, one of such consequences is that the doctor may be liable in battery. We now deal with the definition and components of this tort.

8   A.P. Bell, *Modern Law of Personal Prop-erty in England and Ireland* (Butter-worth, London & Dublin, 1989); A.P. Bell, 'The Doctor and The Supply of Goods and Services Act 1982', *Legal Studies* (1984), Vol. 4, p. 175.

9   A.P. Bell, *Modern Law of Personal Prop-*

erty *in England and Ireland* (Butter-worth, London & Dublin, 1989), p. 331.

10   (1955) 123 NE 2d 792.
11   S. 39(a).
12   S. 39(b).
13   S. 39(c).
14   S. 39(d).

The tort of battery is committed by intentionally bringing about a harmful or offensive contact with the person of another. A more inclusive definition is that of Trindade, who states that . . . '[a] battery is a direct act of the defendant which has the effect of causing contact with the body of the plaintiff without the latter's consent'.[15] The tort of battery represents the importance of the individual patient's right to determine what should or should not be done to his body. It comprises any bodily touching of the person of the plaintiff without the plaintiff's consent.

In *Wilson v. Pringle*[16] the Court of Appeal held that the plaintiff must show that the touching by the defendant was 'hostile'. Hostility in this sense is taken to refer to the defendant doing something to the plaintiff to which the plaintiff may object or which may amount to an intrusion on the plaintiff's right to autonomy. Thus ordinary contact of everyday life would be excluded from the scope of the tort of battery.

However, in the later English case of *In re F. (mental patient: sterilisation)*,[17] Lord Goff, in an *obiter* statement, cast doubt on the decision in *Wilson v. Pringle*. He believed that the requirement that the touching be hostile conflicted with the definition of battery as any touching of the body of the plaintiff without consent or lawful excuse. The imposition of the need for the touching to be hostile, therefore, occluded what should be the primary question: whether the plaintiff consented to the touching or not.

Though in general, acting in what the doctor considers to be the best interests of the patient might negate a finding of battery, it is noteworthy that where a patient fails to give informed consent to treatment, and is subjected to invasive procedures of any sort, the constituents of battery are present. Thus in *Mallette v. Schulman*,[18] the Ontario High Court held that a doctor was liable in damages for giving an unconscious patient a life-saving blood transfusion. The patient carried a card stating that she was a Jehovah's Witness. The doctor saw the card before deciding to give her blood. The card stated that by virtue of her religion, no blood transfusions were to be given to her under any circumstances. The court held that though the doctor had acted promptly and professionally in an emergency situation (the plaintiff had been a passenger in a car involved in a road traffic accident, and was haemorrhaging from the nose and mouth) the doctor was nevertheless guilty of battery. No allowance seems to have been made by the court for the doctor's action in saving the patient's life. The patient was awarded $Can 20,000 for mental distress. (We deal with the question of emergency treatment and consent in chapter 3.)

---

15 F.A. Trindade in *Oxford Journal of Legal Studies* (1982), Vol. 2, No. 1, p. 211 cited in E. McKendrick, *LLB Tort Textbook*, 6th ed. (H.L.T. Publishers,

London, 1992), p. 302.
16 [1986] 2 All ER 440.
17 [1990] 2 AC 1, 72-73.
18 (1988) 47 DLR 18.

The defence of consent allows medical practitioners coming into contact with the person of the patient to practise without fear of committing the tort of battery. To be effective:

(1) consent must be voluntarily given,

(2) the patient must be capable of giving consent, and

(3) the patient's consent must be an informed consent, that is, the patient must have the required amount of information about the nature of the procedure.

Thus, in the English case of *Chatterton v. Gerson*,[19] where the patient lost all sensation in her right leg as a result of an operation to free a trapped nerve, it was held that an action in battery could only succeed where her consent to the operation was not real, and that if the doctor had informed her in general terms of the nature of the operation, then the plaintiff would not succeed. In the subsequent case of *Sidaway v. Governors of Bethlem Royal Hospital*[20] the Court of Appeal asked the question, 'in what circumstances, if any, could failure to disclose information give rise to an action in battery?' Lord Donaldson MR stated that consent is not vitiated by a failure on the part of the doctor to give the patient sufficient information before the consent is given. It is only if consent is obtained by fraud or misrepresentation that it can be said that an apparent consent is not a true consent. The case was appealed to the House of Lords[21] where it was held that English law did not recognise the existence of the doctrine of informed consent. The House of Lords held that the question to be asked in each case was not whether sufficient information had been disclosed to the plaintiff to enable her to make an informed choice about whether or not to have the treatment, but whether a reasonably prudent doctor would have acted as the defendant had done in only releasing a certain amount of information. (For comments about the 'prudent doctor' and the *Salgo* (US) doctrine, see chapter 3).

In *Walsh v. Family Planning Services Ltd*, the plaintiff also sued the defendants for civil assault. At first instance, the plaintiff was successful under the assault heading.[21] On appeal to the Supreme Court the assault finding was reversed. The plaintiff had claimed that he did not consent to one of the defendants performing the operation and this he alleged had amounted to a battery, that is, a non-consensual touching of the plaintiff

19 [1981] QB 432.
20 [1985] AC 871.
21 [1992] 1 IR 496—probably because the procedure was effected by a doctor other than the one who discussed the operation initially with the patient, to whose involvement the patient had not consented and who accordingly had *semble* violated the patient's right to bodily integrity.

which resulted in the injury alleged. The Supreme Court held that a valid consent had been given to the operation and that what the plaintiff had consented to was the carrying out of the operation:

> by a person or persons with the requisite skill and that it should be competently done.[22]

The Supreme Court, in so holding, also discussed the question of the most appropriate action to take in such circumstances. The court held that in such instances the proper form of action was negligence. A battery action would only be appropriate in cases:

> where there is no consent to the particular procedure and where it is feasible to look for consent.[23]

The court used as justification for this decision, the rationale provided by Laskin CJ in the Canadian Supreme Court decision in *Reibl v. Hughes*[24] who said:

> [i]n situations where the allegation is that the attendant risks which have been disclosed were not communicated to the patient and yet the surgery or other medical treatment carried out was that to which the plaintiff consented (there being no negligence basis of liability for the recommended surgery or treatment to deal with the patient's condition), I do not understand how it can be said that the consent was vitiated by the failure of disclosure so as to make the surgery or other treatment an unprivileged, unconsented to and intentional invasion of the patient's bodily integrity. I can appreciate the temptation to say that the genuineness of consent to medical treatment depends on proper disclosure of the risks which it entails, but in my view, unless there has been misrepresentation or fraud to secure consent to the treatment, a failure to disclose the attendant risks, however serious, should go to negligence rather than to battery. Although such a failure relates to an informed choice of submitting to or refusing recommended and appropriate treatment, it arises as the breach of an anterior duty of due care, comparable in legal obligation to the duty of due care in carrying out the particular treatment to which the patient has consented. It is not a test of the validity of consent.[25]

---

22 Ibid., pp. 530-1.
23 Ibid., p. 531.

24 (1980) 112 DLR (3rd), 1.
25 Ibid., *per* Laskin CJC at p. 10.

Medical negligence Most legal actions in Ireland arising from the professional misconduct of a doctor in relation to his patient are brought in the tort of negligence. Negligence actions are a means by which a patient can seek compensation when a duty required of a doctor was carried out in a substandard way, and the patient was injured. At this stage, it should be mentioned that a doctor may be liable for negligence if he does nothing where he ought to have done something, or does part only of what Irish ought to have done completely. In Ireland, as elsewhere, the doctor does not usually undertake to produce a specific result, but to give a particular course of diagnosis and treatment; however, in some cases, a doctor may indeed undertake to produce a specific result. But in most cases, the tort of negligence arises not so much because a particular outcome has not been effected, but rather when the doctor has failed to do competently what should have been done.

It should also be noted that a doctor may be liable in negligence, not only for failure to treat a patient competently, but also for failure to provide proper reports and information.[26]

Most claims are brought by plaintiffs who allege misdiagnosis or mistreatment, by the doctor. However, the doctor's liability is not confined to misdiagnosis or mistreatment. Thus, there have been several cases in Ireland where a medical practitioner has been held liable for failing to furnish a full report on his patient's injuries to the patient's solicitor. It has been claimed that such failure to furnish the report, either at all or in a reasonable time, has resulted in loss. Presumably similar considerations would apply where a doctor failed to complete medical or other certificates correctly, or at all, or unreasonably delayed in so doing.

Since most cases against doctors are concerned with treatment which the patient complains is unsatisfactory, it may be that the patient will claim in the tort of battery, as well as negligence. But claims in battery in common law jurisdictions are no longer the norm, where actions in negligence are possible. In addition, battery has connotations of undesirable or anti-social behaviour, and is increasingly being replaced by negligence as the proper form of action where a doctor is the defendant.

The ever growing area of medical negligence is characterised by a tension between two conflicting policy issues. On the one hand, the importance of the development of medical science to society makes it undesirable that doctors should be obliged to operate under the ever-present threat of litigation. On the other hand, the total dependence of patients on the skill and care of the medical profession and the grave consequences of a failure

---

26 E. Madden (1992), 'The Doctor, the Solicitor and The Expert's Report', *Irish Medical Times*, Vol. 25, No. 8 (21 February), p. 23 considering *McGrath v. Kiely* [1965] IR 497.

in such cases, makes it unacceptable for the law to tolerate a lax standard of care in deciding what is or is not medical negligence. In developing the legal principles outlined, and in applying them to the facts of each case, the courts must strive to give equal regard to both of these conflicting issues. In order to succeed in an action for medical negligence, a patient must establish the following:

(a) that a duty of care was owed by the doctor to the patient;

(b) that the doctor was in breach of the appropriate standard of care imposed by the law;

(c) that the breach of duty caused the patient harm or injury recognised by the law as meriting compensation;

(d) that the extent and quantum of the loss that has flowed from the breach of duty is recoverable in law.[27]

Duty of care A doctor owes a duty to his patient. In general, the scope of the doctor's duty of care will relate to all aspects of care of the patient: diagnosis, treatment, advice and counselling. The essence of the duty in an undertaking by the doctor, once consulted for professional help, is that he possess the requisite skill and knowledge. If the doctor accepts the responsibility and undertakes the treatment and the patient submits to his direction, the doctor owes a duty to that patient to use care, skill and caution in administering treatment.

In practical terms, this applies in many cases where the patient visits a hospital and is treated by one or more doctors in a team. This raises the larger question, of what duty does the hospital owe to the patient in order to provide a safe system of admission, diagnosis, treatment and ancillary matters, which of course includes the duty to provide doctors and other health care professionals who are not negligent.

This question was addressed, but somewhat obliquely, by the Supreme Court in *Kelly v. The Board of Governors of St Laurence's Hospital*.[28] There the plaintiff was admitted as an in-patient to the hospital for tests and observation, presenting with right temporal lobe epilepsy. He was taken off all medication, for the purpose of assessment. On the fifth night of his stay, the plaintiff left his ward, crossed the corridor and entered a toilet. He was observed entering by a staff nurse. In the toilet, the plaintiff removed some bottles from the window sill, and then he placed a mobile commode under the window, which was open. The plaintiff then climbed through the

27 See *Dunne v. National Maternity Hospital* [1989] IR 91; [1989] ILRM 735.
28 [1988] IR 402; [1989] ILRM 437.

window, and fell some twenty feet to the yard, sustaining severe injuries.
In the High Court, the jury found the defendants negligent and awarded
the plaintiff £90,000 damages. In his charge to the jury, the trial judge
stated, 'if you think . . . there was a real possibility of injury to Mr Kelly,
a real possibility that he should suffer injury if he went to the toilet
unaccompanied, you would be entitled to find the hospital guilty of
negligence in that event'. The jury so found.[29]

The defendants appealed the decision to the Supreme Court on the
grounds that the case ought to have been withdrawn from the jury at the
close of all the evidence, as the plaintiff had failed to establish that the
defendant's conduct in the care and treatment of him was inconsistent with
medical practice, or that it was inherently defective.

The trial judge's formulation of negligence might have been interpreted
by the jury so as to conclude that the defendants were negligent if their
conduct gave rise to a mere possibility of the plaintiff suffering injury.

The Supreme Court held, in dismissing the appeal, that there was
sufficient evidence of negligence on the part of the defendants and the case
was properly left to the jury. Henchy J, in a dissenting judgment, outlined
the duty owed to the patient in such a situation as follows:

> the duty the defendants owed to the plaintiffs was to take reasonable
> care to avoid permitting him to be exposed to injury which a reasonable
> person ought to foresee; and in this case the duty of a reasonable
> hospital administration was to provide a reasonable nursing service.[30]

He went on to say that the essential question to be asked was whether
the risk of injury or damage was such that a reasonably careful person in
the position of the defendants would have taken the precautions suggested
by the plaintiff.

Standard of care   The standard of care required of medical practitioners has
been analysed in a number of decisions of the Irish Supreme Court. In
Daniels v. Heskin[31] Maguire CJ stated the general principle that a medical
practitioner is liable for injury caused to another person to whom he owed
a duty to take care if he fails to possess that amount of skill which is usual
in his profession or if he neglects to use the skill which he possesses or the
necessary degree of care demanded or professed.

---

29 For a general discussion of the liability
    of a doctor (especially a psychiatrist) or
    other professional such as a psycholo-
    gist) for failure to take steps to prevent
    suicide, see chapter 8.

30 Ibid., pp. 412-14.
31 [1954] IR 73.

The test laid down in *Daniels v. Heskin* was refined and re-stated in terms which are perhaps more appropriate to contemporary conditions in *Dunne v. National Maternity Hospital*.[32] There the Supreme Court enunciated clear principles relating to the standard of care required by a physician in medical negligence cases.

The case concerned a claim of negligence in the treatment of a birth of twins by Mrs Dunne, one of whom was stillborn, while the other suffered severe brain damage. It was held that the true test for establishing negligence in diagnosis or treatment on the part of a medical practitioner is whether he has been proved to be guilty:

> of such failure as no medical practitioner of equal specialist or general status and skill would be guilty of, if acting with ordinary care.[33]

From this statement of principle it can be seen that, in determining whether a medical practitioner exercised due skill and care, regard must be had to his specialisation (if any) and his status within the medical profession. Therefore, a practitioner who specialises in any particular area of medicine must be judged by the standard of skill and care of that speciality.

The Supreme Court made clear in the *Dunne* case that the court will have regard to the practice of other practitioners of similar status, when trying to determine whether a medical practitioner exercised reasonable skill and care.

In general, if a medical practitioner acts in accordance with the general and approved practice of the profession, or some responsible part of the profession, he will not be held negligent, save in exceptional circumstances. If a medical practitioner departs from the general and approved practice for no good reason, and damage results, he is likely to be held negligent. The Supreme Court in *Dunne* stressed that if the allegation of negligence against a medical practitioner is based on proof that he deviated from a general and approved practice, that will not establish negligence unless it is also proved that the course he did take was one which no medical practitioner of like specialisation and skill would have followed, had he been taking the ordinary care required from a person of his qualifications.

Where there is a difference of opinion as to the practice to be adopted, a physician will not be held to be negligent simply because he chose one alternative over the other. In *Bolam v. Friern Hospital Management Committee*,[34] it was held that the doctor should not be found negligent if he had acted in accordance with the practice accepted by 'a responsible body of

32 [1989] IR 91; [1989] ILRM 735.   34 [1957] 2 All ER 118.
33 Ibid. at 98; 745.

medical men skilled in that particular art'. (For a discission of the *Bolam* test and its progeny in the context of consent, see chapter 3.)

However, the *Dunne* case[35] imposes an important restriction on this dictum from the *Bolam* case. The Supreme Court pointed out in *Dunne* that a court is not obliged to give unreserved and universal approval to all the practices of the medical profession (or some part of the medical profession) whatever those practices may be. Finlay CJ pointed out in *Dunne*[36] that if a medical practitioner charged with negligence defends his conduct by establishing that he followed a practice which was general, and which was approved of by his colleagues of similar specialization and skill, he cannot escape liability if in reply the plaintiff establishes that such practice has inherent defects which ought to be obvious to any person giving the matter due consideration.[37] The courts do not pay such an amount of deference to the medical profession that they would endorse any practice, no matter how unreasonable, which was adopted by medical practitioners.

There is a duty on physicians to keep 'reasonably abreast with the literature in what might be called the mainstream journals although the courts in no sense impose an oppressive burden on medical practitioners in this regard'.[38] Thus, failing to read one particular article may be excusable, while to disregard a series of warnings in the medical press could well amount to negligence.

The *Guide to Ethical Conduct and Behaviour and to Fitness to Practise*[39] issued by the Medical Council stipulates that as part of their responsibility to patients, doctors have a duty to keep informed of current advances in their specialty. It would certainly be negligent to adhere to an out-of-date technique if it has been proved to be discredited by substantially the whole of informed medical opinion.

In *Sidaway v. Board of Governors of The Bethlem Royal Hospital*[40] Lord Bridge divided a doctor's professional functions into three phases: diagnosis, advice and treatment. In performing his functions of diagnosis and treatment, the test is the standard of the ordinary skilled man exercising and professing to have that skill. As regards the doctor's duty to advise, he must inform his patient of the material risks inherent in the treatment. However, he can avoid liability for failure to warn of a material risk if he can show that he reasonably believed that communications to the patient of the existence of the risk would be detrimental to the health of his patient.

---

35 [1989] IR 91; [1989] ILRM 735.
36 Ibid.
37 Ibid.
38 B. McMahon & W. Binchy, *Irish Law of Torts*, 2nd ed. (Butterworth, Dublin, 1990), p. 265.

39 4th ed. (Medical Council, Dublin, 1994).
40 [1985] 1 All ER 118 (HL).

The recent Australian decision in *Rogers v. Whitaker*[41] has changed the position in that jurisdiction in relation to certain aspects of medical negligence. The court there declared that in cases of non-disclosure of medical risks, that the principle laid down in the English case of *Bolam v. Friern Royal Hospital Management Committee*,[42] a principle applied in the *Sidaway* case, was no longer to be applied in Australia. The *Bolam* principle, as formulated by Lord Scarman, in *Sidaway*, stated that:

> a doctor is not negligent if he acts in accordance with a practice accepted at the time as proper by a responsible body of medical opinion, even though other doctors adopt a different practice. In short, the law imposes a duty of care; but the standard of care is a matter of medical judgment.[43]

The new principle laid down in *Rogers v. Whitaker* is that:

> while evidence of acceptable medical practice is a useful guide for the courts, it is for the courts to adjudicate on what is the appropriate standard of care after giving weight to 'the paramount consideration that a person is entitled to make his own decisions about his life'.[44]

This new principle only applies in cases of non-disclosure of medical risk, and not, as of yet, in cases of diagnosis and treatment.

Rogers v. Whitaker clarified the Australian position in relation to providing information and advice concerning risks of medical treatment. The court stated that a medical practitioner would breach his duty of care if he failed to warn a patient of a material risk inherent in the proposed treatment. The court stated that a risk is material if a reasonable person in the patient's position, if warned of the risk, would be likely to attach significance to it.

It is submitted that in both these aspects, Irish courts might reasonably be expected to take *Rogers v. Whitaker* into account, and to this extent *Bolam* and *Sidaway* have limited prospects of being followed.

In the recent Irish case of *Walsh v. Family Planning Services Ltd*[45] the plaintiff, for family planning reasons, elected to undergo a vasectomy operation at the defendant clinic. The plaintiff maintained that at the

---

41 (1992) 67 ALJR 47 and noted by F.A. Trindade, *Law Quarterly Review* (1993), Vol. 109, p. 352.

42 [1957] 1 WLR 582.

43 [1985] 1 All ER 643 at p. 649.

44 67 AJLR 47 at 51, quoting *F v. R* (1983) 33 SASR 189 at 193. See also F.A. Trindade, *Law Quarterly Review* (1993), Vol. 109, p. 352.

45 [1992] 1 IR 496.

consultation which preceded the operation, neither he nor his wife were informed of the possibility of orchalgia (a painful testicular condition), which in fact occurred in this case. As a result of the operation the plaintiff alleged that he had suffered recurring pain in his scrotum. In the years that followed, the plaintiff underwent various treatments for this condition, including the removal of his left testicle. The doctor by whom the plaintiff had been counselled before the operation, stated that she had warned him of the consequences of the surgery. It was established in the High Court hearing of the trial that orchalgia was:

> an extremely rare condition [and] that there is no need to warn a patient prior to an operation of the possibility of its occurrence.[46]

The High Court was of the opinion that the plaintiff had failed to prove negligence on the part of the defendants, stating that:

> . . . the evidence is that the operation was performed properly. Nothing was omitted, nothing that should have been done was not done but it was clumsy, it should have been done under general anaesthetic and it took an inordinately long time and to my mind this harboured up an intense resentment in the plaintiff's mind as to his treatment generally by the medical profession and in that way a great deal of his troubles must relate to what happened in that room on that day.[47]

On the question of the failure to warn the plaintiff of the consequences of the procedure, the High Court held that the doctor at the clinic, with whom the plaintiff had consulted, had given him sufficient warning. The court held that the defendants were liable in civil assault and for violating the plaintiff's constitutional right to bodily integrity.

The defendants appealed this decision to the Supreme Court and the plaintiff cross-appealed on the finding of no negligence. The Supreme Court, on the issue of negligence, found that there was indeed no negligence in the carrying out of the operation. The Supreme Court considered that on the evidence of the case, there was an obligation on the defendants to warn the plaintiff of the possible consequences of any condition such as orchialgia notwithstanding the rarity of its occurrence, particularly since the procedure was elective. Thus, in the words of O'Flaherty J:

> where there is a question of elective surgery which is not essential to health or bodily well-being, if there is a risk – however exceptional or

---

46 Ibid., p. 503.   47 Ibid., p. 504.

remote – of grave consequences involving severe pain stretching for an appreciable time into the future and involving the possibility of further operative procedures, the exercise of the duty of care owed by the defendants requires that such possible consequences should be explained in the clearest language to the plaintiff.[48]

It was held in the circumstances that sufficient warning was given to the patient. As a result the test for negligence in such cases is that the case is to be determined by the trial judge on the ordinary principles of negligence. As we have explained earlier, with certain limited exceptions, only a qualified registered medical practitioner or registered dentist may prescribe drugs, only a registered dentist (or a registered medical practitioner) may perform extractions, and only a registered medical practitioner or registered midwife may assist in the delivery of a baby.

The pattern of medical treatment is changing, and what is called complementary medicine is now widely practised. In this category, acupuncture, herbal therapy, hypnotherapy, and chiropractic are included, to name but a few of the common examples.[49]

The question falls to be considered, what standard of care must an alternative or complementary practitioner reach?

In England, in *Phillips v. William Whitely Ltd*,[50] an action for negligent ear piercing by a jeweller was dismissed. The jeweller, it was held by Goddard J, did not hold himself out as carrying out the procedure with the same degree of skill and care as a qualified doctor.

In Ireland, as McMahon & Binchy[51] point out, the position may be that the practitioner makes no claims to medical *qualifications* but makes definite claims to medical *skill*. In such a case, the law requires that the practitioner should have the competence claimed. 'In truth, this is primarily a case of imposing liability for negligent misstatement, based on the plaintiff's reliance'.[52]

In *Brogan v. Bennett*,[53] the Supreme Court held that a bone setter whose client died of tuberculosis, was liable. He held himself out as having effected cures which were 'scarcely short of miracles'.[54]

The case is authority for the proposition that such a practitioner is not expected to employ the skill which would be expected from a qualified practitioner, but is only liable for failure to employ such skill as he said he

48 Ibid., p. 535.
49 S. Fulder, *The Handbook of Complementary Medicine* (Coronet Books, London, 1988).
50 [1938] 1 All ER 566.
51 B. McMahon & W. Binchy, *Irish Law of Torts*, 2nd ed. (Butterworth, Dublin, 1990), p. 267.
52 Id., p. 267.
53 [1954] IR 119.
54 Ibid., p. 127.

had.

In this context, it should be noted that many complementary practitioners in Ireland possess nursing or medical qualifications, and that this of itself may complicate the issue.

First, will the complementary therapist who is registered as a medical practitioner or nurse and who administers complementary treatment be liable under the *Brogan* test? Not unless he has held out specific promise that such treatment will attain a specific desired effect.

Second, will the complementary therapist with medical or nursing registration be liable if he fails to use orthodox diagnostic or therapeutic procedures, as an adjunct to, or in complementary therapy? It is impossible to generalise about all complementary therapy. Homeopathy is perhaps a good example. Opinions differ about its merits: but many responsible doctors do not accept that it is therapeutically valuable, the placebo effect apart.[55] It has not yet been decided whether a practitioner could make out a case that such therapy is 'in accordance with the practice accepted by a responsible body of medical men skilled in that particular art', as the *Bolam*[56] test describes it.

It would therefore appear as if complementary techniques must be used as an adjunct to conventional diagnosis and therapy by those with medical qualifications.

In the absence of medical or nursing qualifications, a complementary therapist will be liable as discussed above: for failing to deliver whatever skill or end result which was promised.[57]

Causation   There must be a causal connection between the act or omission of the defendant and the injury sustained by the plaintiff.[58]

McMahon & Binchy distinguish between 'factual' and 'legal' causation.[59] The salient feature of this distinction is that the former deals with the scientific aspects of causation (cause and effect), and the latter with the particular policy which is adopted by the courts in determining liability (responsibility and remoteness).[60]

55 P. Skrabanek & J. McCormick, *Follies and Fallacies in Medicine* (Tarragon Press, Glasgow, 1989).
56 [1957] 2 All ER 118.
57 Mr W. O'Dea TD, then Minister of State at the Department of Health and Justice, *Irish Times*, 15 August 1994, p. 10 discusses the need for legal regulation of alternative medical practitioners.
58 *Barnett v. Chelsea and Kensington Hospital Management Committee* [1969] 1 QB 428.
59 B. McMahon & W. Binchy, *Irish Law of Torts*, op. cit. (Butterworth, Dublin, 1990), p. 38-44.
60 Ibid., p. 39.

Kennedy & Grubb, in referring to factual causation in the context of medical treatment, note two main problems. First, that the medical practitioner's conduct 'could' cause the patient harm, as a medical fact. Second, whether or not in the particular case, the harm did arise from the practitioner's conduct.[61]

In *Loveday v. Renton*,[62] the plaintiff alleged that the permanent brain damage that she suffered had been caused by the administration of whooping-cough vaccine. The court held that the scientific evidence did not establish a link between brain damage in young children and the adminstration of the vaccine. This exemplifies the first of the two problems.

The second is demonstrated by *Barnett v. Chelsea and Kensington Management Committee*.[63] There, the plaintiff's husband, B became ill after drinking tea. He went to the casualty department of the defendant hospital. The casualty officer who was himself unwell, did not examine the deceased, but said that he should go home and call his own doctor. B went home, and died some hours later. The cause of death was later discovered to have been arsenic poisoning. The question for determination by the court was whether the cause of death was the negligence of the casualty officer, or whether the deceased would have died in any event due to the poison. It was held that on the evidence, and given the time scale that would have operated if B had been admitted by the casualty officer immediately, it was unlikely that B would have survived. Therefore his death was not attributable to the failure of the casualty officer to examine (and admit) B.

The rule most commonly favoured by the courts in distinguishing the relevant causes from the irrelevant causes is what has come to be known as the 'but for' test. This means that an act is a cause of an event if the event would not have occurred without ('but for') the act in question. If the injury would have occurred in any event, it was not caused by the medical practitioner's breach of duty.

Since it is a necessary element in his claim, the burden normally rests upon the plaintiff to show that he would not have suffered the injury or damage complained of if the defendant had not been negligent. Where, however, the defendant's negligence simply had the effect of increasing the risk of that injury or damage occurring, the question whether the defendant's negligence really 'caused' the injury or damage becomes highly speculative.

If some extraneous event intervenes between the negligence of the medical practitioner and the loss or injury of which the patient complains

---

61 I. Kennedy & A. Grubb, *Medical Law: Text with Materials*, 2nd ed. (Butterworth, London, 1994), p. 468-9.
62 [1990] 1 Med LR 117.
63 [1969] 1 QB 428.

(*novus actus interveniens*), the causal connection may be negatived. (See discussion below at pp. 81-2.)

It is a common feature of medical treatment that the patient's care is shared between a number of different nurses, doctors and specialists. Where more than one person makes a mistake, it is largely a question of fact and degree whether the earlier error is an effective cause of the patient's injury.

In the English case of *Robinson v Post Office*[64] it was held that a doctor who failed to administer a proper test dose of anti-tetanus serum before giving a full ATS injection, was negligent. However, since a proper test dose was subsequently administered to the patient, the failure of the doctor in question had not caused or materially contributed to the encephalitis which the patient contracted 9 days after the injection.

In *Best v. Wellcome Foundation*[65] the High Court, on 11 May 1993 approved an award of £2,740,000 as compensation for brain damage sustained in September 1969 after vaccination with the triple vaccine manufactured by the Wellcome Foundation, which was held to have been negligent in the manufacture and release of the particular batch of vaccine. The decision is based on the finding that the particular batch was below standard, had an unusually high toxicity rating, and should never have been released on to the market. In the High Court, the judge did not accept the evidence of the parents that their son had started to have seizures and to show signs of distress within a few hours of vaccination. The general practitioner's records were however inadequate. Since no such symptoms were recorded until some weeks later, the necessary temporal relation had not been proved. The GP had no recollection of the family, but said in evidence that had he been told of such symptoms he would have recorded them and referred the baby immediately to a hospital. On appeal, the Supreme Court upheld the High Court's findings, that Wellcome had been negligent and that the vaccine was capable of causing brain damage.

However, the Supreme Court took the somewhat unusual step of replacing some of the findings of the High Court judge as to timing by its own conclusion that the baby had seizures and other symptoms within a few hours; that his mother repeatedly sought held from the GP; and that the GP had regarded her as a 'fussy mother', so that the baby was not seen by a specialist until five months after the vaccine was given.

Finlay CJ, in the Supreme Court, placed a different interpretation from that of the High Court judge on the GP's diaries; neither the entries in the diaries, nor the absence of entry from them was a sufficiently strong proof of the date of the first convulsion suffered by the plaintiff, to displace the clear cut evidence of the parents. Finlay CJ was satisfied that the first

64 [1974] 2 All ER 737.   65 [1992] ILRM 609.

convulsion occurred on the evening of the first injection. The plaintiff was thus entitled to a finding against Wellcome of negligence causing personal injury. The claim against the GP was abandoned, since the plaintiff accepted that had the doctor been aware that the vaccine supplied was unusually potent and had failed a toxicity test, he would not have used it.

The case was then referred back to the High Court for a determination of the amount of compensation.

A second aspect of the case is important. It is authority for the proposition that the manufacturers of a vaccine have a duty to exercise all reasonable care to avoid exposing recipients to danger and harm from the use of their products. However, the fact that injuries were proximately caused by the manufacturers' products would not, in itself, establish liability in negligence on the part of a manufacturer, provided that a high degree of care had been exercised in the production and testing of the vaccine. But, merely to comply with mandatory or minimum requirements imposed by national health authorities or merely to rely on one particular point of view in a debated question concerning the risks involved would not necessarily constitute a sufficient degree of care to discharge the legal duty of a manufacturer. This aspect of the case may be important in the current litigation in Ireland in respect of claims by haemophiliacs against those allegedly responsible for providing infected blood, but as this litigation is currently *sub judice*, no confident assertions can yet be made.

Novus actus interveniens This term, literally 'a new intervening act' breaks the causal link between the actor or tortfeasor and the act. An example in point is *Conley v. Strain*.[66] There, the plaintiff was injured in a road traffic accident on 11 June 1984. He was a passenger in a car owned by the first defendant, and driven by the first defendant's son. As a result of the accident an emergency operation was carried out. Sixteen days after the emergency operation, whilst still detained in hospital and having appeared to be recovering, the plaintiff suffered a relapse and underwent a second emergency operation which was performed by the second defendant, a surgeon. The plaintiff remained unconscious from the time of the second operation, until November 1984.

When the plaintiff eventually regained consciousness, he was found to be suffering from severe disabilities. The car owner did not deny negligence, but he sought a contribution from the surgeon and the Western Health Board on the basis that the consequences of the traffic accident were aggravated by the negligence of the surgeon as a servant or agent of the Health Board and that such negligence amounted to a *novus actus interveniens*.

66 [1988] IR 628.

The plaintiff submitted that the surgeon and the Health Board ought to have sought advice from a neuro-surgical centre and ought to have transferred him to such a centre. It was held by Lynch J in the High Court, in giving judgment for the plaintiff against the first defendant (the car owner) and dismissing the action against the surgeon and the Health Board, that on the evidence, the allegation failed that the surgeon had been negligent in failing to seek advice from, or failing to transport the patient to a neuro-surgical centre.

The court held that the surgeon had not been negligent in using the quantities of surgi-cell he deemed necessary in dealing with the emergency of 27 June 1984, even if it was more than would have been used by a neurosurgeon. There was no substance to the criticism of the surgeon that he put too tight a bandage round the patient's skull after this emergency operation. Neither of these actions constituted a *novus actus interveniens*. The only element of erroneous treatment by the surgeon which Lynch J found, was the administration of hypotensive drugs. However this treatment caused no damage to the plaintiff, and Lynch J accordingly dismissed the claim against the surgeon. He said:

> I accept the foregoing evidence of Surgeon Ryan and of the second defendant, and accordingly I have come to the conclusion that the administration of the hypotensive drugs had no adverse effect on the plaintiff and that the plaintiff's present condition arises solely from the road traffic accident of the 11 June 1984, and the secondary haemorrhage of the 27 June 1984, which is of course a consequence of the road traffic accident.
>
> In these circumstances, the only element of erroneous treatment by [the surgeon] which I have found caused no damage to the plaintiff and the plaintiff's action against the [surgeon and the Health Board] must therefore be dismissed.[67]

Remoteness   The test to be applied in determining remoteness of damage is the 'foreseeability' test, as laid down in *Overseas Tankship UK Ltd v. Morts Docks & Engineering Co. Ltd* (known as the *Wagon Mound No. 1* case).[68] In that case, it was stated that the test to be applied in determining liability is whether the damage or injury is of such a kind as the reasonable man should have foreseen and that such foreseeability must be of the damage which in fact happened. This test has been accepted in Ireland in several cases, so, in *Burke v. John Paul & Co. Ltd*,[69] the Supreme Court held that:

67   Ibid. at p. 64.   69   [1967] IR 277.
68   [1961] AC 388.

the test of foreseeability as adopted in [*Wagon Mound No. 1*] has been accepted in this court, (and indeed was accepted in the argument in this case), and I proceed on the basis, that in determining liability for the consequences of a tortious act of negligence, the test is whether the damage is of such a kind as a reasonable man should have foreseen.[70]

An illustrative case in the area of medical treatment and foreseeability of damage is *Reeves v. Carthy & O'Kelly*.[71] Here the plaintiff had suffered severe stomach pains and vomiting. The first defendant, a medical practitioner, attended the plaintiff at his home, and injected him twice with a drug which contained morphine, cyclomorph. He did not advise the plaintiff to go to hospital. The second defendant, another medical practitioner, also attended the plaintiff later on the same day, and injected him with another drug, largactil. The second defendant advised the plaintiff that he required hospitalisation, but the plaintiff refused to go to hospital. He suffered a stroke later on the same day, and was then taken to hospital. There it was discovered that the plaintiff had suffered an abdominal catastrophe by a perforation of the stomach wall. It also appeared that the plaintiff suffered from Crohn's disease, and this had led to the perforation, and abdominal catastrophe. The plaintiff brought an action against both defendants. At trial, the plaintiff adduced evidence that the first defendant failed to carry out an examination of the plaintiff's abdomen, and as a result, failed to recognise the plaintiff as an acutely ill person in need of hospitalisation. In addition, the administration of cyclomorph by the first defendant was in the circumstances contrary to accepted medical practice, because it could mask the plaintiff's symptoms. The plaintiff adduced evidence that the second defendant was negligent in administering largactil, which in the circumstances was dangerous, because it added to the process of circulatory collapse. In addition, the plaintiff alleged that the second defendant failed to realise that the plaintiff was critically ill, and that he had failed to insist on the plaintiff's removal to hospital. The plaintiff also produced evidence that the damage to his brain caused by the stroke was a result of the extended period during which he had suffered from hypotension. The defendants argued that they might have foreseen an abdominal perforation, but they could not have foreseen the occurrence of a stroke, as the stroke was not the consequence of the abdominal perforation but of a perforation with Crohn's Disease. The trial judge appeared to accept the evidence of the defendants, and withdrew the plaintiff's case from the jury, entering judgment for the defendants. The plaintiff appealed to the Supreme Court. The Supreme Court allowed the appeal and directed a re-trial. O'Higgins CJ stated that:

70 Ibid., *per* Budd J at 282.   71 [1984] IR 348.

while undoubtedly Crohn's Disease was a factor, there was a considerable amount of evidence to the effect that, apart altogether from
Crohn's Disease, the subjecting of a patient, even of the plaintiff's age,
to a prolonged period of hypotension, carried with it the risk of a
stroke. There was further evidence that the existence of such a risk
would have been known to any doctor.[72]

Res ipsa loquitur   In certain cases of medical negligence, the patient may be
unable to prove how the injury happened. Here the cause of the injury lies
solely within the knowledge of the medical practitioner. Such eventualities
are covered by the maxim *res ipsa loquitur* (literally, 'the matter speaks for
itself'). The maxim was first authoritatively discussed in the case of *Scott
v. London & St Catherine's Docks Co.*,[73] which stated the rule in such cases
as follows:

> [t]here must be reasonable evidence of negligence. But where the thing
> is shown to be under the management of the defendant or his servants,
> and the accident is such that in the ordinary course of things does not
> happen if those who have the management use proper care, it affords
> reasonable evidence in the absence of explanation by the defendants,
> that the accident arose from want of care.[74]

There are three conditions which must be fulfilled before *res ipsa* can be
applied. These are: (1) the defendant must be in control of the thing which
caused the injury to the plaintiff; (2) the accident must be of such a nature
that it would not have occurred in the ordinary course of events without
negligence; and, (3), there must be no explanation for the accident, that is,
if the court finds on the basis of the evidence how the injury occurred, then
there is no room for inference.

The Supreme Court discussed the doctrine of *res ipsa loquitur* in
Hanrahan v. Merck Sharp & Dohme.[75] Henchy J stated that:

> in the tort of negligence, where damage has been caused to the plaintiff
> in circumstances in which such damage would not usually be caused
> without negligence on the part of the defendant, the rule of *res ipsa
> loquitur* will allow the act relied on to be evidence of negligence in the
> absence of proof by the defendant that it occurred, without want of
> due care on his part. The rationale behind the onus of the shifting of
> the onus of proof to the defendant in such cases would appear to lie

72 Ibid., p. 360.   74 Ibid. *per* Erle CJ at 642.
73 (1865) 3 H & C 596 (Exch D).   75 [1988] ILRM 629.

in the fact that it would be palpably unfair to require a plaintiff to prove something which is beyond his reach and which is peculiarly within the range of the defendant's capacity of proof.

The effect of the application of *res ipsa* is that an onus is put on the defendant to provide a reasonable explanation for the injuries sustained by the plaintiff and to establish that these occurred without negligence on his part.

In the Irish medical negligence case of *Lindsay v. Mid Western Health Board*[76] Morris J in the High Court applied the above conditions in upholding the plaintiff's claim for damages for personal injuries sustained as the result of an operation performed by the defendant surgeon. In that case an emergency appendectomy was carried out, but after the operation the plaintiff experienced a series of seizures and sank into a coma which lasted for 18 years, with complete brain damage. However, in the Supreme Court it was held that the plea of *res ipsa loquitur* should be upheld. While no act of negligence could be identified, it would be in defiance of reason and justice to say that an explanation by the defendant was not called for in circumstances where a patient had undergone a routine medical procedure under general anaesthetic, but did not return to consciousness. The disparity between the situations of the plaintiff, who was a patient in a surgical operation, and the defendant was of crucial importance. But it was held that Morris J was correct regarding this as a *res ipsa loquitur* case.

The Supreme Court stated that the maxim *res ipsa loquitur* was not a rule of substantive law, but simply an aid in the evaluation of evidence which provided a method of inferring a fact or facts in issue from circumstances proved in evidence.

There is still considerable doubt as to what the practical or procedural effect is of the operation of the *res ipsa* doctrine. McMahon & Binchy,[77] attempt to elucidate the practical effect of *res ipsa*. The commentary in Byrne & Binchy[78] on *Lindsay v. Mid Western Health Board* also provides some discussion of the limits of this doctrine. The problem may be that *res ipsa loquitur* is in fact no specific doctrine or policy, but rather a 'species of circumstantial evidence', and as such a catch–all category.

---

76 [1992] 2 IR 147. See C.R. Symmons, 'Medical Negligence and the Doctrine of Res Ipsa Loquitur in Ireland', *Professional Negligence* (1992), Vol. 8, No. 1, pp. 17-19.

77 B. McMahon & W. Binchy, *Irish Law of Torts*, op. cit., pp. 141.

78 R. Byrne & W. Binchy, *1991 Annual Review of Irish Law* (The Round Hall Press, 1993), pp. 415-17.

VICARIOUS LIABILITY

Generally speaking, a person who employs others is 'vicariously liable' for the negligence of his employees, while the employees are acting in the course of their employment. A person who retains an independent contractor, in general will not be 'vicariously liable' for the negligence of that contractor.[79]

For this reason, the law has attached importance to the distinction between an 'employee' and an 'independent contractor'. In general, an independent contractor is one who undertakes to perform a particular task in return for a fixed sum, and who reserves the right to control the manner in which he carries out this task. An employee, on the other hand, is a person who is retained on a long term basis, to carry out a series of specific duties for which he is paid at regular intervals, and who is subject to the dictates of his employer not only as to what tasks he is to perform, but how they are to be executed.

The leading English case of *Hillyer v. Governors of St Bartholomew's Hospital*[80] held that hospital authorities were only liable for the performance by their staff of 'purely ministerial or administrative duties, such as, for example, attendance of nurses in the wards, the summoning of medical aid in cases of emergency, the supply of proper food and the like'.

The reason for this was that vicarious liability was normally determined by the 'control test',[81] that is, that one would only be held vicariously liable for the acts of others, if one had sufficient control over their acts. There is no question of hospital authorities controlling the way in which the surgeon operates. This meant that patients frequently had no redress against the hospital. In *Gold v. Essex CC*[82] and *Cassidy v. Minister for Health*[83] the vicarious responsibility of hospital authorities was gradually enlarged. It was held that the hospital authority was responsible for all medical staff who had treated the plaintiff during the operation and afterwards. That this has been accepted in Ireland can be seen from such cases as *O'Donovan v. Cork Co. Council*.[84] There in an action against the defendant council for the alleged negligence of a surgeon and an anaesthetist, the defendant council, while denying negligence, did not even contest the proposition that it would be vicariously liable if negligence were proved on the part of the surgeon or the anaesthetist.

In *Hay v. O'Grady*[85] the plaintiff was employed by the defendant in his capacity as representative of St Mary's Hospital, Drumcar, in the role of facilitating severely mentally handicapped patients of the hospital to

80 [1909] 2 KB 820.
81 B. McMahon & W. Binchy, *Irish Law of Torts*, op. cit., ch. 43.
82 [1942] 2 KB 293 (CA).
83 [1951] 2 KB 343.
84 [1967] IR 173.
85 [1992] ILRM 689.

re-integrate into the community. Patients were selected by hospital staff to reside in houses in the community, and the plaintiff's role was that of house parent. One particular patient was disruptive and the hospital management decided that a six week hospital stay was necessary. At the end of the six weeks the patient returned to the house. She was again involved in a disturbance in a hotel whilst on a day's outing. A hospital management meeting took place to discuss this incident, but, pending a decision, the patient remained in the house. A week later the patient assaulted the plaintiff. In the High Court, Lynch J rejected the plaintiff's claim that the defendant had been negligent in failing to take the patient away from the house, or in failing to provide two house parents. The plaintiff then appealed to the Supreme Court.

The Supreme Court dismissed the plaintiff's appeal, and held that although there was some confusion as to some of the facts concerning the background of the patient's treatment and behaviour, on the essential facts, there was no dispute. The court stated that Lynch J, in the High Court, concluded that the management of the patient by those concerned did not fall short of the appropriate standard of care. In particular, Lynch J concluded that those concerned with the management of the hospital had not failed to give due consideration to all relevant incidences. There was not therefore an obvious need to transfer the patient back to the hospital after the incident in the hotel. The Supreme Court was of the opinion that such a conclusion was wholly supported by the evidence. McCarthy J stated that if he were to deal with the matter at first instance, he would have come to the same conclusion as Lynch J.

LIABILITY OF DOCTORS FOR ACTS OF OTHER HEALTH CARE PROFESSIONALS

If another person is employed by the doctor, then, in normal circumstances, he is liable for his employee. In its *Guide To Ethical Conduct*, the Medical Council emphasises that whatever deputising arrangements are made by doctors, suitable notice setting out clearly the arrangements for medical care during off-duty time should be displayed prominently in doctor's surgeries, and information sheets on deputising arrangements should be made available to patients.[86] The *Guide* also states that to avail of the services of a deputy does not absolve the principal doctor of final responsibility for his patients. Thus, a principal doctor who contracts for the service of a deputy must ensure that this course of action does not in any way lessen the quality of medical care he is under obligation to provide for his patients. Furthermore,

---

86 4th ed. (Medical Council, Dublin, 1994).

deputy doctors must always act in the knowledge that they are providing medical care on behalf of a principal doctor and must convey to the principal doctor as quickly as possible a report containing the essential details of the home visit.

The overall cost to the medical profession and to the public of medical negligence must be considered in the context of medical indemnity insurance. The most recent statistics suggest that there are three main insurers active in the Republic of Ireland. These are the Medical Defence Union (MDU) the Medical Protection Society (MPS) and the most recent player, Medisec, (until recently called the Irish GP Indemnity Mediation and Advisory Services Ltd). The first two are both mutual organisations, owned by the members and all three are non-profit making. The schemes differ. There is no upper limit in the amount of the indemnity cover of the MDU and the MPS.[87] Although the primary dispute resolution procedure is still litigation, there is a growing interest in alternative dispute resolution as a means of dealing with claims.

DOCTORS AS EXPERT WITNESSES

In October 1993, Costello J by direction made an order about medical witnesses.[88] This direction states that Counsel taking a High Court action in which medical reports are required must consider whether the attendance of medical witnesses is necessary to explain medical reports. (If it is considered that attendance is not necessary, a request should be made to the opposing side to admit in evidence the contents of such reports without the necessity of adducing oral testimony). On the other hand, should the request be acceded to, then copies of all admitted reports should be made available for the court. Before trial, the directive provides additional rules in respect of exchange of medical reports on a reciprocal basis. In addition, the directive introduces new procedures for furnishing medical reports to the other side where evidence is being given orally by a medical witness. If

---

87 See John Daly, 'The Cost of Medical Indemnity', *Irish Medical Times* (1993), Vol. 27, No. 48 (26 November), p. 16; Donal Bergin, 'New Medical Indmnity Service a boon to GPs', *Irish Medical Times* (1994), Vol. 28, No. 20 (20 May), p. 20. Since February 1991, new rules in medical negligence cases have been introduced by hospital authorities and medical insurers in respect of medical negligence claims by patients. Under these rules a similar system will obtain as that which existed in the UK since 1954. The net effect of such an agreement is that it is hoped that it will be unlikely that as a matter of routine, hospital doctors themselves will be joined as parties to actions for medical negligence by hospital authorities, as was the case in the past.

88 This is summarised in F. Bowers, 'Radical Change for Medico-Legal Court System', *Irish Medical News* (1993), Vol. 10, No. 39 (26 October), pp. 1-2.

no objection is taken, then Counsel should indicate to the court whether (a) the report is to be treated as part of the testimony of the witness in which case the witness should be asked to explain or supplement the report or (b) whether it is offered merely for the convenience of the court as an aide memoire.

REMEDIES IN CIVIL LAW

An award of damages is the normal remedy sought by a plaintiff in respect of breach of duty by a medical practitioner whether the claim is brought in contract or tort.

Though different technical rules apply to the calculation and assessment of damages in contract[89] and tort,[90] this difference is largely unimportant in practice, as most claims in medical negligence will be framed in both contract and tort. It is important, for example, to plead breach of contract specifically, so that under O. 31 and O. 63 r.1(6) of the Rules of the Superior Courts, application may be made by notice of motion before the Master's Court for discovery prior to statement of claim. It is believed that as a matter of practice, such an order will only be granted if breach of contract is specifically pleaded.

Assuming therefore that the action is taken in both contract and tort, we comment now upon the question of damages.

In all tort claims, the plaintiff is generally entitled to at least full compensation in respect of his monetary (pecuniary) losses, both past and prospective, which result from destruction or impairment of his ability to earn money because of his injuries.[91]

Recovery for monetary losses, though, is not necessarily limited to lost earnings, but can also include loss of future income from a pension,[92] or loss of the value of a capital asset due to accrue to the plaintiff in the future, but which will now not take place due to the plaintiff's injuries.[93] Recovery for a housewife will be based on the monetary value of her housekeeping capacity.[94]

Limits on pecuniary advantage for which one can recover include illegal earnings.[95] Further, a future loss might be discounted to its present value, because the sum awarded at the judgment is supposed to represent an award

89 See R. Clark, *Contract Law in Ireland*, 3rd ed. (Sweet & Maxwell, London, 1992), pp. 442 and ff.

90 B. McMahon and W. Binchy, *Irish Law of Torts*, 2nd ed., op. cit., ch. 44 *passim.*

91 J.P.M. White, *Irish Law of Damages for Personal Injuries and Death*, Vol. 1, *Law and Practice* (Butterworth (Ireland), Ltd, Dublin), p. 120.

92 See *Parry v. Cleaver* [1970] AC 1 (HL (E)), cited by White, p. 121, fn. 4.

93 White, p. 121.

94 Id.

95 White, p. 130.

for wages lost over many years. Thus, a plaintiff will receive the amount which, if invested at a reasonable interest rate, will equal the amount lost at the future date.[96] Furthermore, if a plaintiff recovers for lost future earnings, and when that sum is not chargeable to income tax at the time of receipt by the plaintiff, a deduction will be made for the tax which the plaintiff would have had to pay if he had earned the money in his usual way.[97]

It should be noted, however, that while capital gains tax exists in Ireland, the legislation expressly excludes damages for loss of earnings recovered in respect of personal injury.[98] In the UK, the situation is the same.[99] So, if the award in respect of loss of earnings is a capital receipt (rather than an income receipt), it is not subject to taxation. The law then demands that a deduction be made to allow for the income tax which the plaintiff would have had to pay, had he earned the money in the ordinary course of employment and earnings.

On the other hand, the plaintiff receives credit, based upon inflation. Irish courts make a direct allowance for the impact of future inflation in the damages calculation; English courts do not.[100] The English approach is articulated by Lord Diplock in *Mallet v. McMonagle*.[101] According to Lord Diplock:

> [M]oney should be treated as retaining its value at the date of judgment, and in calculating the present value of annual payments which would have been received in future years, interest rates appropriate to times of stable currency should be adopted.[102]

The leading Irish case which allows for inflation adjustment is *Cooke v. Walsh*.[103]

A plaintiff might also recover for non-pecuniary loss, that is, for a loss that is not compensation for an economic loss. These damages represent, as much as is possible, monetary compensation for the pain, suffering, inconvenience and loss of the amenities of life which the injury has caused the plaintiff, and will cause the plaintiff in the future.

---

96   Ibid. at p. 143.
97   See *British Transport Commission v. Gourley* [1956] AC 185 HL (E)), in White, p. 173.
98   Capital Gains Tax Act 1975, S. 24(1)(c).
99   Capital Gains Tax Act 1979, S. 19(5).
100 According to White, this leads to serious undercompensation of plaintiffs. See White, p. 187, p. 253.
101 [1970] AC 166 (HL (NI)).
102 Quoted by White, p. 176.
103 [1983] ILRM 429 (HC); [1984] ILRM 208 (SC). Cited by White, p. 189.

White gives two basic theories upon which recovery for non-pecuniary damages can be based, namely, the 'subjective' and the 'objective'.[104] The subjective theory stresses the pain and suffering which the plaintiff has personally experienced, physically and mentally. For example, if a plaintiff successfully recovers for medical negligence which results in his losing a leg, his recovery might include compensation meant to give him some solace for the awareness he will have of his deprivation of life because he has lost a leg. Furthermore, his life-span might have been cut short, and his awareness of that fact is compensable.[105]

The objective theory stresses something like a property interest[106] which a plaintiff has in, again, a lost leg resulting from medical negligence. The compensable injury in this case is the injury itself, the actual loss of the limb and the loss of capacity and the amenities lost (rather than the subjective awareness of the loss).

An example of the distinction is to be inferred from *Cooke v. Walsh*,[107] where the plaintiff, in addition to suffering severe physical injury, also sustained brain damage which made him unaware of his condition. The question of reducing damages in the case of the 'unaware' plaintiff was discussed. The Court held that the damages award should be reduced as a result of the plaintiff's not being aware of his injuries.

The size of medico-legal awards in damages, and the nature of the claims (loss of a specific limb, loss of percentage of hearing etc.) is now recorded in each issue of the *Irish Law Times*.

In the vast majority of medical negligence actions, the principal matter of complaint is that the defendant has caused, aggravated or failed to cure some form of personal injury. The plaintiff ordinarily claims general damages for pain, suffering and loss of amenity and special damages for financial losses suffered in consequence (such as loss of earnings or the cost of medical and nursing care). The same principles apply to the assessment of damages for personal injuries and death, whether resulting from medical negligence or some other form of accident.[108]

It is worth noting that at common law, there did not exist an action for wrongful death, leading to the anomalous result that an injury might be compensable, but a complete (fatal) injury was not. In an infamous passage in *Baker v. Bolton*,[109] it was written that 'the death of a human being could not be complained of as an injury; and in this case the damages . . . must stop with the period of her existence'.[110]

104 White, p. 251.
105 Ibid.
106 See *Arnott v. O'Keeffe* [1977] IR 1 at 15 (SC), cited in White, p. 252.
107 [1984] ILRM 208.
108 *Sinnott v. Quinnsworth Ltd* [1984] ILRM 523 at 531 (SC), in White, p. 248.
109 [1808] 1 Camp. 493.
110 Quoted by White, p. 285.

This situation was alleviated in both England and Ireland by several statutory remedies, the most recent in Ireland being Part IV of the Civil Liability Act 1961, and in England, the Fatal Accidents Act 1976, as amended by s. 3(1) of the Administration of Justice Act 1982.[111]

The essential features of a claim for damages before the Irish courts are fully described in chapter 44 of McMahon & Binchy.[112]

One aspect worth special consideration is that recovery for emotional distress without physical injury is virtually unknown in Ireland. However, recent developments in the US show that there is a trend there allowing for such recovery.[113]

The assessment of damages is subject, in every case, to the overriding principle that the injury in respect of which compensation is sought must be sufficiently proximate to the medical practitioner's breach of duty. This means that the breach of duty must have 'caused' the injury and the injury in question was foreseeable.

LIMITATION OF ACTIONS AT CIVIL LAW

Legal actions are subject to periods of limitation within which proceedings must be taken. The rationale for the existence of limitation periods is that it would be unfair for a person to be subjected to litigation many years after he is alleged to have, for example, committed a tort or acted in breach of contract, where the plaintiff has slept on his rights. Moreover, witnesses may die and the memory of those surviving may be affected by the passage of time. In the context of medical law the limitation periods in relation to tort actions are of most relevance.

S. 11(2) of the Statute of Limitations 1957 provides that an action founded in tort shall not be brought after the expiration of six years from the date on which the cause of action accrued. There are, however, two exceptions to this general rule, where the limitation period is three years. These are actions claiming damages for slander and actions claiming damages for negligence, nuisance or breach of duty where the damages claimed consist of, or include, damages relating to personal injuries. This latter exception would encompass many actions taken against medical practitioners. There has been a great deal of judicial discussion of the question 'at what point

---

111 White, p. 282.

112 B. McMahon & W. Binchy, *Irish Law of Torts*, 2nd ed. (Butterworth, Dublin, 1989).

113 In *Faya v. Almarez* [1993] 329 Md 435, a plaintiff recovered for emotional distress without physical injury after learning that a surgeon with AIDS failed to warn the plaintiff. Similarly, when a recipient of a mechanical heart valve learned of its risk of failure and suffered emotional distress, recovery was also allowed: *Angus v. Shiley Inc* [1993] CCH Prod Liab Rep 13, 453.

does the cause of action accrue? In *Hegarty v O'Loughran*[114] it was stated by Griffin J that:

> there have been cases in which a foreign body was negligently left in a patient after an operation, and the patient had been totally oblivious of its presence for a considerable time before suffering any ill-effects from it. In cases such as these, if time were to run from the date of the occurrence of the wrongful act, the period of limitation of three years might very well expire before there is any manifestation of the damage suffered in consequence of the wrongful act. However, in s. 11(2)(b) of the Act of 1957, time is not expressed to run from the date of the occurrence of the wrongful act and should not in my view be interpreted as if it was. The relevant date under the subsection is the date on which the cause of action accrues. Until and unless the plaintiff is in a position to establish by evidence that damage has been caused to him, his cause of action is not complete and the period of limitation fixed by that subsection does not commence to run.[115]

In that case, the plaintiff underwent surgery on her nose in 1973, carried out by the first defendant. This operation was not entirely successful and in 1974 the plaintiff underwent a second operation performed by the second defendant. In 1976, the plaintiff was still unhappy with the condition of her nose and contemplated further treatment. However, having consulted with another medical practitioner, she decided not to go ahead with further treatment. By 1980, the condition of the plaintiff's nose had deteriorated to such a degree that further surgical intervention was required. In 1982 the plaintiff decided to take legal proceedings against the surgeons who had carried out the first two operations. The question to be decided was whether the plaintiff could take the case or whether it was statute barred. The Supreme Court was of the opinion that the cause of action accrued at the date when the injury or damage manifested itself. Thus, in the case of the first defendant, this point was 1974 and in the case of the second defendant the date was 1976. However, the date of accrual of the cause of action could commence without the patient's knowledge. By the time the plaintiff eventually realised or discovered that such damage or injury had occurred the limitation period may have elapsed.

Among the examples of such latent damage noted by Brady & Kerr in their work *The Limitation of Actions*[116] is the case of *Sykes v Ministry of*

---

114 [1990] 1 IR 148.
115 Ibid., p. 158.

116 J. Brady & A. Kerr, *The Limitation of Actions*, 2nd ed. (The Incorporated Law Society of Ireland, Dublin, 1994).

Defence,[117] a case concerning asbestosis, where it was held that the initial
damage caused by exposure to asbestos particles could constitute actionable
damage, even though such damage to the lungs did not manifest itself in
the physical symptoms of illness. Such symptoms would not become
apparent for many years, by which time the plaintiff's case would be statute
barred.[118]

It may be argued that such a state of affairs deprives the individual of
his constitutional right to litigate.[119] Indeed, the constitutionality of s.
11(1)(a) and 2(a) was challenged in *Tuohy v Courtney (No. 2)*.[119] In this
case the plaintiff was seeking damages against the defendant solicitor for
alleged negligence related to the purchase of a house. The plaintiff's claim
was deemed to be statute barred as the cause of action did not accrue within
six years before the commencement of the action. The plaintiff argued that
those subsections of s. 11 were contrary to the provisions of Article 40.3
and article 43 of the Constitution. Lynch J in the High Court stated that it
was not necessary to determine whether a cause of action was a constitutionally protected right as he did not accept the fact that s. 11 could operate
in a harsh manner was conclusive as to its unconstitutionality.

The law in relation to latent personal injuries was amended by the
introduction of the Statute of Limitations (Amendment) Act 1991. The Act
provides that the three year limitation period in personal injuries actions
will run from the date of the accrual of the cause of action or from the date
of knowledge if this is later. The date of knowledge of an individual is
defined in s. 2(1) of the Act as follows:

> references to that person's date of knowledge are referencees to the
> date on which he first had knowledge of the following facts:
> (a) that the person alleged to have been injured had been injured,
> (b) that the injury in question was significant,
> (c) that the injury was attributable in whole or in part to the act or
> omission which is alleged to constitute negligence, nuisance or breach
> of duty,
> (d) the identity of the defendant, and
> (e) if it is alleged that the act or omission was that of a person other

117   *The Times*, 23 March 1984. The recent litigation in various jurisdictions concerning
      myodil, whose effects were not apparent for many years after its use, may be relevant.
      The English case of *Dobbie v. Medway Health Authority* (CA) 11 May 1994, unreported,
      may be relevant to this issue.
118   See, further, *Macauley v. Minister for Posts and Telegraphs* [1966] IR 345; *O'Brien v.
      Keogh* [1972] IR 144; *O'Brien v. Manufacturing Engineering* [1973] IR 334; *Moynihan
      v. Greensmyth* [1977] IR 75.
119   High Court, unreported, 3 September 1992.

than the defendant, the identity of that person and the additional facts supporting the bringing of an action against the defendant;

and knowledge that any acts or omissions did or did not, as a matter of law, involve negligence, nuisance or breach of duty is irrelevant.

S. 2(2) makes it clear that knowledge also includes knowledge which an individual might reasonably be expected to acquire from facts observable or ascertainable by him or from facts ascertainable by him with the help of medical or other appropriate expert advice, which it is reasonable for him to seek.

S. 3(1) of the Act of 1991 provides that the limitation period in relation to cases in respect of personal injuries caused by negligence, nuisance or breach of duty is three years from the date on which the cause of action accrued or the date of knowledge if later. In *Boylan v. Motor Distributors Ltd*[120] Lynch J held that the words 'if later' meant later than the date on which the cause of action accrued rather than later than three years from the date on which the cause of action accrued.[121]

On the issue of calculating the very last date on which a summons may be issued, it was held in the case of *McGuinness v. Armstrong Patents Ltd*[122] that the day on which the cause of action accrues is to be included in computing the limitation period. However, problems may arise if the last day on which the summons may be issued falls on a day on which the Court Office is closed. In *Poole v. O'Sullivan*[123] the plaintiff sustained a personal injury on 8 July 1987. A summons was transmitted to the plaintiff's solicitors' agents on 4 July 1990. The High Court Central Office would not accept the summons in the form in which it was drafted and as a result the summons could not be issued on that date. Having amended the summons it was eventually issued on 9 July, two days after the expiry of the period of limitation. However, the Central Office was closed on the previous two days, as they fell on a Saturday and a Sunday. Morris J in the High Court held that the summons had been issued within the time limit provided by statute:

> the fact that the Central Office was closed on 7 July 1990 and on 8 July 1990, they being Saturday and Sunday respectively, and since the plaintiff was unable to 'set the Court in motion' on those days it appears to me that in the circumstances of this case the period envisaged by the Statute of Limitations should be construed as ending on the next day upon which the offices of the Court are open and it becomes possible to do the act required.[124]

120 [1994] 1 ILRM 115.
121 J. Brady and A. Kerr, *The Limitation of Actions*, 2nd ed., op. cit., p. 78.
122 [1980] IR 289.
123 [1993] ILRM 55.
124 Ibid., pp. 57-8.

ALTERNATIVES TO TORT LITIGATION: NO-FAULT COMPENSATION SCHEMES

These schemes differ from tort compensation in that one does not have to prove a causal link between an act or omission and the injury in question, and one does not have to find a responsible defendant. In New Zealand the state Accident Compensation Scheme which was set up in 1974 conforms broadly to the no-fault model. This scheme applies to personal injury resulting from accidents. The system was based on the proposals contained in the *Report of the Royal Commission of Inquiry into Compensation for Personal Injury in New Zealand*[125] This scheme is funded by employers' contributions, levies payable on motor vehicles and contributions from the self-employed.[126]

In the United Kingdom, the *Report of the Royal Commission on Civil Liability and Compensation for Personal Injury*[127] was published in 1978 but its recommendations have not been acted upon to any significant degree. In Australia, the 1974 *Report of the National Committee of Inquiry into Compensation and Rehabilitation in Australia*[128] recommended a similar national scheme which would in addition to accidents cover sickness and disease. However, despite being incorporated in draft legislation these recommendations were shelved after a change of Government.

QUALITY ASSURANCE

The responsibility for assuring the quality of the medicine practised in the Irish health care system lies with the Medical Council discussed above. Three aspects of the role and function of this body are particularly relevant: its input into medical education and training, its overall supervision of those admitted to practice medicine, and its powers to discipline, suspend and remove practitioners from the Medical Registers.

It is possible, though debateable, whether or not the Medical Council's *Guide* constitutes another aspect of quality assurance by providing guidelines on expected standards, outlining recommended solutions to some clinical options, and giving broad recommendations on what sort of conduct would be considered disgraceful or dishonourable among 'doctors of experience, competence and good repute'.

It is obvious that quality assurance is impliedly provided by the fact that doctors are subject to the law.

125 (1969), New Zealand Government Printer.
126 See also the amendments made to the scheme by the Accident Rehabilitation and Compensation Insurance Act 1992.
127 (1978), Cmnd 7054, 3 volumes.
128 (1974), Australian Government Publishing Service.

With regard to the more general issue of quality assurance in the health care system generally, the role and function of the Ombudsman should be noted. In 1989, the Ombudsman investigated 237 complaints about the alleged failure of Health Boards to provide payments and services (in particular, to determine correctly eligibility for medical cards, and to deal with patient complaints and grievances within reasonable time periods).

6

LIABILITY FOR DOCTORS: THE CRIMINAL LAW

There is no specific piece of criminal legislation which governs the doctor-patient relationship. There are, however, certain statutes which take into their ambit the doctor-patient relationship, and thereby delimit in a legislative sense the practice of medicine.

CRIMINAL RESPONSIBILITY

It is at this point necessary to give a brief outline of the elements of criminal responsibility in the Anglo-American legal system. In allocating responsibility for a crime, a number of elements must be present.

Firstly, the *actus reus* which can be defined as the external physical circumstances of a criminal act. Thus the physical touching of the patient by the doctor could constitute the *actus reus* of the crime of battery. However, this alone is not sufficient to make this act a crime. There must, in addition be another element present to bring this act within the scope of the criminal law. This second element is referred to as the *mens rea*. The *mens rea* approximates broadly to the psychological attitude of the perpetrator of the act. Put simply, the perpetrator of the act either intends the result brought about by his act or, in the alternative, the perpetrator knows that in the circumstances the result is a virtually certain consequence of such act. Thus in committing the act, the perpetrator acts either intentionally or recklessly.

In a criminal trial the prosecution must establish beyond reasonable doubt that the accused perpetrated the act in question. It must also be established that the act was either intended by the accused or came about as a result of his recklessness. Thus, the criminal act consists of two elements: the actual physical act itself (the stabbing in a murder, or the blow or touch in battery) which is referred to as the *actus reus*; and the accused's state of mind (whether he intended to bring about the criminal act, or was reckless as to whether it occurred or not) referred to as the *mens rea*.

The origin of this distinction lies in the old Latin maxim 'actus non facit reus, nisi sit mens rea', which may be crudely translated as the act does not make the person guilty without the presence of a guilty mind.

CRIMINAL OMISSIONS/FAILURE TO ACT

A person may also be liable in criminal law for failure to act in a particular situation. The question to be asked in the context of medical law is whether the failure to seek medical assistance on the part of a carer of a sick person is of itself a criminal act.

The consensus among legal commentators and judges appears to be that one cannot be liable for a murder by omission unless one was bound by a legal duty to care for the victim.[1] The point is put by Charleton when he states there can be no 'liability for manslaughter by omission unless the accused was under a duty to the victim to perform the act, the neglect of which caused death'.[2] From the decided cases one can see particularly where the carer is a relative of the accused, that a legal duty of care will be implied by the court. In the case of *R. v. Instan*[3] the accused lived with her elderly aunt. In the days leading up to her death, the aunt developed gangrene in one of her legs and was unable to move or seek assistance for herself. The defendant was the only person who was aware of the condition of her aunt, and thus the only person who could seek medical assistance. However, not only did she refrain from obtaining medical assistance, but did not feed her aunt in her last days. In affirming her conviction for manslaughter, Lord Coleridge CJ stated that:

> it was the clear duty of the prisoner to impart to the deceased so much as was necessary to sustain life, of the food which she from time to time took in, and was paid for by the deceased's own money for the purpose of the maintenance of herself and the prisoner; it was only through the instrumentality of the prisoner that the deceased could get the food. There was, therefore, a common law duty imposed upon the prisoner which she did not discharge.[4]

In the more recent case of *R. v. Stone*[5] the first defendant, Stone, was the elder brother of the deceased, Fanny. Stone, it was discovered, was of low intelligence in addition to being partially deaf and very blind. Stone co-habited with the other defendant, Dobinson, who was described as being

1 See P. Charleton, *Offences Against the Person* (The Round Hall Press, Dublin, 1992); Granville Williams, *Textbook of Criminal Law*, 2nd ed. (Sweet & Maxwell, London, 1983).
2 P. Charleton, op. cit., at p. 96. See also Glanville Williams, *Textbook of Criminal Law*, 2nd ed. (Sweet & Maxwell, London, 1983) where he states '. . . a crime can be committed by omission, but there can be no omission in law in the absence of a duty to act'.
3 [1893] 1 QB 450 (Court for Crown Cases Reserved).
4 Ibid.
5 [1977] 2 All ER 341.

'ineffectual and inadequate'. To complete this dysfunctional domestic gathering, there also resided in the dwelling Mr Stone's mentally subnormal son. Fanny, the deceased, came to live there in 1972. Fanny was a victim of anorexia nervosa. In common with the rest of the household, she led a somewhat eccentric existence, spending most of her time in her room, save for the occasional (though rare) foray to the kitchen to cook something to eat, while Stone and Dobinson were at the pub. Over time, Fanny's mental condition deteriorated to such a degree that even Stone and Dobinson, with their limited mental capacity noticed that Fanny needed medical help.

However, it did take them some time to recognise the gravity of Fanny's situation: approximately three years. Thus it was not until the spring of 1975 that the defendants made an attempt to summon Fanny's doctor. They did not meet with success. This may have been due in part to the fact that Fanny refused to tell them his name. As a result, no medical assistance was obtained. It was not until July 1975 that another attempt was made to alleviate Fanny's plight. At that time, Dobinson, with the help of a neighbour, washed Fanny who by now was bed-ridden and lying in her own excrement.

Besides these albeit perfunctory gestures on the part of the defendants, no one was informed of Fanny's condition, not even the social worker who visited Mr Stone's son from time to time. Fanny eventually died in August 1975. Medical reports concluded that she had been in need of urgent medical attention for days, if not for weeks. Both Stone and Dobinson were convicted for manslaughter, notwithstanding their mental deficiencies. Geoffrey Lane LJ, in the Court of Appeal, explained the rationale behind the decision in the following terms:

> whether Fanny or not was a lodger, she was a blood relation of the appellant Stone; she was occupying a room in his house; the appellant Dobinson had undertaken the duty of trying to wash her, of taking such food to her as she required . . . the jury were entitled to find that the duty [to care] had been assumed. They were entitled to conclude that once Fanny became helplessly infirm, as she had by 19 July, the appellants were, in the circumstances, obliged either to summon help or else to care for Fanny themselves.[6]

In the case of *R. v. Sheppard*,[7] the defendants were a young couple of low intelligence, who were charged under s. 1(1) of the Children & Young Persons Act 1933, with the wilful neglect of their sixteen month old son, who died of hypothermia and malnutrition. It was alleged that the defendants

6   Ibid., pp. 345-6.   7   [1980] 3 All ER 899.

had failed to provide the child with adequate medical aid, particularly in the week preceding his death. The defendants claimed that although they noticed the child's loss of appetite and failure to take food, they had thought that this was due to a minor upset which would cure itself. At first instance, the judge directed the jury that the test of guilt was to be judged objectively by whether a reasonable parent, with knowledge of the facts, would have appreciated that failure to have the child examined was likely to cause unnecessary suffering or injury. The defendants were convicted, and subsequently appealed to the Court of Appeal and to the House of Lords. The House of Lords allowed the appeal. In his speech, Lord Diplock held that a failure to provide a child with such medical aid as is needed could not be properly described as 'wilful' unless the parent either had directed his mind to the question, whether there was some risk (though it might fall short of a probability) that the child's health might suffer unless he were examined by a doctor, and treated, or had so refrained because he did not care whether the child might be in need of medical treatment or not.

In *R v. Harris*,[8] a Rastafarian couple who had refused on religious grounds to allow their diabetic nine year old daughter to be given insulin were convicted of manslaughter in Nottingham. The evidence given at the trial was that hospital doctors who had seen the child had said that insulin was the only way to save her. The father had asked whether the insulin came from animals, saying that he was not allowed to eat pork or beef, and told the nurses that he wanted to take his daughter to Africa to see a faith healer. The child was brought back to hospital 6 weeks later in a diabetic coma, and died. Neither parent testified but counsel for the mother told the court that there was no evidence that the couple thought that they were doing harm.

Newspaper accounts of the trial leave several questions unanswered; for example, did the husband inform the child's GP of the parents' refusal and of the danger to the girl if that attitude persisted, and should the child have been made a ward of court so that treatment might be ordered in her best interests?

The main issue, once again, is how the courts should approach the dilemma that arises when a child is put in danger because of misguided but genuinely held religious convictions of his parents.

The United Kingdom has not allowed in this area for legal exemptions based on religious belief. The judge in the Nottingham case will have been hoping to discourage other parents from acting in this way. Prosecutions of this sort for manslaughter rather than breach of duty to care are unusual in Britain.

---

8   D. Brahams, *Medico Legal Journal* (1993), Vol. 61, Pt. 4, pp. 232-4.

In the recent case of *In re S (a minor) (medical treatment)*,[9] S was a four year old child who had been diagnosed as suffering from lukaemia. The condition was treatable by intensified chemotherapy. The transfusion of blood or blood products was a necessary component of this treatment. However the child's parents, who were Jehovah's Witnesses, were opposed to this treatment and refused to give their consent. The local authority sought an order under s. 100 of the Children Act 1989, permitting a blood transfusion. This order had been granted. The following day, the parents issued an application under the 1989 Act for a 'prohibited steps' order. The consultant paediatrician who was charged with S's care, gave evidence to the effect that it was necessary to transfuse blood in this instance. The court eventually granted the local authority the order it sought. Thorpe J posed the question:

> are the religious convictions of the parents to deny their child a 50% chance of survival . . . to deny him that chance, and condemn him to an inevitable and early death? [Counsel for the parents] realistically saw that this was an extreme case, and one in which it is difficult to pursue the argument that the religious convictions should deny the child the chance of treatment . . . if this treatment is applied in the face of parental opposition what would be the difficulties and stresses for S. in years to come – parented by parents who believe that his life was prolonged by an ungodly act? Well – that consideration seems to me one that has little foundation in reality . . . it seems to me that family reaction will recognise that responsibility for consent was taken from them and, as a judicial act, absolved their conscience of responsibility.[10]

In the UK, a statutory duty exists to obtain medical help for a sick child under the Children Act 1989.

In Ireland, there is no similar statutory provision.

CAUSATION IN CRIMINAL LAW

The prosecution must establish that the accused caused the death of the victim within a year and a day. Thus it must be proved that but for the act of the defendant, the death of the victim would not have occurred.[11]

9   [1993] 1 FLR 376.
10 Id. see also *In re E (a minor)* (1990) 9 BMLR 1; *In re O (a minor) (medical treatment)* [1993] 4 Med LR 272; *In re R (a minor)* [1993] 2 FLR 5.
11 See further J.C. Smith & B. Hogan, *Criminal Law*, 7th ed. (Butterworth, London, 1992), pp. 331-46.

In the context of medical treatment, the problem of causation may arise when after the accused inflicts an injury on the victim, the victim receives medical treatment and subsequently dies. The question may then be asked, what was the cause of death? Was it the infliction of the injury by the accused, or was death the result of the negligent medical treatment? In effect, does medical treatment constitute a *novus actus interveniens* which would relieve the accused of liability?

In the case of *R. v. Jordan*[12] the defendant stabbed the victim. The victim was taken to hospital where he died after eight days. The defendant was convicted of murder at first instance, but appealed the decision to the Court of Criminal Appeal. New evidence adduced on appeal established that the stab wound had almost healed at the time of death. Instead, it was submitted that the drug terramycin (which prevented infection) was administered to the victim after it was found that he was intolerant to such a drug. It was also submitted that large quantities of liquid had been administered intravenously, which caused the victim's lungs to become waterlogged, and pulmonary oedema was discovered. The Court of Criminal Appeal found that the treatment was 'palpably wrong' and quashed the defendant's conviction. The court felt that it was the medical treatment that 'produced' the symptoms discovered at the post-mortem examination, which were the direct and immediate cause of death.[13]

This case was distinguished in the subsequent case of *R. v. Smith*,[14] as being 'a very particular case depending upon its exact facts'. In *Smith*, the defendant stabbed the victim in a barrack-room brawl. The defendant argued that the victim would not have died if he had received adequate medical treatment. It transpired that the victim had been dropped twice on the way to the medical station, and that the medical officer was not aware that the victim's lung had been pierced and caused haemorrhage. There were in addition two other stab victims being treated when the victim arrived in the medical station. On finally receiving treatment, it was not of an adequate standard. Indeed, it was argued that if the victim had received adequate treatment in the form of a blood transfusion, he would have had a 75% chance of survival. However, it was held on appeal that the victim's original stab wounds continued to be an operative cause of death.

In the case of *R. v. Malcherek*[15] where the victim was placed on a life support machine as a result of complications which occurred following

12 (1956) 40 Cr Appeal R 153.
13 Hallett J quoted in D.W. Elliott & M.J. Allen in *Elliott & Wood's Casebook on Criminal Law* (Sweet & Maxwell, London, 1993), p. 44.

14 [1959] 2 QB 35.
15 [1981] 2 All ER 422.

injuries inflicted by the defendant, the defendant was not permitted to claim that the cause of the victim's death was the disconnecting of the life-support machine by the victim's doctors. Thus, the original injuries were regarded as the cause of death.

In the more recent case of *R. v. Cheshire*,[16] the victim was shot by the defendant and wounded in the thigh and stomach. In hospital, the victim underwent a tracheotomy due to respiratory problems. The tube was removed after 4 weeks. After it was removed, the victim's windpipe became obstructed. Despite the victim's complaints, the medical staff did not treat this problem and the victim died as a result. The defendant argued that the negligent medical treatment was a sufficient intervening act to relieve him of liability. The Court of Appeal, in its judgment, referred to the Australian case of *R. v. Evans & Gardiner (No. 2)*,[17] stating that it was quite similar on the facts to the instant case. In *Evans & Gardiner* the victim was stabbed in the stomach. After an operation, the victim recovered, and was leading an apparently healthy life. However, approximately a year after the incident, he succumbed to severe abdominal pain and vomiting. He received further medical treatment, but died. It was established that the cause of death was a stricture of the small intestine which was a possible sequel to the operation he underwent for the stab wound. It was claimed that the doctors who carried out the later treatment were negligent in not recognizing the stricture. The Supreme Court of Victoria laid down the test in such a case as being whether the felonious act is still an operating and substantial cause of death; and stated that:

> [t]he failure of the medical practitioners to diagnose correctly the victim's condition, however inept or unskilful, was not the cause of her death. It was the blockage of the bowel which caused death, and the real question for the jury was whether that blockage was due to the stabbing. There was plenty of medical evidence to support such a finding. . . .[18]

After examining *Evans & Gardiner*, and cases such as *Jordan*, *Smith*, and *Malcherek*, Beldam LJ stated in *R. v. Cheshire* that:

> when the victim of a criminal attack is treated for wounds or injuries by doctors or other medical staff attempting to repair the harm done, it will only be in the most extraordinary and unusual case that such treatment can be said to be so independent of the acts of the accused,

16 [1991] 3 All ER 670.   18 [1976] VR 523 at p. 534.
17 [1976] VR 523.

that it could be regarded in law as the cause of the victim's death to the exclusion of the accused's acts.[19]

The court then went on to state the test to be applied in such cases as being '[e]ven though negligence was the immediate cause of his death, the jury should not regard it as excluding the responsibility of the accused unless the negligent treatment was so independent of his acts, and in itself so potent in causing death, that they regard the contribution made by his acts as insignificant'.[20]

In *R. v. McKechnie*[21] the victim was admitted to hospital as a result of head injuries inflicted by the defendant. However, the victim did not die from the head injuries but from a burst duodenal ulcer. The doctors decided that the extent of the victim's injuries prevented them from operating on the ulcer. In this instance, the injury prevented the victim from receiving life-saving treatment, whereas in the other cases noted, the injury caused the victim to receive medical treatment. It was held by the Court of Appeal that the non-intervention on the part of the doctors did not break the causal link between the defendant's act and the victim's death.

Stannard asks the question, 'when, in the light of *Cheshire*, will medical treatment of any injury inflicted by [the defendant] break the chain of causation?' He posits the following principles in reply:

(1) medical treatment will not break the chain of causation simply because [the victim] would have died but for the bad treatment. The injuries inflicted by [the doctor] need not be the sole cause, or even the main cause, of the death, provided they made a significant contribution to it.

(2) Where the original injuries can be categorised as being still 'operative' at the time of the death, the causal chain will not be broken. It will not matter if the medical treatment was incompetent, or even grossly abnormal. Provided the wound is the direct cause of death, [the doctor] will remain responsible for it.

(3) Where the original injuries are no longer operative, the test will be whether the bad medical treatment was reasonably foreseeable. Treatment falling within the 'normal band' of incompetence will be regarded as foreseeable for the purposes of this rule. But where the treatment is so palpably bad as to be outside the bounds of reasonable contemplation, it may break the chain of causation.

(4) Where the death occurs as a result of the treatment of the injury (or

---

19 [1991] 3 All ER 670, 677-8
20 Ibid. at 678.

21 (1991) 94 Cr App Rep 51; (1992) Crim LR 194.

lack of it) by [the victim] himself, [the doctor] may still be responsible on the ground that he must take his victim as he finds him. This may be so even though the original injuries are no longer operative and though the treatment is so grossly wrong as to be unforeseeable.[22]

STATUTORY ASSAULT

The statutory crime of assault is governed by ss. 18 and 20 of The Offences Against the Person Act 1861. Ss. 18 and 20 do not define a criminal assault per se, but rather state that the act of unlawfully and maliciously wounding or inflicting any grievous bodily harm upon another person is a misdemeanour punishable by penal servitude.[23] S. 47 provides that for assault occasioning actual bodily harm or common assault, the perpetrator shall be liable to terms in prison.[24] It would at this juncture be useful to distinguish between grievous and actual bodily harm. Grievous bodily harm was defined in the UK case of *Director of Public Prosecutions v. Smith*[25] as bodily harm of a 'really serious kind'. In Ireland, this definition has been followed by the Supreme Court in the case of *People (AG) v. Messitt*.[26] Actual bodily harm has been described as 'any hurt or injury calculated to interfere with the health or comfort of the victim'.[27]

In the surgical context, the question may be asked as to whether an

---

22 J.E. Stannard, 'Criminal Causation and the Careless Doctor', *Modern Law Review* (1992), Vol. 55, p. 577 at 583.

23 S. 18 states: '[w]hosoever shall unlawfully and maliciously by any means whatsoever wound or cause any grievous bodily harm to any person, or shoot any person, or, by drawing a trigger or in any other manner attempt to discharge any kind of loaded arms at any person, with intent to in any of the cases aforesaid, to maim, disfigure, or disable any person, or to do some other grievous bodily harm to any person, or with intent to resist or prevent the lawful apprehension or detention of any person shall be guilty of a misdeamous, and being convicted thereof shall be kept in penal servitude for life'.

   S. 20 provides: '[w]hosoever shall unlawfully and maliciously wound or inflict any grievous bodily harm upon any other person, either with or without any weapon or instrument, shall be guilty of a misdemeanour, and being convicted thereof shall be liable to be kept in penal servitude for the term of five years'.

24 S. 47 states: '[w]hosoever shall be convicted upon an indictment of any assault occasioning actual bodily harm shall be liable to be kept in penal servitude for the term of five years and whosoever shall be convicted upon an indictment for a common assault, shall be liable for a common assault, shall be liable to be or be imprisoned for any term not exceeding one year, with or without hard labour'.

25 [1961] AC 290.

26 [1974] IR 406.

27 'I see no reason to seek a definition of 'grievous' but if one should be sought, then I think Lord Kilmuir's 'really serious' in *Director of Public Prosecutions v. Smith* [1961] AC 290 at 334 is as simple and effective a description as one could desire' (Ó Dálaigh CJ [1974] IR 406 at 415).

intervention which is intended to improve the health or save the life of a patient can be construed as 'bodily harm'. Where an operation is performed to improve the health of the patient, with the patient's consent, then the law recognises such intervention as being lawful. The lack of consent of the patient is thus an important element of the offence of criminal assault. One can safely say that a surgical procedure intended to benefit the patient and to which the patient has consented does not come within the scope of bodily harm as outlined in the 1861 Act.[28]

Thus, in the surgical context, Irish courts may only construe as 'bodily harm' these procedures to which the patient did not give consent.

COMMON LAW ASSAULT

To find an actual definition of the crime of assault, one must turn to the common or judge-made law. Thus a criminal assault occurs where the accused, intentionally or recklessly, causes force to be applied to the body of the victim. This definition follows the trend now finding favour in criminal legal circles of disregarding the old division of criminal assault and criminal battery where assault constituted the victim being put in fear of the imminent application of force to his or her person, and where the crime of battery involved the actual infliction of injury upon the victim. Thus Glanville Williams has referred to what was previously termed assault as 'psychic assault'.[29] Battery, as a result, is replaced simply by the term 'assault'.

If intentionally or recklessly, a doctor puts his patient in fear of the imminent application of force to that patient's person, that, in law, amounts to the crime of psychic assault. There are no cases of psychic assault in the doctor-patient relationship, but there seems no reason in principle why a doctor could not be guilty of it.[30]

The crime of assault forms an important part of the framework of the law governing the doctor-patient relationship. It consists of the intentional or reckless touching of someone in the absence of legally effective consent. In certain cases, surgical intervention will not have the intended effect of benefitting the patient and will result in 'harm' to the patient. However, as Skegg suggests . . . 'if an application of force was not intended to cause

27 P. Charleton, *Offences Against the Person* op. cit., p. 205.
28 See P.D.G. Skegg, *Law, Ethics and Medicine – Studies in Medical Law* (Clarendon Press, Oxford, 1990) at pp. 35-8, and also P.D.G. Skegg, 'Medical Procedures and the Crime of Battery', *Criminal Law Review* (1974), pp. 699-700.
29 See Glanville Williams, *Textbook of Criminal Law* 2nd ed. (Sweet & Maxwell, London, 1983), p. 173.
30 P. Charleton, *Offences Against the Person* op. cit., p. 195ff.

bodily harm, and the person responsible did not take an unjustifiable risk as to the causing of bodily harm, then the undesired consequence should not render ineffective consent which would otherwise have been effective'.[31]

As many medical procedures involve the touching of the body of the patient then it is conceivable that such 'touching' could come within the ambit of the crime of battery. An important element in this crime is the lack of consent on the part of the patient. A criminal battery requires the application of 'force' to the victim's body. Force in the context of battery may refer to even the lightest of touches. It is only necessary then that such touching be unlawful.

In relation to the crime of battery, courts have held that there are certain applications of force to which one can not give valid consent: public policy precludes such consent. In *R. v. Coney*,[32] the defendant was charged with common assault as a result of having participated in an illegal prize fight. The principle which can be derived from this case is that consent will not legalise an assault, where the action in question has been prohibited by statute. Thus, as the act here constituted a breach of the peace, the public interest dictated that it fell into that category of acts to which the participants could not validly consent. In *R. v. Donovan*,[33] the appellant was convicted of indecent assault and common assault after he had caned a seventeen year old girl in order to obtain sexual gratification. In this case, the court held that:

> [a]s a general rule to which there are well-established exceptions, it is an unlawful act to beat another person with such a degree of violence that the infliction of bodily harm is a probable consequence, and, when such an act is proved, consent is immaterial.[34]

In *Attorney General's Reference No. 6 of 1980*[35] the respondent had been in a public brawl with another, with the result that the respondent caused the other actual bodily harm. At first instance, the respondent was acquitted because of the victim's consent. However, the Attorney General referred to the Court of Appeal the question of whether, when two individuals are involved in a public brawl, it could be a defence to a charge of assault that one party had consented. Lord Lane LCJ held that the normal rule was that the consent of one party vitiated the assault. However, there were exceptions to this rule: where the act was contrary to the public interest. Thus, it was

---

31 See P.D.G. Skegg, *Law, Ethics and Medicine – Studies in Medical Law* (Clarendon Press, Oxford, 1990) at pp. 35-6.

32 (1882) 8 QBD 534.

33 [1934] 2 KB 498.

34 Ibid. at 507.

35 [1981] 2 All ER 1057.

not in the public interest that individuals should, as in this case, cause each other bodily harm for no good reason.[36] The court went on to state that:

> [n]othing which we have said is intended to cast doubt upon the accepted legality of properly conducted games and sports, lawful chastisement or correction, reasonable surgical interference, dangerous exhibitions, etc. These apparent exceptions can be justified as involving the exercise of a legal right, in the case of chastisement or correction, or as needed in the public interest, in the other cases.[37]

In the English case of *R. v. Brown*,[38] a group of men who indulged in consensual sado-masochistic sexual activities was convicted of assault occasioning actual bodily harm, and the wounding of another, contrary to ss. 47 and 20 of The Offences Against the Person Act, 1861. Even though the so-called 'victim' in this case consented to the 'harm' done, the Court of Appeal held that one could not consent to such acts.

The defendants appealed this decision to the House of Lords, which by a three to two majority dismissed the appeal, stating that all causing of bodily harm is *prima facie* unlawful, but that there exist certain exceptions to the rule. Medical treatment to which the patient has consented is one of these exceptions. However sado-masochistic behaviour was not regarded by the House of Lords as an exception to this category.

In the medical or surgical context, the consent must be to the touching which actually takes place. Consent, for example, to a tonsillectomy, is clearly invalid if the surgeon carries out a vasectomy.[39] In the Irish case of *Walsh v. Family Planning Services Ltd*,[40] it was held that civil assault is not committed, however, if the agreed physician does not carry out the operation. Here, the participation of a second doctor in a vasectomy operation did not vitiate the consent of the patient, even if the patient was not informed of this participation beforehand. It was held that the consent given by the patient was a general consent to the carrying out of an operation upon him by a person employed by Family Planning Services Ltd. Therefore, consent

36 Ibid. at 1059.
37 Ibid.
38 [1992] 2 WLR 441.
39 See *Hamilton v. Birmingham Regional Hospital Board and Keates* [1969] 2 Br Med J 456 (sterilisation without consent during the performance of a caesarean section); *Michael v. Molesworth* [1950] 2 Br Med J 171 (operation performed by a different surgeon to the one agreed); and *Cull v. Royal Surrey County Hospital and Butler* [1932] 2 Br Med J 1195 (patient consented to an abortion but the doctor carried out an hysterectomy).
40 [1992] 1 IR 496.

to a medical procedure for a purpose which the law regards as valid is deemed to be genuine consent.

However, one must bear in mind the importance of the public interest criterion. Thus, in Ireland could somebody, for example, give valid consent to a sex-change operation? The ethos of many hospitals and the prevailing moral ethos of the State would lead one to answer in the negative.[41]

MANSLAUGHTER

There has been some recent discussion in England, but none in Ireland, of the circumstances in which professional negligence may give rise to criminal prosecution, as opposed to (or as well as) an action in tort.

The Law Commission's paper, published in 1994, entitled *Involuntary Manslaughter*[42] reviews this entire area in great detail, and reviews most of the recent cases discussed here, but in the context of UK law.

The recent case law provides no real definition of what sort of negligence amounts to justification of a decision to prosecute, let alone a conviction. There is no necessary connection between the nature of the negligent act or omission and the gravity or otherwise of the consequences.

One should bear in mind the words of Lord Denning MR in *Jones v. Manchester Corporation*,[43] where he stated:

> It would be in the highest degree unjust that the hospital board, by getting inexperienced doctors to perform their duties for them without adequate supervision, should be able to throw all the responsibility onto those doctors as if they were fully experienced practitioners.

On this point, in a previous civil case, *Willsher v. Essex Health Authority*[44] where a junior doctor who erroneously inserted a catheter into a premature baby's umbilical vein instead of an artery, but showed what he had done to the senior registrar, was personally absolved of negligence.

However, in *R. v. Prentice, Sullman*,[45] discussed below, there was no senior person present to oversee the treatment.

---

41 See C.N. Armstrong and T. Walton, 'Transsexual Metamorphoses', *New Law Journal* (1992), Vol. 142, No. 6538, pp. 96-7 (24 January).

42 *Involuntary Manslaughter*, Law Commission Consultation Paper No. 135 (Law Commission, London, 1994).

43 [1952] 2 QB 852. See D. Tomkin and R. Pearce, 'Sudden Death, P.M. and a Murder Charge', *Irish Medical Times* (1981), Vol. 15, No. 30, pp. 20, 37; 'Murder. Medical Intervention and The Cause of Death', *Irish Medical Times* (1981), Vol. 15, No. 35, pp. 20-21.

44 [1987] QB 730.

45 [1993] 4 All ER 935.

The issue of seniority did not arise in the most recent criminal cases in England in this area. Thus in *R. v. Saha* and *R. v. Salim*,[46] two general practitioners were convicted of manslaughter for recklessly causing the death of a 23-year-old former heroin addict. The facts involved the police arrest of a man called Rawlinson, in May 1990. He was detained in a succession of police cells, and by September 1990 had been weaned off heroin. On 7 September, it appears that he asked for tranquillisers. He was seen by Dr Saha who initiated benzodiazepines. On 10 Septepmber, Dr Salim added chlorpromazine (300 mg daily from 11 September to a daily intake of 80 mg.) diazepam and 160 mg temazepam at night. Later, Dr Saha added 30 mg Methadone, and 130 mg. co-proxamol. Rawlinson's condition deteriorated, and he was described as shambling about with glazed eyes in a zombie like state. On Sunday 16 September he was found to be comatose and was taken into casualty. The casualty officer discussed the case with the two doctors and Rawlinson was taken back to the cells. At 07.30 the next day, he was found to be unrousable and died about an hour later at hospital from pulmonary oedema.

The defence argued that the drugs prescribed were not the cause of death, and that the inappropriate discharge from hospital was a new factor. It was suggested that had the patient been kept in, he might have survived. It was suggested by a consultant toxicologists that Rawlinson died not from the ingestion of prescribed drugs but from asphyxia; he had recovered from his coma when discharged and had thus obtained more (illicit) drugs or had died during an epileptic seizure. This argument was rejected implicitly.

Curtis J refused to allow leave to the jury to find either further, or as an alternative, that the two doctors had been guilty of gross negligence. D. Brahams states:[47]

> [t]he differentiation between what amounts to negligence that causes death and gross negligence *per se* could in practice cause difficulties in choosing where to draw the line between professional conduct which should be punished by the criminal law and conduct that can be dealt with by the civil courts and/or the General Medical Council.
>
> The 1990s are signalling a new and worrying trend for doctors, in the form of a series of prosecutions for causing death by recklessness in the course of their medical practice. . . . In the summer of 1990 a locum anaesthetist was convicted of the manslaughter of a patient who

46 See D. Brahams (1993), 'Death of a remand prisoner', *Medico Legal Journal*, Vol. 61, Pt. 1, pp. 48-9.
47 Ibid., p. 49.

died in Mayday Hospital, Croydon, as a result of his recklessness and gross negligence; and later that year a locum consultant anaesthetist at Doncaster Royal Infirmary was also convicted of manslaughter when he inflated a patient with oxygen via a pressure pump, which led to fatal barotrauma. Both doctors received suspended prison sentences.

In 1990, the conviction on manslaughter charges of two locum anaesthetists made English legal history. In one of the cases, Dr John Adomako was convicted of manslaughter following the death of a patient to whom he gave an anaesthetic. The doctor was a locum anaesthetist at the Mayday Hospital in Croydon, and had no postgraduate qualifications and his references were never taken up. He was called in to take over the anaesthetic management of a patient half way through an operation for a detached retina as the anaesthetic registrar had left to attend to an obstetric emergency. The Registrar had left the ventilator's alarm turned on, yet when the patient was deprived of oxygen through an unnoticed disconnection, the alarm did not sound. During the operation the Blood Pressure alarm began to sound and the patient's blood pressure was low. Dr Adomako's initial response to the distress signals was to assume that the monitor was faulty and to obtain another blood pressure cuff. He did not check the ventilator hose connections at the patient's end. At the trial, medical expert evidence made it clear that a disconnection in the breathing system is one of the most common problems encountered during anaesthesia. In such circumstances, the anaesthetist should ventilate the patient's lungs by hand in order to ascertain the feel of the patient's lungs and to expose any problem. As a result of the doctor's failure to notice the problem, the patient became cyanosed and pulseless and ultimately died six months later without regaining consciousness. Death was attributed to brain damage from oxygen deprivation.

Dr Adomako appealed his conviction for manslaughter to the Court of Appeal.[48] The court upheld the conviction stating that the jury had been directed according to the proper test and the evidence justified a guilty verdict. Lord Taylor CJ concluded that it was:

> clearly open to the jury to conclude that the appellant's failure to perform his essential and in effect sole duty to see that the patient was breathing satisfactorily and to cope with the breathing emergency which should have been obvious to him, justified a verdict of guilty. They were entitled to conclude his failure was more than mere inadvertence and constituted gross negligence of the degree necessary for manslaughter.[49]

48 [1993] 4 All ER 935.   49 Ibid., p. 954.

The conviction was upheld on appeal to the House of Lords.[50]

In the second case,[51] Dr N. Sargent was convicted of manslaughter following the death of a 55-year-old woman under his care. He was given a six month prison sentence suspended for a year. The prosecution claimed that Dr Sargent had inserted a tube into the patient's throat and inserted the entire contents of an oxygen cylinder (1020 litres) into the patient, inflating her 'until she resembled the Michelin Man advertisements'. The result was fatal barotrauma and the patient died in the operating theatre.

Thus, according to Brahams:[52]

> [d]octors in England and Wales whose patients die due to their recklessness or gross negligence look increasingly likely to be at risk of a charge of manslaughter.

In the case of *R. v. Prentice and Sullman*,[53] a 16-year-old boy suffering from leukaemia was admitted to Peterborough district hospital in March 1990 for his monthly injection of vincristine. Every other month he was given methotrexate, which was injected via a lumbar puncture. On this occasion he was seen by Dr M. Prentice and Dr B. Sullman, who were senior house officers. Both had arrived at the hospital only four weeks earlier. Under the supervision of Dr Sullman, Dr Prentice had injected vincristine for which there is no antidote into the patient's spine, instead of his arm. The boy died two weeks later. The charge was that their action amounted to criminal recklessness. The prosecution accepted that they had not intended to cause harm. Lawyers defending the junior doctors claimed that

50 [1994] 2 All ER 79.
51 See D. Brahams, 'Two locum anaesthetists convicted of Manslaughter', *Lancet* (1990), Vol. 336, p. 431.
52 'Manslaughter and Reckless Medical Treatment', *Medico Legal Journal* (1992), Vol. 60, Pt. 1, p. 73. The recommendations contained in *Involuntary Manslaughter*, Law Commission Consulation Paper No. 135 (Law Commission, London, 1994) deserve considerable debate. The Law Commission points out that instead of the test adopted in *R v. Prentice* and *R v. Sullman*, tests which involve phrases such as, in particular 'gross negligence', or 'indifference to an obvious risk', should be replaced by a test which enables a court to analyse the defendant's conduct to see if it is such that it creates a significant risk of death or (perhaps) serious personal injury. Indeed, the Law Commission suggests that a new test should look at whether the conduct created not only a risk of death but of 'serious injury'. The Law Commission points out that the conclusion of these cases was that two responsible and professional doctors were convicted by failing through 'mere inadvertence' to cope with risks about which, given their particular qualifications, experience, and the harrowing exigencies of the circumstances, in which they were working, they would not be expected to cope. See paras. 3146-48 of the Law Commission paper (pp. 79-80).
53 [1993] 4 All ER 935.

a consultant haematologist in particular had failed to ensure that instructions for the drug administration were clearly understood. However, the court was told and the jury presumably accepted that the doctors had negligently ignored warnings as to how the drug should be injected, although reportedly Dr Prentice realised his mistake shortly afterwards.

The jury found Dr Sullman guilty by unanimous verdict, and convicted Dr Prentice by a majority of ten to two. Both men were sentenced to nine months' imprisonment suspended for one year. Owen J stated as follows:

> [i]t seems to me that you could have been helped much more than you were helped. This could have ensured that this particular tragedy never happened.[54]

Drs Prentice and Sullman subsequently appealed to the Court of Appeal.[55] The Court of Appeal concluded that the Crown Court judge had wrongly directed the jury and the appeal of Drs Prentice and Sullman should be allowed, since if the jury had been directed that the prosecution had to establish gross negligence they might not have convicted. In the words of Taylor LJ:

> [t]he question for the jury should have been whether, in the case of each doctor, they were sure that the failure to ascertain the correct mode of administering the drug and to ensure that only that mode was adopted was grossly negligent to the point of criminality having regard to all the excuses and mitigating circumstances of the case.[56]

The court took the opportunity in this case to answer the question of what is the correct test in cases of involuntary manslaughter by breach of duty. The court went on to hold that the ingredients of involuntary manslaughter by breach of duty which need to be proved are:

(1) the existence of the duty;

(2) a breach of the duty causing death;

(3) gross negligence which the jury considered justified a criminal conviction.

Proof of any of the following states of mind in the defendant could properly lead a jury to make a finding of gross negligence:

(a) indifference to an obvious risk of injury to health;

54 See D. Brahams, 'Manslaughter and Reckless Medical Treatment', *Medico Legal Journal* (1992), Vol. 60, Pt. 1, p. 73.
55 [1993] 4 All ER 935.
56 Ibid., at p. 948-9. This formula is open to objections: see the discussion of the Law Commission paper quoted at footnote 52.

(b) actual foresight of the risk coupled with the determination nevertheless to run it;

(c) an appreciation of the risk coupled with an intention to avoid it but with such a high degree of negligence in the attempted avoidance that the jury considered it justified conviction;

(d) inattention or failure to advert to a serious risk which went beyond 'mere inadvertence' in respect of an obvious and important matter which the defendant's duty demanded he should address.

A further recent case involving the application of criminal sanctions to medical practice is that of Dr Ulmesh Gaud.[57] Here the defendant surgeon was alleged to have put patients at risk by operating on them while knowing that he was a carrier of hepatitis B. The defendant in addition had denied his infection and had substituted patient's blood samples from his own in an attempt to avoid discovery. Dr Gaud's infection had been detected in 1990 while he was working at Killingbeck Hospital in Leeds. However he continued to work as a surgeon for a further three years at the Royal London Hospital and at the London Chest Hospital. A total of nineteen people contacted the virus during his time at the two hospitals. Five of the patients, who agreed to tests, were found to be suffering from a strain of the disease that Dr Gaud carried. The defendant pleaded guilty to the common law charge of causing a public nuisance. The last time the law had been applied in this way was in the case of *R.v. Vantandillo*[58] in 1815. In that case it was held to be a public nuisance to expose on a public highway a child infected with smallpox. In the Canadian case of *R. v. Thornton*[59] the defendant who was HIV positive was held to be a public nuisance under s. 180 of the Canadian Criminal Code. In the *Gaud* case, the defendant surgeon was sentenced to imprisonment for one year. Blofeld J sentenced the defendant on the basis that no conclusive link had been proved between his condition and the contraction by patients upon whom he had operated of the same disease. The essence of the offence of public nuisance with which Dr Gaud was charged is endangering the public. Thus it is enough that he had created a risk of transmission, even if patients had not been infected, for such an offence to be successfully charged.[60]

From the discussion of these cases, it is submitted that any tendency to

---

57 See *The Guardian*, 30 September 1994, p. 2.
58 (1815) 4 M & S 73.
59 [1993] SCR 445.
60 See further, J. Smith & B. Hogan, *Criminal Law*, 7th ed. (Butterworths, 1992); S. Bronnitt, 'Donating HIV-Infected Blood: A Public Nuisance?' (1994), 1 *Journal of Law and Medicine*, p. 245.

attempt to apply the criminal law to similar cases of what are essentially medical malpractice in Ireland should be examined with scepticism. It is difficult to know at this early stage whether the Law Commission's recommendations will be followed, but any attempt to deal with these questions will have to address the Law Commission's expert arguments.[61]

DEFENCES

Consent The defence of consent is discussed fully in Chapter 3, and also in the previous section in this chapter on the crime of battery.

Necessity One aspect of medical care where the conflict between the patient's autonomy and the practitioner's right to intervene is resolved in favour of the latter, is where such intervention is necessary to save the life or preserve the health of the patient. In other words, the balance between preservation of life and self-determination is found in allowing non-consenual medical intervention only when it would be unreasonable to postpone it until consent could be given.

This aspect of non-consensual treatment is discussed in greater detail in Chapter 3. The scope of the defence of necessity at common law is unclear: *R. v. Richards,*[62] where Lord Goff stated (*obiter*):

> that there exists a defence of necessity at common law, which may … be invoked to justify what would otherwise be a trespass to land is not in doubt, but the scope of the defence is by no means clear.

That the defence is available in criminal cases, appears from the decision in *Tudhope v. Grubb.*[63] It was held there that necessity was a valid defence, where the accused drove with excess alcohol in his blood to avoid an assault.

---

61 *Involuntary Manslaughter*, Law Commission Consultation Paper No. 135 (Law Commission, London, 1994). See also S. Lai, 'The Law of Reckless Manslaughter – Swept by the Tide of Change?', *Journal of Criminal Law*, Vol. 58, Pt 3, August 1994, p. 303.
62 (1986) HL (unreported), 10 July, cited in M. Jefferson, *Criminal Law* (Pitman, London, 1992), p. 177.
63 [1983] SCCR 350.

7

THE MENTAL PATIENT

The mentally ill[1] and handicapped[2] have, in the past, been regarded by the law as somehow undeserving of equal treatment.[3] Until the eighteenth century the mentally disordered were not treated *per se*, but were merely locked away from the gaze of society in workhouses or prisons.[4] Alternatively, they were left to fend for themselves on the streets, the baroque equivalent of 'care in the community'. It was not until 1757 and the opening of St Patrick's Hospital in Dublin that provision was made for the care of the mentally disordered.[5] However such care tended to be of a paternalistic nature in that the mentally ill were locked up for their own good and not necessarily for treatment.[6] Control rather then therapy tended to be the objective of the Asylum system.[7]

---

1 There are varying models of mental illness. However a basic definition of mental illness might encompass social and emotional maladjustment which interferes with the ordinary conduct of life. In other words the disorder is psychological in origin rather than organic.

2 When talking of mental handicap, one must distinguish between the mentally retarded individual and the mentally defective individual. A mentally retarded person is essentially sound physically but with a deficiency based on a learning disability with, at least in most cases, no obvious organic damage. A mentally defective person is one whose impairment is caused by brain injury or organic defect.

3 G. Rosen, *Madness in Society* (University of Chicago Press, Chicago, 1966).

4 See J. Robins, *Fools and Mad – A History of the Insane in Ireland* (Institute of Public Administration, Dublin, 1986); J. Masson, *Against Therapy* (Fontana/Collins, London, 1990), chs. 1 and 4.

5 Founded as a result of a provision in the will of Jonathan Swift. He described his own bequest thus:

> He gave the little Wealth he had,
> to build a House for Fools and mad:
> And shew'd by one satyric Touch,
> No nation wanted it so much:
> The Kingdom he hath left his Debtor.

See further E. Malcolm *Swift's Hospital* (Gill & MacMillan, Dublin, 1990).

6 J. Masson, *Against Therapy* (Fontana/Collins, London, 1990), ch. 1.

7 See J. Robins, *Fools and Mad – A History of the Insane in Ireland* (Institute of Public Administration, Dublin, 1986).

Today in Ireland the treatment of the mentally disordered is different. Legal and ethical problems still remain. These include such practices as the involuntary incarceration of the patient and the validity of consent to certain forms of psychiatric treatment. Indeed there has grown up in recent times an 'anti-psychiatry' movement which objects to the accepted treatment of the mentally disordered[8] and in some cases looks on psychiatry as a form of social control.[9] It holds that mental illness is but a label used to control those who do not conform to society's ideal of accepted behaviour.[10]

HEALTH CARE UNDER THE MENTAL HOSPITAL AUTHORITIES

The Mental Treatment Act 1945 forms the legislative basis for the mental health services in Ireland.

In 1981 the Health (Mental Services) Act, (No. 17 of 1981) was passed by the Oireachtas, signed by the President, but has never come into force.

This Act provided for the registration and supervision of psychiatric institutions,[11] introduced new admission and discharge procedures,[12] set out safeguards for patients,[13] and modified the procedure for taking civil proceedings in connection with mental treatment.[14]

The main changes it introduced were the limitation of compulsory powers of admission and detention, the abolition of compulsory powers of treatment of alcoholics and drug addicts, a change in the requirements of two doctors to certify a patient, a requirement that the doctors state reasons for certification, and the establishment of psychiatric review bodies.

As it never became law, and as it is unlikely it will become law in the same form as enacted, we do not deal with it in greater detail.[15]

MENTAL TREATMENT ACT 1945

S. 14 of the Mental Treatment Act 1945 provides that for the purposes of the Act, the state shall be divided into Mental Health Districts. There is a

8 R.D. Laing, *The Politics of Experience* (Ballantine, New York, 1967).
9 See J. Masson, *Against Therapy* (Fontana/Collins, London, 1990) for an incisive criticism of psychotherapy, family therapy, Gestalt therapy.
10 T.S. Szasz, *The myth of mental illness: Foundations of a theory of personal conduct*, revised ed., (Harper & Row, New York, 1974).

11 Part II of the Act.
12 Part III of the Act.
13 Part IV of the 1981 Act.
14 Part V of the 1981 Act.
15 See C. Keane (ed), *Mental Health In Ireland* (Gill & Macmillan/RTE, 1991, p. 120-21), D. Walsh, 'Mental Health Act 1981: a personal view', *Irish Medical Times (1981)*, Vol. 15, No. 28, p. 21.

local administrative authority for each mental health district. There is a general duty on the Mental Hospital Authority to treat, maintain, advise, or provide services for a person who is (a) ordinarily resident in a mental hospital district and (b) requires treatment, maintenance advice or the provision of services and (c) he, or those liable for him, cannot pay.

S. 20 provides that a mental hospital authority shall provide and maintain proper and sufficient accommodation for the exercise of their statutory duties. Every mental hospital authority must provide and maintain a mental hospital for their mental hospital district. A mental hospital authority may, and shall if so directed by the Minister, provide and maintain an auxiliary mental hospital for the reception of patients who, not being dangerous to themselves or others, are certified by the resident medical superintendent of the district medical hospital, as not requiring special care and treatment in a fully equipped mental hospital.

The Health Board hospitals provide the basis for over 80% of in-patient care for the mentally ill. Alongside institutional care for the mentally ill, there also exists community care. Out-patient clinics are arranged in the Health Board hospitals. Facilities for day care are available in some hospitals in Ireland. Hostels for the mentally ill and community workshops are also provided by the Health Boards.

DETENTION OF MENTAL PATIENTS

Article 40.4.2 of the Constitution guarantees that no citizen shall be deprived of his personal liberty save in accordance with law. Thus a mental patient, or someone acting on his behalf, may apply to the court for a judicial review of the decision to detain them in a psychiatric institution under this constitutional provision. The patient, or someone acting on his behalf, can apply to the High Court for an order of *habeas corpus* to release the patient on the grounds that he is being detained unlawfully.

CATEGORIES OF PATIENT

The 1945 Act specifies two main classes of patients received into psychiatric care – voluntary and non-voluntary patients.

There are two categories of non-voluntary patients – temporary patients and those certified as persons of 'unsound mind'.

PROCEDURES FOR ADMISSION

The Act of 1945 sets out the procedures for the admission of voluntary and non-voluntary patients but excludes mentally disordered persons charged with criminal offences and wards of court.

VOLUNTARY DETENTION

This category includes those who enter a psychiatric hospital of their own free will. It is not necessary to produce any written report or recommendation from a medical practitioner. Such a patient can give notice that he wishes to leave the hospital at any time on giving seventy-two hours notice and must be allowed to do so on or after the expiration of the seventy-two hour period. The procedure is slightly different if the patient is under sixteen years of age. In such cases, the application for admission is made by either a parent or guardian and must be accompanied by a recommendation from a medical practitioner. If the child wishes to leave the hospital, the parent or guardian must give seventy-two hours notice. The parent or guardian may then remove the patient at the expiration of the seventy-two hour period.

NON-VOLUNTARY DETENTION

The legislation governing the involuntary incarceration of the mentally ill in the Ireland is to be found in the 1945 Act, as amended by the Mental Treatment Act 1961. This legislation is an example of the *parens patriae* model of committal of the mentally disordered. This model stresses the State's interest in caring for those who cannot care for themselves even if this necessitates acting against the wishes of the patient.[16] The rationale behind this approach is that the patient needs this treatment, but due to his psychiatric condition is unable to seek that treatment voluntarily. This gives the medical practitioner a wide discretion in relation to committing the patient for treatment. Critics of this approach argue that it allows too wide a discretion, in that it enables people to be committed for reasons unrelated to the need for *bona fide* treatment.[17]

Under existing Irish legislation, a person may be admitted to a psychiatric hospital without his consent either as a temporary patient or as a patient of unsound mind.

---

16 See S.K. Hodge, G. Sachs, P.S. Appelbaum, A. Greer and C. Gordon, 'Limitations on psychiatrists' discretionary civil commitment authority by the Stone and dangerousness criteria', *Archives of General Psychiatry* (1988) Vol. 45, pp. 764-9. For a reappraisal of this area see D.B. Wexler and B.J. Winick (eds.), *Essays in Therapeutic Jurisprudence* (Carolina Acadmic Press, Durham, NC, 1991).

17 Ibid. See S.K. Hodge, G. Sachs, P.S. Appelbaum, A. Greer and C. Gordon, op. cit.

There has been considerable judicial comment on this area of the law. In *M v. G*[18] a doctor on call certified a drunk patient whom he believed had been violent, and who he thought was an addict, and who he thought required at least six months' preventative and curative treatment. The patient was taken by ambulance with a police escort to St Brendan's Hospital, but was discharged the next day. The patient sued the doctor for negligence. In such circumstances s. 260 of the Mental Treatment Act requires that a patient bringing such an action must first obtain leave of the High Court. The defendant doctor has the right to receive notice of the application and be heard. In this case, though leave to proceed was given by the High Court, the Supreme Court ultimately held against the patient. When a doctor is called on to deal with a situation such as that described, the law does not require a standard of precision such as might be appropriate in other circumstances. The very urgency, and danger surrounding circumstances where a doctor may need to certify a patient justifies the limited statutory protection afforded to the practitioner.[19]

In a more recent case, *O'R v. M*,[20] the *M v. G* case was judicially considered by the Supreme Court. In the *O'R* case, the appellant was married, and the relationship had broken down. Ultimately, after considerable marital disharmony, the husband and the appellant's father went together to see a local doctor about the appellant's condition.

This doctor was not the appellant's GP, and he did not know the name of the doctor treating her. The doctor was told that the appellant was disturbed, and had threatened to commit suicide. The doctor ultimately went with the husband, but did not go to the front door. However, he did observe from a suitably distant vantage-point, that when the appellant answered the door, and saw her husband, she became 'very agitated and violent'. The doctor felt that it would not be helpful to try and interview her, but decided that she might be a danger to herself. In the High Court, there was a conflict of evidence, and the trial judge said that he had to prefer the evidence of the doctor to that of the appellant or her father.

Satisifed that the appellant was seriously disturbed, the doctor signed the requisite form, asked the Gardaí to provide an escort, and arranged for the admission of the appellant to the Health Board Hospital. Subsequently, Dr M received a call from the hospital doctor, who confirmed with him what had happened.

The majority of the Supreme Court held that the detention had been

18 [1990] 2 IR 566.
19 See E. Madden, 'When the Courts lean Towards the Doctor', *Irish Medical Times* (1991), Vol 25, No. 43 (25 October), p. 14.
20 [1992] 2 IR 145 (HC); (1993) unreported, 16 November (SC).

properly effected. In reply to the contention that the appellant had not been 'examined', Egan J, with whom O'Flaherty J agreed, held that there had been a sufficient examination in the circumstances, taken together with all the information which Dr M had obtained from the appellant's husband and her father.

The majority of the Supreme Court appear to have accepted that the examination by Dr M was not the decisive factor, rather, it was the examination that had occurred in the hospital.

Blayney J, in a powerful dissenting judgment, disagreed. He held that the trial judge, in finding that Dr M did not examine the appellant physically, or even put questions to her 'for the purpose of ascertaining direct evidence as to her mental or emotional well-being' and therefore, it seemed to Blayney J as if there was a 'clear *prima facie* case that he acted without reasonable care'.

Blayney J pointed out that under s. 184 of the 1945 Act, temporary chargeable reception patient orders may be made, resulting in non-voluntary detention, on foot of the certifying doctor, and that a second examination is only required in the case of chargeable patient reception orders. Thus Blayney J held that a special duty lay on the doctor in the position of Dr M to take care to make an accurate certificate (and in Blayney J's view, this necessitated a more comprehensive examination than that in fact accorded to the appellant), and to make a diagnosis of mental illness.

Two aspects of Blayney J's judgment deserve particular consideration.

First, it raises questions about the effect of s. 260 of the 1945 Act. This provides:

> (1) no civil proceedings shall be instituted in respect of an act purporting to have been done in pursuance of this Act save by leave of the High Court and such leave shall not be granted unless the High Court is satisfied that there are substantial grounds for contending that the person against whom the proceedings are to be brought acted in bad faith or without reasonable care.
>
> (2) Notice of an application for leave of the High Court under subs. (1) of this section shall be given to the person against whom it is proposed to institute the proceedings and such person shall be entitled to be heard against the application.

Blayney J reviewed the law on what constitutes such grounds, and cited, in particular, *O'Dowd v. North Western Health Board*[21] where O'Higgins CJ held that the section does no more than to require the applicant for leave

21 [1983] ILRM 186.

to sue to discharge the same onus of proof as he would be required to discharge in pursuing a claim for damages for a tort outside the Act, but to discharge it at an earlier point in time. He held that such an limitation did not seem to be unduly restrictive or unreasonable. Blayney J approved this statement of the law, and as such, it will no doubt continue to be applied until this section is amended.

Second, it is suggested that Blayney J, in holding that this examination was deficient, and that the form was not filled incorrectly, may well be providing an indication of what may in future become the requirement in other cases. In other words, in future, a medical practitioner should probably take care to attempt a fuller examination than that carried out in the *O'R* case, before certifying the patient. Blayney J in *O'R* pointed out that the apellant was given no opportunity to defend herself before being removed from her home. He said that if she had been examined (more fully), she could have put her side of the case to the doctor.

Of course, it may be that those concerned professionally with certification, may take comfort in the fact that the majority of the Supreme Court held that Dr M had properly examined the patient, and that his fear of exacerbating the situation was, in the circumstances quite reasonable. In any future case, it could be argued, it would not be unreasonable to rely on the majority view in *O'R*.

But on the other hand, O'Flaherty J, though concurring with Egan J, did say that 'no two cases are the same, and, most likely, the approach of no two doctors will be the same'. O'Flaherty J held that the doctor in this case 'exercised his best judgment in this case which he believed was fraught with danger'. It will therefore be open to the Courts to use accepted techniques of distinguishing the facts in *O'R* from those in other cases with which they may have to deal, and to hold that a certifying doctor must conduct a fuller examination than that in *O'R*.

Unfortunately, this leaves doctors, and patients too in a dilemma. Failure to certify an ill patient may result in serious harm. Failure to conduct a full examination may well result in the unjust deprivation of liberty of the patient.

Clearly, reform of the law is necessary.

TEMPORARY PATIENT

A temporary patient is defined as a person who requires to be detained for treatment and is believed to require not more than six months suitable treatment for recovery or is, in the alternative, an addict who is believed to require at least six months' preventive and curative treatment.[22] A person

---

22 Mental Treatment Act 1945, ss. 185, 186.

can be detained as a temporary patient under the Act of 1945, as amended by the Act of 1961, using either a 'Temporary Chargeable Patient Reception Order' or a 'Temporary Private Patient Reception Order'.

The Temporary Patient (Chargeable) document consists of three sections. Part I is the application form for the admission of the temporary patient which must be signed by a next-of-kin or, in the alternative, a member of the Garda Síochána, a community welfare officer or another responsible member of the community. Part II is to be completed by the medical practitioner who must examine the patient and recommend his committal. The certifying doctor must not be employed by the psychiatric hospital and is normally a local general practitioner. Part II includes a proviso which allows the doctor in question not to sign, and to give reasons for not doing so. If the doctor refuses to sign, the applicant may go to another doctor, but must inform him of the previous refusal.[23] The form must be used within seven days of Part II being signed and dated.[24] In the event that the patient is deemed to be in need of treatment after examination by the chief medical officer of the psychiatric hospital, then Part III of the document, the 'Order for Reception and Detention', is signed. This order gives authority to bring the patient to the hospital. The maximum period of detention of a temporary patient is six months, but if, towards the end of that period, the chief medical officer of the institution is of the opinion that the patient has not recovered, he may extend the original period of detention to a further six months up to a total of twenty four months, or twelve months in the case of an addict. The only significant difference between the 'Temporary Chargeable Patient Reception Order' and the 'Temporary Private Patient Reception Order' is that in the case of the latter, Part II of the document must be signed by two doctors instead of the one required for the former.

PERSON OF UNSOUND MIND

A 'person of unsound mind' is broadly defined in the Act of 1945 as a person who requires detention for protection and care, and who is unlikely to recover within six months. Section 163 of the 1945 Act (as amended by s. 7 of the Act of 1961) provides that an application for recommendation for reception into a psychiatric hospital may be made by a spouse or other relative. The doctor may refuse the application, but should he grant it, the patient should be medically examined. The recommendation must also certify that the patient is of unsound mind.[25] The medical officer of the psychiatric hospital

23 S. 164 of the 1945 Act.   25 S. 163(2) of the 1945 Act.
24 S. 186 of the 1945 Act.

must examine the person to whom an application for admission as a person of unsound mind refers, before signing the reception order. A person of unsound mind may be detained for an indefinite period. However, there exist a number of safeguards for the patient. Under the *habeas corpus* provisions of Article 40.4.2 of the Constitution, a patient or someone acting on his behalf, may apply to the High Court for an order of *habeas corpus*. If the application were successful, the patient would be released on the grounds that he is being unlawfully detained. In addition, s. 12 of the Act of 1945 provides for the appointment of an Inspector of mental hospitals, who must visit and inspect all health board psychiatric hospitals twice a year. The Inspector has a duty to give special attention to the state of mind of any patient detained where he has grounds to doubt the validity of the detention, or when he is requested to do so by the patient in question or by a third party. The Inspector must also ascertain whether the periods of detention of any temporary patients have been extended since his or her previous visit. The Inspector may report to the Minister for Health on the propriety of any detention, and the Minister, acting on that report, may order the release of the patient.

S. 189 of the Act of 1945 requires the resident medical superintendent of a psychiatric hospital, on extending the period of detention of a temporary patient, to advise the patient and the individual who applied for the original reception order that either of them may appeal to the Inspector of Mental Hospitals. Any relative or friend of the detainee may apply to the resident medical superintendent under s. 220 of the 1945 Act for the release of a patient to his or her care. This application must be granted unless the medical superintendent is of the opinion that the patient will not be properly taken care of or certifies that the patient is dangerous or unfit for discharge. In the latter event, the applicant may appeal to the Minister for Health. Under s. 222 of the 1945 Act, any person may apply to the Minister for Health for an order for the examination of a detained person by two medical practitioners. The report of these practitioners is then sent to the Minister for Health who may direct the discharge of the patient.

Every patient has the right under s. 266 of the Act of 1945 to have a sealed letter forwarded to the Minister for Health, the President of the High Court, the local health board, the Inspector of Mental Hospitals, or if the patient is a ward of court, to the Registrar of Wards of Court. The Inspector of Mental Hospitals may report to the Minister on the propriety of the detention and the Minister may direct the release of the patient. The President of the High Court may require the Inspector to visit and examine any patient detained as a person of unsound mind and to make a report. Under s. 203 of the 1945 Act, a patient who is considered not to be a danger to either himself or others may, with the approval of the resident medical superintendent of the hospital, be allowed to be paroled for a period not exceeding forty-eight hours or to be allowed absence on trial for periods up to ninety days.

To date, the only provision of the Act of 1945 to be subjected to constitutional challenge and fully reported is s. 165. S. 165 of the Act permits a Garda Síochána to detain a person believed to be of unsound mind, where he is of the opinion that it is necessary for the public safety or that of the person concerned, that he be placed under care and control. The Garda officer must immediately apply to a doctor for an order for the reception and detention of that person in the district psychiatric hospital. In the case of *In re Philip Clarke*,[26] an order of *habeas corpus* was sought by the prosecutor who had been detained under this section. Under the *habeas corpus* provisions of Article 40.4 of the Constitution of 1937, a patient so detained or someone acting on his behalf, may apply to the High Court for an order of *habeas corpus* which, if granted, would allow the release of the patient, on the grounds that he is being unlawfully detained. The claim on behalf of the prosecutor was that he had been unlawfully detained as no judicial determination of his case took place between the time of his arrest and the time of his detention in the psychiatric hospital. However, the court held that the section was not repugnant to the Constitution. In delivering the judgment of the Court, O'Byrne J stated:

> [t]hat section is carefully drafted so as to ensure that the person, alleged to be of unsound mind, shall be brought before, and examined by, responsible medical officers with the least possible delay. This seems to us to satisfy every reasonable requirement, and we have not been satisfied, and do not consider that the Constitution requires, that there should be a judicial inquiry or determination before such a person can be placed and detained in a mental hospital.
>
> The section cannot, in our opinion, be construed as an attack upon the personal rights of the citizen. On the contrary it seems to be designed for the protection of the citizen and for the promotion of the common good.[27]

However, it is questionable whether such a stance would be taken by a court today in a similar case, given changing attitudes to the nature of psychiatric care in Ireland and the increasing international obligations of the State in relation to individual human rights. The *European Convention for the Protection of Human Rights and Fundamental Freedoms* of 4 February 1950 is of particular relevance here. The Convention while not being a part of

26 [1950] IR 253.   27 Ibid. at p. 258.

Irish domestic law, certainly influences the approach of the State to questions of individual liberty. Article 29.6 of the *Constitution of Ireland* of 1937 provides that:

> [n]o international agreement shall be part of the domestic law of the State save as may be determined by the Oireachtas.

The rights guaranteed by the *European Convention* are, as a result, not part of Irish law. This is an example of the dualist model of international law, whereby a state is not bound internally by the terms of any Treaty unless it is expressly made a part of its domestic law. The Supreme Court expressed a view as to the relationship of the Convention to Irish domestic law in the case of *In re Ó Laighleis*.[28] Maguire CJ in giving the judgment of the Court, stated:

> [b]y Article 15.2.1 of the Constitution it is provided that "the sole and exclusive power of making laws for the State is hereby vested in the Oireachtas: no other legislative authority has powers to make laws for the State." Moreover, Article 29 . . . provides at s. 6 that "no international agreement shall be part of the domestic law of the State save as may be determined by the Oireachtas." The Oireachtas has not determined that the Convention . . . is part of the domestic law of the State, and accordingly this Court cannot give effect to the Convention if it be contrary to domestic law or purports to grant rights or impose obligations additional to those of domestic law.
>
> No argument can prevail against the express command of Article 29.6.6 of the Constitution, before judges whose declared duty it is to uphold the Constitution and the laws.
>
> The Court accordingly cannot accept the idea that the primacy of domestic legislation is displaced by the State becoming a party to the Convention. . . .[29]

In the case of *Desmond and Dedeir v Glackin, the Minister for Industry and Commerce, Ireland and the Attorney General*[30] O'Hanlon J stated in the High Court that as Ireland had ratified the *European Convention*, it was legitimate to assume that public policy in this country accorded with the Convention. While the Convention itself, he continued, is not a code of principles which is enforceable in Irish courts, this does not prevent a judgment of the European Court of Human Rights in relation to the

28 [1960] IR 93.
29 Ibid. at pp. 124-5.

30 [1992] ILRM 490; (1992) *Irish Times Law Reports* (17 February).

interpretation of the Convention from having persuasive effect in Irish courts.

In the context of committal of the mentally disordered, Article 5(1)(e) of the *European Convention for the Protection of Human Rights and Fundamental Freedoms* provides:

> (1) everyone has the right to liberty and security of the person. No one shall be deprived of his liberty save in the following cases and in accordance with a procedure prescribed by law . . .
>
> (e) the lawful detention of persons for the prevention of the spreading of infectious diseases, of persons of unsound mind, alcoholics or drug addicts or vagrants.

This provision has been interpreted in a number of cases, by the European Court of Human Rights. In the case of *Winterwerp v. The Netherlands*,[31] the plaintiff was committed to a psychiatric hospital on an involuntary basis. The argument made on behalf of the plaintiff was that before the committal orders were made, he had not been notified of the committal proceedings and that he was not afforded the opportunity to contest the orders before a court or to challenge the medical findings on which the courts had founded their decisions to commit him. In interpreting Article 5(1)(e), the court stated that the Convention did not allow the committal of persons because their views or behaviour deviated from the societal norm. A true mental disorder must first be objectively determined and such disorder must be of a kind or degree warranting continuous confinement. The validity of this continuing confinement depended on the persistence of the mental disorder.

In the case of *X v. United Kingdom*,[32] the court was of the opinion that a person of unsound mind who had been detained in a psychiatric institution for an indefinite period, was by virtue of Article 5(4) entitled to take proceedings at reasonable intervals before a court to test the lawfulness of his detention. It was held that the *habeas corpus* provisions of English law were not wide enough to satisfy the requirements of Article 5(4). What was required was an automatic periodic review of the detention, of a judicial character.[33] The United Kingdom has subsequently made provision for such a periodic review in the form of Mental Health Review Tribunals established under the Mental Health Act 1983.[34] It is arguable as to whether the *habeas corpus* provisions of the Constitution would be sufficient to constitute an

31 (1979) 2 EHRR 387.
32 (1981) 4 EHRR 181.
33 Ibid. at p. 207.
34 See P.F. Mawson, 'The function of

mental health review tribunals under the Mental Health Act 1983', *Medicine Science and The Law* (1986), Vol. 26, p. 291.

automatic periodic review of detention required by Article 5(4) of the *European Convention*. Further legislation may be required to satisfy this requirement.[35] In 1992, the Department of Health published a *Green Paper on Mental Health*,[36] which recommended that Irish legislation in this area be brought into line with our international obligations such as, for example, the *European Convention* and the *United Nations Principles for the Protection of Persons with Mental Illness and the Improvement of Mental Health Care*.

At present, a White Paper on Mental Health is in preparation which will provide for new criteria for involuntary admission and automatic periodic review of detention.[37]

Such a reform would arguably entail a change in the philosophy governing involuntary committals. Thus, one may see the introduction of the alternative model of involuntary committal, the 'dangerousness' model. Under this model, a patient may be committed only if he is suffering from a mental illness which causes him to be a danger to himself or to others. This model is the basis for committal law in the US.[38]

The dangerousness model was first given legislative expression in California in 1969 in the form of the Lanterman Petris Short Act of that year. This Act was to become the model for subsequent state legislation in this field;[39] had as its objective the narrowing of the range of criteria under which non-voluntary detention could take place; and provided that there would have to be clear evidence of danger to the patient or to others before a committal order could be made or in the alternative, the patient would

35 An abortive effort was made to introduce legislation providing for such periodic review in the form of the Health (Mental Services) Act 1981. This piece of legislation provided for a limitation of the criteria for involuntary admission, and changed the procedures for involuntary admission and the detention of patients. In particular, the Act of 1981 provided that the patient to be certified should be examined by two doctors and that the initial detention period would be for forty-eight hours, during which time a twenty-eight day reception order could be made if required. In addition, the patient, or someone acting on his behalf, could request a review of his detention within one month by an independent psychiatric review board which would consist of an authorised medical officer, a solicitor or barrister and a lay person. This review board would have the power to discharge the patient. In the event of the applicant's request for discharge being refused by the board, the applicant would have the opportunity to appeal this decision to the Minister of Health. Despite being passed through both Houses of the Oireachtas, this Act never became law.

36 Department of Health, *Green Paper on Mental Health* (Stationery Office, Dublin, 1992, pl. 8918).

37 See Department of Health, *Shaping a healthier future: a strategy for effective healthcare in the 1990s* (Department of Health, Dublin, 1994, pl. 0658), pp. 68-70.

38 S.K. Hodge, G. Sachs, P.S. Applebaum, A. Greer, C. Gordon, 'Limitations on psychiatrists' discretionary civil commitment authority by the Stone and Dangerousness criteria', *Archives of General Psychiatry* (1988) Vol. 45, pp. 764-9.

39 Ibid.

have to be under a 'grave disability' due to his mental disorder. The term 'grave disorder' was judicially defined by the United States Supreme Court in the case of *O'Connor v. Donaldson*,[40] as meaning that the patient must be '. . . incapable of surviving safely in freedom either by himself or with the help of willing and responsible family members'.[41]

The 1969 Act also contained safeguards against unlawful detention. In the case of those who are diagnosed as being a danger to others, after fourteen days a court hearing must be held in order to determine if the patient should be detained for a further period of up to ninety days. At the end of this ninety-day period another court hearing is necessary to determine if further detention is warranted. For those who are diagnosed as being a danger to themselves, the relevant doctor is empowered, at the end of the first fourteen days' detention, to hold the patient for a further fourteen days if necessary, after which, release is generally mandatory. In the case of those diagnosed as being gravely disabled as a result of their mental illness, further detention after the initial fourteen day period requires to be determined by a court, which would allow for further detention up to a period of one year.

Nonetheless, the dangerousness model does not lack critics. Thus, opponents of this model argue that the standards of the criminal law are being imposed on what is supposedly a civil matter.[42] This, the argument goes, radically changes the doctor-patient relationship from one of therapist and patient to one of prosecutor and defendant, where the doctor must prove for the purposes of the law that the patient/defendant is a danger to himself or to others. This obviously has serious implications for the perceived role of the doctor, and the nature of the doctor-patient relationship.[43]

PSYCHOSURGICAL INTERVENTIONS

The use of surgery to modify human behaviour is a topic fraught with ethical problems. In Ireland, psychosurgery is not carried out.[44] However, in a recent Council of Europe report on psychiatry and human rights, the Irish

40 (1945) 422 US 563.
41 Ibid.
42 See A.A. Stone, 'Recent Mental Health litigation: a critical perspective', *American Journal of Psychiatry* (1977), Vol. 134, pp. 273-9.
43 See further P.S. Applebaum, 'The new preventive detention: psychiatry's problematic responsibility for the control of violence', *American Journal of Psychiatry* (1988), Vol. 145, pp. 779-85. For a different approach to the issue, see P. Casey, I. Keilitz and T.L. Hafemeister,

'Toward an agenda for reform of justice and mental health systems interactions' (1992) *Law and Human Behaviour*, Vol. 16, No. 1, pp. 107-28; J. Steadman et al., 'From dangerousness to risk assessment: Implications for appropriate research strategies' in S. Hodgins (ed.), *Mental Disorder and Crime* (Sage, Newbury Park, CA, 1993), pp. 39-62.
44 A. Rogers, 'Legislation on psychiatry In Europe', *Lancet* (1994), Vol. 343, pp. 1027-8 (23 April).

government was reported as stating that patients 'are occasionally referred to Britain for this procedure.'[45] Psychosurgery is used in the treatment of a range of conditions. It appears to be most successful in the treatment of mood disorders such as depression, obsessive-compulsive neuroses and schizo-affective psychoses.[46] However it has also been used in treating conditions such as schizophrenia and *anorexia nervosa* where its effectiveness has been questioned.[47] The use of psychosurgery as a means of controlling violent individuals seems to be even less justifiable. Such an objective brings the practice into the realms of using surgery as a mechanism for social control rather than for the *bona fide* treatment of illness.[48]

As psychosurgery is not performed in Ireland, and some patients are referred to Britain for surgery, we note that relevant legislative provisions in relation to such treatment are to be found in the English Mental Health Act 1983. S. 57 of the 1983 Act does not allow psychosurgery in the absence of the patient's consent. The legal model of consent which applies in England normally requires that consent to surgical procedures be voluntarily given by a patient capable of giving consent in that he understands the nature, purpose and effects of the operation.[49] However, specific legislative guidelines govern the issue of consent in relation to psychosurgery. S. 57 of the Act of 1983 provides that before a patient undergoes psychosurgery, a panel of three persons appointed by the Mental Health Act Commission (an independent multi-disciplinary body appointed by the Secretary of State for Health) must certify that the patient is capable of understanding the nature, purpose and likely effects of the surgery and has consented to it. The surgery may only proceed if the medical practitioner member of the panel has certified that the patient should undergo such surgery. The medical practitioner, in arriving at his decision, must have consulted a nurse and another non-medical professional who have been involved in the care of the patient. In addition, the medical practitioner on the panel is required, under s. 57 of the Act of 1983, to have regard, in coming to his decision, to 'the likelihood of the treatment alleviating or preventing deterioration in the patient's condition.'

45 Ibid. at p. 1027.
46 E.O. Goktepe. L.B. Young, P.K. Bridges, 'A further review of the results of stereotactic subcaudate tractotomy', *British Journal of Psychiatry* (1975), Vol. 126, pp. 270-80; R. Strom-Olsen & S. Carlisle, 'Bifrontal stereodactic tractotomy', *British Journal of Psychiatry* (1971), Vol. 118, pp. 141-54.
47 P.K. Bridges & J.R. Bartlett, 'Psychosurgery Yesterday and Today', *British Journal of Psychiatry* (1977), Vol. 131, pp. 249-60.
48 See for example L.G. Kiloh, R.S. Gye, R.G. Rushworth, D.S. Bell, R.T. White, 'Stereodactic amygdaloidotomy for aggressive behaviour', *Journal of Neurology Neurosurgery and Psychiatry* (1974), Vol. 37, pp. 437-44.
49 See *Sidaway v. Bethlem Royal Hospital Governors and Others* [1985] 1 All ER 643.

The Act, while, in theory, protecting the rights of the patient, may give rise to unintended consequences in practice. These consequences are identified by Dyer & Bloch[50] as including the interposition of:

an overseer in the doctor-patient relationship who may:

(1) Humiliate patients through a public review of their difficulties.
(2) Make the therapeutic alliance difficult or impossible to achieve.
(3) Deprive patients of potentially beneficial treatment.
(4) Add time-consuming, administrative tasks for the psychiatrist to perform.[51]

Thus the autonomy of both patient and doctor is somehow diminished in that the doctor is not free to authorise such surgery without the approval of the Mental Health Act Commission panel, and, the panel may decide not to allow such treatment even when a patient has validly consented to it.[52]

A related issue is that of the modification of the behaviour of sexual offenders through the use of hormonal implants.[53] In Ireland, at present, there exist no legislative provisions in relation to this form of treatment. In practice, this form of treatment does not appear to be available to the sex offender in Ireland. However, in the United Kingdom such treatment is the object of specific legislative provisions. S. 57 of the Mental Health Act 1983 provides that hormone implants for the reduction of the male sex drive may not be administered without the consent of the patient. As in the case of psychosurgery, the administration of hormone implants may not proceed without the authorisation of a panel appointed by the Mental Health Act Commission. The way in which the autonomy of the patient can be diminished by the provisions of the Act of 1983 was demonstrated in the case of *R. v. Mental Health Act Commission ex parte W.*[54] Where, a 26-year-old compulsive paedophile who had recently completed a two-year

50 A.R. Dyer & S. Bloch, 'Informed Consent and The Psychiatric patient', *Journal of Medical Ethics* (1987), Vol. 13, No. 1 (March), pp. 12-16.

51 Ibid., p. 14.

52 See further P. Bridges, 'Psychosurgery and the Mental Health Act Commission', *Bulletin of the Royal College of Psychiatrists* (1984) Vol. 8, pp. 146-8. P.K. Bridges et. al., 'Psychosurgery Stereotactic Subcaudate Tractotony: An Indispensable Treatment', *British Journal of Psychiatry* (1994), Vol. 165, pp. 599-611.

53 S.L. Halleck, 'The ethics of antiandrogen therapy', *American Journal of Psychiatry* (1981), Vol. 138, p. 642; D. Torpy & A. Tomison, 'Sex Offenders and Cyprotene Acetate – A review of clinical care', *Medicine Science and Law* (1986), Vol. 26, p. 279.

54 Unreported, *The Guardian*, 27 May 1988. For further discussion see C. Dyer, 'Mental Health Commission defeated over paedophile', *British Medical Journal* (1988), Vol. 296 p. 1660; P. Fennell, 'Sexual Suppressants and the Mental Health Act', *Criminal Law Review* (1988), p. 660.

prison sentence for indecency offences, had consented to be treated with the drug Goserlin which was administered on a monthly basis by a subcutaneous injection of a thin cylindrical implant.[55] After W had received two injections of the drug, the Mental Health Act Commission became concerned as to the validity of W's consent. The Commission argued that Goserlin came within the category of a hormone and because it was administered in capsule form through an abnormally wide bore syringe, that it was implanted by surgical means. By arguing thus, Goserlin could be brought within the meaning of a hormone implant for the purposes of s. 57 of the Act of 1983. As a consequence the provision of such treatment would have to be authorised by a panel appointed by the Mental Health Act Commission. The panel came to the conclusion that W had not validly consented to the treatment and that such treatment could not, as a result, be given.

W appealed this decision by way of judicial review. The Court quashed the decision of the Commission panel, holding that Goserlin was not a hormone and that its implantation was not surgical. The Court went on to hold that W had consented to the treatment in the knowledge of its nature and likely effect and that he also knew that Goserlin was not routinely sold and used as a sexual suppressant and that the full implications of its use on young males had not been studied. In any case, the Court observed, that s. 1(3) of the Mental Health Act 1983 excluded sexual deviance from the definition of mental disorder for the purposes of the Act. As a result this case was not subject to review by the Commission panel under s. 57 of the Act.

ELECTRO-CONVULSIVE THERAPY

Electroconvulsive therapy (ECT) is provided in Irish psychiatric units.[56] However, there is no specific piece of legislation which governs this form of treatment. As a result, the common law rules in relation to the giving of consent to medical treatment will apply here. In addition to the legal rules, extra-legal guidelines in the form of professional codes are of relevance to the practitioner. In Ireland, the profession of psychiatry does not have a national professional body of its own. Instead, it is governed by the British Royal College of Psychiatrists. The Royal College of Psychiatrists favours the provision of ECT. New guidelines are expected this year from the Royal College specifying that psychiatric clinics should upgrade to newer, more

---

55 Goserlin is not a hormone but a hormone analogue, which is normally used to treat prostate cancer, but which also reduces testosterone to castrate levels.

56 R. Rogers, 'Legislation on psychiatry in Europe', *Lancet* (1994), Vol. 343, pp. 1027-8 (23 April).

efficient ECT machines that deliver electricity in brief bursts; and that psychiatrists should receive more intensive 'hands-on' training in administering the treatment.[57]

The main problem with consent in relation to ECT is that disorders which it is used to treat, such as severe depression and catatonic and affective schizophrenia[58] may interfere with the patient's ability to give valid consent. Legislative intervention is required to give this area of psychiatric medicine more transparency and to avoid as far as is possible using legislative means, the negation of a patient's rights. Indeed, in this regard, the recent *Green Paper on Mental Health*[59] recommended the introduction of legislation which would incorporate the safeguards to be found in the *United Nations Principles for the Protection of Persons with Mental Illness and the Improvement of Mental Health Care* of 1991 in relation to ECT. Principle 11 of the *UN Principles* governs the area of consent. Principle 11(13) provides that:

> A major medical or surgical procedure may be carried out on a person with mental illness only where it is permitted by domestic law, where it is considered that it would best serve the health needs of the patient and where the patient gives informed consent, except that, where the patient is unable to give informed consent, the procedure shall be authorised only after independent review.

Thus, the present void in Irish legislation in relation to the problem of the valid consent of those with a mental disorder would be filled if legislation to this effect were to be introduced. At present, a White Paper on Mental Health is in preparation which will incorporate the recommendations of the *Green Paper*.[60]

If and when such legislation is introduced, one would witness a new phenomenon in Irish psychiatric care; the mental health review board. The objective of such boards is to uphold the rights of the patient by acting as an independent overseer.[61] An example of such an independent review body is to be found in the United Kingdom. S. 58 of the Mental Health Act 1983 provides that ECT may not be given to a patient without his consent. The treatment may only proceed if the patient has consented and the doctor by whom he is being treated, or a second opinion doctor appointed by the

---

57 R. Twombley, 'Shock therapy returns', *New Scientist*, 5 March 1994, pp. 21-23.
58 Ibid. at p. 21.
59 Department of Health (Stationery Office, Dublin, 1992), pl. 8918.
60 Department of Health, *Shaping a healthier future – A strategy for effective healthcare in the 1990s*, (Dublin, 1994), pl. 0658) p. 69.
61 See for example P.F. Mawson, 'The function of Mental Health Review Tribunals under the Mental Health Act 1983', (1986), *Medicine Science and the Law*, Vol. 26, p. 291.

Mental Health Act Commission has verified that consent. If the patient is incapable of consenting, then treatment may only proceed if a panel of three persons appointed by the Mental Health Act Commission is of the opinion that the treatment is required to alleviate the patient's condition or to prevent further deterioration in his condition.

CRIMINAL LAW AND THE INSANITY DEFENCE

In criminal law, an individual is afforded a defence to a particular charge on the grounds of insanity.[62] This is based on the view that a person who is suffering from a mental illness is somehow not in total control of his actions, and therefore not responsible for his crime. However, the problem of defining insanity for the purposes of the criminal law has not been satisfactorily resolved. Thus, the legal definition of insanity does not necessarily correspond to insanity as it is understood by psychiatric medicine.

Modern formulations of the defence of insanity stem from the so-called *M'Naghten Rules* laid down in *M'Naghten's Case*[63] in 1843. Daniel M'Naghten, charged with the murder of the private secretary of the then Prime Minister, Sir Robert Peel, had intended to shoot the Prime Minister, but on the day in question, his private secretary, Edward Drummond, was riding in the Prime Minister's carriage, and M'Naghten shot him by mistake. Medical evidence showed that the accused was suffering from insane delusions. The jury delivered a verdict of not guilty by reason of insanity. However, this verdict caused public disquiet and concern which provoked the House of Lords acting in its capacity as a legislative body to ask the judges of the House of Lords to give an advisory opinion on the question of the insanity defence.

The *M'Naghten Rules* were contained in the advisory opinion of the judges and may be stated as follows:

(i) everyone is to be presumed sane until the contrary is proved.

(ii) To establish a defence on the ground of insanity, it must be clearly proved that, at the time of the committing of the act, the party accused was labouring under such a defect of reason, from disease of the mind, as not

---

62 For a history of the insanity defence, see W. Crotty, 'The History of Insanity as a defence to a Crime in English Criminal Law', *California Law Review* (1924), Vol. 12, p. 105ff.; F. McAuley, *Insanity, Psychiatry and Criminal Responsibility* (The Round Hall Press, Dublin, 1993), pp. 18-39; A. Platt & A. Diamond, 'The origins of the 'Right & Wrong' Test of Criminal Responsibility and its subsequent Development in the United States: An Historical Survey', *California Law Review* (1966), Vol. 54, p. 1227 & ff.

63 10 Cl & F 200; 8 Eng Rep 718 (HL 1843).

to know the nature and quality of the act he was doing; or if he did know it, that he did not know that what he was doing was wrong.

However, the *M'Naghten* rules place the term 'insanity' within very narrow definitional limits, which may not correspond to accepted psychiatric thinking.[64] As a result, such conditions as arteriosclerosis,[65] and epilepsy,[66] have been held to amount to diseases of the mind for the purposes of the criminal law. Thus in *R. v. Sullivan*, Lord Diplock put the legal position as follows:

> '[m]ind' in the *M'Naghten* rules is used in the ordinary sense of the mental faculties of reason, memory and understanding. If the effect of a disease is to impair these faculties . . . it matters not whether the aetiology of the impairment is organic, as in epilepsy, or functional, or whether the impairment itself is permanent or is transient and intermittent, provided it subsisted at the time of the commission of the act.[67]

Thus there is a divergence between legal thinking on insanity and that of psychiatry. As McAuley has observed:

> [t]his follows from the fact that, unlike its psychiatric counterpart, the legal criterion of insanity is essentially a test of moral responsibility. The question is whether illness exonerates the defendant from blame for his actions, not whether he is suffering from a recognised mental illness.[68]

Having established that the accused is suffering from a disease of the mind in the legal sense, one must then establish that such disease prevented the accused from knowing the nature and quality of the act, or that it was wrong. The *M'Naghten* rules do not furnish one with a definition of knowledge as to the nature and quality of one's act. However, in the case of *R. v. Codere*[69] the English Court of Appeal held the phrase 'nature and quality' referred to the physical quality of the act as opposed to the moral character. Thus, someone who cut off the head of a sleeping person because 'it would be great fun to see him looking for it when he woke up',[70] or

---

64 See G. Williams, *Textbook of Criminal Law*, 2nd ed. (Stevens, London, 1983), p. 643.
65 See *R. v. Kemp* [1956] 3 All ER 249.
66 See *R. v. Sullivan* [1983] 2 All ER 673.
67 [1983] 2 All ER 673 at 677.

68 F. McAuley, *Insanity, Psychiatry and Criminal Responsibility* (op. cit.), p. 5.
69 (1916) 12 Cr App Rep 21.
70 J. Stephen, *History of the Criminal Law* (London, 1899), Vol. 11, p. 166.

someone who cuts another's throat thinking that he was slicing an onion would not know the 'nature and quality' of the act for the purposes of the *M'Naghten* rules.

The alternative limb (if so infelicitous a pun may be permitted) of the responsibility test provides that where the accused knew what he was doing, did he know that it was wrong? Thus, if the accused knew that his act was prohibited by law, then he is not insane for the purposes of the *M'Naghten* rules. In *R. v. Windle*[71] the accused persuaded his wife, who had suicidal tendencies, to swallow one hundred aspirins, because he thought it would be in her best interests to die. It was established in evidence that the accused had stated that he would be hanged for what he had done, thus implying that he knew that his conduct was contrary to the law. The Court of Appeal held that the word 'wrong' in the context of the *M'Naghten* rules meant 'contrary to law'.

In Ireland, the judiciary has questioned the use of the *M'Naghten* rules as the exclusive test for insanity. Thus in the case of *Attorney General v. O'Brien*[72] O'Kennedy CJ held that since the *M'Naghten* rules were developed in reply to a number of questions in relation to insane delusions, then their application should be limited to cases of insane delusion, stating:

> [t]he questions related to crimes committed by persons afflicted with insane delusions in respect of one or more particular subjects or questions. It follows, in our opinion, that the opinions given by the Judges must in every case be read with the like specific limitation. ... Hence the dissatisfaction expressed by many legal and medical persons with the opinions as so read with the wide and general interpretation wrongly given to them.

In the later case of *People (Attorney General) v. Hayes*,[73] Henchy J commented further on the insanity defence:

> [i]n the normal case, tried in accordance with the *M'Naghten* rules the test is solely one of knowledge; did he know the nature and quality of his act, or did he know that the act was wrong? The rules do not take into account the capacity of a man on the basis of his knowledge to act or to refrain from acting, and I believe it to be correct psychiatric science to accept that certain serious mental diseases, such as paranoia or schizophrenia, in certain cases enable a man to understand the morality or immorality of his act, or the nature and quality of it, but

71 [1952] 2 All ER 1.
72 [1936] IR 263.

73 Unreported, Central Criminal Court, 30 November 1967.

nevertheless prevent him from exercising a free volition as to whether he should or should not do the act. In the present case, the medical witnesses were unanimous in saying that the accused man was, in medical terms, insane at the time of the act. However, legal insanity does not necessarily coincide with what medical men would call insanity, but if it is open to the jury to say, as say they must, on the evidence, that this man understood the nature and quality of his act, and understood its wrongfulness, morally and legally, but that nevertheless he was debarred from refraining from assaulting his wife fatally because of a defect of reason, due to his mental illness, it seems to me that it would be unjust, in the circumstances of this case, not to allow the jury to consider the case on those grounds.[74]

This approach was approved by the Supreme Court in *Doyle v Wicklow County Council*.[75] In this case, a seventeen year old youth had set fire to, and burned down an abattoir. It had been established that the youth was suffering from a mental disorder which caused him to believe that the burning down of the abattoir would not lead to his being punished by the law. He believed that, in effect, his love of animals gave him the right to burn down the abattoir without incurring the wrath of the law, even though he knew the act of arson was contrary to the law. Certain questions were referred to the Supreme Court by the Circuit Court by way of case stated. One of these questions referred to the correct test to be applied in relation to the defence of insanity. Griffin J, in giving the opinion of the Court, stated:

[i]n my opinion, the *M'Naghten* rules do not provide the sole or exclusive test for determining the sanity or insanity of an accused. The questions put to the judges were limited to the effect of insane delusions and I would agree with the opinion expressed by the Court of Criminal Appeal in *Attorney General v O'Brien*, that the opinions given by the judges must be read with the like specific limitation.[76]

Griffin J then went on to approve the above-quoted passage from Henchy J's judgment in *People (A.G.) v Hayes*.

Notwithstanding this verdict, the issue requires clarification. This may only be achieved through the introduction of legislation. The courts may only interpret the law in the light of previous decisions; in this instance, the *M'Naghten* decision. However, the legal definition of insanity in *M'Naghten*

74 Quoted by Griffin J in *Doyle v. Wicklow*   75 [1974] IR 55.
    County Council [1974] IR 55 at 71.   76 Ibid., pp. 70-1.

may no longer be adequate given the subsequent development of psychiatric medicine. Thus, the better approach to take, is to introduce legislation which would define insanity for the purposes of the defence, and delineate the situations in which the insanity defence would be available.[77]

CONSEQUENCES OF THE VERDICT

Those who are found guilty but insane at trial are the object of a special verdict under s. 2 of the Trial of Lunatics Act 1883. S. 2(1) provides that if the accused is found to be:

> . . . insane, so as not to be responsible, according to the law, for his actions at the time when the act was done or omission made, then, if it appears to the jury before whom such person is tried that he did the act or made the omission charged, but was insane as aforesaid at the time when he did or made the same, the jury shall return a special verdict to the effect that the accused was guilty of the act or omission charged against him, but was insane as aforesaid at the time when he did the act or made the omission.

Such a verdict is regarded as an acquittal for procedural purposes and as such the Court has no power to detain the person in question. S. 2(2) of the 1883 Act provides therefore that:

> Where such special verdict is found, the court shall order the accused to be kept in custody as a criminal lunatic, in such place and in such manner as the court shall direct till the pleasure of the Lord Lieutenant shall be known; and it shall be lawful for the Lord Lieutenant thereupon, and from time to time, to give such order for the safe custody of the said person during pleasure and in such place and in such manner as to the Lord Lieutenant may seem fit.

Since Independence the writ of the Crown no longer runs in Ireland. S. 11(1) of the Adaptation of Enactments Act 1922 provided for the transfer of Crown function to the Government of the new state. Thus, as it stood it was a matter exclusively for the Government if, and for how long such detention should continue. However this practice was amended as a result of a number of later decisions. In the case of *The State (C) v. Minister for*

---

77 For a full discussion of the issues involved see F. McAuley, *Insanity, Psychiatry and Criminal Responsibility*, op. cit.

Justice[78] the appellant was charged with having committed indictable offences and during the preliminary investigation of the charges, the court remanded the appellant in custody to St Patrick's Institution until 13 September 1965. He was certified insane on 10 September and was removed to St Brendan's Hospital, as directed by the Minister for Justice pursuant to s. 13 of the Lunatic Asylums Act 1875. This section enabled the Minister to order that a person who had been remanded by a court for further examination and who had been certified during that period to be insane, be removed to a district lunatic asylum. On an application for *habeas corpus* on the part of the appellant, the Supreme Court held that the provisions of s. 13 of the Act of 1875 would prevent an accused person from appearing before a court on the return date of his remand and as such would be a legislative interference with the power of the judiciary. The Supreme held that in this respect the provisions of s. 13 were inconsistent with the Constitution.

In the later case of *The State (O) v. O'Brien*[79] the appellant had been convicted of murder in 1956. As a minor the accused was at the time subject to the provisions of s. 103 of the Children Act 1908. S. 103 provided that a sentence of death should not be pronounced against any 'young person' but that in its stead the court should sentence the 'young person' involved to be detained 'during His Majesty's pleasure'. The appellant was, as a result, sentenced to be detained 'until the pleasure of the Government be made known'. In 1969, the appellant applied for an order of *habeas corpus*. The Supreme Court held that the sentence was unlawful stating that:

> neither the Government nor any member of the Executive can be substituted for the words 'His Majesty' in s. 103 of the Act of 1908, and the power to sentence the convicted person to detention under that section and to determine the duration of the detention is vested exclusively in the courts.[80]

As a result of these cases the practice grew up of detaining those found to be 'guilty but insane' under the Trial of Lunatics Act 1883, in the Central Mental Hospital until further order of the court. This practice allowed those detained as a result of the 'guilty but insane' verdict to apply to the courts for release on the grounds that they were no longer a danger to themselves or others. This practice was declared to be invalid by the Supreme Court in the case of *Director of Public Prosecutions v. Gallagher*[81] The accused had been found guilty but insane on a charge of murder in July 1989, and was ordered to be detained in the Central Mental Hospital until further order

78 [1967] IR 106.   80 *Per* Walsh J at p. 76.
79 [1973] IR 50.   81 [1991] ILRM 339.

of the court. In January 1990, the appellant applied to Johnson J in the Central Criminal Court for a release order. Johnson J amended the original order of the Central Criminal Court to the effect that the appellant be detained in the Central Mental Hospital until the pleasure of the Government be known. The appellant appealed this decision on the grounds that it was for the courts to decide on his continued detention. The Supreme Court held that the role of the court in such cases was to order the detention of such persons until the Government decides the question of his continued detention or release, stating:

> [w]hen the special verdict is returned, the court has no function of inquiry into the then mental state of the former accused; that role is given to the executive. Pursuant to subs. 2 [of the Act of 1883] the only order that could be made was an order that the accused be kept in custody as a criminal lunatic in such place and in such manner as the court should direct; immediately after the making of the order or 'thereupon' as stated in the subsection, the role of the executive arose – to provide an appropriate place for the safe custody of the accused in such place and in such manner as the executive thought appropriate, until such time as the executive was satisfied that having regard to the mental health of the accused it was, for both public and private considerations, safe to release him. . . . If and when a person detained pursuant to s. 2(2) of the Act of 1883 seeks to secure release from detention, as in the instant case, for his release on the grounds that he is not suffering from any mental disorder warranting his continued detention in the public and private interests, then the executive, in the person of the Government or the Minister for Justice, as may be, must inquire into all of the relevant circumstances.[82]

Despite the resolution of the procedural issues in such cases, the difficulty of the mandatory detention of all those found 'guilty but insane' remains. In the words of McAuley, a leading commentator on this issue:[83]

> the court has no discretion to release the defendant either absolutely or conditionally. This arrangement is usually justified on the grounds of social defence: the insane defendant is subject to automatic detention on the presumption that he is dangerous, ie, because it is taken for granted that a defendant whose pathological beliefs and attitudes led him to kill on one occasion may be driven to do so again.[84]

82 *Per* McCarthy J at pp. 344-5.   84 Ibid., p. 115.
83 F. McAuley, op. cit. at chapter 6.

McAuley also submits that such automatic hospitalisation may be in breach of Article 5 of the *European Convention on Human Rights and Fundamental Freedoms*, which guarantees the right to liberty of the individual.[85]

85 Ibid., p. 121.

8

THE DYING PATIENT

There is no Irish case law specifically in the area of treatment of the dying patient, either in relation to the rights guaranteed in the Constitution, or at common law generally. The apparent conflict between the right to life and bodily integrity of each citizen and the respect that the common law pays to the autonomy of the individual heightens the difficulty of this issue.

THE CONCEPT OF A RIGHT TO DIE

When one speaks of a right, to what is one referring? The conceptualisation of rights does not seem to have occurred until the sixteenth and seventeenth centuries. The growth of the nation state and the move from absolutist to democratic ideals brought the idea of individual rights into sharp focus.[1] However, in a democratic society it must be asked if one may be possessed of absolute 'rights', given the competing interests of both the State and of other citizens. In the context of the right to die this conflict was addressed in the American case of *Cruzan v. Director, Missouri Department of Health*[2] the Supreme Court raised the point that the existence of a constitutionally protected right does not prevent the State from curtailing such right, because the State's interest in this area may override those of the individual.[3] At the state and federal court level, specific instances in which the interests of the State would outweigh the right of the competent patient to refuse medical treatment have been outlined. These include the State's interest in preserving life; its interest in preventing suicide; its interest in protecting the interest of innocent third parties; and its interest in maintaining the ethical integrity of the medical profession.[4]

---

1 See, in general, J.M. Kelly, *A Short History Of Western Legal Theory* (Clarendon Press, Oxford 1992), chs. 6 and 7; F. Kratochwil, *Rules, Norms and Decisions – On the conditions of practical and legal reasoning In international relations and domestic affairs* (Cambridge University Press, Cambridge, 1989), ch. 6.
2 110 S Ct 2841 (1990).
3 Ibid. at p. 2852.
4 See *Superintendent of Belchertown State Sch. v. Saikewicz* 370 NE 2d 417 (1977); *In re Conroy*, 486 A 2d 1209, 1223 (1985); *Bartling v. Superior Court*, 209 Cal Rptr 220, 225 (1984); *Brophy v. New England Sinai Hospital*, 497 NE 2d 626, 635-38 (1986).

On the philosophical plane, the conception of rights which one adopts will have an impact on the stance which one takes in relation to the right to die. In philosophical debate, an important issue is how rights are to be conceived. Are they on the one hand to be seen as focusing on interests and benefits or alternatively are they to be seen as focusing on individual choice?[5] If one looks on a right as focusing on interests then the individual may not have a right to die as he has an interest in maintaining his life whether or not he wishes to continue living. Thus, the focus is on duties rather than on individual freedom to act. This view of rights has been defined by Feinberg[6] as 'mandatory' rights. In the context of euthanasia, Feinberg states that this conception of rights would prevent the individual from refusing life-sustaining treatment and would, in addition, prevent the medical practitioner from acting on a request from a patient to terminate treatment. Thus, this view of the right to life would imply:

> a duty not to take one's own life or not to cooperate with others in its taking.[7]

If the concept of a right is viewed as focusing on individual choice, then it is, in Feinberg's phrase, a discretionary right. Thus, in the context of euthanasia, the individual is free to choose to die. As Feinberg notes:

> [t]he right to die is simply the other side of the coin of the right to live. The basic right underlying each is the right to be one's own master, to dispose of one's own lot as one chooses, subject of course to the limits imposed by the like rights of others.[8]

However, as this statement suggests, even if one holds the right to live to be a discretionary right, it may only be exercised by an individual who can voluntarily and competently exercise that right. Thus, as Childress[9] points out, this discretionary or option right may be overridden in situations where (i) there is a defect in the rightholder's deciding, willing or acting; (ii) there is a risk of harm if the rightholder's choice is not overridden; (iii) there is no proportionality between the harm prevented and the benefits provided by the intervention.[10] Therefore, even on the liberal analysis of

5   See J. Finnis, *Natural Law and Natural Rights* (Clarendon Press Oxford, 1980) p. 227.
6   J. Feinberg, 'Voluntary Euthanasia and the Inalienable Right to Life', *Philosophy and Public Affairs* (1978), Vol. 7, p. 110 (Winter).
7   Ibid.
8   Ibid., p. 121.
9   J.F. Childress, *Who Should Decide? Paternalism in Health Care* (Oxford University Press, New York, 1982).
10 Ibid., chs. 5 and 6.

rights one may be constrained from acting freely if one is not competent.

In the medical context, this will have practical implications for the mentally incompetent patient or the patient in a persistent vegetative state, for example. As a result, courts will have to adopt appropriate decision-making standards in relation to the question of treatment withdrawal in the case of the incompetent patient. It is the practical legal ramifications of such philosophical quandaries which form the basis for discussion in this chapter.

A CONSTITUTIONAL RIGHT TO DIE?

In order to find some guidance in this analysis, a number of US cases will be referred to, since that jurisdiction is, like Ireland, a common law system with a Constitution at its apex.

The common law has been slow to develop, but building on the constitutional right to privacy the US courts in a number of jurisdictions have turned to the Constitution to determine the rights of patients and doctors in disputed areas.

In the United States, the right to die, as well as being incorporated in legislation,[11] has been the subject of constitutional analysis.[12] In the New Jersey Supreme Court case of *In re Quinlan*,[13] the Court concluded that the recently developed constitutional right to privacy[14] could be extended to the patient who refused life-sustaining treatment, stating that:

> [p]resumably this right is broad enough to encompass a patient's decision to decline medical treatment under certain circumstances, in much the same way as it is broad enough to encompass a woman's decision to terminate pregnancy under certain conditions.[15]

In this case, the patient was in a chronic persistent vegetative state. On

---

11 See, for example, the California Health and Safety Code 1977, paras. 7185-95; Missouri Uniform Rights of the Terminally Ill Act, Missouri Annotated Statutes paragraphs 459.010-.005; C.J. Dufraine, 'Living Wills – A Need For Statewide Legislation or a Federally Recognised Right?', *Detroit College of Law Review* (1983), Vol. 3, p. 781, 788-94; S. Morgan, 'Does Arizona's Living Will Statute Help Enforce Decisions?', *Arizona Law Journal* (1986), pp. 275-95.

12 See, *inter alia*, *In re Quinlan*, 355 A 2d 647 (NJ), cert denied, 429 US 922 (1976); *In re Conroy*, 486 A 2d 1209, 1223 (NJ 1985); *Cruzan v. Director, Missouri Department of Health* 110 S Ct 2841 (1990).

13 355 A 2d 647 (NJ), cert denied, 429 US 922 (1976).

14 See, *Griswold v. Connecticut*, 381 US 479, 85 SCt 1678, 14 L Ed 2d 510 (1965); *Eisenstadt v. Baird*, 405 US 438, 92 S Ct 1029, 31 L Ed 2d 349 (1972); *Stanley v. Georgia 394* US 557, 89 SCt 1243, 22 L Ed 2d 542 (1969).

15 *In re Quinlan*, 355 A 2d 647 (NJ) cert denied 429 US 922 (1976) p. 663.

the evidence, it was believed that the patient would never return to a sentient condition. The New Jersey Supreme Court, having concluded that there existed a right to privacy that may allow the termination of treatment in certain circumstances, then turned to the question of the possible criminal liability of those involved in withdrawing such treatment. The Court concluded that:

> there would be no criminal homicide in the circumstances of this case. We believe, first, that the ensuing death would not be homicide but rather expiration from existing natural causes. Secondly, even if it were to be regarded as homicide, it would not be unlawful. These conclusions rest upon definitional and constitutional bases. The termination of treatment pursuant to the right to privacy is, within the limitations of this case, *ipso facto* lawful. Thus, a death resulting from such an act would not come within the scope of homicide statutes proscribing only the unlawful killing of another. There is a real and in this case determinative distinction between the unlawful taking of the life of another and the ending of artificial life-support systems as matter of self-determination.[16]

However, this approach to the question of refusal of life-sustaining medical treatment has not gained universal acceptance among the members of the United States judiciary. In the later case of *Cruzan v. Director, Missouri Department of Health*,[17] the United States Supreme Court upheld the decision of the Supreme Court of Missouri and refused to allow the family of a patient in a persistent vegetative state from withdrawing artificial nutrition and hydration from the patient. The case involved the Missouri Uniform Rights of the Terminally Ill Act, which required certain formalities to be fulfilled, so that a living will be deemed valid. Here, the patient's previously expressed wish to a friend in relation to the withdrawal of medical treatment in the case of her becoming incapable of caring for herself was deemed not to have fulfilled these formalities.[18] The Supreme Court did, however, hold that States were allowed to require clear and convincing evidence before a patient's alleged wishes could be acted upon. This could lead to a situation where, even though a patient may not have fulfilled the formalities laid down in a State's living will legislation, a court may nonetheless order the withdrawal of life-sustaining treatment if it can be demonstrated that there was clear and convincing evidence of the patient's wishes in this regard. In the *Cruzan* case, the Court was not satisfied as to

16 355 A 2d 647 (NJ) p. 664.   18 Ibid., p. 2854.
17 110 SCt 2841 (1990).

the existence of such clear and convincing evidence. One outcome of this case was the enactment of the Patient Self-Determination Act 1990, a federal statute which requires hospitals in receipt of federal funding in the form of Medicaid or Medicare funds to furnish all patients with written information of their rights under state law to refuse medical care. Thus in the United States, patients with a terminal illness have a right to die by having life saving treatment withheld or withdrawn, provided clear and convincing proof of the patient's wishes exist.

THE POSITION IN IRELAND

In Ireland, although there exists no legislation on the issue of refusal of life-sustaining medical treatment, it is possible that such a right may be derived from the constitutional right to privacy. Article 40.3.1 of the Constitution of Ireland 1937 provides that the State:

> guarantees in its laws to respect, and, as far as practicable, by its laws to defend and vindicate the personal rights of the citizen.

From this general injunction, the Supreme Court has derived a number of unennumerated rights which though not listed in the Constitution, nonetheless exist and are protected by the Constitution. Thus, the court has held, in common with the United States Supreme Court, that a right to privacy exists in certain specified circumstances.[19] Also, of relevance to the field of medicine is the judicial recognition of a right to bodily integrity in the case of *Ryan v. Attorney General*.[20] The Supreme Court stated that in upholding this right, the State had:

> the duty of protecting the citizens from dangers to health in a manner not incompatible or inconsistent with the rights of those citizens as human persons.

Professor Casey, in his analysis of this utterance, believes that:

> neither the State nor anyone else may insist upon a person undergoing medical treatment that he/she wishes to decline–even if death may result. To do so would surely trench impermissibly upon the right of privacy.[21]

19 See *McGee v. Attorney General* [1974] IR 284 and the discussion on the topic of personal rights and the Constitution in J. Casey, *Constitutional Law In Ire-land*, 2nd ed. (Sweet & Maxwell, London 1992) pp. 309-58.
20 [1965] IR 294.
21 J. Casey, op. cit., pp. 334-5.

This argument was elaborated upon by Mr Justice Costello of the Irish High Court, in an important article on the issue of refusal of medical treatment.[22] Mr Justice Costello argued that:

> the dignity and autonomy of the human person (as constitutionally predicated) require the State to recognise that decisions relating to life and death are, generally speaking, ones which a competent adult should be free to make without outside restraint and that this freedom should be regarded as an aspect of the right to privacy which should be protected as a 'personal' right by Article 40.3.1.[23]

However, Judge Costello goes on to state that such a right is not absolute. Thus, he states that if one is to define a right to die as a:

> 'right' to procure death by his or her [the patient's] hand or by means of someone else, then it cannot be said that there is a constitutionally protected 'right to die', for it is a reasonable conclusion from the nature of man as envisaged in the Constitution that he may not kill himself or ask others to assist him to do so.[24]

Nonetheless, he states that one can make a distinction between the above conception of the right to die and the concept of allowing the patient to die by discontinuing life-sustaining treatment. Judge Costello provides the following rationale for this position:

> [i]n the case of the competent patient discontinuance would be in response to a request which the patient was constitutionally entitled to make, and no 'unlawful' act would occur. In the case of the incompetent patient discontinuance in the proper discharge of the a duty of care would likewise involve no legal fault and the patient's death could not be an 'unlawful' homicide.[25]

Thus, according to Judge Costello, the right of the terminally ill patient to forego life-sustaining medical treatment is compatible with the provisions of the Constitution. In addition, the doctor who discontinues such treatment does not perpetrate a criminal act. This analysis of the right to die while moving towards a situation where the patient is treated as an autonomous agent is not however, an ideal solution. The individual patient may only

22 D. Costello, 'The Terminally Ill: The Law's Concerns', *Irish Jurist* (1986), Vol. 21 (ns), p. 35.

23 Ibid., p. 42.
24 Id.
25 Id., p. 44.

exercise his right to die in limited circumstances, that is, only when no active measures are used to hasten the patient's death. This is arguably not a right to die in the true sense of the word but a conditional right to die. The individual is restricted in his scope of action and cannot therefore be said to be truly autonomous.

It is clear that, under the Constitution, there is no 'right to die' in the sense of a 'right' to procure death by one's own hand or by means of someone else. But the law can make a distinction, as the courts in the USA have done, between the reasoned choice of a competent terminally ill person to discontinue medical treatment because its burdens are out of all proportion to the benefits conferred by it and a decision to take steps deliberately to terminate life.

EUTHANASIA AND THE COMMON LAW

Euthanasia may either be active or passive. Active euthanasia occurs when the doctor carries out an act which brings about a patient's death. In other words, (in the vocabulary of the criminal law) the doctor murders the patient. This act may be carried out at the patient's request: voluntary euthanasia. If such act is not carried out at the patient's request then it may be termed either involuntary or non-voluntary euthanasia. Involuntary euthanasia refers to the situation where a patient who could meaningfully consent, did not do so before his or her life was terminated. Non-voluntary euthanasia occurs when the life of a patient, who was not capable of giving consent to his death, is terminated.

Passive euthanasia involves not acting, or omitting to perform a life-saving act or withdrawing medical treatment.

Active Euthanasia Euthanasia is derived from the Greek words, 'eu' meaning 'well' and 'thanatos' meaning 'death'. Thus in English one could state that it means to die well.

However, in Ireland, a doctor who gives his terminally ill patient a lethal drug for the purpose of killing him is guilty of the crime of murder. The Medical Council looks on active euthanasia as professional misconduct.[26]

A person who intends to kill, or has not substantial doubt that his act will kill, has the fault element for murder. Thus if a doctor gave an injection for the purpose of hastening death, or if he administered a drug which he knew would have this effect, he would be guilty of murder if the patient died as a consequence. An intention to cause a patient with a curable

---

26 *A Guide to Ethical Conduct and Behaviour and to Fitness to Practise*, 4th ed. (Medical Council, Dublin, 1994), p. 38.

condition serious bodily harm is also a sufficient element for murder. However, as Charleton states, a doctor 'will have no criminal liability if he acts without criminal negligence and without intent to kill or cause serious injuries'.[27] Charleton goes on to say that a doctor who prescribes 'a treatment to ease terminal suffering may realise that a risk of an earlier death is thereby created. His purpose is not to kill but to comfort his patient. That cannot be murder'.[28]

This is an argument of the 'double effect' variety. The intention was to ease pain and not to kill, thus, the argument goes, murder has not been committed.

The doctrine of double effect has been defined 'crudely' by Glover[29] as:

> saying that it is always wrong intentionally to do a bad act for the sake of good consequences that will ensue, but that it may be permissable to do a good act in the knowledge that bad consequences will ensue.[30]

Implicit in the doctrine is the idea that there are unequivocally 'good' and 'bad' acts. Thus, the classical model of the double effect doctrine[31] would allow for an abortion which resulted from a hysterectomy which was necessary to treat uterine cancer. The abortion would be justified on the grounds that what the doctor directly intended was the removal of the cancer and not the termination of the pregnancy. However, the double effect doctrine would not allow an abortion to save the life of a woman suffering from kidney disease on the grounds that in this instance it would be necessary for the doctor to directly intended the termination of the pregnancy as an 'evil' means to a 'good' end.[32] The Roman Catholic Church in the Congregation for the Doctrine of the Faith's *Declaration on Euthanasia* uses the double effect doctrine to justify the death of a patient who has died as a result of being administered a pain-killing drug, where the doctor's intention was to relieve pain and not to kill:

> But the intensive use of painkillers is not without difficulties, because

27 P. Charleton, *Offences Against the Person* (The Round Hall Press Dublin, 1991) p. 23.
28 Ibid.
29 See J. Glover, *Causing Death And Saving Lives* (Penguin, Harmondsworth, 1977).
30 Ibid., p. 87.
31 For a full account see F. Connell, 'Principle of Double Effect', *New Catholic Encyclopaedia* (Vol. 4, McGraw-Hill, New York, 1968); D. Kelly, *The Emergence of Roman Catholic Medical Ethics in North America* (Edwin Mullen Press, New York, 1979); J. Mangan, 'An Historical Analysis of the Principle of Double Effect', *Theological Studies* (1949), Vol. 10, pp. 40-61.
32 See Pope John Paul II, 'On Reconciliation and Penance', *Origins* (1984), Vol. 74, No. 27, p. 442 (20 December).

the phenomenon of habituation generally makes it necessary to increase their dosage in order to maintain their efficacy. At this point it is fitting to recall a declaration by Pius XII, which retains its full force. In answer to a group of doctors who had put the question: 'Is the suppression of pain and consciousness by the use of narcotics . . . permitted by religion and morality to the doctor and the patient (even at the approach of death and if one foresees that the use of narcotics will shorten life)?'

The Pope said 'If no other means exist, and if, in the given circumstances, this does not prevent the carrying out of other religious and moral duties: "Yes".' In this case, of course, death is in no way intended or sought even if the risk of it is reasonably taken; the intention is simply to relieve pain effectively, using for this purpose painkillers available to medicine.[33]

However, an alternative model of the double effect doctrine has been formulated by thinkers such as Knauer[34] and Fuchs[35] whereby human acts *per se* cannot be said to be intrinsically 'good' or 'evil'. Rather, the object of a human act is a 'premoral' object that involves certain values and disvalues. The object only becomes moral ('good' or 'bad') when one considers the proportion of beneficial to detrimental consequences of the act itself in the light of the actor's intentions. Thus, for example, capital punishment may be justified on this analysis if in the particular circumstances, the value of 'justice' outweighs the disvalue of the death of a criminal. Similarly, in the context of abortion, the termination of a pregnancy may be justified if the value of saving the life of the mother outweighs the disvalue of aborting the foetus. This model of the double effect doctrine is less absolutist than the classical model and takes account of the individual circumstances of a particular ethical dilemma rather than holding that certain acts are either morally 'good' or 'evil' without taking into account the particular circumstances of the case.

However, the difficulties inherent in the double effect argument have been described as:

arguing that, if a wasp were to land on your mother-in-law's scalp, it would be defensible to hit her over the head with a spade provided

33 See Sacred Congregation for the Doctrine of the Faith' *Declaration on Euthanasia* (Vatican City, 1980).

34 P. Knauer, 'The Hermeneutic Function of the Principle of Double Effect', *Natural Law Forum* (1967), Vol. 12, pp. 132-62.

35 J. Fuchs, SJ, *Christian Ethics in a Secular Arena* (Georgetown University Press, Washington DC, 1984).

that you claimed your intent was to rid her of the wasp, and that this was an effective method of doing so.[36]

A doctor who participates in active euthanasia may also come within the scope of two of the three available categories of manslaughter.

These are manslaughter by criminal negligence and manslaughter by a criminal and dangerous act.

Manslaughter by criminal negligence occurs where death is brought about by the defendant's gross negligence.[37] Manslaughter by a criminal and dangerous act has been defined as follows:

> [w]here the act which a person is engaged in performing is unlawful, then, if it is at the same time a dangerous act, that is an act which is likely to injure another person, and quite inadvertently he causes the death of that other person by that act, then he is guilty of manslaughter.[38]

Although the presence or absence of consent will affect liability for murder and manslaughter, consent to being killed is no defence to a charge of murder or manslaughter. Even if the patient pleaded with the doctor to terminate his life this would not provide a defence at law.

There have been no Irish cases specifically on the issue of active euthanasia, nor does there exist specific legislation on the point. However, Irish courts may look for guidance to the English precedents in this area. The intention of the doctor in this regard would appear to be of vital importance. Thus, in the case of *R. v. Adams*,[39] Devlin J stated the law as follows:

> [i]f the acts done intended to kill and did, in fact, kill, it did not matter if a life were cut short by weeks or months, it was just as much murder as if it were cut short by years.[40]

In that case, the defendant doctor was alleged to have treated an incurable patient with large doses of heroin and morphia. On the death of the patient,

36 T. Helme and N. Padmore, 'Safeguarding Euthanasia', *New Law Journal* (1992), Vol. 142, No. 6570, p. 1335 (2 October).

37 The test for this type of manslaughter was laid down in the case of *State (Attorney General) v. Dunleavy* [1948] IR 95 (CCA).

38 *R. v. Larkin* [1943] KB 174.

39 See H. Palmer, 'Dr Adams' Trial for Murder', *Criminal Law Review* (1957), p. 365.

40 Ibid., p. 375.

Dr Adams was charged with her murder. Here the accused was acquitted as the intention required was not present. In his summing up to the jury, Devlin J stated:

> [t]he doctor is entitled to relieve pain and suffering even if the measures he takes may incidentally shorten life.[41]

One may detect here an argument similar to that of the principle of double effect.

In the later case of *R. v. Cox*,[42] the defendant was unable to avail of this argument as it was his intention to cause the death of the patient in question. In that case, Dr Cox had been treating the deceased, Mrs Lillian Boyes, for some three years. She suffered from rheumatoid arthritis and was reported to have been in severe pain as her condition deteriorated. The accused prescribed increasing doses of morphine based drugs until the patient expressed her wish to die. As a result, Dr Cox injected the patient with a lethal dose of potassium chloride which brought about her death. Dr Cox was charged with attempted murder rather than murder. This, the prosecution claimed, was due to their inability to prove conclusively that the cause of death was the injection of potassium chloride as the body had been promptly cremated. However, the prosecution may have been trying to avoid a repetition of the *Adams* verdict. Dr Cox was found guilty and given a suspended sentence of one year's imprisonment. However, if Dr Cox had administered an analgesic cocktail, which has the secondary effect of hastening death, he may have escaped liability by arguing that his primary intention was to relieve pain. By using potassium chloride, which is a poison with no therapeutic qualities, he could not avail of the double effect argument.

In the case of *R. v. Lodwig*,[43] the accused was cleared of murdering a patient when the prosecution offered no evidence. The patient was suffering from terminal pancreatic cancer and was in continuous pain. His death was imminent. The patient's family asked Dr Lodwig to do something to relieve the pain. Dr Lodwig injected the patient with a lethal dose of potassium chloride and lignocaine. Dr Lodwig claimed that it was his intention to kill the pain and not the patient, stating that the combination of drugs which he used had been the subject of experiments conducted at St Bartholomew's Hospital, London. The object of these experiments had been to mix potassium chloride with painkillers to accelerate their analgesic effect.

41 Ibid., p. 375.
42 Unreported, 18 September 1992, Ognall J (English HC).
43 See *The Times*, 16 March 1990, p. 3.

From the foregoing, it would appear that if such a case came to be decided in Ireland, a substantially similar approach would be taken.

In Ireland, the Medical Council has drawn up, in the 4th edition of its Ethical guide, the following statement on Euthanasia:

> 43.01 Where death is imminent, it is the doctor's responsibility to take care that a patient dies with dignity and with as little suffering as possible. Euthanasia, which involves deliberately causing the death of a patient, is professional misconduct and is illegal in Ireland.[44]

Passive euthanasia In the law of homicide, a distinction is made between positive acts and omissions. Where a person is under a duty of care recognised by the criminal law, an omission to act, which causes the death of the patient, if made with intent to kill or cause serious injury is murder.[45] If a person is under a duty of care recognised by the criminal law, an omission to act, which causes the patient's death, if made by failing to observe the ordinary and necessary care expected in the circumstances, provided that a high degree of negligence on his part can be proved, and which results in a very high degree of risk of substantial personal injury to others, then such an omission is manslaughter.

Where a person is not under any duty to act, recognised by the criminal law, his omission to save or prolong the life of a patient will not be regarded as a cause of death. However, making the distinction between an act and an omission is not an easy task. Thus Smith & Hogan pose the question of whether switching off a functioning machine is different in principle from, say, a scenario where a doctor who has been keeping a patient alive by cranking the handle of a machine stops?[46] There is no substantial literature on the approach that Irish law should take to the problems raised in these extreme circumstances. It is therefore appropriate to examine some of the cases and periodical literature derived from other jurisdictions, which at some stage, the Irish courts may be forced to consider.

---

44 *A Guide To Ethical Conduct and Behaviour and to Fitness to Practise*, 4th ed. (Medical Council, Dublin, 1994) p. 38.

45 A duty of care has been recognised in the following circumstances: (a) Parents owe such a duty to their children. (b) A person who undertakes to care for an infirm relative owes such a duty. (c) Medical practitioners will also be under a duty to keep a patient alive.

46 See Glanville Williams, in *Criminal Law Review* (1977) pp. 443-52, and *Textbook of Criminal Law*, 2nd ed. (Sweet & Maxwell, London, 1983) pp. 236-7 both cited and discussed in J.C. Smith & B. Hogan, *Criminal Law*, 7th ed. (Butterworth, London 1992) at p. 49.

INCOMPETENT PATIENT AND TREATMENT WITHDRAWAL

Decisions to discontinue measures supporting the life of an incompetent patient require the application of very high standards of care, and a failure to comply with such standards could amount to negligence.[47]

In the United States, courts have laid down two different standards in relation to withdrawal of life-prolonging treatment from incompetent patients. These are the tests of (i) 'substituted judgement' and (ii) 'best interests'.[48] These standards allow a concerned party to decide on behalf of the incompetent patient.

SUBSTITUTED JUDGEMENT

With regard to 'substituted judgement' it has been held that the surrogate decision maker must make the decision the incompetent patient would make, if he were able to choose himself. This will involve examining evidence of the patient's attitude to life-sustaining treatment when that patient was in a position to express that attitude. One approach requires clear evidence of the patient's previous wishes. Thus in the cases of *In re Storar (Eichner)*[49] and *In Re Westchester County Medical Center (O'Connor)*[50] the New York Court of Appeals required evidence of prior statements of the patient which expressed a 'firm and settled commitment' to the withdrawal of life-prolonging medical treatment and must be more than immediate reactions to the unsettling experience of seeing or hearing of another's unnecessarily prolonged death.

A more relaxed approach to the substituted judgement standard has been evidenced in other cases. In the Massachusetts case of *Superintendent of*

---

47 Thus in *Airedale NHS Trust v. Bland* [1993] 1 All ER 821, at 839, Sir Thomas Bingham MR, re-stating the argument of counsel for the plaintiff (with which he said counsel for the defendant agreed) stated that the question of discontinuance of artificial feeding and antibiotic treatment 'is one to be resolved by the doctors in charge of his case, in consultation with independent medical experts, conscientiously exercising a careful and informed judgement of what the best interests of their patient require'. What is perhaps more difficult to translate into an Irish context is the Master of the Rolls' next statement, that it is appropriate for the doctors to 'take full account of the family's wishes' in reaching that decision. It is submitted however that a principled decision made by doctors, in conformity with a responsible body of medical opinion, made in what they consider to be the best interests of the patient could not be negligent.

48 A brief account of these two tests, and how they are interpreted by U.K. courts, may be found in *Airedale NHS Trust v. Bland* [1993] 1 All ER 821 at 843, where Butler Sloss LJ prefers the 'best interests' test over the 'substituted judgement' test; saying that the latter 'appears to have little in common with the trend discernible in recent decisions'.

49 52 NY 2d 363, 420 NE 2d 64, 438 NYS 2d 266, cert. denied, 454 US 858 (1981).

50 72 NY 2d 517, 531, NE 2d 607, 534 NYS 2d 886 (1988).

Belchertown State School v. Saikewicz[51] the patient had never been competent and therefore never in a position to express his wishes in relation to the termination of life prolonging medical treatment. However, the court applied the substituted judgement standard, despite this fact, stating that any such treatment should be based on the decision the incompetent patient would make if the patient 'were competent, but taking into account the present and future incompetency of the individual as one of the factors which would necessarily enter into the decision making process of the competent person'.[52] The inclusion of such a circumstance in the substituted judgement category has been much criticised. Indeed it appears completely illogical that a court would place such a case in this category.[53]

Even in cases in this category where the patient was once competent, hard evidence will be difficult to ascertain in relation to the patient's opinion on withdrawal of treatment, absent a valid written intention or living will. Thus such a standard will be based on the evidence of relatives whose decision may be actuated by such factors as the cost of further treatment and their relationship with the patient. Thus, this standard may not always lead to a decision which is true to the needs or interest of the patient.

'BEST INTERESTS'

With regard to the 'best interests' standard, it should be noted that this standard has been less widely applied by courts than the substituted judgement standard. This standard involves the surrogate decision maker coming to a decision based on what he considers the benefits or otherwise of continued treatment. Thus such factors as the present condition of the patient, the degree of pain, the loss of dignity, the prognosis, and the benefits and risks of the various treatments available will be of relevance. For example, in the case of *In Re Conroy*[54] the court required that cessation of treatment under the best interests standard would only be countenanced where 'recurring, unavoidable and severe pain' would make the treatment inhumane. Courts applying this standard may also consider quality of life and the interests of the patient's family.[55] This issue was recently discussed

51 373 Mass. 728, 370 NE 2d 417 (1977).
52 Id., pp. 752-3 and p. 431.
53 Thus Butler Sloss LJ in *Airedaile NHS Trust v. Bland* [1993] 1 All ER 821 at 843 could see no reason to extend the substituted judgement test beyond the Court of Protection.
54 98 NJ 321, 486 A 2d 1209, (1985).
55 For a discussion of these and other issues relating in particular to English

decisions on the termination of a feeding supply by means of a nasogastric tube, as applied to the Irish context, see W. Binchy, 'Irish Implications of the Bland Case', *Irish Medical Times* (1993), Vol. 27, No. 7 (12 February), p. 22. For a discussion of the Bland case In general see D. Brahams 'Persistent Vegetative State', *Medico Legal Journal* (1993), Vol. 61, pt. 1 p. 50.

again in the case of *Frenchay Health Care NHS Trust v. S.*[56] In *Frenchay*, the Court of Appeal upheld a decision of the High Court to the effect that it would be lawful for doctors not to re-insert a feeding tube into the stomach of a patient which had become accidentally dislodged. They confirmed that where a health authority made an application in an urgent situation, the court would not refuse the declaration solely on the grounds that it had not been possible, in the time available, to obtain independent medical opinions on the patient's behalf. However, this case leaves open for decision by an Irish court some of the larger issues: that is, what precisely precipitates the medical emergency which in its turn requires an application to court (in this case it was a simple dislodgment of a feeding tube), and what within the context of a medical emergency can be said to constitute the 'best interests' of a patient in a persistent vegetative state other than life preservation.[57]

The concept of passive euthanasia can be compared to the idea of omitting to act as the doctor in this instance discontinues treatment which would, if continued, keep the patient alive. This analogy was discussed by the House of Lords in their decision in the case of *Airedale NHS Trust v. Bland.*[58] The case concerned Tony Bland, who at the age of seventeen, was seriously injured in the Hillsborough football disaster in 1989. He suffered brain damage which left him in a persistent vegetative state, PVS. The condition was described thus by Sir Thomas Bingham MR in his judgment in the Court of Appeal decision on the case:

> the brain stem remains alive and functioning while the cortex of the brain loses its function and activity. Thus the PVS patient continues to breathe unaided and his digestion continues to function. But although his eyes are open, he cannot see. He cannot hear. Although capable of reflex movement, particularly in response to painful stimuli, the patient is incapable of voluntary movement and can feel no pain. He cannot taste or smell. He cannot speak or communicate in any way. He has no cognitive function and can thus feel no emotion, whether pleasure or distress. The absence of cerebral function is not a matter of surmise; it can be scientifically demonstrated. The space which the brain should occupy is full of watery fluid.[59]

56 [1994] 2 All ER 403 discussed in J. Stone, 'Withholding Life-Sustaining Treatment: The Ultimate Decision', *New Law Journal*, (1994), Vol. 144 No. 6635 (11 February) pp. 205-96. See also *New Law Journal Law Reports*, Vol. 144, No. 6637, (25 February 1994). Since writing this, a Practice Note has issued dealing with the procedure to be fol-lowed in cases of applications for the termination of artificial feeding and hydration for patients in a persistent vegetative state. This is reported at [1994] 2 All ER 413.

57 Ibid.

58 [1993] 2 WLR 316.

59 Ibid., p. 333.

The question to be decided in the case was whether it was in the best interests of Mr Bland to continue feeding him artificially. Lord Goff of Chieveley was of the opinion that:

> a doctor's conduct in discontinuing life support can properly be categorised as an omission. It is true that it may be difficult to describe what the doctor actually does as an omission, for example, where he takes some positive step to bring the life support to an end. But discontinuation of life support is, for present purposes, no different from not initiating life support in the first place. In each case, the doctor is simply allowing his patient to die in the sense that he is desisting from taking a step which might, in certain circumstances, prevent his patient from dying as a result of his pre-existing condition; and as a matter of general principle an omission such as this will not be unlawful unless it constitutes a breach of duty to the patient.[60]

Thus, in the United Kingdom the duty of care imposed on the doctor will not extend to keeping a patient, with no possibility of ever regaining sentience, alive. Therefore, in the words of Lord Browne-Wilkinson:

> if there comes a stage where the responsible doctor comes to the reasonable conclusion (which accords with the views of a responsible body of medical opinion) that further continuance of an intrusive life support system is not in the best interests of the patient, he can no longer lawfully continue that life support system: to do so would constitute the crime of battery and the tort of trespass to the person. Therefore he cannot be in breach of any duty to maintain the patient's life. Therefore he is not guilty of murder by omission.[61]

In the later case of *Frenchay Healthcare NHS Trust v. S*,[62] S was suffering from severe brain damage as a result of a drug overdose. Like Tony Bland, he was in a persistent vegetative state. He was fed by means of a gastronomy tube which was inserted through his stomach wall. In January 1994, it was discovered that the gastronomy tube had become detached from his body. The medical team felt that it was not medically practicable to reinsert the tube. The surgeon in charge of S's case was of the opinion that it was in S's best interests that the medical team should refrain from intervening in S's case and to allow him to die naturally. The surgeon in question felt that the option of reinserting the gastronomy tube would not be beneficial to S, stating that:

60 Ibid., p. 369.
61 Ibid., p. 385

62 [1994] 2 All ER 403.

[t]o reinsert the tube now that we have such certainty about the state of his brain, his function and prospects would, in my opinion be a criminal act as it would be being done against the best interests of S.[63]

In this case the Court of Appeal further elaborated on the role of the courts in this area of medical decision-making. Sir Thomas Bingham MR stated:

[i]t is, I think, important that there should not be a belief that what the doctor says is the patient's best interest *is* the patient's best interest. For my part I would certainly reserve to the court the ultimate power and duty to review the doctor's decision in the light of all the facts.[64]

This statement demonstrates how the law presumes to interpose itself between the doctor and the patient in his care. The doctor can no longer decide independently on how he should treat such a patient but must defer to the judiciary for the ultimate decision. This however may not be as great an erosion of medical autonomy as it might at first sight seem. This can be seen from the judgment of Lord Goff of Chieveley in the *Bland* case where he offered a thoughtful contribution on the relationship between the law and the medical profession in relation to clinical decision-making.

The truth is that, in the course of their work, doctors frequently have to make decisions which may affect the continued survival of their patients, and are in reality far more experienced in matters of this kind than are the judges. It is nevertheless the function of the judges to state the legal principles upon which the lawfulness of the actions of doctors depend; but in the end the decisions to be made in individual cases must rest with the doctors themselves. In these circumstances, what is required is a sensitive understanding by both the judges and the doctors of each other's respective functions, and in particular a determination by the judges not merely to understand the problems facing the medical profession in cases of this kind, but also to regard their professional standards with respect. Mutual understanding between the doctors and the judges is the best way to ensure the evolution of a sensitive and sensible legal framework for the treatment and care of patients, with a sound ethical base, in the interest of the patients themselves.[65]

63 Ibid., p. 406-7.
64 Ibid., p. 411.

65 Ibid., p. 374.

This is an important contribution to the debate on the resolution of medico-legal dilemmas, as it takes cognisance of the importance of professional autonomy, the need for a sound framework for the resolution of such disputes and perhaps most importantly of all, the interests of the patient. How such good intentions can be transformed into a workable mechanism remains to be seen, but at least it gives rise to a certain degree of optimism that such intractable moral dilemmas are not only receiving judicial attention, but are being dealt with in a humane and equitable manner. As a result of the *Bland* and *S* cases, a *Practice Note*[66] was issued in the UK by the official solicitor in March 1994 which laid down the correct procedures to be followed in relation to terminating the artificial feeding and hydration of patients in a persistent vegetative state. Briefly the *Practice Note* upholds the approach taken in both of the aforementioned cases, to the effect that such termination of care will require the prior sanction of a High Court judge. In diagnosing persistent vegetative state, doctors should pay heed to the guidelines laid down on the issue by the British Medical Association in July 1993. Thus, such a diagnosis should not be considered confirmed until the patient has been insentient for at least twelve months. The proper forum for the hearing of such applications is the Family Division of the High Court. In addition the Court should consider carefully the previously expressed views of the patient, if any, on the issue of continuing life-sustaining treatment in the event of his entering a persistent vegetative state.

THE COMPETENT PATIENT AND TREATMENT REFUSAL

Little specific relevant Irish authority exists in this area. However, the following discussion attempts to indicate what principal considerations may be relevant to any future Irish judicial discussion of problems which will undoubtedly arise for resolution before the courts.

The main issue governing refusal of treatment by the competent patient is that of patient autonomy. Is the competent patient to be permitted to make an independent decision to terminate his suffering? How does this desire on the part of the patient affect the duty of the individual doctor to continue life-sustaining treatment?

In the United States since the decision of the New Jersey Supreme Court in the case of *In re Quinlan*[67] courts have permitted competent patients who are terminally ill to refuse life-prolonging treatment.[68] In addition courts have allowed patients suffering from fatal as opposed to terminal illnesses

---

66 [1994] 2 All ER 413.
67 70 NJ 10, 355 A 2d 647, cert. denied, 429 US 922.

68 See *Bartling v. Superior Court*, 163 Cal App 3d 186, 209 Cal Rptr 220 (1984).

to exercise this right to refuse treatment. Courts have, in many cases, cited the constitutional right to privacy as a basis for the competent patient's right to refuse treatment. However, this basis for refusal of treatment has been criticised as being too cursory. Thus, for example, in the hearing of the case of *Cruzan v. Harmon*[69] in the Supreme Court of the state of Missouri, it was stated that the 'bare statement that a right of privacy extends to treatment decisions is seldom accompanied by any reasoned analysis as to the scope of that right or its application to the refusal of life-sustaining treatment'. The *Quinlan* case itself contained little reasoned analysis of why the right of privacy should extend to cases of refusal of life-sustaining medical treatment. There it was stated that just as the privacy right extended to a woman's decision on whether to have an abortion[70] so it is 'broad enough to encompass a patient's decision to decline medical treatment under certain circumstances'.[71] In the New Jersey case of *In re Conroy*[72] it was held that the constitutional right to privacy is broad enough to encompass a patient's decision to decline medical treatment under certain circumstances. However such cases will now have to be looked at in the light of *Cruzan* and subsequent cases in which the constitutional right to privacy has been narrowed.[73]

Apart from the privacy basis, the right to decline medical treatment in the US is embraced by the common law right to self-determination. The patient's interest in freedom from invasion of his bodily integrity would outweigh any state interest in preserving life or in safeguarding the integrity of the medical profession. In the case of *Bouvia v. Superior Court*[74] it was emphasised that a person of adult years and of sound mind, has the right, in the exercise of control over his own body, to determine whether or not to submit to lawful medical treatment. It follows that such a patient has the right to refuse any medical treatment, even that which may save or prolong his life. In this case, the court stated that it would be 'incongruous, if not monstrous' for doctors to force a woman suffering from quadriplegia and cerebral palsy to live 'imprisoned . . . physically helpless (and) subject to the ignominy, embarrassment, humiliation and dehumanising aspects created by her helplessness'.[75] In the subsequent case of *In re Rodas*,[76] the court allowed a non-terminally ill and competent patient who was paralysed from

69 760 SW 2d 408, 417, (Mo 1988).
70 See *Roe v. Wade*, 410 US 113 (1973).
71 See *In re Quinlan* 70 NJ 10, 40, 355 a 2d 647, 663, Cert Denied, 429 US 922 (1976).
72 98 NJ 321, 360-64, 486 A. 2d 1209, 1229-31 (1985).
73 See *Webster v. Reproductive Health Services* 109 SCt 3040 (1989); *Michael H. v. Gerald D.* 109 SCt 2333 (1989); *De Shaney v. Department of Social Services* 109 S. Ct. 998 (1989).
74 179 Cal App 3D 1127, 225 Cal Rptr 297 (1986).
75 Id. at 1143, 225 Cal Rptr at 305.
76 No. 86 PR 139 (Colo Dist Ct Apr, 3, 1987).

the neck down to refuse artificial feeding. However, there is a particular circumstance in which courts will refuse such a request on the part of a competent patient. This is where the patient is also a prisoner. In such a case the state can argue that it is upholding the public interest in the preservation of prison order and discipline.[77]

Of course, what appears to be the decision of a competent patient may require analysis, and may prove to be a decision vitiated by undue influence or other factors.

To sum up, it is suggested that Irish law in this area should probably accept that the voluntary choice of a competent and informed patient must determine whether or not life-sustaining therapy will be undertaken, just as such choices provide the basis for other decisions about medical treatment. A doctor is rarely if ever entitled to administer treatment against the patient's wishes.

The question remains to be answered, in the Irish courts, whether the doctor who turns off a life-support machine is guilty of murder under Irish law.

The prevailing view held among legal writers in this area is that even if the patient's death is homicide, the homicide would not be unlawful and it is submitted that Irish courts would adopt the view of the court in *Quinlan*. For example, Costello J has stated, extra-judicially, that the right to privacy may extend to permit a competent patient to decide to dispense with life-prolonging treatment.[78] Therefore, in the case of the competent patient, termination of treatment would be in response to a request which the patient was constitutionally entitled to make and no 'unlawful' act would occur.

In the United Kingdom, it has fallen to the courts to decide on this issue. In the case of *In re T (Adult: Refusal of Treatment)*[79] the patient was a 20-year-old female who had been injured in a traffic accident when she was thirty four weeks pregnant. T was diagnosed as having pneumonia and was prescribed large doses of pethidine, oxygen and antibiotics. She subsequently went into labour. Before the delivery, T was visited by her mother, a Jehovah's Witness. T herself was not a member of the sect. After conversations with her mother, T told the midwife that she did not want blood transfusions. The obstetrician told T that a caesarian section did not normally require a blood transfusion. After the obstetrician had left, the

---

77 See e.g. *O'Lone v. Estate of Shabazz* 482 US 342, 349 (1987); *Washington v. Harper* 110 SCt 1028 (1990); *Commissioner of Correction v. Myers* 379 Mass 255, 399 NE 2d 452 (1979).

78 In the *Irish Times*, 9 September, 1987. See also P. Lanham, 'The Right to Choose to Die with Dignity', *Criminal Law Journal* (1990) Vol. 14, No. 3, p. 401. See discussion of Costello J's views at p. 147.

79 [1992] 4 All ER 649.

midwife furnished T with a form which provided for the refusal to consent to blood transfusions. This form was required to be countersigned by the attending doctor, but in this case, the medical practitioner did not sign the document. There followed an emergency caesarian section operation, T's condition deteriorated and the medical team was of the opinion that blood and plasma transfusions were necessary. She was placed on a ventilator and was administered sedatives. However her situation was critical and transfusions of blood and plasma were required for her survival.

T's father joined with the father of the child in applying to the court for a declaration that it would not be unlawful for the medical team to give T such transfusions without her consent. At the hearing it was adduced that T's parents were separated since T was three years old. Custody was eventually granted to her mother. The custody order prohibited the mother from rearing T as a Jehovah's Witness. However, T's mother had forced her daughter to live by the tenets of the sect. It was argued on T's behalf that her decision to forego blood transfusions had been made under undue influence from her mother, who had encouraged her to refuse blood transfusions. At first instance, Ward J held, that because of her medical condition, and due to the effect of the medication which had been administered to her, she was not in a rational state when she signed the consent refusal form. The court granted an interlocutory order allowing the transfusions to be given.

However, the Official Solicitor appealed this decision to the Court of Appeal. The case was important in that it would provide guidance for hospital authorities faced with such a dilemma. The Court of Appeal dismissed the appeal of the Official Solicitor. The court affirmed the right of the patient to decide whether or not to undergo a particular form of treatment. However, in order for this right to be upheld, it must be validly exercised. In this case, it was found, that the form signed by T was found to be invalid as it had not been signed by a medical practitioner and because its significance had not been properly explained to her.

The case of *In re C (Adult: Refusal of Treatment)*[80] provides one with yet another variation on the general theme of treatment refusal and the consequences for the medical practitioner. In this case, the patient, though a sentient adult, was suffering from chronic paranoid schizophrenia. C had been sentenced to seven years imprisonment in 1962 for stabbing a former lover. It was discovered, during the currency of his sentence, that C was mentally ill. He was, as a result, transferred to Broadmoor. It was there that he was diagnosed as being a chronic paranoid schizophrenic, and remained institutionalised ever since. In September 1993, the surgeon at Broadmoor

80 [1994] 1 WLR 290.

diagnosed C as suffering from gangrene of the foot, whereupon C was transferred to Heatherwood Hospital. At the hospital, the consultant vascular surgeon found C's leg to be severely infected with a necrotic ulcer covering the dorsum. He was of the opinion that C would die quite shortly if the leg was not amputated below the knee. C refused to consent to the amputation, claiming that he would rather die with two feet than live with one. The surgeon then, in the light of the gravity of C's condition, tried to obtain his consent to less radical surgery. On 22 September, he succeeded in obtaining C's consent to debridement of the dead tissue under general anaesthetic. There followed an improvement in C's condition and the risk of imminent death had been averted. Nonetheless, the patient applied for an injunction to prevent any future attempt to amputate his leg without his consent. In applying the principles laid down in both *Bland* and *In re T*, Thorpe J allowed the application. The question of C's capacity to consent was discussed and it was found that C was capable of managing his own affairs and was thus not precluded from giving valid consent. Thorpe J concluded that the correct question to be addressed in determining C's capacity was:

> whether it has been established that C's capacity is so reduced by his chronic mental illness that he does not sufficiently understand the nature, purpose and effects of the proffered amputation.[81]

Thorpe J was satisfied that, on the evidence, C though suffering from schizophrenia:

> understood and retained the relevant treatment information [and] that in his own way he believes it, and that in the same fashion he has arrived at a clear choice.[82]

This decision confirms the autonomy of the patient in deciding whether or not to undergo life-saving medical treatment. More importantly it confirms the autonomy of the mental patient in relation to consenting to medical treatment.[83] Thus, in this conflict between the medical professional's view of what was in the best interests of the patient and the patient's own decision on what is best for him, the Court favoured the latter.

---

81 Ibid., p. 295.
82 Ibid., p. 295.
83 See the general discussion on consent in ch. 3 and the more specific discussion of consent in relation to the mental patient in ch. 7.

THE MINOR PATIENT

In the United Kingdom, the question of the minor patient and the refusal of treatment leading to the possible death of the patient has been broached in the case of *In re W (a minor) (medical treatment)*.[84] In that case, a sixteen-year-old girl who suffered from *anorexia nervosa* was the subject of an application by her local authority under s. 100(3) and (4) of the Children Act 1989 for a court order that it be free to place W in a hospital specialising in eating disorders and that she be given medical treatment without her consent if necessary. At first instance, it was held that although W had sufficient understanding to make an informed decision, the Court had inherent jurisdiction to make the order sought. W appealed the decision to the Court of Appeal. The Court of Appeal dismissed W's appeal, holding that it had an unlimited inherent jurisdiction over minors and as such could, in the child's best interests, override the child's wishes even where the child was capable of understanding the nature and consequences of her refusal to accept treatment where such refusal would lead to the death of the child or to severe permanent injury. However, the Court did point out that:

> [n]evertheless such a refusal is a very important consideration in making clinical judgments and for parents and the court in deciding whether themselves to give consent. Its importance increases with the age and maturity of the minor.[85]

This decision considerably narrows the freedom of action of the minor as laid down in *Gillick v. West Norfolk and Wisbech Area Health Authority*.[86] Given the approach to the autonomy of the child in Irish law, as discussed previously in this book, it is likely that an Irish court faced with a question such as that raised in *In re W* would follow the more restrictive line adopted in that case rather than the *Gillick* model of child autonomy in the context of medical treatment.

In some circumstances, a doctor who has agreed to provide a particular life-prolonging treatment, may be under a contractual duty to give that treatment, although if it were not for that undertaking he would have been free to omit to do so. Having expressly agreed to provide particular treatment, there are circumstances where any reasonable doctor would comply with that undertaking. Furthermore, a doctor who has started on a particular course of action will often be obliged to complete it, or to arrange for someone else to do so. There is an important additional issue: anyone is

---

84 [1992] 4 All ER 627.
85 Ibid. per Lord Donaldson MR, p. 639-40.

86 [1985] 3 All ER 402.

free to waive that right, and place decision making in the hands of another, such as a doctor or parent. In England, the *Gillick* case[87] points out that parental rights should yield to that of the child when the child 'reaches a sufficient understanding and intelligence which would render him capable of making up his own mind'.

The inference from *Gillick* is that there is no defined age limit for consent, and so presumably refusal of treatment. But these waters have been muddied by the case of *In Re W*.[88] This challenges the relative independence from parental interference of 16 to 18-year-olds on the issue of consent, established by the Family Law Reform Act 1969, the *Gillick* case, and the Children's Act 1989.

Although it could be said that *In re W* may muddy the English waters, it is probable that in this context the *In re W* decision would weigh more heavily with an Irish court than *Gillick*.[89]

The duty on a doctor's part to keep a patient alive is different from a duty not to kill. A doctor has a duty to maintain life. But does a duty not to kill consist of the same elements? In another relationship, where a legally recognised duty of care arises, that of parent and child, parents, by not acting, may not always be guilty of homicide. Thus in the English case of *In Re B (a minor)*,[90] where the parents of a child refused to give consent to an operation, in the knowledge that without such operation the child would die, the court was of the opinion that the decision of the parents was 'entirely responsible'. It was a decision which the parents could lawfully take without the refusal constituting homicide for the purposes of the criminal law. In this case, the child was made a ward of court, and the court gave consent to the operation in question. On the other hand, if the parents committed a positive act which led to the death of the child, then the parents would be guilty of murder. In this instance, the duty to preserve life is different from the duty not to kill.

In Ireland, in cases where a parent refuses such treatment when refusal might lead to the child's death, a Health Board or other concerned party may seek a court order under the Children's Act 1908.[91]

In the case of the minor patient who is incapable of giving consent and where neither parent is willing to consent to life-prolonging treatment of the child, the parent's refusal to consent will release a doctor from an obligation to provide particular medical treatment for the child. Where a child's life is in immediate danger and his parents refuse to consent to

87 Ibid.
88 [1992] 4 All ER 627.
89 For a discussion of the minor and medical treatment, see ch. 3.

90 [1981] 1 WLR 1421.
91 See *F. v. The Eastern Health Board and Ors.*, [1990] ILRM 767 (SC).

life-saving treatment, a doctor will often be legally justified in proceeding despite the parent's objection.

MEDICAL COUNCIL GUIDELINES

The Medical Council in *A Guide to Ethical Conduct and Behaviour and to Fitness to Practise*[92] suggests that where death is imminent, it is the doctor's responsibility to take care that a patient dies with dignity and with as little suffering as possible. 'The Principles of Medical Ethics in Europe',[93] endorsed by the Irish Medical Council, states in Article 12 that the practice of medicine entails in all circumstances constant respect for the life, the moral autonomy and the free choice of the patient. However, the doctor may, in the case of an incurable and terminal illness, alleviate the physical and emotional suffering of the patient by restricting his intervention to such treatment as is appropriate to preserve, so far as possible, the quality of a life which is drawing to its close. It is essential to care for the dying patient right to the end and to take such action as will permit the patient to retain his dignity. It is implicit in this statement that if the restoration of health can no longer be achieved, there is still much for a doctor to do, and he is entitled to do all that is proper and necessary to relieve pain and suffering, even if the measures he takes may incidentally shorten life.

THE AUSTRALIAN MODEL

In certain states in Australia an attempt has been made to frame legislation which would go some way towards providing a practical resolution to the dilemma posed by passive euthanasia. The Natural Death Act 1983 of South Australia is the piece of legislation which has acted as a model for subsequent legislative intervention by certain other Australian states.[94] The Natural Death Act 1983 enables the terminally ill patient in specific circumstances to forego life-sustaining treatment. In addition the Act provides for immunity from civil and criminal liability for doctors, who, acting without negligence, follow the directions of such patients. The Act only applies to terminally ill patients who are defined in s. 3 as those people who are suffering from:

any illness, injury or degeneration of mental or physical faculties—

---

92 *A Guide to Ethical Conduct and Behaviour and to Fitness to Practice*, 4th ed. (Medical Council, Dublin, 1994).
93 'Principles of Medical Ethics in Europe' in *A Guide to Ethical Conduct*, op. cit., p. 38.
94 See, for example the Northern Territory Natural Death Act 1988.

(a) such that death would, if extraordinary measures were not undertaken, be imminent; and

(b) from which there is no reasonable prospect of temporary recovery, even if extraordinary measures were undertaken.

The term 'extraordinary measures' is taken to mean:

medical or surgical measures that prolong life, or are intended to prolong life, by supplanting or maintaining the operation of bodily functions that are temporarily or permanently incapable of independent operation.[95]

This would include such measures as artificial ventilation, artificial feeding and artificial hydration.

The capacity of the patient is important in exercising this right to forego treatment under the 1983 Act. Thus, the Act will only apply to the patient who:

is conscious and capable of exercising a rational judgment of all the various forms of treatment that may be available in his particular case so that the patient may make an informed judgment as to whether a particular form of treatment should, or should not, be undertaken.[96]

Thus, the category of patients who may avail of this right to forego life sustaining treatment is quite narrow. In effect it is confined to the competent adult and does not make provision for the minor or the incompetent adult. The Act allows the defined category of patients to make a living will or advance directive outlining how the medical practitioner should proceed in the event of the patient suffering a terminal illness necessitating his being kept alive by artificial means. The Act itself does not specify when the will should be made but it would appear that it should be made before the patient succumbs to the terminal illness. This would avoid the problem of pressure being exerted on the patient by avaricious relatives when the patient is in a vulnerable state as a result of the illness. However the Act does not lay down requirements in relation to those persons who may validly witness the advance directive. This may raise the problem of the witnesses being related to the patient which would cast doubt on whether the patient freely signed the document or was badgered by relatives into doing so.

Once made, the living will becomes effective indefinitely, unless of course it is revoked. The Natural Death Act 1983 provides that such an advance

95 Natural Death Act 1983, s. 3.   96 S. 4(4), id.

directive will become effective in the event of the patient suffering from a terminal illness which would necessitate the use of life-sustaining medical intervention.[97]

The medical practitioner who acts in compliance with the wishes of the patient as expressed in the advance directive will not be deemed liable for causing the patient's death.[98] In addition the medical practitioner who is faced with the decision as to whether:

(a) a patient is, or is not, suffering from terminal illness;
(b) a patient revoked, or intended to revoke, the direction not to have the extraordinary measures applied or undertaken;
(c) a patient was, or was not, at the time of giving direction, capable of understanding the nature and consequences of the direction.[99]

makes such decision in good faith and without negligence, will be deemed to be immune from criminal liability. The Act does not grant immunity in civil law for the practitioner. The Act only applies to the withdrawal of life-sustaining measures and does not provide immunity in cases where the doctor performs an act which:

causes or accelerates death, as distinct from an act that permits the dying process to take its natural course.[100]

In the Australian state of Victoria, the Medical Treatment Act 1988 as amended by the Medical Treatment (Enduring Power of Attorney) Act 1990 and by the Medical Treatment (Agents) Act 1992 allows a competent adult to refuse consent to treatment for a condition from which he is currently suffering. The major impetus for the 1988 Act was the decision of the coroner in the inquest into the death of a former water-skiing champion, John McEwan, who suffered from quadriplegia as a result of a diving accident.[101] He had expressed a wish to die and that he not be revived if he became unconscious, in a document drawn up by his solicitor. Having refused to take all food and medication, he was certified under the Victorian Mental Health Act 1958 on the grounds that he was not capable of making a rational decision due to his suffering from severe depression. He eventually

97 S. 4(1), id.
98 S. 6 of id.
99 S. 5 of id.
100 South Australia (1983) *Parliamentary Debatres*, House of Assembly, 4 May, 1167. See also Natural Death Act 1983, s. 6(1).
101 See D. Lanham & S. Woodford, 'Refusal by agents of life-sustaining medical treatment', *Melbourne University Law Review* (1992), Vol. 18, p. 659.

agreed to take food and medication and the certification was revoked. He was discharged from hospital, whereupon he discontinued taking anti-depressant medication. His respirator was disconnected in April 1986. At the inquest, the coroner found that death was not due to the disconnection of the respirator but was caused by heart failure resulting from the diving accident. This decision provoked public debate on the issue and it was thought that the current legislation did not adequately uphold the patient's right to die. The Victorian Parliament commissioned two reports into the issue[102] before enacting the Medical Treatment Act in 1988.

The Act provided for procedures for the drawing up of refusal of treatment certificates on the part of patients and also created a statutory offence of medical trespass for those who do not comply with the wishes of the patient as expressed in the refusal of treatment certificate. The patient in question must be an adult of sound mind who has understood the information on the nature of his condition and has voluntarily expressed a wish to forego life-sustaining treatment for a current condition.[103] The refusal of treatment certificate must be signed by two witnesses, one of whom must be a medical practitioner. The Act does not provide a definition of 'sound mind' for the purposes of refusing medical treatment. For guidance on who may be deemed to be competent for the purposes of creating a valid refusal of treatment certificate, one may look to the Victorian Parliament's *Second and Final Report upon Inquiry into Options of Dying with Dignity* wherein an incompetent patient (either adult or minor) is defined as:

> a patient who is not capable of understanding the nature, consequences and risks of the proposed medical treatment and the consequences of non-treatment, and who is thus incapable of consenting to, or refusing, medical treatment.[104]

In opposition to the Natural Death Act in South Australia, the Medical Treatment Act includes in its scope any patient of sound mind who suffers from an illness requiring treatment regardless of whether the illness is terminal. Those who fail to adhere to the refusal of treatment certificate under the Medical Treatment Act will be guilty of the criminal offence of medical trespass. This is a summary offence which attracts a maximum fine of A$500. In addition, the patient whose wishes have not been complied

---

102   Victoria, (1986), *First Report of the Social Development Committee upon the Inquiry Into Options for Dying with Dignity*; Victoria, (1987), *Second and Final Report of the Social Development Committee upon the Inquiry Into Options for Dying with Dignity*.

103   S. 5(1) Medical Treatment Act 1988.

104   Victoria, (1987), *Second and Final Report of the Social Development upon the Inquiry into Options of Dying with Dignity*, p. 174.

with, may sue the doctor in the tort of trespass or may lodge a complaint with the Medical Board of Victoria.

The approach of the various state legislatures in Australia to the issue of the autonomy of the dying patient whilst not free from imperfection, certainly shows a willingness on the part of government to provide practical solutions to complex medical dilemmas. These developments also give societal recognition to the right of the patient to die with dignity. The advantage of a legislative solution to such issues is that it allows the interests of all parties involved to be represented. In addition, it should allow those involved to be provided with clear guidelines as to their respective rights and duties in such a situation.

ASSISTING SUICIDE

In the United States, the right to die has not yet been extended to physician-assisted suicide. As of the end May 1994,[105] the position appears to be that a federal district court in Seattle, Judge Barbara J. Rothstein, has struck down a 140-year old state ban on assisted suicide, saying that the law violated the 14th Amendment by restricting a person's liberty. Judge Rothstein based her decision on the 1992 Supreme Court decision in *Planned Parenthood v Casey*, which re-affirmed *Roe v. Wade*. In *Casey*, the Supreme Court held that 'matters involved in the most intimate and personal choices a person may make in a lifetime . . . are central to the liberty protected by the 14th Amendment. At the heart of liberty is the right to define one's own concept of existence, of meaning, of the universe, and of the mystery of human life'.

The Court of Appeals of Michigan ruled on the constitutionality of a statute designed to restrict and regulate physician-assisted suicide. A lower court Michigan judge declared the act unconstitutional, dismissed the criminal charges against the famous defendant, Dr Kevorkian, and held that individuals have a constitutional right to commit suicide under the Fourteenth Amendment of the US Constitution.

The Court of Appeals declared the act unconstitutional, but on technical grounds which do not address the deeper issues, namely, that the legislation violates a Michigan constitutional provision which mandates that all legislation must only have one object. (In short, the legislation was not written correctly).

Nonetheless, in dictum the Court commented on the federal constitutional questions, and sharply disagreed with the lower courts which found

105 See E. Goodman, 'The right to end life is about to divide the nation again', *Boston Globe* 17 May 1994.

a federal constitutional right to commit suicide: 'The scope of rights encompassed by the concept of ordered liberty does not include the right to commit suicide, much less the right to assisted suicide. . . . Judicial discovery of a right to terminate one's life is not a logical extension of this catalog of rights. Liberty and justice will not cease if a right to commit suicide is not recognised'.[106]

In a separate decision, *People v. Kevorkian*,[107] the Court of Appeals determined whether a murder statute applies to the conduct of a physician who assists another in voluntarily committing suicide. The Circuit Court dismissed the charges against Kevorkian. The Court of Appeals held that in so doing, they were in error:

> The act provides that one who provides the physical means by which a person attempts to commit suicide or for participating in the physical act by which another attempts to commit suicide is guilty of a felony punishable by up to four years' imprisonment. Defendant's argument that he cannot be charged with murder because the Legislature subsequently enacted a law criminalising assisted suicide is misplaced. The Legislature is not prohibited from providing a specific and lesser penalty for actions that could be punished under another statute with a harsher penalty. . . . If the laws here in question involved any wrong or unnecessary harshness, it was for Congress or the people who make congresses, to see that the evil was corrected. The remedy does not lie with the judicial branch of the government. We conclude that the circuit court erred in dismissing the murder charges against the defendant.[108]

In *Kane v. Kulongoski*,[109] the Supreme Court of Oregon addressed challenges to a proposed initiative measure certified by the Attorney General, which affirmatively authorises and creates standards for physician assisted suicide.

The proposed initiative is entitled 'The Oregon Death with Dignity Act'. It would create a statutory regime that 'permits an adult resident of Oregon, who has been diagnosed as suffering from an incurable and irreversible disease that will . . . cause that person's death within six months, to obtain and take lethal medication.'[110]

After rejecting some challenges to the wording of the initiative, the Court addresses the point that the certified question is deficient because its main

---

106 *Hobbins v. Attorney General* [1994] Mich App LEXIS 232 at 15.
107 [1994] Mich App LEXIS 237.
108 [1994] Mich App LEXIS 237 at 16.
109 [1994] 318 Ore 593.
110 Ibid., p. 596.

purpose is to remove criminal sanctions to physician-assisted suicide.[111] The Court rejected this argument, as it overstates the purpose of the initiative. They argue that the purpose of the initiative is to authorise and to create standards for physician-assisted suicide, and is limited to certain categories of terminally ill adults.[112]

The initiative, then, will proceed, with a few changes in wording, and Oregon voters will vote directly on the issue of adopting a statutory scheme to regulate physician-assisted suicide for terminally ill patients.

This measure was approved in November 1994 and is due to become law on 8 December 1994.

FAILURE TO PREVENT SUICIDE

In a related issue, in a number of cases recovery has been sought from a doctor, psychiatrist or a psychologist for failure to take steps to prevent a patient's suicide.[113] Cases seem to fall into one of three classifications:[114]

First, where it is alleged that the doctor, psychiatrist or psychologist generally failed to take precautions to prevent a patient's suicide, liability was found in some cases, with other cases reaching the opposite result.[115]

Second, in cases where recovery is sought based on failure to disclose information concerning the patient's condition or failure to warn persons of the patient's condition, it is generally held that the health carer is not

---

111 Ibid., p. 600.

112 Ibid.

113 A conclusion that a deceased committed suicide is made by a coroner. (See the discussion of coroners in general, ch. 12. Suicide is never presumed, and a conclusion of suicide must be based on some evidence that the deceased intended to take his or her life. P. Matthews and J. Foreman, *Jervis on the Office and Duties of Coroners* (Sweet & Maxwell, London, 1993) p. 249. Although there is no crime involved, since suicide ceased to be a crime in Ireland with the Criminal Law (Suicide) Act of 1993, the standard of proof in the coroner's verdict of suicide is the same as in a criminal prosecution: beyond a reasonable doubt. Cf. *R. v. West London Coroner, ex p. Gray* [1988] QB 467 at 477; *R. v. North Northumberland Coroner, ex p. Armstrong* [1987] 151 JP 773, 785; *R. v. Wolverhampton Coroner, ex p. McCurbin* [1990] 1 WLR 719, 728; *R. v. Newbury Coroner, ex p. John* (1991) 156 J.P. 456, 457; *In re Beckon* [1992] 93 DLR (4th), 161 (Ontario CA), cited by Matthews and Foreman, p. 249, fn. 55.

114 See J.L. Rigelhaupt, Jr., Annotation. *Liability of Doctor, Psychiatrist, or Psychologist for Failure to Take Steps to Prevent Patlent's Suicide* [1993] 17 ALR 4th 1128.

115 In *Meier v. Ross General Hospital* (1968) Cal 2d 420, 445 P 2d 519, liability was found based upon a duty to protect the decedent from his own actions, after he had previously attempted suicide. However, in *North Miami General Hospital v. Krakower* (1981) 393 So 2d 57 (Fla App D3) 393, no recovery was allowed for a widow of a patient of suicidal tendencies who committed suicide, after requesting the attendant to leave. 17 ALR 1128.

liable.[116] Similarly, a failure to administer or continue administering drugs for the patient resulting in the patient's suicide has not resulted in liability. In *Fernandez v. Baruch*, the court held that a psychiatrist who discontinued the use of the drug Thorazine, violated no professional standards in doing so, even though the patient later committed suicide. The court further rejected the plaintiff's argument that the psychiatrist breached a duty to inform the police that Thorazine had been used, and that its discontinuance might result in the decedent harming himself.[117]

Third, liability has also not been found in cases where it is alleged that the doctor, psychologist or psychiatrist failed to confine or commit the patient, or failed to locate a hospital for the patient. In *Dillman v Hellman*,[118] the court held that a psychiatrist should not be held liable, having thought that the patient had progressed enough to be transferred to a less secure wing of a hospital. The psychiatrist's treatment of the patient conformed to the medical standards of the community.

SUICIDE IN IRELAND

Until the enactment of The Criminal Law (Suicide) Act 1993, suicide was a felony at common law. The 1993 Act provided that suicide 'shall no longer be an offence'.[119]

S. 2(2) of the Act provides that a person who aids, abets, counsels or procures[120] the suicide of another, or an attempt by another to commit suicide, shall be liable on conviction on indictment for a term not exceeding fourteen years.[121] Thus one can conclude that physician-assisted suicide

116 In *Bellah v. Greenson* (1978) 81 Cal App 3d 614, 146 Cal Rptr 535, the court rejected the plaintiffs' contention that a psychiatrist had a duty to breach doctor-patient confidentiality in order to reveal to the plaintiffs (the parents of the psychiatrist's client) that the daughter might commit suicide. 17 ALR 4th 1128.

117 (1968) 52 NJ 127, 244 A 2d 109, see also 17 ALR 4th. 1128.

118 Cited by LEXIS as (1973) 282 So 2d 388 (Fla App D2) (17 ALR 4th 1128).

119 For a discussion of the Irish position in the context of assisted suicide and euthanasia in Europe, see the discussion by J. Hennigan, 'Assisted Suicide and Euthanasia in Europe', Irish Medical Times (1993) Vol. 27, No. 15 (9 April) p. 15, which in particular criticises the position adopted by the Royal Dutch Medical Association; and an earlier article 'Doctors' Concern Over Proposals on Euthanasia', *Irish Medical Times* (1991), Vol. 25, No. 44 (1 November) p. 19.

120 The provisions in regard to aiding and abetting suicide could arguably leave the authors and publishers and distributors of books and other material promoting suicide liable. See *Irish Medical News* (1993), Vol. 10, No. 25 (28 June), pp. 1, 2.

121 For a vividly written and interesting review of some of the social implications of suicide in Ireland, see F. Bowers, *Suicide in Ireland* (Irish Medical Organisation, Dublin, 1994). As Bowers notes, statistics on suicide have long been acknowledged to be problematical in Ireland: the estimate of 4,114 suicides over the twenty year period culminating in

would be regarded in Ireland as a criminal offence. From the foregoing account of the law in this area, one can see that, in most circumstances, a doctor may not carry out treatment involving the bodily touching of a patient who is capable of consenting, if the patient's consent has not been sought, or if the patient has refused to give consent. Where someone attempts to commit suicide, the doctor is free and indeed sometimes under a duty to prevent the suicide attempt.

The rationale behind the fourteen-year term of imprisonment was explained by the Minister for Justice in the Dáil discussion on the Bill as being:

> to cover situations where a person deliberately procures the suicide of another for his own motives. For example, a dominant personality, rather than committing murder, might induce his intended victim to commit suicide. A depressed person with suicidal tendencies, if caught in a moment of despair, would be easy prey for a manipulative person who had anything to gain from his death.[122]

DIAGNOSIS OF DEATH

In Ireland, the Medical Council's guidelines define death as 'brain death', and, in the context of donor organ procurement, endorse Arts 13, 14, and 15 of the *Principles of Medical Ethics in Europe*. The Guidelines therefore state that:

> [i]n a case where it is impossible to reverse the terminal processes leading to the cessation of a patient's vital functions which are being artificially maintained, doctors will satisfy themselves that death has occurred, taking account of the most recent scientific data. At least two doctors, acting individually should take meticulous steps to verify their findings in writing. They should be independent of [any] team

1991 are probably incorrect. Official statistics state that in the period from 1987 to June 1991, there were 1,230 suicides: 245 in 1987, 166 in 1988, 255 in 1989, and 311 in 1990. The 1990 figures break down as follows: 114 were between the ages of 15 and 34, while 110 were aged between 35-54, while 110 were over the age of 55. See *Irish Medical Times* (1991) Vol. 25, No. 50 (13 December) p. 2 (1991) Vol. 25, No. 27 (5 July) p. 5.

In this context, the Samaritan telephone service, which produces annual reports stated in its 1992 report that in 1992 'one in every hundred callers to the Dublin Samaritans had attempted suicide before phoning'. Of the 74,197 calls, 6% were actively contemplating suicide and 27% had less specific suicidal feelings. Most of the callers were aged 20-29 years: *Irish Medical News* (1993), Vol. 10, No. 25, (28 June) p. 4.

122   430 Dáil Debates, col. 659.

which is to carry out [a] transplantation . . . [d]octors should take all
practicable steps to satisfy themselves that the donor had not expressed
an opinion, or left instructions, on the matter either in writing or with
his/her family.[123]

The development of a definition of death, based on brain function
commenced in France in 1959,[124] when two neurologists, Mollard and
Goulon, wrote of the *coma dépassé*. In this state, the patient was in an
irreversible coma, and had lost the capacity to breathe unaided by a
ventilator. However, the idea of *coma dépassé* was never to be generally
adopted as a means of defining death.

The next significant development in relation to the definition of death
based on brain function occurred when such a definition was advocated in
the *Report of the Ad Hoc Committee of the Harvard Medical School to examine
the Definition of Brain Death*.[125] The Harvard criteria for brain death are (i)
the absence of cerebral responsiveness; (ii) the absence of induced or
spontaneous movement, (iii) the absence of spontaneous respiration; and
(iv), the absence of brain stem and deep tendon reflexes.

Following this report, the definition of death based on brain function
was further refined to that of brain stem death.[126] The rationale for basing
the diagnosis of death on brain stem criteria is that irreversible loss of brain
stem function results in the inability to breathe, which in turn deprives the
heart and the cerebral hemispheres of oxygen.[127] In the United Kingdom,
the Conference of Medical Royal Colleges and their Faculties have recognised that death of the brain stem is synonymous with death of the person.[128]
Thus, once the medical practitioners in question are satisfied that brain stem

---

123 *A Guide to Ethical Conduct and Behaviour and to Fitness to Practise* 4th ed. (Medical
      Council, Dublin, 1994), pp. 37-8.
124 P. Mollaret and M. Goulon, 'Le Coma Dépassé' *Revue Neurologique* (1959), Vol. 101,
      pp. 3-15. But note earlier references to states akin to brain death; for example, Sir
      Dyce Duckworth 'Some Cases of cerebral disease in which the function of respiration
      entirely ceases for some hours before that of the circulation', *Edinburgh Medical Journal*
      (1898), Vol. 3, pp. 145-52.
125 H.K. Beecher (chairman) 'A definition of Irreversible Coma', Report of the ad hoc
      committee of the Harvard Medical School to examine the definition of brain death,
      Journal of American Medical Association (1968), Vol. 205, p. 337.
126 A. Mohandas & S.N. Chou, *Journal of Neurosurgery*, 'Brain Stem Death' (1971), Vol.
      35, pp. 211-18.
127 See, for example, C. Pallis, *The ABC of brainstem death* (The British Medical
      Association, London, 1983).
128 Conference of the Medical Royal Colleges and their Faculties in the United Kingdom,
      'Diagnosis of Brain Death', *British Medical Journal* (1976), Vol. 2, p. 1187; Conference
      of the Medical Royal Colleges and their Faculties in The United Kingdom 'Diagnosis
      of Death', *British Medical Journal* (1979) Vol. 1, p. 332.

death has occurred, they may diagnose death. In practice, the diagnosis of brain stem death will include the primary diagnosis of the cause of the coma, and the establishment of its irreversible nature. Thus, there should be evidence that all reversible causes of coma such as hypothermia and drug overdose have been ruled out.[129]

The connection with euthanasia and brain death is complex, and recently, the Medical Council has proposed that doctors in each hospital should draw up guidelines in keeping with current medical practice for the purposes of diagnosing brain death.[130]

129 See J.K. Mason & R.A. McCall Smith, *Law and Medical Ethics*, 3rd ed. (Butterworth, London, 1991), pp. 290-6.

130 'Medical Council Proposes Brain Death Guidelines For Hospitals', *Irish Medical Times* (1993), Vol. 27, No. 41 (8 October), p. 6. For further detailed discussion see, D. Lamb, *Death, Brain Death and Ethics* (Croom Helm, London, 1985).

9

SEX, MEDICAL INTERVENTION
AND THE LAW

CONTRACEPTION: CONSTITUTIONAL BACKGROUND

The 1960s and 1970s saw what appeared to be a liberalising of Irish society. In the forefront of this movement was the Supreme Court, whose judgments demonstrated an innovative approach to interpretation of the Constitution. One topic which fell to be reviewed by the Court was contraception. This topic was the source of continued controversy. The basis of the legal prohibition on the sale of contraceptives was to be found in The Criminal Law Amendment Act 1935. S. 17(1) of the 1935 Act provided that:

> [i]t shall not be lawful for any person to sell, or expose, offer, advertise, or keep for sale or to import or attempt to import into . . . [Ireland] for sale, any contraceptive.

In addition, s. 17(2) provided that anyone who contravened s. 17(1) would be liable to a fine or imprisonment for up to six months or both.

In effect, these provisions prevented people from gaining access to contraceptives. As Walsh J put it in his judgment in the case of *McGee v. Attorney General*:[1]

> the effect of s. 17 of the Act of 1935 . . . is effectively to make contraceptives unavailable to persons within the State without an infringement of the law and the possibility of a criminal prosecution and conviction.[2]

Therefore, it was apparent that not only were persons denied autonomy over an aspect of their private sexual behaviour, but were subject to criminal sanctions if they tried to exert control over their fertility.

In a case heard in 1973, the Supreme Court was given the opportunity to adjudicate on the issue. The plaintiff in *McGee v. Attorney General*[3] was

1 [1974] IR 284.
2 Ibid., p. 308.

3 [1974] IR 284.

a married woman, who was told by her doctor that a further pregnancy would put her life at risk. As a result, the plaintiff decided to use artificial contraceptives to prevent this contingency. As a consequence of the provisions of the Criminal Law Amendment Act 1935 the plaintiff was forced to import the required contraceptive jelly from England. However, the customs authorities seized the jelly on its arrival in Ireland. The plaintiff commenced an action in the High Court, claiming that s. 17 of the 1935 Act was inconsistent with the Constitution. The action was dismissed by the High Court, whereupon the plaintiff appealed to the Supreme Court. The Supreme Court allowed the appeal and in the process held that the impugned provisions of the Act of 1935 were inconsistent with the provisions of Article 40.3.1 of the Constitution, in that they constituted an unjustified invasion of the plaintiff's personal right to privacy in her marriage. The Supreme Court in effect held that a constitutional right to privacy existed in the context of marriage. As Walsh J stated:

> [t]he sexual life of a husband and wife is of necessity and by its nature an area of particular privacy. If the husband and wife decide to limit their family or to avoid having children by use of contraceptives, it is a matter peculiarly within the joint decision of the husband and wife and one into which the State cannot intrude unless its intrusion can be justified by the exigencies of the common good. The question of whether the use of contraceptives by married couples within their marriage is or is not contrary to the moral code or codes to which they profess to subscribe, or is or is not regarded by them as being against their conscience, could not justify State intervention. Similarly the fact that the use of contraceptives may offend against the moral code of the majority of the citizens of the State would not *per se* justify an intervention by the State to prohibit their use within marriage.[4]

It may be that this was a coded signal to the legislature that it was time for change. Walsh J was of the opinion that:

> [s.] 17 of of the Act of 1935, in so far as it unreasonably restricts the availability of contraceptives for use within marriage, is inconsistent with the provisions of Article 41 of the Constitution for being an unjustified invasion of the privacy of husband and wife in their sexual relations with one another. The fundamental restriction is contained in the provisions of s 17(3) of the Act of 1935 which lists contraceptives among the prohibited articles which may not be imported for any

4 Ibid., p. 312.

purposes whatsoever. On the present state of facts, I am of opinion that this provision is inconsistent with the Constitution and is no longer in force.[5]

Five years were to pass before legislation on the issue was introduced. When the legislation eventually came, in the form of The Health (Family Planning) Act 1979, it was far from satisfactory. In the *McGee* case, the Supreme Court declared that the decision to use contraceptives was:

a matter peculiarly within the joint decision of the husband and wife.[6]

However, the final decision under the Act of 1979 lay with the medical practitioner, who could provide a prescription for contraceptives only if satisfied that the contraceptives were for *bona fide* family planning or for adequate medical reasons.[7]

The 1979 Act has been the subject of significant modification since its introduction, leading to a less restrictive regime in relation to contraceptive availability.

The Health (Family Planning) (Amendment) Act 1985 provided for the availability of contraceptive sheaths and spermicides. However, those who required contraceptives for medical purposes were still obliged to obtain a prescription from a medical practitioner. In addition, the outlets from which contraceptives were obtainable continued to be restricted. Indeed, the sale of contraceptives by bodies or individuals not entitled to do so under the 1979 and 1985 Acts constituted a criminal offence. This led to the situation where a *bona fide* family planning body, the Irish Family Planning Association was charged and convicted for the unlawful sale of contraceptives contrary to the Acts, in 1991.[8] The law was clearly unsatisfactory.

The Health (Family Planning) (Amendment) Act 1992 recognised the role of contraception in the area of public health, by increasing the number of outlets through which contraceptives could be sold. Those who can now lawfully sell contraceptives are pharmacists, registered medical practitioners, employees of health boards, family planning clinics and employees of hospitals providing treatment for sexually transmitted diseases and maternity services.[9] In addition, the legislation provides for the sale of contraceptives to all those of seventeen years of age and over.

However, the Act, while purporting to be a public health measure, refused to recognise the incidence of sexual intercourse amongst minors, by

5   Ibid., p. 314.
6   Ibid., p. 312.
7   Health (Family Planning) Act 1979, s. 4.

8   *Irish Times*, 15 and 27 February 1991.
9   S. 4 of the 1992 Act.

continuing the prohibition on the sale of condoms in places frequented by those under seventeen or through condom-vending machines.[10]

The Health (Family Planning) (Amendment) Act 1993 provides that 'condoms' no longer come under the definition of 'contraceptive' in the Health (Family Planning) Act 1979. The effect of this amendment is to allow for the sale of condoms in outlets other than pharmacies or family planning centres.

The Minister for Health is still obliged to prescribe standards for condoms, by regulations and is empowered to prohibit the sale or the offering for sale of contraceptive sheaths (condoms) by vending machines at a place or a class specified in the regulations.

TERMINATION OF PREGNANCY

Historic overview   Prior to 1983, the law governing abortion was contained solely in ss. 58 and 59 of the Offences Against The Persons Act 1861,[11] and s. 10 of the Health (Family Planning) Act 1979.[12] The 1861 Act prohibited the administering of drugs or the use of instruments to procure abortion or the supplying of drugs or instruments to procure abortion. The wording of the sections was wide enough to make the act of the prospective mother or anyone taking part in the procedure, guilty of an offence.

10 In many countries, on the advice of best medical opinion, the sale of condoms to young people is actively encouraged, as a practical measure to diminish the risk of contracting the HIV/AIDS virus, and (possibly) other STDs. The Department of Health's *Shaping a healthier future* (Department of Health, Dublin, 1994, pn. 0685), p. 65 expressly states that one of its objectives is 'to prevent the spread of HIV infection'.

11 24 & 25 Vict. c. 100. S. 58 states that '[e]very woman, being with child, who, with intent to procure her own miscarriage shall unlawfully administer to herself any poison or other noxious thing, or shall unlawfully use any instrument or other means whatsoever with the like intent, and whosoever, with intent to procure the miscarriage of any woman, whether she be or be not with child, shall unlawfully administer to her or cause to be taken by her any poison or other noxious thing, or shall unlawfully use any Instrument or other means whatsoever with the like intent, shall be guilty of felony, and on being convicted thereof shall be liable to be kept in penal servitude for life.'

S. 59 states that '[w]hosoever shall unlawfully supply or procure any poison or other noxious thing, or any instrument or thing whatsoever, knowing that the same is intended to be unlawfully used or employed with Intent to procure the miscarriage of any woman, whether she be or not with child, shall be guilty of a misdemeanour, and being convicted thereof shall be liable to be kept in penal servitude for any period not less than three years and not exceeding five years'.

12 S. 10 states that '[n]othing in this Act shall be construed as authorising: (a) the procuring of an abortion, (b) the doing of any other thing the doing of which is prohibited by s. 58 or s. 59 of the Offences Against the Person Act 1861 (which sections prohibit the administration of drugs and the use of instruments to procure abortion or the supplying of drugs or instruments to procure abortion) or (c) the sale, importation into the State, manufacture, advertising or display of abortifacient.'

The 8th Amendment to the Constitution was enacted on 7 September 1983, and supplemented the existing legislation on abortion. The Amendment guaranteed a right to life to the unborn. The amended Article 40.3.3 read as follows:

> the State acknowledges the right to life of the unborn and, with due regard to the equal right to life of the mother, guarantees in its laws to respect, and as far as practicable, to vindicate that right.

The amendment was the result of a sustained campaign in which Roman Catholic pressure groups played the dominant part. As a response to the liberal mood in Ireland in the 1970s, a referendum on the controversial religious and ethical issue of abortion was mooted.

Perhaps it was not the specific constitutional prohibition on abortion which was important to those involved, as abortion was already illegal, but rather that it was an issue which could be used to stem the tide of liberalism. In spite of the fact that the 1861 statute outlawed abortion, the anti-abortion lobby decided that the time had come to take a stance.

It was feared that the Supreme Court might use the fundamental rights articles of the Constitution to allow for abortion in certain circumstances. This had occurred in the USA in *Roe v. Wade*.[13] The debate in Ireland was at least ostensibly about abortion, and on both sides of the argument there was much well-informed and legitimate argument about this area. There is evidence to suggest that the debate, at a different level, was also about fundamental and opposing views about the direction of Irish society, and the position of traditional Roman Catholic values in Irish law.[14]

Politicians were concerned, and there was a measure of agreement to the holding of a referendum so that the rights of the foetus could, if desired, be protected by a specific amendment to the Constitution. The terms that were selected were not neutral. The proposed amendment referred to 'the right to life' of the 'unborn'.

Surprisingly, objections to the wording of the referendum came both from some of the Protestant churches, and also from a distinguished Roman Catholic psychologist. The Protestant churches argued for freedom of conscience in the matter. The Roman Catholic academic, Rev Professor Brendan O'Mahony, stated that it was strange that the wording allowed only those exceptions permitted by Roman Catholic moral teaching, and that the

13 (1973) 410 US 113.
14 See further J.P. O'Carroll, 'Bishops, Knights – and Pawns? Traditional Thought on the Irish Abortion Referendum Debate of 1983', *Irish Political Studies* (1991), Vol. 6, pp. 53-71; R. Pearce, 'Abortion and the Right to Life under the Irish Constitution', *Journal of Social Welfare and Family Law* (1993), pp. 386-402, who describes the campaign leading up to the referendum as 'heated, vitriolic and extremely divisive' (p. 390).

success of the campaign could lead to a form of 'moral imperialism'.[15]

The words in Article 40.3.3 – 'with due regard to the equal right to the life of the mother' was calculated to add to the Constitution the philosophical principle of double effect, (discussed in chapter 8) which in relation to abortion holds that where a foetus is removed to save the life of a mother, then abortion is therefore permissible.

The Amendment was carried. It was of merely symbolic effect, and did not alter the trend of Irish women seeking abortions in the neighbouring jurisdiction of England, where termination of pregnancy is practised lawfully.[16] Indeed statistics have shown that the numbers continue to increase with, for example, a pre-amendment figure in 1982 of 3650 rising by 1989, to 3721.[17] Indeed, perhaps to the surprise of those who advocated the amendment to the Constitution, the Supreme Court declared in 1992 in the case of *Attorney General v. X* that abortion in Ireland could be lawful in certain instances.[18]

Attorney General v. X   In the case of *Attorney General v. X*,[19] the Supreme Court considered the case of a fourteen year old girl, who was raped in December 1991, and who, as a result, became pregnant. The girl and her parents proposed to travel to England to obtain an abortion. The Attorney General applied *ex parte* for an injunction, on 7 February 1992, which he obtained. The injunction restrained the girl and her parents from leaving the jurisdiction for the purposes of obtaining an abortion.

It was argued on behalf of X that there was a risk that she would commit suicide if the pregnancy were allowed to go to term. The Supreme Court held, by a majority of 4-1, that the proper test to be applied is that 'if it is established as a matter of probability that there is a real and substantial risk to the life as distinct from the health of the mother which can only be avoided by the termination of her pregnancy . . . such termination is permissible'. It was held that there was a 'real and substantial risk' to the life of the mother by suicide, which could only be avoided by termination

15 *Irish Times*, 14 May 1982, quoted in B. Girvin, 'Social Change and Moral Politics; the Irish Constitutional Referendum 1983' in *Political Studies* (1986), Vol. 34, p. 73.

16 See the (UK) Abortion Act 1967. According to *Irish Medical Times*, Vol. 27, No. 44 (29 October 1993), statistics published by the UK office of Population Censuses and Surveys, state that since 1970, more than 63,000 women giving Irish addresses have procured abortions there. From 1 April to 30 June 1992, 1,040 such abortions were performed, bringing the total to 63,015. However the article points out that 'the actual number ... is thought to be higher' (pp. 1-2).

17 UK Office of Censuses and Surveys published in the *Irish Times*, 5 January and 17 February 1990 quoted in Peter Charleton, *Offences Against the Person* (The Round Hall Press, Dublin, 1992), p. 188.

18 *Attorney General v. X* [1992] IR 1.

19 [1992] IR 1.

of her pregnancy. This judgment attracted international attention. It was not immediately clear whether this judgment had, in some senses, changed the law, by permitting abortion in circumstances where the life as distinct from the health of the mother was at risk, or whether the law was unchanged by this judgment.

One part of this judgment, which would seem to support the view that the 8th Amendment was of merely symbolic importance, was the speech of O'Flaherty J, who claimed that the 'enactment of Article 40.3.3 did not [sic] bring about any fundamental change' in the law. He stated that the 1861 Act, and also s. 58 of the Civil Liability Act 1961 already protected the unborn. It is therefore of interest to compare the approach of the judiciary in the UK to the particular section of the 1861 Act, which applied there until 1967.

In *R. v. Bourne*[20] a surgeon terminated the pregnancy of a fourteen-year-old victim of a multiple rape. McNaghten J held that the defence of aborting the foetus for the purpose of saving the mother had existed under sec. 58 of the 1861 Act, and that this was implied by the inclusion in the section of the word 'unlawful'. The significance of the case for the medical profession was to be found in the following statement of McNaghten J which outlined the circumstances in which a doctor could lawfully carry out an abortion: 'There are . . . cases . . . where it is reasonably certain that a woman will not be able to deliver the child with which she is pregnant. In such a case, where the doctor expects, basing his opinion upon the experience and knowledge of the profession, that the child cannot be delivered without the death of the mother, in these circumstances the doctor is entitled—and, indeed, it is his duty—to perform this operation with a view to saving the life of the mother, and in such a case it is obvious that the sooner the operation is performed the better. The law is not that the doctor has got to wait until the unfortunate woman is in peril of immediate death and then at the last moment snatch her from the jaws of death. He is not only entitled, but it is his duty, to perform the operation with a view to saving her life.'[21] Indeed, McNaghten J contended that the defence of aborting the foetus for the purpose of saving the life of the mother had always existed under s. 58 of the Act of 1861, and that this was implied by the inclusion in the section of the word 'unlawful'. He believed that: '. . . it has always been the law that the Crown has got to prove the offence beyond reasonable doubt, and it has always been the law that on a charge of procuring abortion, the Crown has got to prove that the act was not done in good faith for the purpose of preserving the life of the mother.'[22]

In the Australian case of *R. v. Davidson*,[23] the case was decided on

20 [1939] 1 KB 687 [1938] 3 All ER 615   22 Ibid. at 617
      (CCA).   23 (1969) VR 667.
21 [1938] 3 All ER 615 at 678.

legislation similar to s. 58 of the Offences Against the Person Act 1861 (s. 69 of the Crimes Act 1958).[24] There, the implications of the word 'unlawful' were also considered. Mehennitt J ruled that 'the accused must have honestly believed on reasonable grounds that the act done by him was necessary to preserve the woman from some serious danger. As to this element of danger, it appears to me in principle that it should not be confined to danger to life but should apply equally to danger to physical or mental health provided it is a serious danger not being merely the normal dangers of pregnancy and childbirth'.[25]

He then went on to outline the criteria which must be present in order to constitute the act as being unlawful. These were (1), that the accused did not honestly believe on reasonable grounds that the abortion was necessary to preserve the woman from a serious danger to her life or her physical or mental health which the continuance of the pregnancy would entail or (2), that the accused did not honestly believe on reasonable grounds, that the act done by him was in the circumstances proportionate to the need to preserve the woman from serious danger to her life or her physical or mental health.

It would seem then, if O'Flaherty J's view is correct, that abortion is permissible under the Constitution and under s. 58. However, it would appear that the circumstances in which it would be allowed are far more limited than in pre-1967 UK and in Australia. The current Irish test would appear to discount such factors as the mental and emotional well-being of the woman, and to concentrate merely on her continued physical existence. This explains the origin of Finlay CJ's frequently quoted guideline of the life as opposed to the health of the woman, cited from the Supreme Court decision above.

After the *X* case, the Medical Council in Ireland issued guidelines on abortion to the following effect:

> 39.03 It has always been the tradition of the medical profession to preserve life and health. Situations arise in medical practice where the life and/or health of the mother or of the unborn, or both, are endangered. In these situations it is imperative ethically that doctors shall endeavour to preserve life and health. This is in accordance with the International Code of Ethics where the English text states: 'A doctor must always bear in mind the obligation of preserving human

---

24 'Whosoever . . . with intent to procure the miscarriage of any woman whether she is or is not with child unlawfully administers to her or causes to be taken by her any poison or other noxious thing, or unlawfully uses any instrument or other means with like intent shall be guilty of felony and shall be liable. . . .'

25 At pp. 671-2.

life' and the Declaration of Geneva which in 1983 stated "I WILL
MAINTAIN [*sic*]" the utmost respect for human life from its
beginning even under threat and I will not use my medical knowledge
contrary to the laws of humanity.

39.04 While the necessity for abortion to preserve the life or health of
the sick mother remains to be proved, it is unethical always to withhold
treatment beneficial to a pregnant woman, by reason of her pregnancy.

39.05 Departure from these principles in practice may leave the doctor
open to a charge of medical misconduct.[26]

The effect, as well as the propriety of the issue of the Guidelines have
been the subject of intensive debate inside and outside the Medical
Profession.[27] In general, it was thought that some doctors who considered
that the *X* case would open the floodgates welcomed the Guidelines, but
others were worried by the ambiguous nature of the statement, considering
on the one hand that if they undertook terminations they would be in breach
of the Medical Council Guidelines, but if they refused to undertake such
terminations, they might be liable legally, if ill effects ensued to mother or
foetus.[28] What was clearly required in the wake of the *X* case was legislation
which would give statutory force to the Supreme Court's decision. This was
not forthcoming. Instead the Government held a referendum on the
substantive issue of pregnancy termination, and on the related rights to travel
and to information, on 25 November 1992.[29] The electorate rejected the
proposal on the substantive issue of abortion, which would have inserted
the following wording into Article 43.3:

> It shall be unlawful to terminate the life of an unborn unless such
> termination is necessary to save the life, as distinct from the health, of
> the mother where there is an illness or disorder of the mother giving
> rise to a real and substantial risk to her life, not being a risk of
> self-destruction.

The electorate accepted the clauses in relation to the provision of
information, and of freedom to travel.

---

26 *A Guide to Ethical Conduct and Behaviour and to Fitness to Practise*, 4th ed. (Medical
    Council, Dublin, 1994), p. 36.
27 See *Irish Times*, 30 March 1994, p. 1; M. Browne, 'Some Doctors May Resign From
    Council Over Guidelines', *Irish Medical Times* (1993), Vol. 27, No. 11 (12 March) p. 24.
28 F. Bowers 'New Legal Risk For Irish Doctors on Abortion', *Irish Medical News* (1993),
    Vol. 10, No. 9 (8 March), pp. 1-2.
29 B. Girvan 'Moral Politics and the Irish abortion referendums of 1992', *Parliamentary
    Affairs* (1994), Vol. 47, No. 2 (April) p. 203.

ABORTION AND FREEDOM OF INFORMATION

In a series of cases decided before the *X* decision, the courts held that non-directive pregnancy counselling which included the option of pregnancy termination was contrary to Irish law as it then stood. In *Attorney General (SPUC (Ireland) Ltd) v. Open Door Counselling Ltd*,[30] an injunction was sought by the plaintiffs against the defendant pregnancy counselling service which would prevent the defendants from providing pregnant women with information on the pregnancy termination option. The Supreme Court held in favour of the plaintiffs, stating that:

> The performing of an abortion on a pregnant woman terminates the unborn life which she is carrying. Within the terms of Art 40.3.3 it is a direct destruction of the constitutionally guaranteed right to life of the unborn child.
>
> It must follow from this that there could not be an implied and unenumerated constitutional right to information about the availability of a service of abortion outside the state which, if availed of, would have the direct consequence of destroying the expressly guaranteed constitutional life of the unborn . . . no right could constitutionally arise to obtain information. The purpose of the obtaining of which was to defeat the costitutional right to life of the unborn child.[31]

In the subsequent case of *SPUC (Ireland) Ltd v. Grogan*,[32] the plaintiffs brought proceedings against the defendants, who were officers of students' associations, preventing them from providing information on pregnancy termination services located outside the state. The High Court in this case decided to refer certain questions to the European Court of Justice before ruling on the issue, and refused the plaintiff's application for an interlocutory injunction. The plaintiffs appealed this decision to the Supreme Court. The Supreme Court granted an interlocutory injunction, preventing the defendants from distributing information on pregnancy termination. However, the Supreme Court did not overturn the High Court's decision to refer certain questions to the European Court of Justice. On the question of the provision of information on pregnancy termination services, the European Court of Justice[33] held that it was not contrary to European Community Law for a member state in which abortion was outlawed to prohibit the defendants from distributing information about the provision of pregnancy termination services in clinics in other member states, where the provision of such services is lawful. This was provided that such clinics have no involvement in the distribution of such information.

30 [1988] IR 593.
31 Ibid. per Finlay CJ at p. 65.

32 [1989] IR 753.
33 [1992] ILRM 461.

It was held that such information was not distributed by the representatives of the students' associations involved on behalf of an 'economic operator' established in another member state, but constituted a manifestation of freedom of expression and of freedom to impart and receive information which was independent of the economic activity carried on by clinics in another member state. Consequently, a prohibition on the distribution of such information could not be regarded as a restriction on the freedom to supply services within the meaning of Article 59 of the Treaty of Rome, and was not, therefore, protected. It should be stressed that the restriction on the provision of information on abortion discussed in this case was based on Irish law prior to the *X* case.

As a result of this decision, the Government was prompted to add a Protocol to the Maastricht Treaty which states:

> nothing in the Treaty on the European Union or in the Treaties establishing the European Communities, or in the Treaties or Acts modifying or supplementing those Treaties shall affect the application in Ireland of Article 40.3.3 of the Constitution of Ireland.[34]

These decisions raised the question of whether the right of the defendants to freedom of expression was being infringed. The defendants in the *Attorney General (SPUC (Ireland) Ltd) v. Open Door Counselling Ltd* case referred to above, appealed the decision of the Supreme Court to the European Court of Human Rights on the grounds that the prohibition on the provision of information on pregnancy termination violated Article 10 of the *European Convention for the Protection of Human Rights & Fundamental Freedoms*.

In the appeal, (reported as *Open Door Counselling Ltd and Dublin Well Woman Centre Ltd v. Ireland*)[35] the European Court of Human Rights held that the prohibition on information and assistance to pregnant women in regard to obtaining pregnancy terminations abroad was a violation of Article 10 of the European Convention. The court held by 15 votes to 8 that the protection afforded by Irish law to the right to life of the unborn was based on profound moral values concerning the nature of life which were reflected in the stance of the majority of the Irish people against abortion, as expressed in the 1983 referendum. The restriction thus pursued the legitimate aim of the protection of morals of which the protection in Ireland of the right to life of the unborn was one aspect. However, the Court went on to state that the discretion of Ireland in the field of the protection of morals was not unfettered and unreviewable. The national authorities enjoyed a wide margin

---

34 Protocol No. 17 to the Treaty on European Union of 7 February 1992. See further discussion in G. Hogan & G. Whyte, *J.M. Kelly's Irish Constitution,* 3rd ed.) (Butterworth Dublin, 1994), p. 795-796.

35 [1992] 15 EHRR 244.

of appreciation in matters of morals, particularly in areas such as the present one, which concerned matters of belief about the nature of human life. However that margin of appreciation was not unlimited. The court was struck by the absolute nature of the Supreme Court's injunction, which imposed a perpetual restraint on the provision of information to pregnant women concerning abortion facilities abroad, regardless of the woman's age, state of health, or reasons for seeking counselling on the termination of pregnancy. The court concluded that on that ground alone, the restriction appeared too broad and disproportionate.

In the wake of the Supreme Court decision in the *X* case, which revealed that Article 40.3.3 did not impose a total ban on the provision of pregnancy termination services in the state, the question of the provision of information was further clouded. If abortion were legal in Ireland, albeit in limited circumstances, could counselling which included the abortion option, or indeed the distribution of information on preganancy termination services, be considered repugnant to the law?

In the subsequent referendum on the issues of pregnancy termination, the right to travel, and the right to information, the electorate accepted the proposed amendment to Article 40.3 in relation to the right to disseminate information on pregnancy termination. This clause, which became the 14th Amendment to the Constitution, states that:

> Subsection 3 of this section shall not limit freeedom to obtain or make available, in the state, subject to such conditions as may be laid down by law, information relating to services in another state.

Confusion still reigned as to the exact status of the 14th Amendment in relation to information. In the light of the *X* case, and the amendment in relation to information, the defendants (Open Door Counselling and the Well Woman Centre) who had been the subject of the Supreme Court injunction in the case of *Attorney General (SPUC (Ireland) Ltd) v. Open Door Counselling*,[36] applied to the Supreme Court to overturn that decision injucting them from assisting pregnant women to travel abroad for terminations, or from giving information on pregnancy termination services outside the State. In this application, reported as *Attorney General (SPUC (Ireland) Ltd. v. Open Door Counselling and Dublin Well Woman Centre*,[37] the second named defendant claimed that the restraints contained in the Supreme Court order were not now maintainable following the Constitutional Amendments. The plaintiff contended that the Supreme Court Order should remain in force until legislation was introduced to deal with the

36 [1988] IR 593.
37 ILT Digest, in *Irish Law Times* (1994), Vol. 12, No. 8, p 204; also reported at [1994] 1 ILRM 256.

implementation of the 14th Amendment to the Constitution. The Supreme Court refused the application, holding that this application should have been brought before the High Court in the first instance. The Court stated that under the terms of Article 34 of the Constitution, the Supreme Court is a court of appeal only, and does not have any originating jurisdiction of any kind other than that expressly provided for in Article 12.3 and Article 26.

Denham J gave the only dissenting judgment in the case, holding that what was at issue was whether an extant order of the Supreme Court which was contrary to the Constitution should stand. She was satisfied that it should not. She said that the Supreme Court has an original (non-appellate) jurisdiction which is explicit under Articles 12.3 and 26 of the Constitution, and an implicit jurisdiction in certain rare instances to determine an issue not decided by the High Court.[38] The Supreme Court has an inherent jurisdiction that justice should be done and that the Constitution, and constitutional rights are not circumvented. The absence of legislation giving effect to the constitutional right to freedom of information, and to travel, does not nullify or postpone the constitutional right.

Following this case, the Attorney General, in a letter to the Council For the Status of Women, stated that the Order of the Supreme Court in the original case of *Attorney General (SPUC (Ireland) Ltd) v. Open Door Counselling Ltd*,[39] was correct when it was made, that is, before the decision in the *X* case. ' . . . But that it is now inconsistent with the Constitution because of the amendments'.[40] It has been reported that the Government has prepared a bill in relation to freedom of information in respect of pregancy termination.[41] The Bill, if passed, would give legislative form to the 14th Amendment to the Constitution. As presently drafted, the Bill would allow for advertisements in journals detailing the names, addresses, and telephone numbers of clinics outside Ireland which offer pregnancy termination services, advertisements giving details of public meetings at which abortion would be discussed, and consultations between a doctor and a woman contemplating termination of pregancy whereby the doctor may make an appointment for the woman if she decides to seek a termination of her pregnancy abroad. The Bill would prohibit advertising of pregnancy termination information in the form of leaflets distributed in the streets, home delivered mail shots, and large-scale poster displays. The Bill would also outlaw any advertising which attempted to persuade women to seek

---

38 See *State (Browne) v. Feran* [1967] IR 147; *Murphy v. Attorney General* [1982] IR 241; *K.D. (C.) v. M.C.* [1985] IR 697; *B. v. B.* [1975] IR 54.
39 [1988] IR 593.
40 *Irish Times*, 6 August 1993.

41 See J. Joyce, 'Revealed: Details of Bill On Abortion' *Sunday Tribune*, 3 June 1994; M.M. Tynan 'Bill would let doctors make appointments for abortions abroad', *Irish Times*, 4 June 1994.

terminations of pregnancy, and medical or other counselling that seeks to persuade rather than to inform. The Bill is expected to be introduced to the Dáil in the current parliamentary session.

STERILISATION

The process of sterilisation has as its end the cessation of the human reproductive function.[42] It is also known as surgical contraception.[43] The crucial difference between surgical contraception and the use of contraceptive devices is that the former is irreversible. We consider here the process of male sterilisation (vasectomy) and also female sterilisation involving procedures either tying and dividing or removing the Fallopian tubes.

Sterilisation is not regulated by statute in Ireland. However the operation is available on a limited basis. The fact that some hospitals expressly profess to a Roman Catholic ethos, may account for the limited availability of this service.

Roman Catholic doctrine views sterilisation as the deliberate destruction of the procreative function and as such is not generally permissible. Nonetheless, the doctrine of double effect allows for sterilisation in circumstances where it will benefit the life or health of the individual; it is argued that in such an instance the intention of the doctor is to benefit the health of the person involved and not to sterilise *per se*.

There is a question whether such limitations on the availability of treatment (unless exclusively justifiable as contra-indicated for medical reasons) in institutions which are in part funded by the State, should be allowed, given that the personal rights articles of the Constitution have been interpreted to allow freedom of procreative choice.[44]

On the ground, the position is somewhat different. In 1991, in 11 public and private hospitals, 1745 sterilisations were carried out. In addition, 220 such procedures were carried out in one private clinic, and 150 in Clane General Hospital, Co. Kildare, according to a survey by the Irish Association of Family Planning Doctors.

This body stated that the criteria varied from hospital to hospital, from 'extremely restrictive' to 'very liberal'. Since that survey was done, female sterilisations have markedly increased at the Coombe Hospital, which altered its guidelines in 1992. From a figure of 58 procedures in 1991, the figure rose to 225 in 1992.

---

42 Joan E. Mulligan, 'Professional Transition: Nurse to Nurse Midwife', *Nursing Outlook* (1976), Vol. 24, No, 4, pp. 228-33.
43 See A. Haverty, 'Don't Say Sterilisation, Say Surgical Contraception', *Irish Times*, 28 August 1982.
44 *McGee v. Attorney General* [1974] IR 284.

The new guidelines for the Coombe Hospital are worth quoting. They permit sterilisations if:

(1) in the stated opinion of a consultant obstetrician/gynaecologist, a future pregnancy would result in undue risk to the physical health of a woman.

(2) in the stated opinion of a consultant obstetrician/gynaecologist, a future pregnancy would have a serious psychological impact on a woman's health.

(3) in the stated opinion of a consultant obstetrician/gynaecologist, a future pregnancy would be unlikely to conclude successfully due to fetal problems.[45]

STERILISATION OF THE MENTALLY HANDICAPPED

The issue of sterilisation gives rise to even more contentious legal and ethical dilemmas when the procedure is carried out on an individual who cannot give valid consent to this procedure. Thus, in the case of the mentally handicapped female, sterilisation procedures are carried out on her for no other reason than that the law deems it to be in her best interests. The notion of non-consensual sterilisation with its connotations of eugenics is indeed an undesirable one. What justification then do courts offer for condoning non-consenual sterilisations, and what if any are the legal arguments against such a procedure? In the absence of a developed jurisprudence on the issue in Ireland, one must look to the approach of the judiciary in other common law jurisdictions in order to proffer an opinion on the possible approach of the Irish judiciary to the question.

As part of their programme for the 'improvement' of the human race, eugenicists have advocated the compulsory sterilisation of certain groups in society. Such groups included, amongst others, the mentally handicapped. In America in the early part of this century such ideas were in vogue among many advocates of social reform. Such ideas eventually were included in the compulsory sterilisation statutes of many US states. By the 1920s, twenty-eight states had passed legislation providing for the sterilisation of the mentally handicapped.[46] In 1927 the constitutionality of one such statute came before the US Supreme Court for review, in the case of *Buck v. Bell*.[47]

---

45 *Irish Medical Times* (1993), Vol. 27, No. 21 (21 May), p. 10, Id. (1993), Vol. 27, No. 23 (4 June) p. 11.
46 M. Sherlock & J. Sherlock 'Sterilizing The Retarded: Constitutional Statutory and Policy Alternatives', *National Civil Liberties Review* (1982), Vol. 60, p. 943.
47 (1927) 274 US 200.

In that case the compulsory sterilisation statute of the state of Virginia was challenged on the grounds that it violated procedural and substantive due process as well as the equal protection rights of the handicapped. The challenge failed and the court was seen to be wholeheartedly in favour of the eugenics movement as the judgment of Holmes J shows:

> [i]t is better for all the world, if instead of waiting to execute degenerate offspring for crime, or to let them starve for their imbecility, society can prevent those who are manifestly unfit from continuing their kind. The principle that sustains compulsory vaccination is broad enough to cover cutting the Fallopian tubes . . . Three generations of imbeciles are enough.[48]

Today, although the *Buck* decision has not been overruled, US courts are reluctant to order the sterilisation of the mentally handicapped in the absence of specific legislative provision. Thus, in *In re Guardianship of Tully*[49] it was stated that 'the awesome power to deprive a human being of his or her fundamental right to bear or beget offspring must be based on the explicit authorisation by the legislature'.[50]

Nonetheless, other courts have been willing to order the sterilisation of the mentally handicapped, using as a justification for so doing, the court's inherent jurisdiction, either by way of the doctrine of *parens patriae* or otherwise.[51]

The origin of the *parens patriae* jurisdiction over the mentally incompetent is 'lost in the mists of antiquity' according to the commentator Sir Henry Theobald, in his book *The Law Relating To Lunacy* (1924). *De Prerogativa Regis*, an instrument regarded as a statute that dates from the late thirteenth century, recognised the Crown's *parens patriae* jurisdiction, but did not create it. Theobald speculates that 'the most probable theory [of its origin] is that either by general assent or by some statute, now lost, the care of persons of unsound mind was taken from the feudal lords by Edward I, who would naturally take possession of the land of a tenant unable to perform his feudal duties.[52] So in the 1540s the *parens patriae* jurisdiction was transferred to the Court of Wards and Liveries, where it remained until that court was wound up in 1660. From 1660, the crown exercised its jurisdiction through the Lord Chancellor, to whom, by letters patent, under the sign manual procedure, was granted the care and custody of the persons and the estate of persons of unsound mind.

By the early part of the nineteenth century, the work arising out of the

48 Ibid., p. 207.
49 (1978), 146 Cal Rptr 266 (CA).
50 Ibid., p. 270.
51 See *Stump v. Sparkman* (1978) 435 US 349.
52 See Theobald, op. cit., p. 1.

Lord Chancellor's jurisdiction became more than one judge could handle, and the Chancery court was re-organised and the work reassigned to several justices.

In 1852, under the Act for the Relief of the suitors of the High Court of Chancery, the jurisdiction of the Lord Chancellor regarding 'the custody of the persons and estates of persons found idiot, lunatic, or of unsound mind' was authorised to be exercised by anyone for the time being entrusted by virtue of the sign manual.

The *parens patriae* jurisdiction was entrusted to the courts of equity after the Supreme Court of Judicature (Ireland) Act 1877. In the US, The majority of state courts before which the matter has been raised have held that they have equitable authority in the absence of statute to order such sterilisations.[53] In such cases courts have adopted two different approaches, that is, the 'best interests' and the 'substituted judgement' approaches, discussed in Chapter 8. It has been argued by Cooney[54] that Irish courts would appear to possess such inherent jurisdiction in relation to the ordering or otherwise of sterilisations of the mentally handicapped. Article 34 of the constitution gives the High Court full jurisdiction on all matters of law and fact. Also the personal rights articles of the Constitution place a duty on the courts to uphold the rights of the individual. In *In re Application by The Midland Health Board*[55] it was held by the Supreme Court that a person of unsound mind could be made a ward of court even though such a person has no property. Finlay CJ held that such jurisdiction sprang from the court's duty to protect individual rights under Article 40.3 of the Constitution.

Cooney argues that applications to authorise the non-voluntary sterilisation of incompetent mentally handicapped persons would seem, logically, 'to be covered by the same protective principle'.[56]

What justification then do courts offer for condoning non-consenual sterilisations, and what if any are the legal arguments against such a procedure?

In the UK, the judicial trend is in favour of such procedures. The case of *In re D (A minor) (Wardship: Sterilisation)*[57] brought the issue to legal prominence there. This case, unlike later decisions, held against the sterilisation of an eleven year old girl. The girl in question suffered from

---

53 See *In re Guardianship of Eberhardy* (1981) 307 NW 2d 881 (Wisc SC); *In re Grady* (1981) 426 A 2d 467 (NJSC); *In re CDM* (1981), 627 P 2d 607 (Alaska SC); *In re Moe* (1982), 432 NE 2d 712 (Mass SC).

54 T. Cooney, 'Sterilisation and the men-

tally handicapped', *Dublin University Law Journal* (ns) (1989), Vol. 11, p. 56.

55 [1988] ILRM 251.

56 T. Cooney 'Sterilisation and the mentally handicapped', *Dublin University Law Journal* (ns) (1989), Vol. 11, p. 56.

57 [1976] Fam 185; [1976] 1 All ER 326.

Soto's syndrome which manifested itself in personality dysfunction, epileptic fits, and intellectual dysfunction. The child's mother was of the opinion that the child should be sterilised, citing such reasons as the risk that the child could in the future give birth to a physically or mentally defective child, that D's epilepsy might cause her to injure the baby and that in the circumstances the only appropriate form of birth control would be sterilisation. There was evidence however that D's condition might improve slightly and that it was not beyond the bounds of possibility that she could successfully care for a child. Heilbron J was of the opinion that sterilisation was not the appropriate solution in this case, stating that:

> . . . where the evidence shows that her mental and physical condition and attainments have already improved, and where her future prospects are as yet unpredictable, where the evidence also shows that she is unable as yet to understand and appreciate the implications of this operation and could not give valid or informed consent, that the likelihood is that in later years she will be able to make her own choice, where, I believe, the frustration and resentment of realising (as she would one day) what happened could be devastating, an operation of this nature is, in my view contra-indicated.[58]

Heilbron J also drew the distinction between therapeutic and non-therapeutic sterilisations. Thus, she contended that the decision to carry out a sterilisation for non-therapeutic purposes was not a decision which lay with the doctor alone. As a result, the intervention of the law was necessary to decide on the validity of such a procedure.

Given subsequent judicial pronouncements on the issue, *In re D* can be taken as but a brief nod in the direction of the reproductive autonomy of the mentally handicapped. In 1987 the House of Lords came to decide on the issue in the case of *In re B (A Minor) (Wardship: Sterilisation)*.[59] In this case, a seventeen year old mentally handicapped girl was the subject of an application by her local authority to have her made a ward of court and for leave to allow her to undergo a sterilisation operation. The child's mother was in favour of such a course of action. The House of Lords held that it was in the best interests of the girl to undergo such an operation. Referring to Heilbron J's statement in *In re D* to the effect that the sterilisation operation in such a case would amount to the deprivation of a basic human right,[60] the House of Lords came to the conclusion that because B was unable to appreciate the existence and significance of such a right that in

58 Ibid. at p. 213.
59 [1987] 2 All ER 206.
60 Ibid., p. 214.

effect this right did not inhere in her. Thus, Lord Hailsham states that the significant difference between the case of *In re D* and the present case was in terms of degree. Because D's condition was not as severe as that of B, Lord Hailsham claimed, this was justification for the conflicting decisions in both cases. In effect what the House of Lords decision is saying is that certain individuals, due to their mental incapacity, are not capable of appreciating or conceptualising the significance of a particular human right and as such are not capable of enjoying this right.

Lord Hailsham appealed to reality in arguing against the reproductive right inhering in such an individual:

> [t]o talk of the 'basic right' to reproduce of an individual who is not capable of knowing the causal connection between intercourse and childbirth, the nature of pregnancy, what is involved in delivery, unable to form maternal instincts or to care for a child appears to me wholly to part company with reality.[61]

It must be suggested that to argue, as the House of Lords does in this case, that these particular rights should not be accorded to certain members of society is unsatisfactory. Such persons are human, and (it could be argued) as such, are entitled to the deprivation of these rights only in the most convincing and uniform circumstances. Michael Freeman takes a contrasting view to that adopted by the judgments in this case.[62] Freeman, in an argument that the present authors find convincing, favours the model of rights which:

> [a]ccepts that rights may conflict with each other, in which case the preferred solution is one which maximises the fulfilment of rights and minimises their violations.[63]

This model is antithetical to the model which the House of Lords appears to be espousing in this case, a model which would as Freeman states:

> adopt a conception of rights as a very important interest, weighted as against other calculations. As such it could be knocked off its pedestal by a goal of special urgency.[64]

---

61 Ibid., p. 213.
62 M.D.A. Freeman, 'Sterilising the mentally handicapped' in M.D.A. Freeman (ed.), *Medicine Ethics and The Law* (Current Legal Problems, Stevens, London, 1988).
63 Ibid., p. 77.
64 Id.

The House of Lords' reason for 'knocking B's right to reproduce off its pedestal' was that in doing so it was acting in the perceived best interests of the individual in question. Such a reason, it may be argued, is unconvincing, because judicial perceptions of 'best interests' tend to differ from judge to judge, and from time to time. Such approaches, no matter how well-intentioned, are the *apotheosis* of a particular philosophical stance, that stance being paternalism. The 'best interests' are thus what the court representing a particular viewpoint believes is the best interest of the individual.

It is thus interesting to look at how a court in the common law system in a substantially similar fact situation can arrive at a diametrically opposing solution. In the Canadian Supreme Court case of *In re Eve*[65] the question was whether a mentally retarded adult female, Eve, should undergo an involuntary sterilisation operation. La Forest J, for the court, made the distinction between therapeutic and non-therapeutic sterilisation, stating that:

> [t]he grave intrusion on a person's rights and the certain physical damage that ensues from non-therapeutic sterilisation without consent, when compared to the highly questionable advantages that can result from it, have persuaded me that it can never safely be determined that such a procedure is for the benefit of that person. Accordingly, procedure should never be authorised for non-therapeutic purposes under the *parens patriae* jurisdiction.[66]

La Forest J went on to state that the proper forum to rule on this was the legislature and not the courts. He spoke of the lack of knowledge of the judiciary of the concept of mental illness and the fact that the legislature is:

> . . . in a position to inform itself and it is attuned to the feelings of the public in making policy in this sensitive area.[67]

Thus the Canadian Supreme Court has recognised, unlike the House of Lords, the inherent right of the mentally handicapped to procreate and indeed adverted to the dangers of treating the mentally handicapped as less than human. In this the judgment is similar to that of Heilbron J in the case of *In re D*. Indeed La Forest J in *In re Eve* takes the same stance as Heilbron J even though dealing with the case of a mentally handicapped adult.

---

65 (1986) 31 DLR (4th) 1.
66 ibid. at p. 32.

67 Id., p. 33.

[T]he importance of maintaining the physical integrity of a human being ranks high in our scale of values, particularly as it affects the privilege of giving life. I cannot agree that a court can deprive a woman of that privilege for purely social or other non-therapeutic purposes without her consent. The fact that others may suffer inconvenience or hardship from failure to do so cannot be taken into account.[68]

Both La Forest J and Heilbron J were of the opinion that the sterilisation of those who are not capable of giving consent may only be carried out if it is required for *bona fide* medical treatment. Again because of the importance of the right protected, such therapeutic sterilisations should only be performed where:

such treatment is necessary in dealing with a serious condition.[69]

This approach to the protection of individual rights was further rejected by the House of Lords in the case of *F. v. West Berkshire Health Authority and another (Mental Health Act Commission intervening)*.[70] This case gave the opportunity to the House of Lords to pronounce on the validity of ordering the sterilisation of a mentally handicapped adult. The person involved was thirty-six years of age and it was established that she had a verbal capacity of a child of two and the mental capacity of a child of four to five. F had developed a relationship with a male patient at the hospital at which she was an in-patient. The hospital authorities were concerned about the consequences of a sexual relationship between F and the other patient. The House of Lords came to the conclusion that a sterilisation operation should be allowed in the circumstances. The Court considered that a difference arose in the case of a mentally incompetent adult, as opposed to a mentally incompetent minor. Unlike the case of a minor, the court, in the case of an adult, could not purport to make such an order in exercise of its *parens patriae* jurisdiction. In England that jurisdiction no longer governs the affairs of a mentally incompetent adult, since the Mental Health Act 1959,[71] and the revocation by warrant under the sign manual procedure

68 Id., p. 33.
69 Id., p. 34.
70 [1989] 2 All ER 545.
71 S. 1 of which provides: 'Subject to the transitional provisions contained in this Act, the Lunacy and Mental Treatment Acts 1890 to 1930, and the Mental Deficiency Acts 1913 to 1938, shall cease to have effect, and the following provisions of this Act shall have effect in lieu of those enactments with respect to the reception, care and treatment of mentally disordered patients, the management of their property, and other matters related thereto.' See in addition B. Hoggett, 'The Royal Prerogative in Relation to the Mentally Disordered: Resurrection, Resuscitation or Rejection' in M.D.A. Freeman (ed.), *Medicine, Ethics and The Law*, op. cit.

of the last warrant dated 10 April 1956. By this, the jurisdiction of the Crown over the persons and property of the mentally incompetent had been assigned to the Lord Chancellor and the Chancery Division of the High Court.

Nonetheless, the court declared that it had an inherent jurisdiction to make a declaration in relation to the sterilisation of a mentally handicapped adult. In addition, the court held that while such a declaration was not strictly necessary in order to make such a procedure lawful, in practice an application should be made to a court before such treatment was undertaken as it would establish by judicial process whether the operation was in the individual's best interests and therefore lawful.

Unlike the Canadian Supreme Court, the House of Lords chose to treat the issue as one which was susceptible to resolution by the courts. In addition, the philosophical approach which the House of Lords took was that of 'best interests'. Again, as with Lord Hailsham's decision in *In re B.*, the best interests here appear to be those of others such as parents and medical professionals rather than the interests of the individual on whom the operation would be performed. The focus in *F.* tended to be fixed on the peripheral issues of the jurisdiction of the court to declare the carrying out of such an operation and the interests of third parties rather than on the rights of the individual concerned.

Thus, Lord Goff applied the common law concept of necessity to the situation.[72] At common law, necessity provides a defence to a doctor who operates on a patient who is incapable of giving consent if it can be demonstrated that the operation is in the best interests of the patient. The language of Lord Goff is framed in paternalistic terms when he speaks of the best interests of the individual concerned.

> [N]o doubt, in practice, a decision may involve others beside the doctor. It must surely be good practice to consult relatives and others who are concerned with the care of the patient . . . [*sic*] . . . the overriding consideration is that they should act in the best interests of the person who suffers from the misfortune of being prevented by incapacity from deciding for himself what should be done to his own body in his own best interests.[73]

The necessity argument is quite tenuous in respect of a non-therapeutic sterilisation. The defence of necessity would apply in cases of genuine

---

72 Ibid., pp. 564-7. 73 Ibid., p. 567.

medical necessity. It is doubtful that one could place a non-therapeutic sterilisation in the category of a medical necessity. Indeed La Forest J in *In re Eve* stated (quoting a Law Reform of Canada Working Paper on sterilisation)[74] as follows:

> [s]terilisation as a medical procedure is distinct, because except in rare cases, if the operation is not performed, the physical health of the person involved is not in danger, necessity or emergency not normally being factors in the decision to undertake the procedure.

Thus, one can conclude that the particular philosophical approach adopted by the judiciary will affect to a material degree the outcome of such a case. The 'best interests' model as espoused by Lord Hailsham in *In re B.* and Lord Goff in *F.* tends to uphold the interests of those other than the patient whereas the approach of Heilbron, J in *in re D.* and La Forest J in *In re Eve* recognises the right to reproductive autonomy of the mentally handicapped.

The issue of non-therapeutic sterilisation of the mentally handicapped has not come to be decided before the courts of Ireland, nor indeed does any legislation exist in relation to it. Therefore, if such a case ever arose for decision before the Irish courts, it is to be hoped that the position taken in *In re Eve* will be adopted.

IN-VITRO FERTILISATION

In-vitro fertilisation (IVF)[75] has not been regulated by statute in Ireland, nor has it come for consideration before the courts. It has been accepted by the Irish Medical Council that the method of IVF is a significant advance

---

74 The Law Reform Commission of Canada, *Sterilization*, Working Paper 24 (Ottawa, Canada, 1979).

75 IVF is the procedure whereby fertilisation occurs outside the body. Fertilisation in fact occurs in a small glass dish, known as a petri-dish, hence the Latin description of the process 'in vitro' as opposed to the more traditional means of fertilisation 'in vivo' in the body. The procedure involves extracting a ripe human egg or ovum from the ovary shortly before it would have been released naturally. Ultrasound is used to place a needle through the wall of the abdomen and over a ripe follicle in the ovary. The ovum Is flushed from the ovary into a receiving tube. The ovum is then frozen. It is common practice to extract more than one ovum to increase the possibility of a successful pregnancy. In order to stimulate the production of several ripe eggs in one cycle, the woman may undergo a course of hormone treatment. The ovum is kept in the frozen state until it matures fully. Fertilisation is the next step in the process. The mature ova are placed in a petri-dish, where they are mixed with male sperm. The hope is that at

in the treatment of certain cases of infertility. It has accepted the guidelines promulgated by the Institute of Obstetricians and Gynaecologists of the Royal College of Physicians of Ireland.

Guidelines exist for physicians practising IVF. Within the framework proposed by the Institute of Obstetricians and Gynaecologists,[76] therapeutic application of IVF is acceptable. Experimentation on fertilised embryos at any stage of development, or the storage or freezing of spare embryos is unacceptable. It is emphasised that IVF is a clinical technique used for the treatment of selected cases of human infertility: in no circumstances should it be used to produce or store human embryos for research purposes. According to the Institute, the method is most suitable for treatment of the woman who has a normal uterus and produces healthy eggs but has damaged, diseased or absent fallopian tubes. IVF in these circumstances may be the appropriate treatment for about 5% of infertile couples. Recent claims that IVF may be used to treat other causes of infertility such as reduced or defective sperm have still to be confirmed but if substantiated, could lead to the use of IVF in a larger percentage of cases of infertility.

The guidelines provide that the technique of IVF should be offered to married couples who have been appropriately counselled, understand the method and give informed consent. All fertilised embryos produced by IVF should be replaced in the potential mother's uterus. Only sperms and eggs from the consenting couple will be used in all IVF procedures.

The national centre for IVF is based in the Human Assisted Reproduction Institute at the Rotunda Hospital, Dublin. Approximately 300 women receive IVF treatment there annually.[77] The treatment is free to medical card holders, and costs about £1,500 in the case of private patients.[78]

---

least one of the sperm will penetrate the egg, causing it to be fertilised. A number of days are allowed to be passed in order to enable fertilisation to take place. If fertilisation occurs, a further number of days are allowed to elapse so that the embryo may develop. It is then that the embryo is transferred into the womb, using a speculum, a thin tube which is pushed through the vagina. The embryo is injected down this tube, through the vagina into the womb. Several days will then elapse before one can determine whether the embryo has embedded itself in the womb lining, and pregnancy has commenced.

76 'Institute of Obstetricians and Gynaecologists. In-Vitro Fertilisation' in *A Guide to Ethical Conduct and Behaviour and to Fitness To Practice*, 4th ed. (Medical Council, Dublin, 1994) pp. 36-7, and Appendix G, pp. 62-63.

77 Over the last three years, the unit in the Rotunda Hospital has had a 34% take-home baby rate. In 1992, IVF cycles were undergone in 188 couples with a 32.9 pregnancy rate achieved. Irish Medical Times, Vol. 27, No. 47 (19 November 1993) p. 2. See also Ed. O'Loughlin, 'Medical Council Would Forbid Post-Menopausal Mothers', *Irish Times*, 29 December 1993, p. 4.

78 Ibid. See also F. Bowers, 'The GIFT of life', *Irish Medical News* (1993) Vol. 10, No. 25 (28 June) p. 8.

SURROGACY

Surrogacy is the term given to the procedure whereby an infertile woman and her partner arrange with another woman that she will carry a child conceived by artificial insemination with the husband's semen and hand the child over to the child's genetic father after birth. The process may also be carried out by creating an embryo in-vitro from the gametes of a husband and wife, which is then implanted in the womb of a surrogate mother.

Surrogacy is neither regulated nor prohibited in Ireland by specific legislative provisions. Nevertheless, at common law, it is clear that an agreement for surrogate motherhood is against public policy, since it is a purported contract for the sale and purchase of a child. In the United States, the New Jersey Supreme Court in *In the matter of Baby M* ruled that surrogacy contracts are not enforceable. Wilentz J, in delivering the judgment, stated that the court invalidated:

> the surrogacy contract because it conflicts with the law and public policy of this state. While we recognise the depth of the yearning of infertile couples to have their own children, we find payment of money to a surrogate mother illegal, perhaps criminal, and potentially degrading to women.[79]

However, note the differing approach taken in *Johnson v. Calvert*,[80] where the Supreme Court of California upheld a surrogacy agreement between biological parents and a gestational surrogate mother. The dispositive factor for the court was the intent of the parties to the agreement, which was clearly that the gestational surrogate mother deliver the child to the biological parents, in exchange for a payment. The court concluded that the gestational surrogate mother had no parental rights to the child, as agreed. The court did not see surrogacy agreements on their face as contrary to public policy. Thus, like other contracts, they may be enforceable. It is not anticipated that this approach will be taken by the Irish courts.It is submitted that a substantially similar approach would be taken by the Irish courts if this matter were to be brought before them.

ARTIFICAL INSEMINATION

Artificial insemination can be accomplished by either of two methods. Artificial insemination by donor (AID) involves obtaining semen from a donor who is not the woman's husband and injecting it into the woman.

79 537 A 2d 1227 NJ (1988).   80 (1993) 5 Cal 4th 84.

This method is used where the husband is infertile. Artificial insemination by husband (AIH) occurs where the husband's semen is introduced into his wife's uterus by injection. This method is used where the couple's inability to conceive is not due to the infertility of the husband.

In some cases the couple in which the husband is infertile would still like to believe that the ovum may have been fertilised by the husband's sperm. In such cases the semen of the husband and the semen of the donor is mixed together and is then injected into the woman. This is known as artificial insemination by donor and husband (AIDH).

In the United Kingdom, the Human Fertilisation and Embryology Act 1990 provides for the legal status of children conceived by such processes. S. 27 of the act provides that the birth mother is to be the mother in the legal sense. S. 28(2) provides that the husband of a woman medically assisted to carry a child will be treated in law as the father unless he did not consent to the assistance. A man who donates sperm may be excused from parenthood under the provisions of s. 28(6) of the act.

In Ireland, there are no specific legislative provisions in relation to artificial insemination in humans.

PRENATAL DIAGNOSIS (GENETICS IN GENERAL)

Medical technology now enables the identification of parents whose offspring will be at high risk of certain genetic diseases. Such parents may be faced with a choice as to whether the pregnancy should continue. In Ireland, given the specific protection accorded the foetus in the Constitution, such parents would be unable to choose the option of terminating the pregnancy.

Prior to 1994, there was no full medical genetics service, supervised by a consultant in medical genetics. In 1988, the holder of a medical geneticist post in Temple Street Hospital, Dublin, resigned because she claimed the service was underfunded. She obtained a post in Trinity College Dublin.

In July 1994, Our Lady's Hospital in Crumlin set up a laboratory, and a consultant post in this speciality. A new neurogenetic facility has also begun at the Adelaide Hospital, Dublin, whereby predictive testing is carried out on patients over eighteen, to assess the potential risk of inheriting neurological conditions.[81]

This genetic counselling service takes the form of non-directive counselling session(s). This form of couselling is based on the client-centred therapy of Carl Rogers developed in the 1940s.[82] Rogers believed that the

---

81 *Irish Medical Times* (1993), Vol. 27, No. 17 (23 April), p. 12; (1994), Vol. 28, No. 21 (27 May) p. 9.

82 See C.R. Rogers, *Counselling and psychotherapy: new concepts in practice* (Houghton

relationship of therapist and patient (or as Rogers termed it, the 'client') should be based on equality. The therapist should not tell the patient what treatment he should follow in his best interests. Rather, the therapist should endeavour to help the patient or client help himself. The essence of non-directive counselling is that the therapist does not directly advise the patient, but endeavours to draw out the patient's true feelings on a particular issue. Thus the director should not allow his personal views on a particular treatment option to colour the therapeutic relationship. This is especially true in the area of genetic counselling, where one of the options which is open to the patient on discovering that the foetus has a genetic disease, is pregnancy termination. In Ireland, pregnancy termination is only permissible in order to preserve the life or health of the mother if at all.[83] The judiciary's approach to non-directive counselling in the context of abortion is discussed in the section on preganany termination and the right to information, on p. 185. It is to be hoped that the proposed legislation on pregnancy termination and freedom of information will be introduced in the near future in order to end confusion in this area of the law.[84]

PATENTABILITY OF GENETIC MATERIAL

S. 10 of the Patents Act 1992 states that a plant or animal variety or an essentially biological process for the production of plants or animals other than a microbiological process or the products thereof is not patentable.

This wording reflects the exception to patentability found in Article 53(b) of the European Patent Convention of the 5 October 1973, which states that patents shall not be given to '(b) . . . plant or animal varieties or essentially biological processes for the production of plants or animals; this provision does not apply to microbiological processes or to products thereof'.

Thus under s. 10(b) and Article 53(b) microbiological processes and their products are patentable. However it is no longer certain if the prohibition of the patenting of animals is definite. This doubt comes about as the result

Mifflin, Boston, Mass. 1942); C.R. Rogers, *On becoming a person: a therapist's view of psychotherapy* (Houghton Mifflin, Boston, Mass, 1961).

83 *Attorney General v. X* [1992] 1 IR 1. See p. 155 and ff..

84 See for a discussion of this area *inter alia*, G.R. Dunstan, 'Screening for foetal and genetic abnormality: social and ethical issues', *Journal of Medical Genetics* (1988), Vol. 25, No. 5, pp. 290-3; R. Gillon, 'Genetic Counselling, Confidentiality and The Medical Interests of Relatives', *Journal of Medical Ethics* (1988), Vol. 14, No. 4, 171-172; B.M. Dickens 'Pre-natal Diagnosis and Female Abortion: A Case Study in Medical Law and Ethics', *Journal of Medical Ethics* (1986) Vol. 12, p. 143; 'Conference Report on the Workshop of The Commission of the European Communities on ethics of human genome analysis: Survey of the European Discussion', *Journal of Medical Genetics* (1993), Vol. 30, No. 3. p. 257

of a decision of the Technical Board of Appeal of the European Patent Office. In the case of *HARVARD/Oncomouse*[85] it was held by the Technical Board of Appeal that Article 53(b) of the European Patent Convention did not prohibit the patenting of animals as a whole. The Board stated that there was a distinction between animal varieties and other animals, in relation to patentability. They based this on the wording employed in Article 53(b). The wording of the European Patent Convention appears in three languages – English, French and German. Article 177(1) of the European Patent Convention provides that the English French and German texts are all equally authentic.

The texts of Article 53(b) appears as follows:

European Patents shall not be granted in respect of . . .

(b) plant or animal varieties or essentially biological processes for the production of plants or animals'.

(b) les varietes vegetales ou les races animales ainsi que les procedes essentiellement biologiques d'obtention de vegetaux ou d'animaux;

(b) Pflanzensorten oder Tierarten sowie fur im wesentlichen biologische Verfahren zur Zuchtung von Pflanzen oder Tieren.

Thus, the Board points out the reference to both animals (*animaux, Tiere*) and animal varieties (*races animales, Tierarten*) would lead to a distinction between both concepts. The Board was of the opinion that animals as such were not excluded from patentability and that animal varieties were. The Board remitted the case to the Examining Division of the European Patent Office. The Examining Division held that the onco-mouse, defined as:

a transgenic non-human mammalian animal whose germ cells and somatic cells contain an activated oncogene sequence introduced into said animal, or an ancestor of said animal, at a stage not later that the 8 cell stage, said oncogene optionally being further defined according to any one of claims 3-10

did not constitute an animal variety.

On this point, an amount of uncertainty has arisen due to the tenuous distinction between the words 'animal' and 'animal variety'. Applying this view to s. 10(b) of the Irish Act, then animals as such would appear to be patentable. The Oncomouse patent was granted in October 1991.

---

85 Case Number T 0019/90 [1990] European Patent Office Reports, 501.

In addition to the exception set out in Article 53(b), Article 53(a) states that inventions which are prejudicial to public order and morality are not patentable. The EPO appeals board decided that the role of the oncomouse in advancing cancer research was of such importance to the welfare of mankind that it far outweighed its drawbacks in terms of pain and suffering to the individual mouse, and was not therefore a threat public order or morality.

However, the EPO is currently hearing objections in relation to the granting of the patent and has called an unofficial halt to all animal patents to allow a discussion on the ethical dimensions in relation to the granting of such patents.[86] Critics of the oncomouse patent claim that a healthy mouse might expect a lifespan of 18 months. But a genetically modified oncomouse develops fatal tumours within 6 months of birth. Thus, critics argue that such mice are designed to suffer and that this violates standards of public morality.

TRANSSEXUAL INTERVENTIONS

The transsexual feels an all-consuming desire to become a member of the opposite sex, and feels trapped within an inappropriate sexual persona.

The surgical procedure required to fulfil the desire of the transsexual involves castration in both males and females. In the case of males a synthetic vagina is fitted in place of the original sex organs. However, in females the fitting of a replacement male organ is not feasible.

Some commentators[87] have argued that this is a case where consent is not possible. The argument runs that since the process involves castration, this may constitute 'maim', and 'maim' is a crime at common law. However in England, gender reassignment surgery is carried out quite legally. Within the UK National Health Service, over two thousand people have undergone such surgery.[88] Indeed certain countries have introduced legislation which deals specifically with this topic. Sweden has such legislation on the statute books, which provides that the age of consent for such surgery is eighteen.

However, the recognition of transsexuals in the UK for marriage purposes has not been forthcoming. In the case of *Corbett v. Corbett*,[89] it was held that despite gender reassignment surgery, the transsexual was not

---

86 See Susan Watts, 'Ethics of DNA Ownership Under Scrutiny', *The Independent*, 8 January 1994.

87 See the discussion in D.W. Mayers, *The Human Body and The Law* (Edinburgh University Press, Edinburgh, 1970), ch. 8.

88 J.K. Mason & R.A. McCall Smith, *Law and Medical Ethics*, 2nd ed. (Butterworth, London, 1987).

89 [1970] 2 All ER 33.

a woman for the purposes of marriage and in the eyes of the law was a biological male. It was further held that a transsexual 'wife' was not capable of consummating the marriage by the use of an artificial vagina. The findings in this case were based on the pre-operative gonadal complement, the chromosomal make-up, and genital appearance. These attributes constitute the so-called Ormrod test (after the deciding judge) which is thus purely a biological test for determining sexual identity, based solely on the congruence of the three biological factors we have mentioned in the previous sentence, as at the time of birth of the individual concerned. This test does not take into account the transsexual's psychological sexual identity 'a passionate, lifelong conviction that one's psychological gender – that indefinable feeling of maleness or femaleness – is opposite to one's anatomic sex'.[90]

In view of this non-recognition of the new identity of transsexuals a number of British transsexuals have made applications to the European Court of Human Rights. In the case of *Rees v. United Kingdom*[91] the European Court of Human Rights concluded that the right to marry under Article 12 of the European convention on human rights and fundamental freedoms referred to the traditional marriage between persons of opposite biological sex. Accordingly UK marriage laws did not impair the right under Article 12.

In the subsequent case of *Cossey v. UK*[92] the applicant claimed that under English law she was not free to marry a man and could not realistically marry another woman. This she claimed breached her right to marry under Article 12. The court held however that the criteria of English law were in conformity with the concept to which the right guaranteed by Article 12 referred.

In the UK case of *R. v. Tan & Ors.*[93] the decision was the first in which the sexual identity of a post-operative transsexual was material to a criminal charge. One of the accused, Gloria Greaves, a post-operative female transsexual, was charged with having contravened s. 30 of the Sexual Offences Act 1956. The relevant section provides *inter alia*:

> It is an offence for a man knowingly to live wholly or in part on the earnings of prostitution.

The accused contended that she was a post-operative female and

---

90 M.M. Belli 'Transsexual surgery', *Journal of the American Medical Association* (1978) Vol. 239, p. 2143.
91 [1986] judgment of 17 October 1986 (Plenary session).
92 [1990] (Plenary Court, series A no. 184).
93 [1983] 2 All ER 12.

therefore beyond the scope of the offence. Furthermore she had married a biological male who at all times regarded her as a female. Her counsel urged the court not to apply the decision in *Corbett v. Corbett* to a criminal law issue. However, this argument did not persuade the Court of Appeal which held that:

> both common sense and the desirability of certainty and consistency demand that the decision of *Corbett v. Corbett* should apply not only for marriage but also for a charge under s. 30 of the Sexual Offences Act.[94]

To have found Gloria Greaves to be a female would have led to an acquittal.

The decision has been criticised by J. L-Taitz[95] and by Pace.[96] The facts of the case were not perhaps such as would obviously be calculated to provoke sympathy from a court. The courts' attempt to achieve certainty and consistency between the criminal law and the civil law is, it has been argued, unnecessary, since many other inconsistencies between criminal and civil law exist, which have caused no inordinate legal problems.

In Australia, the courts have taken a different approach to transsexuals, which differs from the Ormrod test, taking into account psychological and related factors.

In *R. v Cogley*,[97] the accused, a biological male, was charged with *inter alia* assault with intent to commit rape with aggravating circumstances on the complainant, who was a post operative transsexual female. For the purposes of the charge, there had to have been an attempt to penetrate the vagina of the complainant. Before the trial court, the defence took the point that being a post-operative female transsexual, the complainant was a male and did not have a vagina for the purposes of the offence. The Supreme Court of Victoria overruled this objection, and instructed the jury that the complainant was a woman and possessed a vagina. Therefore the accused was found guilty of the charge. In giving his reasons for the judgment, Cummins J found that the charge was competent and that:

> the law should regard as a woman, a male to female transsexual where core identity is established (i.e. the psychological personality or character of the person concerned) and where sexual reassignment surgery has taken place.[98]

94 Ibid., p. 18.
95 'Confronting transsexualism, sexual Identity and the criminal law', *Medico Legal Journal* (1992), Vol. 60, Pt. 1, pp. 60-72.
96 'Sexual identity & the criminal law', *Criminal Law Review* 1983, p. 317.
97 (1989) 41 Crim R 198.
98 Ibid., p. 198.

The accused appealed against the conviction on the ground that the trial judge had erred in law in finding that the complainant was a woman and had a vagina capable of being penetrated in circumstances amounting to rape. The Victorian Court of Criminal Appeal agreed in a collegiate judgment, that the trial judge had erred in finding that the complainant was a woman on the ground that sexual identity is a matter of fact which should have been decided by the jury and not by him. Nonetheless it dismissed the appeal. It found that irrespective of the finding by the trial judge that the complainant was a woman there was clear evidence which justified the finding that the accused had intended to rape the complainant who he believed to be a woman and that there was evidence of aggravating circumstances.

The later Australian case of *R. v. Harris & McGuinness*[99] was heard before the Court of Criminal Appeal of New South Wales. It concerned the sexual identity of the two accused who were alleged to have contravened s. 81A of (New South Wales) Crimes Act 1900 which provides:

> whosoever, being a male person, in public or private, commits or is a party to the commission of or procures or attempts to procure the commission by any male person to any act of indecency with another male person shall be liable to imprisonment for two years.

Each of the accused had offered to engage in acts of indecency with male police officers attached to the vice squad, who were acting as 'traps'. There would appear to be no doubt regarding the facts, however, the separate defence of each of the accused, was that they were not 'male persons' in that the first accused, Harris, was a post operative female transsexual, who had undergone 'sex change treatment'. The second accused, McGuinness, was a transsexual female, who, although she had not as yet undergone sex change procedures, considered herself a female. The offence in question, as with the offence in *Tan* can only be committed by males. Accordingly, the central issue before the court was the sexual identity of each of the accused. The majority judgment of the Court of Criminal Appeal answered the following essential question of law stated by the lower court as follows:

> Q.I.A. Is the test laid out in *Corbett v. Corbett* [1971] P 83 and *Tan* [1983] QB 1053 76 Crim App Rep 300 (the Ormrod biological test) the only test to be applied in determining the question of sex in New South Wales, and if not, what other criteria should be considered?

> Answer: No.

99 (1988) 35 Austr Crim Rep 146.

(It is not the only test.)

The other criteria referred to therein should be whether, through medical interaction or otherwise, the person has assumed the external genital features of the opposite sex, thereby bringing those genital features into conformity with the person's psychological sex.

Mathews J rejected the formalistic approach by Ormrod J in *Corbett* and strongly criticised his findings concerning the essential role of woman in marriage. She found that the state of a person's chromosomes can not be relevant in the determination of his or her criminal liability, and that it is equally unrealistic to treat as relevant the fact that a person has acquired his or her external attributes as a result of operative procedure. She decided that the time had come when the courts must, for the purposes of the criminal law, give proper effect to successful reassignment surgery undertaken by transsexuals.

In relation to the second accused, McGuinness, who, while being a transsexual, had not undergone the sex-change procedure. Mathews J found McGuinness to be a male person for the purposes of the offence. Mathews J stated that she was not prepared to limit the criteria for the determination of sexual identity solely to that of the individual's psychological sex. She thought that were it to be the sole criterion, the situation would be abused by persons who were not true transsexuals.

In Ireland, transsexual surgery is not the subject of specific legislative control nor has the issue come before the courts. However, given the prevailing moral climate, it is unlikely that such surgery would be performed in Irish hospitals. It is very unlikely indeed that a marriage involving a transsexual partner would come within the ambit of marriage as conceived in the Constitution. Moreover, the common law crime of maim may be cited by those who oppose such procedures to the effect that this surgery is a bodily touching to which valid legal consent is impossible.

However, despite what has been written above, there is some anecdotal evidence to suggest that patients are being referred for transsexual interventive surgery to other jurisdictions. In what circumstances is it permissible for (say) a Health Board to fund an Irish patient for an operation or procedure to be performed abroad, where the operation constitutes a transgression of the Irish criminal law of 'maim'? Presumably some of the same issues ventilated in the paragraphs on termination of pregnancy above may apply, *mutatis mutandis.*

10

DRUG EXPERIMENTATION AND PRESCRIPTION

The leading textbook on Medical Law, Kennedy & Grubb[1] states:

> [i]t is a truism that for medical practice to develop and improve in any
> systematic and ordered way research must be carried out. It is equally
> a truism that such research must include research on human beings
> whether they are patients or are healthy.

In the context of Irish medical law, three aspects of Kennedy & Grubb's
discussion must be addressed, before passing to a detailed consideration of
the legal position in Ireland.

First, Kennedy & Grubb describe fully the process whereby the
randomised controlled clinical trial has become the key method whereby
methods of treatment of ill patients are analysed, refined and ultimately
implemented throughout the scientific community.[2]

Secondly, the authors provide a description of, and further references
to, the history and the evolution of clinical trials, including the way in which
the Nuremberg Military Tribunals dealt with the Nazi experiments on live
subjects and high-altitude, Malaria, Sulfanilamide, epidemic jaundice, spot-
ted fever, and poison. In the context of the Nuremberg Trials, they discuss,
and provide illustrative quotations from the discussions of others, about the
role of the Declaration of Helsinki.[3]

Thirdly, the authors review and discuss certain distinctions: the distinction between 'therapeutic' research, 'non-therapeutic' research, and 'innovative therapy'.

The authorities cited by Kennedy & Grubb do not present any
completely satisfactory definition of these terms, but, for the purpose of the

---

1   *Medical Law: Text with Materials*, 2nd ed. (Butterworth, London, 1994) p. 1009ff.
2   See I. Kennedy & A. Grubb, *Medical Law*, op. cit. p. 1009, citing Nicholson (ed.), *Medical Research with Children* (1986) pp. 24-26.
3   Kennedy & Grubb, ibid., at p. 1012-29.

present work, we offer the following definitions adapted from those discussed in Kennedy & Grubb.

Thus, it is clear that 'therapeutic research' is an activity or procedure which involves, in relation to a single act or series of acts, the twin motivation of therapy and research.

'Non-therapeutic research' involves (a) not only an activity or procedure which does not have therapy as its aim, but (b) research or procedure which is undertaken on a patient, to whom therapy may have been or will be administered, but to whose therapy the instant research or procedure is not directed, and which therefore is unconnected with the therapeutic intention.

'Innovative therapy' is, by its nature, the performance of some procedure which is new, non-standard, non-proven. The primary motive for its use is therapeutic, but it has not been tried and tested, so in this sense it may be termed experimental. However, unlike the accepted form of controlled randomised double-blind clinical trial, innovative therapy does not have to be, and usually is not part of some formal scientific project.

APPLICATION TO IRELAND

In Ireland, 'innovative therapy' is not subject to legal controls, though prior to 1987, it was not unknown for doctors to seek approval from ethics committees for innovative therapy. Essentially, this is treatment: if it fails, and the patient makes a claim in tort, the doctor runs a higher risk of being sued in negligence, than if he adopts a conservative approach, always assuming such an option is realistically open to the treating doctor.

As we shall show, the position with regard to 'non-therapeutic research' on human beings is regulated by the Control of Clinical Trials Acts 1987 and 1990.

Though the same acts apply to 'therapeutic research', the position is complex, as the legislation seeks to distinguish between therapeutic and non-therapeutic intervention, and in a perhaps artificial and unsatisfactory way, seeks to exclude from statutory control, administration of substances or preparations where the 'principal purpose' is 'to prevent disease in or save the life, restore the health, alleviate the condition or relieve the suffering of, the patient'.[4] Though the reader is referred to the works cited in Kennedy & Grubb for a fuller picture, the point we make here is that in many cases, therapeutic activity may involve some preliminary non-therapeutic investigation as a pre-requisite, and the distinction between therapy and experiment by reference to the 'primary purpose' of the doctor may be criticised as artificial.

4   Control of Clinical Trials and Drugs Act 1990, s. 2(ii).

BACKGROUND TO THE LEGISLATION

In Ireland, in 1984, a 'healthy' participant took part in a controlled trial. He did so apparently because the trialists perfectly properly paid such participants a small amount of money. Such participants were used as controls, and it was intended to test the same or similar treatment on a selection of ill people, and compare the results. Unfortunately, the participant in question failed to disclose to the investigating physician the fact that he had been taking certain drugs, other than the drugs the subject of the controlled clinical trial in question. He fell ill and died. There was a perceived gap in the law, as such trials were not expressly regulated by legislation.

There was considerable public debate on the whole issue of clinical trials. It was felt appropriate to introduce regulation in this area, and eventually, a bill was proposed in the usual manner, discussed, and the Control of Clinical Trials Act 1987 was passed. The Act became fully effective on 6 December 1988.

Prior to the passing of the Act, certain deficiencies in the then draft legislation were noticed, and the Minister for Health received submissions *inter alia* from certain Irish hospitals, who were active in the field of research and clinical trials, and who were concerned about problems which were anticipated.

The first problem was that the Bill imposed liability on the members of ethics committees, where such committees allowed clinical trials to proceed, without ensuring that sufficient arrangements for compensation in the event of claims for negligence were in place.

Though it might seem strange that members of ethics committees were anxious about what would happen in the event of their negligently approving clinical trials, two factors should be recalled.

First, though some members of ethics committees were full time medical professionals, others were volunteers (unpaid members of the general public, or in professions other than medicine) and such members were sometimes ill-equipped to understand the ramifications of clinical trials whose nature, purpose, and function were not fully explained to them. They would be in the position of approving what they could perhaps understand only in part, but they had no means of knowing whether what they understood was the complete picture or not. They felt, therefore, that they might be liable for consequences which they could not fully appreciate.[5]

---

5   They may have been right, but it is still uncertain. Kennedy & Grubb in *Medical Law: Text with Materials*, op. cit., p. 1037 review the position of ethics committee members in England, and state '[t]hus, failure on the part of a Committee member to satisfy himself . . . may render him liable to a legal claim in negligence at the suit of a research subject. . . . Notice however that the law does not require the Committee member

Second, it was quite unclear what degree of insurance cover would be available to members individually, and ethics committees collectively. Some members of ethics committees sought further clarification from those expert in the insurance market, and were unable to ascertain what insurance, if any, they could take out against such liability, and the reports they received from experienced professional advisers were not sanguine. The idea of a broad indemnity by the Minister for Health was canvassed, but it was not clear whether such an indemnity would be reliable, in the absence of specific statutory authorisation.

It was suggested that if the 1987 Act was passed in the form that it ultimately took, clinical trials of new products in Ireland would effectively cease. This fear ultimately proved to be not without justification, and in the period 1987-1990, most clinical trials in Ireland were concerned with different dosages or applications of products which already had product authorisation, rather than new drugs.

In 1990, the Control of Clinical Trials and Drugs Act was passed. It became operative on 11 July 1990. This legislation requires trialists to satisfy the Minister for Health that adequate security exists to provide payments to persons who suffer loss or injury as a result of negligence, a burden which under the 1987 the ethics committees were supposed to shoulder. It went some way to meeting the objections to the 1987 Act.

The legislation also provided immunity from suit for the Minister for Health, The National Drugs Advisory Board, and ethics committees, which was substantially what was suggested to the then Minister For Health, when he was lobbied about the 1987 Act.

THE LEGISLATION

The legislation compels all proposed clinical trials to obtain prior approval from the Minister for Health, and from an Ethics Committee whose composition and whose individual members have been approved by the Minister. The trial must be conducted by a qualified doctor or dentist. The participants must give their informed consent. The conduct of a clinical trial otherwise than as permitted by the Act constitutes a criminal offence. The legislation embodies the basic principles for the guidance of medical doctors in biomedical research involving human subjects adopted by the 18th World

---

to get things right. Rather . . . the obligation is to behave reasonably. Clearly, the expertise of the member may limit what he can do, but the law is likely to require that any reasonable member finding a matter on which he was unsure, should seek advice'. However, in the Irish context, it was difficult to know from whom a lay member of the ethics committee should have sought such advice.

Medical Assembly in Helsinki in 1964, as amended in Tokyo 1975, Venice 1983 and Hong Kong 1989. These principles are supported by the (Irish) Medical Council.

CLINICAL TRIALS AND CONDUCTING A CLINICAL TRIAL

A clinical trial may only be conducted by a registered medical practitioner or registered dentist.[6] The requirement is that such a person must (a) conduct the trial and (b) do so, as described below.

The full definition of conduct[ing] a clinical trial' in the Control of Clinical Trials Acts is:

> the conducting of a systematic investigation or series of investigations for the purpose of ascertaining the effects (including the kinetic effects) of the administration of one or more substances where such administration may have a pharmacological or harmful effect, but does not include the conducting of such a systematic investigation or series of investigations as aforesaid:
>
> (a) where
>
>> (i) the administration of one or more substances or preparations, as the case may be, is on a patient in the ordinary course of medical practice (in the case of a registered medical practitioner) or of dental practice (in the case of a registered dentist) and
>> (ii) the principal purpose of that adminstration is to prevent disease in, or to save the life, restore the health, alleviate the condition or relieve the suffering of, the patient,

or

> (b) where the substance or preparation concerned is to be administered to persons undergoing a course of training leading to a qualification which will entitle such a person to be registered as a registered medical practitioner or as a registered dentist or as a registered pharmaceutical

6   The World Medical Association recommends that biomedical research involving human subjects must conform to generally accepted scientific principles and should be based on adequately performed laboratory and animal experimentation and on a thorough knowledge of the scientific literature. It should be conducted only by scientifically qualified persons and under the supervision of a clinically competent medical person and never rest on the subject of the research, even though the subject has given his or her consent.

chemist and where it is to be administered as part of such a course of
training, or

(c) for the purpose of examining the nutritional effect of the substance
or preparation concerned where that substance or preparation is a
normal dietary constituent.

The first question relates to the definition of 'systematic investigation
or series of investigations'.

R.A. Pearce[7] points out that the word 'systematic' was added to this
phrase in the Seanad. The intention appears to have been to exclude from
the definition *ad hoc* uses of a particular drug. He continues to suggest that
this would not exclude systematic investigations of a single participant
suffering from an unusual condition, but *pace* Pearce, it seems hard to accept
that any clinical trial on one participant could really have any scientific
validity.

The next relates to 'effects (including kinetic effects)'. This would seem
to cover the ways in which a drug moves through the human body, as Pearce[8]
notes.

'Administration of one or more substances or preparations' is a phrase
which has given rise to difficulty. Pearce[9] suggests that though the definition
clearly covers oral, or injected ingestions, the expression could only 'with
difficulty be interpreted to include radiation, light or heat'. He adds that
the reasons for not including treatments involving these, or 'surgical
treatment and manipulative treatments . . . such as physiotherapy' are
unclear.

'Pharmacological or harmful effect': Pearce argues that the definition of
such effects is lacking; he compares the definition to that provided in the
(UK) Medicines Act 1968, which regulates clinical trials involving medicinal
products, that is, products to be used for a 'medicinal purpose', being defined
(in s. 130(2) of the 1986 Act) as:

(a) treating or preventing disease;

(b) diagnosing disease, or ascertaining the existence, degree or extent
of a physiological condition;

(c) contraception;

(d) inducing anaesthesia;

(e) otherwise preventing or interfering with the normal operation of a
physiological function, whether permanently or temporarily, and

7   See his annotation in *Irish Current Law*   8   Pearce, ibid.
    Statutes Annotated, 1987-88 (Sweet &   9   Id.
    Maxwell, London, 1988).

whether by way of terminating, reducing or postponing, or increasing or accelerating, the operation of that function or in any other way.

Next, the question of 'the ordinary course of medical practice . . . or dental practice', where the principal purpose is 'to prevent disease in or to save the life, restore the health . . .' of the patient

It should be noted that the criterion of 'the ordinary course' of treatment and 'the principal purpose' of such treatment are conjunctive: the treatment must satisfy both limbs of the test.

The first question that may arise with this test is: what constitutes 'the ordinary course of medical/dental practice'? Is this exemption limited to the administration of substances which are recognised as conventional treatment, or would it include a novel treatment for a routine condition, or any treatment for an exceptional or rare condition? It is tentatively suggested that the Act attempts to exclude all treatments for routine conditions (novel or otherwise), but may not include treatments for exceptional or rare conditions.

WHERE THE CONTROL OF CLINICAL TRIALS ACTS 1987-1990 DO NOT APPLY

It is now clear beyond doubt that the Act does not apply to investigations on a patient in the ordinary course of medical or dental practice by a registered medical practitioner or dentist, where the principal purpose of that administration is to prevent disease in, or save the life of, or to restore the health of, the patient.[10]

In the following situations the full rigour of the 1987 Act does not apply:

(a) where a clinical trial had already begun at the date of the introduction of the 1987 Act;[11]

(b) where a clinical trial had not actually begun but appropriate arrangements were in place;[12]

---

10 This is taken from the definition of 'conduct a clinical trial' contained in s. 6 of the 1987 Act, as amended by s. 2 of the 1990 Act. The full definition is set out in the Table to s. 2 of the 1990 Act. It should be noted that this amendment to the 1987 Act was passed to make it quite clear that where the principal purpose of the adminstration of the drug is therapeutic or palliative, no coexisting systematic investigation of the treatment will constitute the therapy or palliative care a clinical trial. In his annotation to the 1990 Act, Dr R. Clark states that '[t]he experience of some AIDS patients who were not able to obtain a particular treatment, the drug DDI, was the primary impetus for this amendment'. (*Irish Current Law Statutes Annotated*, 1989-90 (Sweet & Maxwell, London, 1990).

11 Control of Clinical Trials Act 1987, s. 2(1)(a).

12 Ibid., s. 2(1)(b). The arrangements were deemed to comply with s. 3 even if that was not the case.

(c) where there is an existing product authorisation in respect of a product, then clinical trials involving the use of that product in compliance with the conditions of the authorisation are governed by s. 2(2) of the Act;[13]

(d) where there is an existing product authorisation in respect of a product, and a clinical trial is carried out to test new uses for the product, then, provided that the dosage is in the same form and does not exceed the level specified in the authorisation, permission may be given by the Minister.[14]

A potentially controversial section provides a complete exception for clinical trials where the substance or preparation is to be administered to medical, dental or pharmacy (undergraduate) students.[15] The students in question are defined as 'persons undergoing a course of training leading to a qualification which will entitle such a person to be registered as a registered medical practitioner, or as a registered dentist or as a registered pharmaceutical chemist'. The substance or preparation must be administered 'as part of such a course of training'.

It is surprising, to say the least, that this exemption applies irrespective of the nature of the substance or preparation.

It is also surprising that the legislation does not accord undergraduate students protection, but this comment should not be taken to suggest that there is evidence that any abuse of this section exists. However the authors submit that this section is perhaps inappropriate; and it might be more acceptable if the exemption was confined to doctors, dentists and chemists, who, having qualified, might be expected to be better aware of the nature and effects of such trials, and to only certain substances or preparations. We question whether in fact such an exception meets the requirements of Article 40 of the Constitution; but this has not yet been decided.

13 S. 2(2) of the 1987 Act involves: (a) Product authorisation under the Medical Preparations (Licensing, Advertisement and Sale) Regulations (SI No. 21 of 1984); (b) Notification of the National Drugs Advisory Board in writing in advance; (c) Approval of the National Drugs Advisory Board of the composition of a committee appointed to consider the justification for conducting the proposed clinical trial and the circumstances under which the proposed trial is to be conducted; (d) Receipt by the National Drugs Advisory Board of such information, evidence, documents, samples or other materials that they may have, not later than four weeks after being so notified, requested in relation to the proposed clinical trial; and (e) the conditions under which the product authorisation was granted are complied with in respect of the substance or preparation concerned.

14 However, the recommendation of the National Drugs Advisory Board must be sought, see s. 2(3) of the 1987 Act. The Minister may revoke permission under s. 7 of the 1987 Act.

15 S. 6(2)(b) of the 1987 Act.

A less tendentious exception excludes from the definition of clinical trials, substances or preparations which are normal dietary constituents. Thus a trial of one kind of diet would be exempt from clinical trials legislation, provided that only ordinary foodstuffs were being consumed.

APPLICATIONS FOR PERMISSION

Application must be made to the Minister for permission to conduct a clinical trial.[16] The application must include:

(a) the name and address and description of the applicant,
(b) sufficient information to enable a scientific evaluation to be made of the proposed clinical trial and of the substance or preparation which it is proposed to administer in the course of that trial,
(c) the identity and qualifications of the ethics committee members,
(d) name, address and qualification of each person who will conduct the clinical trial,
(e) criteria used for recruitment and selection of participants,
(f) details of any proposed inducements or rewards, whether monetary or otherwise, to be made for becoming or being a participant,
(g) such further information, evidence, documents or samples and other materials as may be necessary to indicate the nature of the trial, and
(h) the appropriate fee (if any) specified by the Minister.

The Minister has power, before approval of the trial to request 'such further information, evidence, documents, samples, and other materials as may in his opinion assist him in making such a decision'.[17]

DECISION

Within twelve weeks of the application, or twelve weeks of the request by the Minister for further information being acceded to, the Minister must issue a decision. This decision must be made after consultation with the National Drugs Advisory Board. The decision must be either to:

— grant permission for the proposed clinical trial to be undertaken in accordance with the application, or

— grant permission for the proposed clinical trial to be undertaken in accordance with the application subject to such modifications as he may specify or

---

16 S. 3 of the 1987 Act.   17 See s. 3 of the 1987 Act.

— refuse to grant permission for the proposed clinical trial to be undertaken.[18]

Prior to the conducting of the trial, Ministerial approval of the
composition of the ethics committee must be sought and obtained.[19]

If the Minister refuses to grant permission, he must, when so refusing,
inform the applicant of the grounds for such refusal.[20]

This part of the legislation has been criticised by Hodges,[21] because, like
the French legislation, it does not state what criteria the Minister for Health
must apply in considering the proposed trial, in contrast to the Spanish
legislation.

AMENDMENT OF PERMISSION

If there is subsisting permission for a clinical trial, and it is proposed to
alter the trial, then permission must be sought for the trial as amended.[22]

S. 5(1) refers to a proposal 'to do, or to refrain from doing any act in
relation to the proposed clinical trial or the clinical trial otherwise than in
accordance with the permission'. This covers any amendment to the trial.
It covers a proposal to modify a future trial or an ongoing trial.

The trialist must apply to the Minister. The Minister is obliged to consult
the National Drugs Advisory Board. Not later than six weeks after the
application for amendment was made, the Minister must agree or not agree
the amendment of the permission.

If the Minister agrees to the amendment, it shall not be acted upon until
the ethics committee for the proposed trial has given its approval to the
proposed trial as amended.[23] In the case of a clinical trial which has already
been approved by the ethics committee, the committee must give its approval
and each person to whom substance(s) or preparation(s) are being administered has been 'made aware of such matters (if any) as the committee
considers he should be made aware of having regard to the amendment'.[24]

CONSENT

The reader is referred to chapter 3 for a discussion of consent generally.

With regard to consent to participate in a clinical trial, the Act attempts
to ensure that participants in all clinical trials must give prior valid consent.

18 See s. 4(1) of the 1987 Act.
19 S. 4(2)(a) of the 1990 Act.
20 S. 4(2)(b) of the 1990 Act.
21 C. Hodges, 'Harmonisation of European
    Controls over Research: Ethics Com-
    mittees, Consent, Compensation and In-
    demnity' in A. Goldberg & I. Dodds
    Smith, *Pharmaceutical Medicine and The
    Law* (London, 1991).
22 S. 5 of the 1987 Act.
23 S. 5(2)(a) of the 1987 Act.
24 S. 5(2)(b)(ii) of the 1987 Act.

The consent, to be valid, must be given in writing and signed by the participant. Signature alone is not sufficient to render the consent valid.

A general question arises at this stage as to what kind and degree of information must be given to a participant in a clinical trial. It is suggested that in common law, no distinction exists between the doctor's duty of disclosure where the doctor is treating a patient, and is engaged in non-therapeutic intervention (such as providing contraception). Elsewhere, we have indicated that, at common law, the standard which obtains in Ireland, certainly for therapeutic intervention, is that proposed by *Sidaway v. Bethlem Royal Hospital,*[25] where it was stated that the appropriate standard of disclosure is that accepted as proper by a responsible body of competent medical practitioners, subject to an overriding jurisdiction on the part of the court to consider a matter to be of such importance to a proper decision on the part of the patient that no responsible doctor would have failed to disclose it.

The common law position has now been statutorily modified for clinical trials: the criterion is no longer 'that accepted as proper by a responsible body of competent medical practitioners', it is instead a statutory checklist. What is surprising about this is that in some clinical trials, the main or ancillary purpose may be therapeutic, and if so, what non-disclosure is permitted the doctor who is also a trialist?

The following are the statutory criteria:[26]

(a) The person is capable of comprehending the nature, significance and scope of his consent and
(b) It is obtained by or on behalf of the person conducting the clinical trial.

It is submitted that the general consent form for treatment would not be apt to elicit appropriate consent. A special form should be drafted, and the procedures specially explained, if not by the trialist, then by some person qualified and suitable to explain in detail what is proposed.

The explanation must include:

the objectives of the trial,

the manner in which the substance or preparation is to be administered,

the risks and any discomfort involved in, and the possible side-effects of the trial,

whether or not a placebo ('pharmaceutically inactive substance or

25 [1985] AC 871.   26 S. 9(3) of the 1987 Act.

preparation') is to be administered to some persons in respect of each of whom a consent has been given to being a participant in the trial in accordance with this section, and

such other matters (if any) as may be prescribed by Ministerial regulations or specified in the Ministerial permission.[27]

A clinical trial shall not be conducted on any person within the period of six days after that day on which the person has been given this information and has consented.[28] However, in exceptional circumstances, this requirement may be waived if the Minister gives his permission for this in the permission for the clinical trial.[29]

Any person who has given his consent to participate in a clinical trial may withdraw consent at any time without incurring contractual liability.[30]

Special considerations apply where the participant in the clinical trial is either incapable of expressing his consent, or incapable of understanding comprehending the nature, significance and scope of the consent.

If the trial is conducted on a person who suffering from an illness and 'an' objective of the trial is to obtain a remedy for or the alleviation of such an illness, then consent by proxy may be obtained.[31] This qualification is reiterated and expanded at the end of s. 9: '[p]rovided that a clinical trial to which this subsection relates may be conducted only if the substance or preparation under trial is to be administered for the purpose of saving the life of such a person, restoring his health, alleviating his condition or relieving his suffering'.

What two circumstances may justify consent by proxy?

Either the person may understand the nature significance and scope of consent, but be physically unable to give such consent. In such circumstance, his consent clearly given in the presence of two witnesses present at the same time to a registered medical practitioner shall be sufficient. Such consent must be expressed in writing and be attested by the signatures of other witnesses.[32]

Alternatively, the person the subject of the trial may be incapable of comprehending the nature, significance and scope of consent to be given. If this is the case, the person may only be a participant in a clinical trial if a written and signed consent is given by a person or persons competent to give a decision on such participation. The person(s) giving consent must be independent of the person who applied to undertake or is conducting the trial.[33]

27 S. 9(4) of the 1987 Act.
28 S. 9(5) of the 1987 Act.
29 S. 9(6) of the 1987 Act.
30 S. 9(6) of the 1987 Act.

31 S. 9(7) of the 1987 Act.
32 S. 9(7)(a) of the 1987 Act.
33 S. 9(7)(b) of the 1987 Act.

It follows from this, and it is reasonably clear, that clinical trials may be conducted on minors or mentally incapacitated patients who are themselves incapable of consent, provided that such subjects are ill, that the clinical trial's objective is to provide a remedy for or to alleviate the illness from which they suffer, and that the substance under trial is to be administered for the purpose of saving the participant's life, restoring his health, alleviating his condition or relieving his suffering.

This of course depends on the ethics committee being of the view that such a clinical trial is justifiable; the criterion being 'that the risks to be incurred by participants would be commensurate with the objectives of the trial'.[34]

ROLE OF THE MINISTER AND THE ETHICS COMMITTEE

In Ireland, the Medical Council explicitly supports the formation of ethical committees in all institutions where human research is undertaken, and advises them to seek approval from an appropriate supervisory organisation before undertaking any research project involving risks to human subjects.

The 1987 and 1990 Acts provide for the setting up of ethics committees to monitor the conduct of clinical trials in Ireland.[35]

The Minister is obliged to approve the proposed ethics committee considering the trial. In determining whether the ethics committee should be approved or not, the Minister for Health must first be satisfied that a proposed ethics committee for a clinical trial is competent to consider the justification for conducting the proposed clinical trial and the circumstances under which it is to be conducted.

The function of the ethics committee is to 'consider the justification for conducting the proposed clinical trial and the circumstances under which it is proposed to be conducted'. The criterion for this consideration is that the ethics committee shall not consider the proposed clinical trial justified unless it is satisfied that the risks to be incurred by participants would be commensurate with the objectives of the trial. The Act specifies the matters to which the ethics committee must have regard. These are:

(a) the objectives of the proposed trial and its planning and organisational structure;

(b) the qualifications and competence of each person who would

---

34 S. 8(3) of the 1987 Act.
35 In so providing, account is taken of the Declaration of Helslnki on Biomedical Research involving Human Subjects, adopted by the 18th World Medical Assembly in 1964, as amended in Tokyo 1975, Venice 1983 and Hong Kong 1989.

conduct the trial and, where appropriate, the resources available to him;

(c) the criteria to be used for the recruitment and selection of participants;

(d) the procedures proposed for compliance with the choice of participants;

(e) the extent to which participants' health will be monitored during and after the clinical trial;

(f) the extent and nature of any medical examination accorded to potential participants;

(g) whether or not the persons selected as participants are to undergo independent medical examination before, during or after the clinical trial;

(h) details of the proposed method or methods by which participants are to be recruited;

(i) details of any proposed inducements or rewards, whether monetary or otherwise, to be made for becoming or being a participant;

(j) any payments, whether monetary or otherwise, to be made to any person for conducting the clinical trial or any part of the trial;

(k) the criteria to ensure that the identity of each participant remains confidential;

(l) any payments, whether monetary or otherwise, to be made to any person for facilities used for the purposes of the clinical trial;

(m) such other matters as may be prescribed by regulations made by the Minister under the 1987 Act.[36]

S. 8 of the 1987 Act allows the composition of an ethics committee to be changed with the approval of the Minister.

The Minister has issued non-statutory guidelines about the composition of ethics committees, and recommends, *inter alia*, that the composition should include at least the following:

> Two medical practitioners neither of whom is personally involved in the study to be conducted. One should be independent of the institution in which the study is to be conducted, and one should be personally familiar with the conduct of clinical trials.
>
> A nurse actively involved in patient care.
>
> A professional, non-medical person who is involved in administration or business.

36 S. 8(3) and (4) of the 1987 Act.

A person with legal training.

A member of the lay public whose competence and integrity the public might be expected to respect.

As R.A. Pearce points out in his annotation to the 1987 Act,[37] there is some duplication between the vetting functions of the ethics committees and the Minister for Health, in regard to the scientific evaluation of the trial, the recruitment and selection of participants, and the inducements or rewards offered to them.

Ethics committees are protected by the 1987 and 1990 Acts, by s. 10 of the 1987 Act as amended by s. 3 of the 1990 Act, which provides that '[n]othing in this section shall be construed as requiring, by virtue of s. 8, an ethics committee to have regard to any security . . . [as set out] in subsection (1) or (2)'.

S. 5 of the 1990 Act provides an immunity in respect of actions (except in the case of wilful neglect or default) against the Minister for Health, the National Drugs Advisory Board, and its members acting as such, its officers or servants, and ethics committees or any member thereof. The immunity is for actions for damages 'in respect of any injury to persons or property alleged to have been caused or contributed to by reason of or arising from the discharge of any of their functions imposed by the' 1987 and 1990 Acts.

S. 5(2) provides a similar indemnity in respect of claims against the National Drugs Advisory Board.

A question must be asked about the constitutionality of this section. It provides an immunity from suit on a subordinate body created by the Oireachtas, and, since the State itself is not constitutionally entitled to avail of immunity from suit since *Byrne v. Ireland*,[38] it follows that any subordinate body might not be so entitled. This view would seem to be supported by Hogan & Whyte, who discuss immunities in the context of the inconsistency of the State's obligation under Article 40.3 to defend and vindicate the citizen's personal rights.[39]

OFFENCES

The 1987 Act has been amended by the 1990 Act, to provide that the following are offences:

failure to apply to the Minister for Health to conduct a clinical trial;[40]

37 *Irish Current Law Statutes Annotated*, op. cit., p. 28-92.
38 [1972] IR 241.
39 G. Hogan & G. Whyte, *J.M. Kelly's The*

Irish Constitution (Butterworth, Dublin, 1994), p. 1152.
40 S. 3 of the 1987 Act.

conducting a clinical trial without the approval of the ethics committee;[41]

failing to communicate the ethics committee's approval to the Minister;[42]

contravening the terms of the Minister's permission without proper authorisation;[43]

failing to comply with the requirements for obtaining consent from the participants;[44]

failing to report an adverse drug reaction;[45]

supplying incorrect or misleading information.[46]

The offences are punishable, on summary conviction, by a fine not exceeding one thousand pounds, or imprisonment for a term not exceeding twelve months or both. On conviction on indictment, the offences are punishable by a fine not exceeding ten thousand pounds, or at the discretion of the court, to imprisonment for a term not exceeding three years.

NATIONAL DRUGS ADVISORY BOARD

The main functions of the National Drugs Advisory Board, established in 1966 as a corporate body, are fourfold. They are:

(1) organisation and administration of a service to assess information on the safety, quality and efficacy of all medicinal products intended for human or veterinary use in order to advise the Minister for Health on their authorisation for marketing;

(2) organisation and administration of services for obtaining and assessing reports on the adverse effects of medicinal products in use in Ireland, and to take whatever steps are judged necessary, either to advise the Minister concerning necessary action, or to inform the relevant professions, and on occasion the public, of changes and procedures necessary to improve the safety in use of medicinal products in Ireland;

(3) organisation and maintenance of a system for the inspection, both initial and continued, of manufacturers of medicinal products and of wholesalers of medicinal products for human use. The recommenda-

---

41 S. 4(2) and s. 6(1)(c) of the 1987 Act.   44 S. 9 of the 1987 Act.
42 S. 8(2) of the 1987 Act.   45 S. 11 of the 1987 Act.
43 S. 5 of the 1987 Act.   46 S. 12 of the 1987 Act.

tions consequent on this system are made to the Minister for the purposes of licensing;

(4) organisation and administration of procedures for evaluation of the scientific content of applications for clinical trial approval, to establish the safety of the trial proposals for the purposes of advising the Minister of their acceptability.

Assuming that the clinical trials have been effected, and the drug is available for commercial use, questions arise of how such drugs should be controlled.

It is proposed that a new 'one stop' drug licensing agency will be established shortly, for the purpose of providing a system throughout the entire EU for the licensing and control of new drugs.[47]

PRESCRIPTION OF DRUGS

There is a multiplicity of regulations on the manufacture, advertisement and sale of pharmacologically active substances in Ireland.[48] Much of this law is outside the scope of this work. We concentrate here on the prescription, sale and dispensing of medicines.

The Minister for Health is empowered to 'make regulations for the control of the . . . sale of medical preparations'.[49]

Of the many regulations so made, The Medical Preparations (Licensing, Advertisement and Sale) Regulations 1958 prohibit misleading claims about the efficacy of medicines, and the Medical Preparations (Licensing, Advertisement & Sale Regulations 1984 introduce a common statutory licensing system for all medical preparations, both proprietary and non-proprietary. The Medical Preparations (Control of Sale) Regulations 1987 restrict the sale of certain drugs, so that they must be prescribed by a registered medical practitioner, or dentist, and dispensed by a pharmacist. Such drugs include those containing substances set out in the first schedule to the Regulations,

47 'New Drug Licensing Agency to be established shortly', *Irish Medical Times* (1993), Vol. 27, No. 34 (20 August) p. 10; V. Ryan 'NDAB gears up for Major Changes In EC Drug Licensing' *Irish Medical News* (1993), Vol. 10, No. 37 (12 October), p. 10.

48 For a full account see P.B. Weedle & M.J. Cahill, *Medicines and Pharmacy Law in Ireland* (Kenlis Press, Dublin 1991). See also the useful synopsis in B. Hensey, *The Health Services of Ireland*, 4th ed. (IPA, Dublin, 1988 repr. 1990), which the authors have found so helpful on this, as on other topics. Practitioners should note that the Misuse of Drugs (Scheduled Substances) Regulations 1993, and the Misuse of Drugs (Scheduled Substances) (Exemption) Order 1993 are not included in either of these works, and are not specifically addressed here, but must be consulted, together with all other regulations made both before or after publication of this work, if a problem arises to be addressed.

49 The statutory authority for such regulations derives from s. 65 of the Health Act 1947, as amended by s. 39 of the Health Act 1953, and s. 36 of the Misuse of Drugs Act 1977.

those intended for use by means of parenteral administration, and those which are or contain new drug substances.

Dealing with those drugs which are listed in the first schedule to the Regulations, different rules apply to the sale of drugs according to whether they are listed in Part A, or Part B. Prescriptions for Part A drugs may, unless otherwise directed by the prescribing physician, be dispensed on one occasion only. Prescriptions for Part B preparations may, unless otherwise directed, be dispensed as often as the pharmacist deems appropriate within a period of 6 months from the date of issue of the prescription.

New drugs, and drugs administered by parenteral administration are dispensed only on one occasion, unless the physician directs otherwise.

The Misuse of Drugs Act 1977, and orders made thereunder, among other things impose extra controls on the prescription or sale of controlled drugs. The kinds of control differ depending on which category the controlled drug falls. There are five groupings.

The first, CD1, contains drugs such as cannabis and LSD. A special licence is required for any activity in respect of such drugs, which are properly used more for forensic and scientific than therapeutic purposes.

The second, CD2, comprises such drugs as morphine, heroin, and seconal. Drugs in this category may be prescribed and dispensed, but the physician can only write the prescription in a specified form if it is to be dispensed, and the pharmacist must note the sale in a special controlled drugs register, and stringent controls apply to the storing and destruction of such drugs. If the prescription is not in the correct form, the pharmacist is not permitted to sell the drug in question.

The third category, CD3, includes most potent analgesics and some barbiturates. The pharmacist does not have to record their sale in a register.

The fourth category, CD4, comprises drugs such as the benzodiazepine tranquillisers, and phenobarbitone preparations containing less than 100mg. In practice these are prescribed and dispensed in the same manner as those drugs listed in schedule 1 of the 1987 Regulations mentioned above.

The fifth category, CD5, contains preparations exempt from most restrictions. In this category are included, for example, preparations of cocaine containing not more than 1% calculated as cocaine base, preparations of medicinal opium or morphine containing not more than 0.2% calculated as anhydrous morphine base.

Special regulations apply to the sale of rectified spirits, wine and methylated spirits: the main provision is that the pharmacist must keep a register of sales of methylated spirits, and there are certain hours within which such spirits can not be sold.[50] Similarly, poisons (weedkillers and the

50 See P.B. Weedle & M.J. Cahill, *Medicines and Pharmacy Law in Ireland*, op. cit., pp. 123-31.

like) are subject to statutory control in respect not only of labelling but also of sale, and a register must also be kept.[51]

Exceptions to the sale of prescribed drugs exist; these are really outside the scope of this work, but it should be noted that a registered medical practitioner, the matron of a nursing home, a midwife, a person in charge of a laboratory, the owner or master of a ship and the manager of an off-shore installation may all be supplied with certain drugs by a pharmacist on a requisition. This requisition must be written, and if an undertaking is given to supply such a requisition after the supply of the drug in question (as in an emergency), the requisition must be given within twenty-four hours, otherwise an offence is committed.[52]

The pharmacist may supply the drugs to a messenger, if satisfied that the messenger is *bona fide*. The messenger must produce a statement in writing from the purchaser that the messenger is authorised.[53]

As well as statutory restrictions, the Medical Council, in *A Guide to Ethical Conduct and Behaviour and to Fitness to Practise*[54] lays down ethical guidelines about prescription. These guidelines specify that the doctor must 'prescribe the most appropriate medicine to suit the patient's condition and best interests'. The Guide continues to prohibit 'irresponsible prescribing' specifying the requirement to observe 'published protocol' on treating drug dependent or addicted patients. Further, the Guide refers to its own recommendations issued with the Department of Health and The Pharmaceutical Society of Ireland.

PRESCRIPTIONS

There are at least three good reasons why this work must stress that every health care professional is legally obliged to write prescriptions in the correct form. First, it is a breach of the law for the pharmacist to sell controlled drugs unless the prescription satisfies the requirements of the Misuse of Drugs Act 1977, and, in particular, the 1987 regulations.[55] Second, it is suggested that an action for negligence will lie if the prescription is not written correctly, and the prescription is not dispensed, and as a result, the patient suffers damage.[56] Third, where the prescription has not been written

---

51 The sale of poisons is regulated by the Poisons Act 1961 and the Poisons Regulations 1982, as amended in 1983, 1984, and 1986.
52 See the Misuse of Drugs Act 1977 and the 1987 Regulations made thereunder.
53 See the Misuse of Drugs Act 1977 and the 1987 Regulations made thereunder.
54 *A Guide to Ethical Conduct and Behaviour and to Fitness To Practise*, 4th ed. (Medical Council, Dublin, 1994).
55 See Misuse of Drugs Regulations 1988, Article 14.
56 *Pharmaceutical Society of Great Britain v. Storkwain Ltd* [1985] 3 All ER 4.

correctly, or is ambiguous, and a pharmacist dispenses what he thinks is the correct drug, it is possible that the practitioner might be liable in negligence, or, contributorily liable with the pharmacist.[57]

The 1987 regulations require that the prescription must:

(a) be in ink or otherwise so as to be indelible and signed by the practitioner with his usual signature and dated by him;

(b) except in the case of a health prescription, specify the address of the person issuing it;

(c) specify in the prescriber's handwriting the name and address of the person for whose treatment it is issued . . . in the case of a patient in a hospital or nursing home, the address of the patient need not be specified provided the prescription is written on the patient's bed card or case sheet;

(d) clearly indicate the name of the person issuing it and state whether that person is a registered medical practitioner. . . .

(e) specify a telephone number at which the prescriber may be contacted;

(f) specify (in the prescriber's handwriting) (i) the dose to be taken, (ii) the form in the case of preparations, (iii) the strength (when appropriate), and (iv) in both words and figures, either the total quantity of the drug or preparation or the number of dosage units to be supplied;

(g) in the case of a total quantity intended to be dispensed by instalments, specify the quantity, the number of instalments, and the intervals to be observed when dispensing.

If the drug to be dispensed is a CD2 or CD3 drug, the physician must appreciate that the pharmacist has to fulfil certain extra requirements, and, presumably, the physician has to ensure that his prescription is written so as to enable the pharmacist in his turn, to satisfy the legal requirements.

The pharmacist has an overriding obligation to ensure that the prescription conforms with the requirements mentioned above, and that:

(a) the address of the prescriber as written on the prescription is one within the State;

(b) he is acquainted with the signature of the prescriber and has no reason to believe it is not genuine, or else takes reasonable steps to ensure that it is genuine;

---

57 *Pharmaceutical Society of Great Britain v. Storkwain Ltd* [1985] 3 All ER 4.

(c) the prescription is not dispensed before the date specified on it or later than fourteen days afterwards;

(d) in the case of a prescription to be dispensed by instalments, the first instalment is not dispensed later than fourteen days from the date on the prescription, and no instalment is dispensed later than two months after that date;

(e) he is satisfied as to the identity of the patient or patient's representative as appropriate;

(f) the date of supply is marked on the prescription and on each occasion an instalment is supplied;

(g) the prescription or duplicate copy of a GMS prescription is retained on the premises for two years.

Weedle & Cahill point out that the prescriber's telephone number as it appears on a prescription should not be relied on alone.[58]

Beyond what has been discussed above, there is no legislation in Ireland specifically on the relationship between physicians and pharmacists. Their relationship has been developed in practice in areas such as the provision and supply of drugs.[59] Retail pharmacists are the main channels of supply for drugs, medicines and appliances prescribed for eligible persons. Since 1972, when the General Medical Services Scheme was set up, a doctor issues a prescription on a special form and this can be fulfilled by any pharmacist who has an agreement under the service (there are limitations on the list of drugs which may be prescribed). The pharmacist is reimbursed for the cost of the drugs and is paid a fee for dispensing them.

Where the operation of this system of supply would cause hardship, either because there is no retail pharmaceutical chemist in an area or because of special circumstances in the case of a particular patient, it is part of the physician's contract that he will arrange for the supply of drugs, etc. He is paid a special annual fee for this responsibility. He requisitions his drugs from a convenient retail pharmacist participating in the General Medical Services Scheme.

Under this scheme, every medical practitioner in the general medical service is expected to provide, within reason, within his area of practice, emergency services for cases arising from accidents or otherwise of eligible persons who are not on his list. When a physician considers it necessary to supply a person on his list with drugs or appliances for immediate use he is empowered to do so and can recoup the items from a participating retail pharmacist three miles or more from the nearest retail pharmacist, any

58 P.B. Weedle & M.J. Cahill, *Medicines and Pharmacy Law in Ireland* op. cit., p. 63.
59 *A Guide to Ethical Conduct*, op. cit.

patient on his panel may opt to have prescriptions dispensed by the physician or by a retail pharmacist. Physicians who dispense prescriptions in this way are paid an annual fee in respect of these prescriptions.[60]

THE ADVERTISING AND PROMOTION OF MEDICINAL PRODUCTS

The Medical Preparations (Advertising) Regulations 1993 give effect to EC Council Directive 92/28 of 31 March 1992 on the advertising of medicinal products for human use. The regulations govern the advertising of medicinal products to both health professionals and to the general public. Notably, the Regulations state that representatives of pharmaceutical companies shall not supply, offer or promise to a health professional (defined in the regulations as registered medical practitioners, registered dentists or persons registered in any of the registers provided for in the Pharmacy Acts 1875-1977) gifts or other benefits unless they are inexpensive and relevant to the practice of medicine or pharmacy. The level of hospitality which is to be extended to health professionals at sales promotions or scientific conferences must be 'reasonable' and 'secondary to the main purpose of the meeting'. In addition, such hospitality must not be extended to non-health professionals. This, for example, would prevent pharmaceutical companies from entertaining the spouses or friends of health professionals in an effort to induce the doctor, dentist or pharmacist to purchase and promote a particular product.

The Regulations provide, moreover, that the provision of free samples of medical products to either registered medical practitioners or registered dentists shall be limited to a maximum of six single treatment samples in any one year.

The format and content of advertisements of medical products, aimed at the general public, is also governed by the regulations. The product must be clearly identified by name, and, where the preparation contains only one active ingredient, and is a medical preparation with both a common and a 'medical' name, this must be made clear. A warning stating that the consumer should carefully read the instructions must be printed on the advertisement. The public advertising of prescription drugs or controlled drugs (as identified in s. 2 of the Misuse of Drugs Act 1977) is prohibited. The advertisement for medical preparations shall not make exaggerated claims about the efficacy of products. The use of recommendations by scientists, health professionals, or celebrities which could encourage the consumption of medical preparations shall not be allowed. Advertisements which suggest

60 B. Hensey, op. cit., p. 84-6.

that product's safety or efficacy is due to the fact that it is 'natural' shall be prohibited other regulations concerning the format and content of advertisements of medical products and described furher in Weedle & Cahill.[61]

61   P.B. Weedle & M.J. Cahill, *Medicines and Pharmacy Law in Ireland*, op. cit.

11

VOLUNTARY HEALTH INSURANCE

The Voluntary Health Insurance (VHI) Board was set up in 1957 primarily to cover the fifteen per cent. of the population not entitled to public health care.

Prior to 1957, voluntary health insurance benefits were provided on a very limited scale. In the report of the advisory body to the Minister for Health[1] in May 1956, it was pointed out that few of the commercial insurance companies transacted health insurance business and that none did so to any material extent. The advisory body assumed that the primary objective on which they were asked to advise was protection against the high and unforeseeable cost of ill-health and not against the minor costs which can readily be allowed for in the family budget.[2] The benefits which the advisory body thought should be given under such a scheme were maintenance in hospital or nursing home, surgical and medical fees, maternity benefit, drugs and medicines for hospital in-patients, medical and surgical appliances, and various specialist services for in-patients in hospitals.

The body advised that the State should provide for a scheme of voluntary insurance since it seemed unlikely that any private company would undertake such a business. The recommendations of the advisory body were accepted, with some exceptions, and were the basis of the Voluntary Health Insurance Act 1957.

By 1992, membership of the VHI had reached 1,193,965 persons, representing approximately thirty-four per cent. of the population.[3] This substantially exceeds the original fifteen per cent. target; hence many VHI members are paying for private insurance cover and are entitled to public hospital care in a public ward at the State's expense.

---

1   *Report of Advisory Body on Voluntary Health Insurance Scheme* (Stationery Office, Dublin, 1956).
2   B. Hensey, *The Health Services of Ireland*, op. cit., pp. 84-6; Oireachtas Seventh Joint Committee on Commercial State Sponsored Bodies, *First Report on VHI* (Stationery Office, Dublin, 1994, pl. 6763), p. 10.
3   *1992 VHI Annual Report* (VHI, Dublin, 1992).

Personal income tax relief is available on the full amount of the premium.[4] Thus, some private spending is supported indirectly from the public purse. However with the pay-related contributions all income earners are liable to pay the health contributions, except category I candidates and persons in receipt of welfare benefits.[5] By law, employers are liable to pay health contributions for employees with full eligibility.[6]

LICENSE

In general, the provider of Health Insurance must be licensed.[7] To provide health insurance without a licence is a criminal offence, carrying a fine not exceeding one hundred pounds together with a further fine not exceeding five pounds for every day on which the offence is committed.[8] S. 23(1) of the Voluntary Health Insurance Act 1957, makes it unlawful

> to provide by means of insurance or otherwise, in consideration of the payment by any person, of a subscription or premium, benefits to defray the whole or part of the cost incurred by the person paying the subscription or premium, if any medical, surgical, hospital or other health service, unless the person providing the benefits holds a health insurance licence for the time being in force.

Indeed it is also a criminal offence to pay subscriptions or premiums to, or receive benefits from an unlicensed provider of health insurance.[9] The penalty is a maximum of fifty pounds.[10]

There are, however exceptions, which effectively permit certain bodies to provide health insurance without being licensed.

The exceptions enable some categories of person to provide health insurance without a licence. These are (a) the VHI Board, (b) a Minister of State, (c) a Trade Union or Friendly Society registered before the coming into force of the 1957 Act.[11]

The exceptions also include certain kinds of assurance schemes. These involve contracts of human life assurance which are non-cancellable, and which also provide for payment of moneys in case of sickness, injury or

---

4   Income Tax Act 1967, s. 145, see N. Judge, *Irish Income Tax* (Butterworth, London, 1986), p. 606-7.

5   Health Contributions Act 1979 and Health Contributions Regulations 1979 as amended: see N. Judge, *Irish Income Tax*, op. cit., p. 754.

6   See N. Judge, op. cit., p. 757.

7   Voluntary Health Insurance Act 1957, s. 23(1).

8   Voluntary Health Insurance Act, 1957, s. 23(1) of ibid.

9   S. 24(1), (2) of ibid.

10   S. 24(2) ibid.

11   S. 23(3)(a) of ibid.

disease of the insured.[12] Certain insurance[13] schemes are also excepted, under which

> benefits are payable in respect of sickness, injury, or disease of an amount calculated by reference to the duration of the sickness, injury or disease and not to the nature or cost of any hospital, medical, surgical or other health service, provided in respect of sickness, injury or disease.

Contracts of insurance are excepted in relation to accidents causing or contributing to sickness, injury or disease, which give rise to payment 'to the person insured or to any other person' of benefits.[14]

There is a general exception for contracts of insurance made before the introduction of the Act.[15]

THE VHI

By far the greatest volume of health insurance in Ireland is conducted through the Voluntary Health Insurance Scheme. The Voluntary Health Insurance Act 1957 set up the Voluntary Health Insurance Board as a body corporate. Its function is:

> to make and carry out a scheme of voluntary health insurance for defraying . . . the cost . . . of such medical, surgical, hospital and other health services as the Minister may from time to time specify.[16]

The Minister appoints the chairman,[17] determines the number of members of the Board,[18] and appoints its members.[19] The Minister has powers of removal of members of the Board.[20] The Act specifies in outline how the Board shall regulate the conduct of its business: empowering it to employ officers and servants,[21] pay pensions,[22] present accounts, provide for these to be audited, and make annual reports which are laid before the Oireachtas.[23] The Board has the power to borrow 'temporarily by arrangement with bankers such sums as it may require for the purpose of providing for current expenditure'.[24]

12 S. 23(3)(b)(i) of ibid.
13 S. 23(3)(b)(ii), (iii), and (iv) of ibid.
14 S. 23(3)(b)(iii) of ibid.
15 S. 23(3)(b)(iv) of ibid.
16 S. 4(1) of ibid.
17 S. 5(2) of ibid.
18 S. 5(1) of ibid.
19 S. 6 of ibid.
20 S. 7 of ibid.
21 S. 13 of ibid.
22 S. 15 of ibid.
23 S. 19 of ibid.
24 S. 18 of ibid.

The VHI is a non-profit making body: any surplus on its income is devoted to the reduction of premiums or increase in benefits.[25] However, the comments of the Oireachtas Joint Committee on the VHI should be noted:

> [t]he VHI has no share capital and, in this respect, resembles a mutual insurance company where retained earnings surplus to reserve requirements are available for the benefit of members in terms of reduced premiums or improved benefits. This appears to be supported by the provisions of s. 4 of the 1957 Act. However, the imposition of the three million pound levy on the VHI by the Minister for Health in 1992 would suggest that the Department views the VHI's reserves as the property of the Minister for Health and thus they are not necessarily for the benefit of the members.[26]

Its main purpose is to give insurance cover against unforeseen hospital and out-patient costs and to provide this cover at reasonable rates.[27] It is not an alternative to the payment of health contributions which are obligatory payments and which must be paid irrespective of voluntary health insurance membership.

The VHI has been described as:

> essentially commercial in nature, though with a virtual monopoly of the market, offering health insurance on a community rating basis, with a financial framework similar to that of a Friendly Society, but largely controlled by the Minister for Health.[28]

PURPOSE AND BENEFITS OF VHI

The VHI's schemes were aimed at alleviating the high cost of health care associated with hospital treatment and hospital stays.[29]

Initially, the VHI provided a scheme comprising three plans covering treatment in a public ward, a semi-private room and a private room. These

---

25 See Member Update MUAE 16 'VHI, as a not-for-profit co-operative fund, is committed to ensuring that members receive the highest quality healthcare at an affordable price'.
26 Oireachtas Seventh Joint Committee on Commercial State Sponsored Bodies, *First Report on VHI*, Stationery Office, (Dublin, 1994, Pn. 0408), p. 23.
27 *Report of the Commission on Health Funding* (Stationery Office, Dublin, 1989, pl. 6763), p. 123-5, pp. 389-94.
28 *First Report on VHI*, op. cit., p. 10.
29 Ibid., pp. 10-13.

three plans were limited to in-patient hospital and consultant charges and fees and to medical and surgical appliances.[30]

This scheme was replaced in 1962 by the unit system, whereby subscribers could choose from one to twelve units of each of one or two types of unit. Unit M provided for hospital maintenance charges and the other one, unit T, provided for treatment charges. The basis for this scheme was that subscribers would be able to choose the amount of care that they needed.[31]

In 1979, a new scheme of premiums and benefits was introduced by the VHI. The scheme was comprised of two sections: doctors' fees and hospital plans. Under the doctors' fees section, subscribers had to purchase fourteen units of cover, with the possibility of purchasing more. The rationale for the minimum of fourteen units was, according to the VHI, that it was considered adequate to cover professional fees in most cases. The hospital plan section covered hospital charges, and subscribers could elect for one of three different levels of benefit: plans A, B, or C.[32]

Plan A gave full cover for semi-private accommodation and partial cover for private accommodation in those hospitals and for care in private hospitals. Plan B covered private or semi-private accommodation in public hospitals and semi-private accommodation in private hospitals, and partially covering care in private rooms generally. Plan C covered private and semi-private accommodation in all classes of hospitals.[33]

In 1986, two new private institutions were opened in Dublin, the Mater Private Hospital and the Blackrock Clinic. These institutions comprise suites of consulting rooms where consultants see patients, and also private hospital facilities. They both offer a number of treatments not available or not readily available in other hospitals. They also operate at higher cost levels. The VHI deemed it impossible to fully accommodate these hospitals in its existing hospital plans, although plans B and C partially cover care in the new private institutions.

Consequently, two new schemes were introduced – plans D and E.

Plan D provides cover as in Plan C, but also covers fully semi-private accommodation in the Blackrock Clinic and the Mater Private Hospital.

Plan E covers private or semi-private accommodation in all hospitals including the Blackrock Clinic and the Mater Private Hospital.[34]

---

30 B. Hensey, *The Health Services of Ire-land*, op. cit., ch. 16.

31 *First Report on VHI*, op. cit., pp. 10-11.

32 Id.

33 B. Hensey, op. cit., p. 189-90.

34 *A Guide To Plans A, B, C, D, E,: Rules* (VHI Board Dublin, 1992), as amended in 1993 and 1994.

DOCTORS' FEES

The VHI attempted to tackle the problem of limited indemnity for doctors' fees in 1991, with the introduction of the full cover scheme. Under this scheme, the VHI negotiated a differential fee structure whereby doctors who accepted the VHI fee schedule as full payment for their services to subscribers received a higher level of remuneration than those that did not. Subscribers attending such 'participating doctors' have one hundred per cent. indemnity for both hospital charges and doctors' fees. Those doctors who are not willing to accept the VHI schedule receive a lower payment and are free to charge their patients additional amounts. At present, approximately sixty-five per cent. of all consultants participate in this scheme, although, in December 1993, no anaesthetists and pathologists were members, and there were at that date relatively speaking few urologists, gastroenterologists and obstetricians.[35]

Before 1991, the VHI paid a scale of fees to consultants which was believed to be in line with the going rate for each medical procedure. However, some consultants' fees were about fifteen to twenty per cent. above the VHI rates. This resulted in patients being underinsured, and the patients had to pay the balance due out of their own pockets. The so-called 'balance bills' which are the result of this practice are the subject of controversy.

The VHI has tried to introduce total indemnity. However, consultants claim that their relations with the VHI are difficult. They argue that there is an unwillingness on the part of the VHI to negotiate realistic rates for fees.[36] On the other hand, the VHI justifies total indemnity with the following reasons. First, VHI subscribers complain about the practice of being billed for a service which, they argue, they have already paid for through their VHI subscriptions. Second, the VHI sees 'balance billing' as making its product less attractive in the market place. Third, the VHI claims that without having a ceiling on the upward movement of consultant's fees, there is a risk that the VHI's reimbursement rates will simply be a 'floor' which will enable consultants to charge a higher overall fee.[37]

MEMBERSHIP OF THE VHI

The VHI operates on the basis of community rating principles. In other words all subscribers pay the same premium regardless of the risk of their making a claim. As such risks increase with age, this system involves a

---

35 Ibid., p. 37. See the report in the *Irish Medical Times* (1994), Vol. 28, No. 4 (28 January), pp. 1-2. It should be noted that the number of participants will inevitably vary.

36 Ibid., p. 37.

37 Ibid., p. 38-9.

transfer from the young to the old. The VHI justifies this by arguing that the elderly are deemed to be more vulnerable economically than the young. The VHI limits to a certain extent this principle. Those over sixty-five years of age cannot join the VHI, while all have to go through a waiting period before gaining eligibility for benefit.

The alternative to community rating is risk rating. This system involves the calculation of premiums in relation to the probability that a class of subscriber will make a claim. In a non-monopolistic situation such as that which should obtain from July 1994 as a result of the introduction of the EC Third Non Life Directive. This Directive, discussed below, effectively abolishes the monopoly position of the VHI allowing insurance companies from other EU states to offer insurance in this country. However, as a result of lobbying by the Irish Government, this Directive provides that EU Member State Governments can require health insurers to market policies based on the principles of community rating, open enrollment,[38] and lifetime membership.[39] It is believed that new entrants to the health insurance market would offer lower risk related schemes which would lead to lower rates for young people.[40]

The Joint Oireachtas Committee in its report on the VHI, recommends[41] that community rating should be preserved as much as possible in order that vulnerable groups should not be exposed to large increases in subscriptions, and recommended that the Government should set up an equalisation mechanism to preserve the benefits of a competitive market and community rating.[42]

The VHI ceased publishing socio-economic information on its clientele in 1984. Since that date, the only source of such information is contained in a sample survey undertaken by the Economic and Social Research Institute (ESRI) in 1987, as part of a wider study of health services in Ireland.[43] The ESRI study provides the most comprehensive account of the membership profile of the VHI presently available.

It should be noted that there is a close association between income, when adjusted for family size, and membership of the VHI. Yet 25% of the top 10% of the population in income adjusted terms are not members of the VHI. About 7% of the bottom 10% are VHI members.[44]

38 All persons who apply for membership of an insurance scheme are entitled to membership as is noted by the Joint Oireachtas Committee Report on The VHI.

39 *First Report on VHI*, op. cit., ch. 7.

40 Ibid., p. 50.

41 Ibid., ch. 7.

42 Ibid., pp. 49-53.

43 See Brian Nolan, *The Utilisation and Financing of Health Services in Ireland* General Research Series, Paper No. 155 (Economic and Social Research Institute, Dublin, 1991).

44 *First Report on VHI*, op. cit., p. 16.

There is a positive association between social class and VHI membership. Thus 69.2% of the Higher Professional/Managerial group have VHI cover, and 58.3% of lower professional/managerial group are in the VHI. This falls to 3.2% in the case of the unskilled manual worker category.[45]

LICENSING OF OTHER INSURERS

Although not stated in the 1957 Act, it seems to have been understood that Ireland was not large enough to allow more than one health insurance body to operate effectively. Since the passing of the Act, successive Ministers for Health have tended to refuse licences to such bodies. However, by virtue of membership of the European Union, Ireland now faces the prospect of the opening up of its domestic insurance market to insurers from other member states. The First EC Non-Life Directive established common rules for calculating solvency margins and made it easier for insurers from one member state to establish business in another. However, member states were allowed to exempt certain institutions form these regulations, and the Irish government exempted the VHI.

The Second EC Non-Life Directive allows insurance companies to offer insurance in the member states. Here, responsibility for ensuring that solvency margins are respected rests with the 'home' country. The VHI was exempted from the provisions of this Directive also. The Third EC Non-Life Directive abolishes the exemptions, so that from July 1994, the VHI and health insurance in general will be subject to the provisions of the First and Second Non-Life Directives. However, due in large part to representations made by the Irish Government, the Directive provides that the governments of member states can require health insurers to market policies based on the principles of community rating, open enrolment (open to all) and life time membership (one cannot have one's membership withdrawn on age grounds). These insurers do not have to be established in Ireland.

DEANE & ORS. v. VHI BOARD

The VHI scheme has however been subject to litigation: in *Deane & Ors. v VHI Board*[46] the Supreme Court has held that certain activities of the

---

45 Id., p. 16.

46 [1992] 2 IR 319. For comment and analysis of this decision, see E. Madden, 'Further Battles on Irish Medical Insurance Are Likely After Ruling', *Irish Medical Times (1993)*, Vol. 26, No. 32 (7 August), p. 12. Insurance is a critical factor in Irish medicine. Not only are a relatively large proportion covered by insurance schemes of one sort or another for illness, but in a common law adversarial system such as Ireland's where negligence cases arising out of accidents at work and motoring are currently resolved by law cases,

VHI Board may constitute a breach of the Competition Act, 1991, by being an abuse of a dominant position within a national context. In the case of *Deane v VHI*[47] the question of the status of the VHI arose for decision. The plaintiff alleged that the VHI was breaching section 5 of the Competition Act 1991. The plaintiff's argument revolved around the definition of the word 'undertaking' for the purposes of the Act of 1991. If the VHI, as alleged by the plaintiff, came within this definition then it was in breach of s. 5 of the Act of 1991. S. 5(1) of the Act provides that:

> [a]ny abuse by one or more undertakings of a dominant position in trade for any goods or services in the state or in a substantial part of the State is prohibited.

S. 3(1) of the Act of 1991 defines an 'undertaking' as:

> a person, being an individual, a body corporate or an unincorporated body of persons engaged for gain in the production, supply or distribution of goods or the provision of a service.

The question for decision was therefore whether the VHI was a body corporate engaged for gain in the supply of a service. The VHI argued on its part that s. 4(4) of the Voluntary Health Insurance Act 1957 supported its contention that it was not an undertaking in that it did not supply the service of health insurance for gain.

In deciding the issue, Finlay CJ referred to the definition of the word 'gain' supplied by Sir George Jessel MR in his judgment in the case of *In re Arthur Average Association for British, Foreign and Colonial Ships*.[48] In that case, Jessel MR defined 'gain' as meaning:

> acquisition. It has no other meaning that I am aware of. Gain is something obtained or acquired. It is not limited to pecuniary gain. We should have to add the word 'pecuniary' so to limit it. And still less is it limited to commercial profits. The word used, it must be observed, is not 'gains' but 'gain' in the singular. Commercial profits, no doubt, are gain but I cannot find anything limiting gain simply to a commercial profit. I take the words as referring to a company which

medical evidence is critical to the resolution of many disputes which are essentially between insurers. It is significant that Irish injury awards are said to be the highest in Europe according to a study of EU jurisdictions undertaken by Davies Arnold Cooper, and reported in *Irish Medical Times* (1991), Vol. 25, No. 41 (11 October), pp. 1, 2.

47 [1992] 2 IR 319.
48 (1875) LR 10 Ch App 542.

is formed to acquire something or in which the individual members are similarly to give something away or to spend something and do not gain anything.[49]

Finlay CJ approved of this definition of the word 'gain' in holding that the VHI came within the definition of the word 'undertaking' for the purposes of s. 3(1) of the Act of 1991, stating:

> the true construction of this section [s. 3(1)] is that the words 'for gain' connote merely an activity carried on or a service supplied, as it is in this case, which is done in return for a charge or payment, and that, accordingly, the defendant does come within the definition of an undertaking in the Act of 1991. What would be saved from application of the Act, by reason of the insertion of the words 'engaged for gain' is, in my view, what is referred to in the judgment of Jessel MR in *In re Arthur Average Association for British, Foreign and Colonial Ships* ... namely, a charitable association providing the spending of money and the supply of goods or services free of any charge or payment.[50]

Nevertheless the *de facto* monopoly situation of the VHI is unlikely to be threatened, at least in the short term, as a derogation was sought and granted from the EC's Third Non-Life Directive, for a continuation of the current system of community rating, which is not widely prevalent internationally.[51]

49 Ibid. at p. 546.
50 [1992] 2 IR 319 at p. 332.
51 *First Report on VHI*, op. cit., ch. 57.

12

STATUTORY CONTROLS OF MISCELLANEOUS MEDICO-LEGAL AREAS

ORGAN TRANSPLANTS

Ireland has no specific legislative provisions[1] in relation to organ transplants, nor to donor organ transplants,[2] nor to donor organ procurement. It is submitted, however, that there is a need for a legislative framework to control the harvesting and transplant of organs.

The general legal principles in relation to consent and the right to be informed will apply, *mutatis mutandis*, to organ transplant, as will the limits placed on the actions of physicians by the principles of tort and criminal law.

The Medical Council has endorsed Articles 13, 14, and 15 of the Principles of Medical Ethics in Europe in relation to this matter.[3]

Article 13 provides that in a case where it is impossible to reverse the terminal processes leading to the cessation of a patient's vital functions which are being artificially maintained, doctors will satisfy themselves that death has occurred. At least two doctors acting independently of each other should take meticulous steps to verify this situation and record their findings in writing. They shall be independent of the team which is to carry out the

---

1   Note however the provisions of the Liability for Defective Products Act 1991. For a general view of the medico-legal problems involved in this area which will doubtless be relevant to Irish judicial considerations of these issues, see P.D.G. Skegg, 'The Use of Corpses for Medical education and Research: The Legal Requirements', *Medicine Science and The Law* (1991) Vol. 31, No. 4 (October) p. 345.

2   There exist four different types of transplant. There are (i) autografts, which involve the transplant of tissue of an organ within the same individual from one part of the body to the other; (ii) homografts, which are transplants from one individual to another within the same species (iii) heterografts, involving transplants between individuals of different species; and (iv) isografts, which are transplants between genetically identical individuals, such as identical twins.

3   The Medical Council, *A Guide to Ethical Conduct and Behaviour and to Fitness to Practise*, 4th ed. (Medical Council, Dublin, 1994).

transplantation. (See chapter 8 for a more extensive discussion on the definition of 'death').

Article 14 provides that doctors removing an organ for transplantation may give particular treatment designed to maintain the condition of that organ.

Article 15 states that doctors must also take all practical steps to satisfy themselves that the donor had not expressed an opinion, or left instructions on the matter either in writing or with his or her family.

The European Parliament passed a resolution on 14 September 1993 which prohibited the trade in transplant organs.[4] There currently exists a great shortage of transplant organs[5] which has led many developing countries to legalise trade in organs by offering payment to live donors.

Thus many health care professionals and politicians see a need to prevent a market in organs developing on a grand scale. Indeed the Report of the Conference of European Health Ministers of November 1987 was strongly opposed to such a development. It was stated in the Report that:

> [t]he sale of human organs is no longer a myth and the wealthiest can buy life at the expense of the most underprivileged. That is where we have been led by an act of which ethics approves, and we are only at the beginning of a venture fraught with dangers. Organ donation is undoubtedly a profoundly humane gesture, but its legislation and use without major restrictions involve one of the greatest risks man has ever run, that of giving a value to his body, a price to his life.[6]

CADAVER DONATIONS

This aspect of organ donation is not regulated by statute in Ireland. It is, however, governed by professional ethical guidelines, laid down in the Medical Council's Guidelines.[7] These Guidelines provide that the body of the deceased may be used as a source of transplant organs provided that two doctors who are not part of the transplant team and who are acting independently of each other are satisfied that the donor is dead. Secondly, the transplant team must satisfy themselves that the deceased had not expressed any opinion on the issue of organ donation nor had left any instructions on the matter.[8]

---

4 See *Irish Times*, 15 September 1993, p. 2.

5 See Sir R. Hoffenberg, *Report of the Working Party on Supply of Donor Organs For Transplantation* (HMSO, London, 1987).

6 *Report of the Conference of European Health Ministers* (EU, Brussels, November 1987) p. 15.

7 *A Guide to Ethical Conduct*, op. cit., pp. 37-8.

8 Ibid., p. 38.

THE SALE OF HUMAN TISSUE AND ORGANS

Due to the short supply or suitable organs for donation, individuals may involve themselves in less than ethical means of obtaining such organs.[9] In nations where economic and social deprivation is the norm for the majority of the population, the sale of organs is not rare.[10] In Ireland, there has been no specific legislative intervention, but perhaps, as there is international concern about the extent of the problem in this area, legislation governing cross-national traffic in organs should be introduced. Such legislation may become necessary in any event because of EU developments. On 14 December 1993, the EU Parliament adopted a resolution on the prohibition of trade in transplant organs.[11] However the resolution is merely of symbolic importance at the moment; and will only acquire statutory force if for example it is implemented in the terms of a Directive.

FOETUS

Given the present position with regard to pregnancy termination in Ireland,[12] it is unlikely that foetal material may lawfully be used in transplant or experimental procedures. This is due to the fact that foetal transplantation is dependent on a supply of foetal tissue which comes in the main from induced abortions.[13] Tissue from spontaneous abortions is not considered suitable due to the high incidence of viral infections and chromosomal abnormalities.[14] Despite the scientific arguments for and against the use of foetal material, in Ireland, the constitutional protection of the right to life of the unborn contained in Article 40.3.3, and the ethical guidelines would appear to preclude the use of such material.

It may be possible to regulate this area of medical practice to prevent abuse and also to separate it from the issue of abortion. This could be done

---

9 B. Brecher, 'The Kidney Trade: or the Customer is always wrong', *Journal of Medical Ethics* (1990), Vol. 16, pp. 120-3; L. Cohen, 'Increasing the supply of transplant organs: the virtues of a futures market', *George Washington Law Review* (1989), Vol. 58, No. 1, p. 1-51.

10 See C. Hedges, 'Egypt's Desperate Trade: Body Parts for Sale', *New York Times*, 23 September 1991; W. Land and J.B. Dosseter (eds.), *Organ Replacement Therapy: Ethics Justice Commerce (Springer Verlag, Heidelberg, 1991)*.

11 WHO *International Digest of Health Legislation* (1994), Vol. 45, No. 1, pp. 111-4.

12 Discussed in ch. 9.

13 G.J. Annas and S. Elias, 'The politics of transplantation of human foetal tissue', *New England Journal of Medicine* (1989) Vol. 320, p. 1079-82.

14 Id; The National Institutes of Health, *Report of The Human Foetal Tissue Research Transplantation Panel* (National Institutes of Health, Bethesda, Maryland, 1988).

using as a basis the recommendations raised by The National Institutes of Health *Report of The Human Foetal Tissue Research Transplantation Panel.*[15]

ANENCEPHALIC NEONATES

The use of the anencephalic neonate as a source of transplant organs has yet to be considered by the Irish legislature or courts. The medical profession in Ireland has not introduced specific ethical directions on the issue, apart from the general statements to be found in the Medical Council's Guidelines.[16] However, the Conference of Medical Royal Colleges in the UK has provided a set of guidelines.[17] The Conference is of the view that organs for transplantation can be removed from anencephalic infants when two doctors who are not members of the transplant team agree that spontaneous respiration has ceased.[18]

REGISTRATION OF BIRTHS AND DEATHS

Births (including stillbirths) The registration of births and deaths in Ireland is compulsory. The legislation provides for official registration, the Registrar of Births and Deaths, and the maintenance of a Register of Births and Deaths, and, since the 1994 Act, a Register of Stillbirths.[19]

The topic is dealt with in this work, because, as we shall explain in this section, hospital authorities and registered medical practitioners in charge of hospitals where a birth or stillbirth takes place, have registration obligations in connection with the registration of such births. It is important to note that whenever a birth occurs in Ireland, and a hospital or a medical

---

15 National Institutes For Health, Bethesda, Maryland, 1988. The recommendations stated that payments and other forms of remuneration and compensation (reimbursement of expenses etc. apart) associated with the procurement of foetal tissue should be prohibited. The decision and consent to abort must precede discussion of the possible foetal tissue for transplantation purposes. The pregnant woman should be prohibited from designating the transplant recipient of the foetal tissue. Anonymity between donor and recipient should be maintained. Finally, the timing and method of abortion should not be influenced by the potential uses of foetal tissue for transplantation or medical research.

16 *A Guide to Ethical Conduct*, op. cit., pp. 37-38.

17 The Conference of Medical Royal Colleges and Their Faculties in the UK, *Report of the working party on organ transplantation in neonates* (London, 1988).

18 M. Harrison, 'Organ procurement for children: The anencephalic foetus as donor', *Lancet* (1986), Vol. 2, p. 1383.

19 Births and Deaths Registration Act (Ireland) 1880, as amended by the Vital Statistics on Births Deaths and Marriages Registration Act, 1962, the Births Deaths and Marriages Registration Act 1972, and the Stillbirths Act 1994, and acts referred to therein.

practitioner is involved either at the birth or afterwards, then an obligation arises or may arise.

The law requires that all live births[20] and stillbirths[21] must be registered.

The definition of 'birth' in this context poses no difficulty, but it should be noted that s. 1 provides that a stillbirth for registration purposes is one where the child is born weighing five hundred grammes or more or has a gestational age of twenty four weeks or more who shows no sign of life.

A primary duty of registration of births is statutorily placed on the father and mother of the child. In default of the father and mother, it is the duty of 'the occupier in the house in which to his knowledge the child is born, and of each person present at the birth, and of the person having charge of the child' to notify the birth to the Registrar in the prescribed manner within forty-two days.[22] Presumably, this section applies to a registered medical practitioner attending a birth, or to a doctor or nurse or midwife employed by a hospital or health authority, or to a nursing home proprietor, or the person in charge of any institution where the birth has taken place. Where a living newly born child is found exposed, the finder, and the person taking charge of the infant, has a duty to notify the registrar within seven days.[23]

Where there is default, the registrar may by written notice require information from 'any persons required by this Act'. In this connection, it should be explained that under s. 4 of the 1880 Act,[24] the Registrar of births and the Registrar of Deaths of the district must 'inform himself carefully of every birth which happens within his district', and to register the birth, and likewise, with every death.[25]

The Registrar may not register any child three months after its birth: however an exception is made for registration up to a year after birth, but a special procedure applies to such registration.[26]

The procedure for the registration of stillbirths is slightly different.[27] The duty of registration devolves on the mother or father,[28] and there is no supplementary provision for registration by the occupier of the house or each person present at the birth.

Where a stillbirth is registered by the mother or father, specified details[29]

20 S. 1 of the 1880 Act.
21 S. 6 of the 1994 Act.
22 Ss. 2, 3, 4 of the 1880 Act.
23 S. 3 of the 1880 Act.
24 S. 3 of the 1880 Act defines these persons.
25 The obligation of the registrar to register births and deaths is respectively contained in ss. 4 and 14 of the 1880 Act.
26 S. 5 of the 1880 Act.

27 S. 6 of the 1994 Act.
28 S. 6(1) of the 1994 Act.
29 See the schedule to the 1994 Act. This specifies: date and place of birth, sex of child, weight, gestational age, forename and surname of child, mother and father's forename, surname, address, occupation and former names (if any), signature, qualification & address of informant, and when registered.

must be given to the Registrar. The certificate must be signed by a registered medical practitioner who has attended the birth or who has examined the child, and must certify 'in the opinion of the medical practitioner, the weight and gestational age of the child and naming, where applicable, the hospital in which the birth occurred or which had care of the mother following the birth'.[30]

As part of the statutory duty of the Registrar under the 1880 Act to register all births, the 1994 Act provides that the Registrar must notify the hospital named in the certificate, or, where none, the relevant medical practitioner, that registration has taken place.[31]

If no such notification is received by the hospital or by the medical practitioner within three months of the stillbirth, a duty is imposed on the hospital or medical practitioner concerned. An authorised member of the staff of the hospital, or, if the birth did not take place in hospital, the medical practitioner involved, must give the required particulars to the Registrar (of Births and Deaths) and sign the register.[32]

Where there is uncertainty in the case of the birth whether or not the infant is stillborn, the medical practitioner must refer the matter to the coroner, and if the coroner finds that there was a stillbirth, the coroner must, within one month or so of finding, notify the Registrar.[33]

Deaths All deaths must be registered. In the preponderance of cases, where death takes place in hospitals, the hospital will register the death. If death takes place at home, the nearest relative(s) will obtain a certificate of cause of death from the attending doctor, and will proceed to register the death. Though in fact this is sometimes done by the undertakers concerned, it should be noted that, under the 1880 Act, the duty of registration devolves on the nearest relatives of the deceased present at the death, or those relatives in attendance during the last illness of the deceased, or in default of such relatives, of every other relative of the deceased living in the same district. In default of these, the responsibility devolves on persons present at the death or the occupier of the house where the deceased was believed to have died.[34]

Special provisions apply where a person dies elsewhere than in a house, or a dead body is found somewhere other than in a house. In practical terms, such deaths invariably come under the coroner's jurisdiction. The relatives of the deceased having knowledge of any particulars of the death, or, in default, any person present at the death, or the finder, or the person taking

---

30 S. 6(1) of the 1994 Act.
31 S. 6(3) of the 1994 Act.
32 S. 6(4) of the 1994 Act.

33 S. 6(6) of the 1994 Act.
34 S. 10 of the 1880 Act.

charge of the body must notify the registrar within five days of the death or the finding of the body.[35] S. 12 of the 1880 Act provides an extension of this period where a death may be properly registered and accompanied by the requisite medical certificate. It is assumed that in this case, the extension applies only where a registered medical practitioner is prepared to certify the death, and does not consider it necessary to inform the coroner.

In default of the statutory registration procedure, the registrar is accorded certain powers of requiring the attendance at his registry of those who may know about the death, and requiring them to sign the register. These powers may be exercised at any time up to twelve months after the death or finding of the body, whichever is latest.

The 1880 Act specifies that no death may be registered after twelve months 'where [the] death has from the default of the persons required to give information concerning it not been registered'.[36] In practice, this does not mean that late deaths are not registered: late registrations do take place by special authorisation of the Registrar General and are recorded separately at the end of the annual book of statistics.

In general, the procedure for certification of death by a registered medical practitioner, is that the attending doctor will fill in a medical certificate of the cause of death which specifies that the doctor attended the deceased and the dates on which he was seen. The certificate provides for the disease or condition leading to death and other significant conditions contributing to the death but not related to the disease or condition causing it. The certificate of the cause of death is then taken to the registrar of births and deaths who will in turn issue a death certificate.

CREMATIONS

Until the nineteen seventies, cremations were not performed in Ireland. There is now a crematorium based at Glasnevin, Dublin. The Dublin Cemeteries Committee has made rules governing cremation. These rules were made pursuant to the Dublin Cemeteries Committee Act 1970.[37]

Under these rules, a medical referee authorised by the Committee or his deputy must authorise each cremation. Before so doing the medical referee of deputy must be satisfied that the attending doctor must have been registered for at least three years and has completed and signed a form stating the cause of death. If the attending doctor is not available or has not been registered for at least three years a certificate must be obtained from

35 S. 11 of the 1880 Act.
36 S. 13 of the 1880 Act.
37 *The Dublin Cemeteries Committee Rules*

(1989) made pursuant to s. 8 and s. 9 of the Dublin Cemeteries Committee Act 1970.

another doctor who has been registered for three years, who has viewed the body, and made such enquiries as he deems necessary to satisfy himself as to the cause of death before signing the certificate.[38] Alternatively, a cremation may be performed if the death was reported to the coroner, who has given a certificate to the medical referee that the cremation can go ahead. The medical referee has obligations to satisfy himself both by enquiry and also by commissioning or performing an external examination or an internal dissection or autopsy in order to ensure that no reason exists that the body should not be cremated.

Special rules apply whereby a Garda superintendent of the district where the death took place may inform the committee that further examination or investigation is or may be required, and cremation may not take place without the consent of the superintendent or his authorised deputy or without the authority of a court order or coroner's order, where such consent has been refused.[39]

CORONERS

General The legislation governing the function, powers, duties and terms and conditions of appointment of coroners in Ireland is principally contained in the Coroners Act 1962.[40]

We do not deal here with the power of the coroner to conduct an inquest into 'treasure trove', as it is outside the remit of medical law.[41]

38 As the crematorium insists that the certifying doctor has seen the deceased in life as well as after death, for identification purposes, this clause can rarely be used. While this is not specified in the regulations or bye laws, it is now embodied in Form C.

39 In effect this is so that all necessary samples may be taken by the pathologist concerned prior to cremation.

40 Terms and conditions of tenure of the offices of coroner and deputy coroner, including matters such as payment, residence, qualifications, appointment and removal are set out in Part II and part V of the Act.

  In particular, the Act specifies some of the particular duties of coroners: that coroners must either take depositions or keep notes of the names and addresses of witnesses in an inquest, (s. 28), they must preserve documents (s. 29), furnish particulars to other state bodies (s. 50), make returns (s. 55), and certify sums to be paid by local authorities (s. 58).

  The law in England governing coroners is in some respects similar. In *R. v. Bristol Coroner, ex p. Kerr* [1974] QB 652, the functions of the coroner in relation to inquests under English law is discussed.

41 N.E. Palmer et. al., *Bailment*, 2nd ed. (Law Book Co. Ltd, Australia, 1991). See also *Webb v. Ireland* [1988] ILRM 19, where the High and Supreme Courts dealt with the issue of ownership of the Derrynaflan Hoard, which was at least initially thought to be treasure trove. Though the High Court held that the Crown's prerogative of treasure trove had not survived the 1922 Constitution, and therefore the status and rights in the

The State is divided into Coroners' Districts.[42]

The principal duty of the coroner is to inquire into uncertified deaths and deaths in suspicious circumstances or in particular places (such as mental hospitals) where the law imposes such an obligation. The inquiry may involve an inquest.

Inquests   There are some circumstances where a coroner is obliged to hold an inquest[43] and others where he may hold an inquest if he thinks it necessary.[44] These requirements are apart from what obtains under other legislation such as Road Traffic Act legislation, or Safety at Work legislation.[45]

The function of the inquest is 'to (ascertain) the identity of the person in relation to whose death the inquest is being held and how, when, and where the death occurred'.

The coroner of the relevant district must be informed if certain deaths have taken place. Two are instanced here as being of the most importance, practically.

First, an inspector or other officer of the Gardaí is obliged to notify the coroner if he becomes aware that a death has occurred, and a medical certificate of cause of death is not procurable. The Gardaí will investigate such deaths, and, where necessary, summon the state pathologist. As a courtesy, the Gardaí will inform the coroner.

Second, every medical practitioner, registrar of deaths, funeral undertaker, house or mobile home occupier and every person in charge of any institution or premises who becomes aware that any deceased died directly

Derrynaflan Hoard was uncertain, the Supreme Court, on appeal held that the State had a right to claim the hoard, though it is uncertain precisely on what basis the right exists, and whether the right to treasure trove, and indeed the nature of treasure trove itself, is still the same under Irish law as in English law. It is unlikely, however that the procedures involved in a coroner's inquest on treasure trove are directly affected by any change In the status or nature of treasure trove itself.

42 In general, where the Act provides for or permits the performance of specified acts by the coroner, it is the coroner of the district in which the death has occurred who is liable to discharge the obligations laid down for the coroner to perform.

43 Coroners Act 1962, s. 17. S. 17 lays down a general duty to hold an inquest, where the coroner is informed that the body of a deceased person is lying within his district, if he is of the opinion that death 'may have occurred in a violent or unnatural manner, or suddenly, or from unknown causes, or in a place or in circumstances which . . . require that an inquest should be held'.

44 S. 18 provides that 'a coroner may inquire into the circumstances of death', of a person whose body is within his district and for whom a medical certificate of cause of death is not 'procurable', and if unable to ascertain the cause of death, the coroner may hold an inquest.

45 S. 30, ibid.

or indirectly as a result of violence, misadventure, unfair means, negligence, misconduct, malpractice on the part of others, or any cause other than natural illness or disease for which he had been seen and treated by a registered medical practitioner within one month before his death or in such circumstances as may require an investigation, including death from anaesthetic, must notify the coroner.[46]

The notification required must include the facts and circumstances relating to the death.

Failure to comply with this requirement is a criminal offence; the penalty on summary conviction may not exceed twenty pounds.

Having been so notified, the coroner has options as to what should be done. A coroner may decide that an examination *post mortem* should be made, and if this shows that an inquest is unnecessary, the coroner is not obliged to hold an inquest. However, a coroner may not dispense with the holding of an inquest, if he is of the opinion that death had occurred 'in a violent or unnatural manner, or in a place or circumstances which, under provisions in that behalf contained in any other enactment, require that an inquest should be held'.[47]

Practically speaking the authors understand that about fifteen per cent of cases dealt with by coroners are inquested. Most are either referred back to the medical practitioner involved, so that he may complete the requisite certificate, or are registered as natural deaths under s. 50(1)(c) by the coroner.

Though an inquest will normally be ordered informally by the coroner, his powers include the capacity to hold an inquest without ordering an exhumation 'where the coroner knows that no good purpose will be effected by exhuming the body'.[48]

The Minister may direct a coroner to hold an inquest where the relevant body has been destroyed or is irrecoverable.[49] The Attorney General may direct any coroner to hold an inquest 'in circumstances which, in his opinion, make the holding of an inquest advisable', and provision is made for the payment of fees to the coroner by the local authority.[50]

Provision is made for the conduct of an inquest by the coroner of an adjoining district where the coroner or deputy coroner is 'absent, ill, incapacitated or disqualified' from the conduct of the inquest. Similarly special rules permit the Minister to arrange for inquests to be held by one coroner in respect of several deaths from the same cause.

---

46 See Coroners Act 1962, s. 18. It should be noted that where an obligation exists to notify the coroner, this may be discharged by notifying a member of the Gardaí not below the rank of sergeant (s. 18(5)).

47 Coroners Act 1962, s. 19(2).
48 S. 22 of Ibid.
49 S. 23 of Ibid.
50 S. 24 of Ibid.

An inquest may be adjourned, where criminal proceedings are being considered or have been instituted, and a request for adjournment is made by a member of the Gardaí 'not below the rank of inspector'. If criminal proceedings in relation to the death have been instituted, the coroner must adjourn the proceedings but does not have to resume them.[51] An inquest which has been adjourned, and at which only evidence of identification has been given, may be resumed with a different jury.

A coroner may, at any time, before or during an inquest, cause a *post mortem* examination to be made of the body, and the coroner may request the Minister to arrange post mortems or special examinations or both.[52] The Coroner *must* so request the Minister where a Garda not below the rank of Inspector so requests him, stating reasons therefor.[53]

Certain powers are accorded the coroner in respect of the holding of an inquest. The coroner also has certain powers to summon witnesses,[54] and examine them on oath[55] but special rules apply in respect of the summoning to an inquest of a second registered medical practitioner. A summons may not be issued for such a second doctor unless either (a) a majority of jurors requisition that doctor's attendance, or (b) the second doctor[56] attended the *post mortem* examination.[57]

The coroner conducting an inquest must view the body unless it has first been viewed by a member of the Gardaí, another coroner or deputy coroner. If the coroner sits with a jury, the jury are only required to view the body if the coroner directs or a majority of the jury so desires.[58]

51 An adjournment *sine die*, is no longer allowed: *State (Costello) v. Bofin* [1980] ILRM 233.
52 It is under this power, contained In s. 33(2) of the Act, that the State Pathologist is appointed for each case.
53 The Coroner may commission a registered medical practitioner, or in exceptional circumstances, two to perform *post mortems*. It prohibits such *post mortems* to be conducted by any doctor who had attended the deceased within one month before the death. It permits a hospital pathologist who had attended the deceased within the last month of the deceased's life, to perform the *post mortem* 'save where the coroner considers that the conduct of such practitioner in relation to his attendance on the deceased is likely to be called in question'.
54 The method of service of such witness summons is set out in s. 36.
55 S. 38 provides that a witness is guilty of an offence if he fails to take an oath legally required, or answer a question or do anything which would equate to contempt of court. However it is thought that this section may be unconstitutional.
56 This may be of importance in cases such as those where a pathologist has died after the post mortem but before the inquest, where another doctor happened to be present.
57 Coroners Act 1962, s. 52. This may apply either where the second doctor assists the first in the one *post mortem*, or where a second post-mortem is performed by e.g. the State Pathologist after the first *post mortem*, which for example might be inadequate. In Scotland, such a second post mortem is routine in 'suspicious death' post mortems.
58 S. 27, ibid.

Findings of the coroner Practically, one of the most important issues relating to coroner's inquests has been the issue of the findings. The findings must include the full name of the deceased, or the sex if unknown, the medical cause of the death, and the time, place and circumstances of the injury and death, and the 'verdict' of the coroner or jury.

Because the coroner's verdict proceeds from the coroner's court which is inquisitorial, not accusatorial, the findings of the coroner are not binding in later criminal or civil proceedings.[59] For example, a conclusion of 'murder' by the coroner, does not convict anyone of murder. The verdict of the coroner merely can be used formally to charge that individual with murder, thus beginning the normal criminal procedure. The conclusion must not be framed in such a way that it appears to make legal conclusions, civil or criminal.[60]

This is not to say that a coroner's verdict is irrelevant to all later legal proceedings. For example, a verdict of suicide might be relevant to an insurance company.[61] On the whole, however, documents generated by the coroner are used only as the basis for further inquiry or cross-examination at trial by interested parties. They are not admissible as evidence of the facts stated therein.[62]

An appeal may be taken from the coroner's court, but the usual procedure has been to remit the case to the coroner for re-hearing.

Provision is made for the preservation of documents by the Coroner and County Registrar.

The Coroners' legislation is in need of radical reform.[63] In the Dáil on 19 May 1994 Deputy Dr R. O'Hanlon raised the question of the difficulties being experienced by coroners in performing *post mortem* examinations, and indicated that delays in performing post mortems were attributable in part

---

59 See P. Matthews and J. Foreman, *Jervis on the Office and Duties of Coroners* (Sweet & Maxwell, London, 1993) ch. 20.

60 Ibid. at p. 363-4. It should be noted that previously a coroner's verdict could impute a conclusion against a named individual, although it remained legally non-binding. Today in the UK even this possibility has been eliminated; no conclusory assertions as to the legal responsibility of a named person may be made by the coroner. This reform was carried out by the Criminal Law Act 1977, s. 56 and s. 55, cited by Matthews and Foreman, p. 8.

61 Ibid., p. 364.

62 *Grime v. Fletcher* [1915] 1 KB 634; *Bird v. Keep* [1918] 2 KB 292, CA; *Calmenson v. Merchants' Warehousing Co.* (1921) 90 LJPC 134, HL; *Barnett v. Cohen* [1921] 2 KB 461; *In re Sigsworth* [1935] Ch. 89, *In re Pollock* [1941] Ch 219. Cited by Matthews and Foreman, p. 365, fn. 19.

63 See the interview with Dr Brian Farrell, Dublin City Coroner reported in D. Bergin, 'Coroners' Legislation Needs to be updated', *Irish Medical Times* (1994), Vol. 28, No. 2 (14 January), p. 19.

to the administrative difficuties because both local authority and health board resources are required.[64]

CHILD CARE; CHILD SEX ABUSE

At present, no duty is imposed, either by legislation or by the common law, on the medical health practitioner or other health care professional, to report cases of child sexual abuse. The law in relation to the protection of children is still contained in the Children Act 1908. This shall remain the case until the Government implements all the relevant provisions of the Child Care Act 1991, the statute introduced to amend the law in relation to the protection of 'at risk' children. However, the 1991 Act is to be introduced on a piece-meal basis by Ministerial order, until 1996, when, as the Department of Health has stated, its provisions shall be fully implemented.[65]

The 1908 Act provides for the removal of at risk children from their homes to the care of a relative or other fit person (usually the local health board). S. 20 of the 1908 Act provides that a member of the Gardaí who believes that a child has been the victim of a crime perpetrated by a parent, may remove the child to a place of safety (Garda station, doctor's surgery, hospital, or any other appropriate place), without the need to obtain a warrant. S. 24 of the Act allows a fit person to apply to the District Court on an *ex parte* basis (ie without having to give notice of the application to the child's parents), for a warrant authorising a member of the Gardaí to search for the child in question, and to bring the child to a place of safety. In practice, the 'fit person' is invariably the local health board. After the issuing of that warrant, and the placing of the child in a place of safety, the Health Board must return to the District Court, this time with the child, in order to obtain an order which would allow the child to be placed in the care of either the health board or a relative. This hearing affords the parents the opportunity to rebut the arguments of the Health Board. The order will only be granted if it is shown to the satisfaction of the Court that the child's welfare would be at risk if the child were returned to the care of the parents.

The Child Care Act 1991 provides for substantial changes in relation to the care of children. The Government's rationale in introducing the Act in a manner is economic, in that the resources required to effect such radical changes could not be provided immediately. S. 1(2) of the Act provides that the act shall come into effect on a gradual basis by ministerial orders.

S. 2 defines a 'child' for the purposes of the act as a person under the

64 See *Dáil Debates*, Vol. 442, No. 10 (19 May 1994), cols. 1845-8.
65 Department of Health, *Shaping a healthier future – A strategy for effective healthcare in the 1990* (Stationery Office, Dublin, 1994), pp. 58-9.

age of eighteen years, other than one who has married. Under the Act, every Health Board has as a function the promotion of the welfare of children in its area who are at risk. S. 3(2) states that the Health Board shall 'take such steps as it considers requisite to identify children who are not receiving adequate care and protection'. S. 4(1) places a duty on the Health Board to take a child into its care where it is apparent that such child requires care and protection which he would not otherwise receive. However, s. 4(2) provides that a Health Board may not take such a child into care if it is contrary to the wishes of the parent who has custody of the child or someone *in loco parentis*.

Under s. 13(1), an emergency care order may be applied for by a Health Board. Such order may be granted by a District Court Judge if he is of the opinion that there is either an immediate and serious risk to the health or welfare of a child which requires his being placed in the care of a Health Board or if there is likely to be such a risk if the child is not removed from where he is for the time being. Such order if granted allows the child to be placed under the care of the Health Board for a maximum period of eight days.

A further duty is imposed on the Health Board by virtue of s. 16. If it appears that a child requires care or protection, then the Health Board is under a duty to apply for a care order or a supervision order. S. 18(1) provides that the court may make a care order where, on the application of a Health Board, the court is satisfied that either:

(a) The child has been or is being assaulted, ill-treated, neglected or sexually abused; or

(b) the child's health, development or welfare has been or is being avoidably impaired or neglected; or

(c) the child's health, development or welfare is likely to be avoidably impaired or neglected, and that the child requires care or protection which he is unlikely to receive unless the court makes an order under the section.

The care order commits the child to the care of the Health Board for as long as that person remains a child or for such shorter period as the court may determine.

S. 19 deals with supervision orders. Where, on the application of a Health Board, with respect to a child residing in its area, the court is satisfied that one of the three conditions identical to those set out in s. 18(1) exist and that it is desirable that the child be visited periodically by or on behalf of the Health Board, the court may make a supervision order. A supervision order directs the Health Board to have the child visited on such periodical occasions as the court may determine, in order to satisfy the board as to the welfare of the child and to give to his or her parents or to a person acting *in loco parentis* any necessary advice as to the care of the child. A supervision order remains in force for a maximum period of twelve months.

At common law, certain persons failing to report child sexual abuse may be exposed to a possible civil action. It is arguable that liability in tort for negligence and breach of statutory duty would extend to the medical practitioner who fails to diagnose child sexual abuse.

The Child Care Act 1991 does not, however, provide for the mandatory reporting of child sexual abuse. In 1993, the *Report of the Kilkenny Incest Investigation*[66] recommended the introduction of a system of mandatory reporting of cases of suspected child sex abuse.[67] The Department of Health has responded to this recommendation by promising in 1994 a discussion paper on the issue of mandatory reporting.[68]

However, non-statutory guidelines governing the issue of child abuse exist. These were issued by the Department of Health in 1987, under the imaginative title, *Guidelines on Procedures for the Identification, Investigation and Management of Child Abuse*.[69] These Guidelines place the responsibility for the monitoring and co-ordinating cases of child abuse with the Health Boards. Overall responsibility for the handling of such cases is entrusted to the Director of Community Care and the Medical Officer of Health in the particular Health Board area. In addition, the Guidelines provide for the roles of other health professionals, such as general practitioners, social workers, and public health nurses, in the management of a child abuse case. An inter-disciplinary approach is stressed, as being the most effective way of dealing with such cases. Thus, the Guidelines promote liaison between health care professionals, Gardaí and schools. However, in practice, these guidelines do not appear to be adhered to uniformly by all eight Health Boards.[70] The guidelines also provide that in cases where there are reasonable grounds for suspecting child abuse, the Director of Community Care should report the matter to the Gardaí. However, the guidelines do not impose a legal duty on the Director of Community Care to report such cases. The *Report of the Kilkenny Incest Investigation*[71] has recommended that the Minister For Health prepare 'revised procedures for the identification, investigation and management of child abuse to replace the current guidelines'.[72] The Report goes on to specify the revised procedures. These

66 Department of Health, *Report of the Kilkenny Incest Investigation* (Stationery Office, Dublin, 1993).
67 Ibid., pp. 99-101.
68 Department of Health, *Shaping a healthier future*, op. cit., p. 59.
69 Department of Health (Stationery Office, Dublin, 1987).
70 See Department of Health, *Report of the Kilkenny Incest Investigation* (Stationery Office, Dublin, 1993) at pp. 96-7.
71 Department of Health (Stationery Office, Dublin, 1993).
72 Ibid., pp. 96-7.

would include a mandatory system of reporting, the maintenance of standardised child abuse registers in each community care area, and written agreed protocols for the investigation and management of child abuse cases.[73]

NOTIFIABLE DISEASES

In Ireland, certain infectious diseases[74] are subject to specific regulations, designed to protect public health.

The regulations[75] permit the Minister to require 'registered medical practitioners and any other persons' to notify medical officers of health of the disease in question.[76] They may also 'requir[e] adult persons to submit themselves, or the parents of children to medical examination . . . including the permission to take blood or other specimens for examinations or tests'.[77] The Schedule to the Act does not specifically enable the Minister to make regulations for compulsory treatment. However, the regulations may require:

73 Id., pp. 96-110.
74 S. 29 of the Health Act 1947 entitles the Minister of Health to specify by regulation which diseases are designated as infectious diseases.

The principal current regulations are contained in the Infectious Diseases Regulations 1981 (SI No. 390 of 1981) as amended by the Infectious Diseases (Amendment) Regulations 1985 (SI No. 268 of 1985).

The diseases currently the subject of regulation are: acute anterior poliomyelitis, acute encephalitis, acute viral meningitis, anthrax, bacillary dysentery, bacterial meningitis (including meningococcal septicaemia), brucellosis, cholera, diphtheria, food poisoning (bacterial other than salmonella) gastroenteritis (when contracted by children under two years of age), infective mononucleosis, influenza, pneumonia, legionnaires disease, leptospirosis, malaria, measles, ornithosis, plague, rabies, rubella, salmonellosis (other than typhoid or paratyphoid) sexually transmissible diseases (syphilis, gonorrhoea, chancroid, lymphogranuloma venereum, granuloma inguinale, non-specific urethritis, chlamydia trachomatis, trachomoniasis, candidiasis, pediculosis pubis, ano-genital warts, molluscum contagiosum, genital herpes simplex), smallpox, tetanus, tuberculosis, typhoid and paratyphoid, typhus, viral haemorrhagic diseases, viral hepatitis (type A, type B & type unspecified), whooping cough, yellow fever.
75 The scope of any such regulations are defined in the Second Schedule to the Health Act 1947.
76 Regulation 1 of the Second Schedule of ibid. The current regulation (Art 11 of the 1981 regulations) state: 'On becoming aware, whether from a notification or intimation under these regulations or otherwise, of a case or a suspected case of infectious disease or a probable source of infection with such disease, a medical officer of health, or a health officer on the advice of a medical officer of health, shall make such enquiries and take such steps as are necessary or desirable for investigating the nature and source of such infection and for removing conditions favourable to such infection'. Under Article 18 a medical officer of health is required to make weekly returns to the Minister of cases of infectious disease notified to him, and to make detailed reports on cases of specified infections.
77 Regulation 2 of ibid.

specified measures to be seen in relation to the protection or immunisation of such adult persons or children against a particular infectious disease.[78]

S. 30(a) of the Health Act 1947 imposes a duty on a person who knows he is a probable source of infection to take reasonable precaution to prevent his infecting others with such disease by his presence or conduct, or by means of any article with which he has been in contact. S. 30(b) imposes a similar restriction on 'a person having the care of another . . . and knowing that such other person is a probable source of such infection'.

S. 43 of the Health Act 1947 provides that where a civil action arises out of A infecting B through not taking prescribed precautions, the court may assume that the infection was caused by A's failure to take precautions, unless A can prove that his failure was 'unlikely' to have caused the disease.

If a person is considered to be a probable source of infection of acute anterior poliomyelitis, cholera, diphtheria, plague, smallpox, tuberculosis, typhoid, paratyphoid, typhus, and viral haemorrhagic diseases (including lassa fever and marburg disease) a chief medical officer (with the agreement of a second registered medical practitioner) may certify that the person should be detained in a hospital or other suitable place.[79] Certain legal safeguards exist. The certification must be notified to the Minister, the patient (or if a child, his parent) may appeal to the Minister in writing, and the appeal must be determined by the Minister and the decision communicated to the appellant.[80]

In addition to this, certain other regulations specify the precautions that must be taken relating to the sale and letting of dwellings,[81] verminous 'persons and articles',[82] and the burial of bodies.[83]

Certain nursing and accommodation facilities and maintenance allowances are available for patients in the relevant category.[84]

Health Boards are obliged to make arrangement for the diagnosis and treatment of infectious diseases,[85] to keep supply of medical agents,

---

78 Regulation 3 of ibid.
79 S. 38 of the Health Act 1947 as amended by s. 35 of the Health Act 1953.
80 Ibid. S. 38(2) of the 1947 Act.
81 S. 33-36 of the Health Act 1947. Note comments by B. Hensey, *The Health Services of Ireland*, 4th ed. (IPA, Dublin, 1990) p. 211.
82 S. 46-50 of the Health Act 1947.
83 S. 39 ibid.
84 S. 40 of the Health Act 1947 gives power to arrange rehabilitation services to persons suffering or recovering form infectious diseases. S. 42 provides for nursing services. S. 44 provides for maintenance allowances.
85 Regulation 10 of the Infectious Diseases Regulations.

instruments and equipment,[86] and keep records.[87] Special regulations too govern infectious diseases in the context of shipping and aircraft.[88]

The constitutionality of the regulations which involve issues such as deprivation of personal liberty and invasive diagnosis in the contexts discussed above has not yet been tested, but it is thought that where the provisions can be shown not merely not to be harmful to health, but designed to protect public health generally, that they would not be impeachable, representing a balance between public health requirements and incursion into private liberty.[89]

HIV/AIDS

The HIV/AIDS condition is not a notifiable disease in Ireland. That the pandemic is evident in Ireland may be deduced from the official statistics from the Department of Health. These suggest that as of 5 April 1992 there were 103 deaths from AIDS, and 258 cases of the condition diagnosed. At the end of 1993, 378 people had developed AIDS, of whom 182 had died. The figure for those testing HIV positive at end 1993 was 1,449. As of 15 June 1994, a total of 399 cases of AIDS have been confirmed in Ireland. Of these 172 constitute intravenous drug abusers, 133 homosexual or bisexual, 44 heterosexual, 28 haemophiliacs, 8 homosexual/bisexual/intravenous drug abusers, 8 babies born to drug abusers, and 1 baby born to heterosexual parents. 201 people have died from the disease: of these 82 were intravenous drug abusers, 63 were homosexual or bisexual, 21 heterosexual, 20 haemophiliac, 6 were babies born to intravenous drug abusers, and 3 were of undetermined category. As of May 1994, a total of 101 Irish children have now tested positive for the infection. It should be noted that the Department of Health states that the numbers of those presumed to be infected with HIV are understated, and it may be presumed that even the figure for death from AIDS does not take into account all deaths from AIDS-related illnesses.[90]

86 Regulation 13 of ibid.
87 Regulation 20 of ibid.
88 See the Infectious Diseases (Shipplng) Regulations 1948 (SI No. 170 of 1948), and the Infectious Diseases (Aircraft) Regulations, 1948 (SI No. 136 of 1948).
89 *Ryan v. Attorney General* [1965] IR 294. This case dealt with the compulsory fluoridation of water supplies: however, in that case, the Supreme Court held that the statutory level of fluoridation was not harmful to health. The decision might have been different if it could have been shown that there were no positive benefits to fluoridation. Also relevant are issues of personal freedom under Art 40 of the Constitution of Ireland, 1937.
90 The 1992 figures appear in National Aids Strategy Committee (1992), *Reports and Recommendations of the Sub-Committees of the National Strategy Committee* (Department of Health, Hawkins House, Dublin), pp. 7-8. The end 1993 figures are taken from *Shaping*

Though considerable public attention has been paid to the issues raised by the condition, no specific Irish legislation exists according protection to those with the virus.

The principal Irish policy recommendations, which to some degree the Government now follows, and which will probably provide the direction for future policy, have been proposed by the National AIDS Strategy Committee. This body, chaired by the then Minister for Health, at its first Committee Meeting on 20 December 1991, decided to establish Sub-Committees to examine various aspects of its brief. The four sub-committees examined respectively (1) care and management of persons with HIV/AIDS; (2) HIV/AIDS surveillance; (3) Education and prevention strategies and (4) Measures to avoid discrimination against persons with HIV/AIDS. Sub-Committees (1), (3) and (4) published their reports, and sub-committee (2) its interim report, on 13 April 1992.[91]

A full review of its recommendations is beyond the scope of this work, but four aspects of the reports deserve mention as raising issues which involve the law.

First, it was recommended that decriminalisation of homosexual acts between male adults should be given priority.[92] This was effected by s. 2 and s. 4 of the Criminal Law (Sexual Offences) Act 1993, which legalises consensual homosexual acts ('buggery' and 'gross indecency') between persons where (a) both parties are aged seventeen years or more and (b) neither party is mentally impaired, and probably, but not certainly (c) the acts are committed in private.[93]

Second, the report adverted in terms which give rise to concern about the existence of discrimination against HIV/AIDS sufferers in several areas; principally, discrimination at work, in housing, in prisons and hospitals, and by the Medical Profession.[94]

---

a healthier future: a strategy for effective healthcare in the 1990s (Department of Health, Dublin, 1994, Pn. 0658) p. 65, which includes the suggestion that the numbers of those suffering wlth HIV virus may be underestimated. The figures for June 1994 are those taken from figures released by the Department of Health and published by *Irish Medical Times* (1994), Vol. 28 No. 24, p. 3, (17 June), and the *Irish Times*, 15 June 1992.

91 Ibid.

92 Ibid., p. 84.

93 It is thought that though the 1993 Act does not specifically advert to the commission of acts in private, this requirement derives from s. 18 of the Criminal Law (Amendment) Act 1935 as amended by the Criminal Law (Rape) (Amendment) Act 1990, and the exlstence of common law offences. See T. O'Malley, *Irish Statutes Annotated*, Vol. 1993-1994, p. 20-6 (Commentary on s. 4).

94 National Aids Strategy Committee (1992) *Reports and Recommendations of the Sub-Committees of the National Strategy Committee* (Department of Health, Hawkins House, Dublin), p. 8485.

Third, the report suggests that the special needs of persons with HIV/AIDS were not being fully met by the provisions implemented by the Department of Social Welfare and the Health Boards.[95]

Fourth, the report drew attention to the fact that legislation did not enable condoms to be sold as widely as the sub-committee considered appropriate.[96] The position has been ameliorated by the Health (Family Planning) (Amendment) Act 1992, which permit the sale of condoms in all places except those specifically prohibited by the Act (where persons under the age of seventeen would be likely to obtain them, such as sports centres, primary and secondary schools, and vending machines). It could be argued that it is this part of the population that most requires protection, and that a problem still remains.[97]

In terms of education about HIV/AIDS and STD generally, some difficulties have been experienced in Ireland with the dissemination of literature relating to sexually transmitted diseases. Until a decade ago, it was thought that there was a ban on the advertisement of information about treatment of certain diseases, contained in the Indecent Advertisements Act 1889 as amended by the Censorship of Publications Act 1929. However, Schedule 2 of the Health Act 1947 specifically permits the dissemination about certain information about notifiable diseases, by providing that regulations may be made concerning:

> 21. The giving to the public of information and advice with respect to infectious disease by advertisements, notices, pamphlets, lectures, radio, cinema exhibitions or by any other means.

It is open to debate how efficient these provisions are in the Irish context.[98]

Though the issue has not arisen in Ireland, it should be noted that health

---

95 Ibid.

96 Ibid. p. 68, recommendation (3). 'The legislation should be amended to allow for sale of condoms from vending machines, and also to allow for free distribution of free condoms'.

97 See Paul Ward's comments to the Act in *Irish Statutes Annotated* (Sweet & Maxwell, 1991-1992), pp. 21-01.

98 See T.J. Phillipson & R.A. Posner, *Private Choices and Public Health: The Aids Epidemic in an Economic Perspective* (Harvard University Press, Cambridge, Mass., 1993). The arguments that AIDS will reach a maximum level in the US, and then decline. This is in part attributable to the alteration of behaviour, caused by the availability of information on AIDS. In Ireland, where information levels are different, their argument would raise very worrying implications. However, Phlllipson & Posner's argument has been criticised heavily by *inter alia* W. N. Eskridge Jr. & Brian D. Weimer 'The Economic Epidemic in An AIDS perspective', *University of Chicago Law Review* (1994) Vol. 61, No. 2, pp. 733-74.

carers with HIV/AIDS might be liable to patients in respect not merely of harm caused to them, but also in respect of failure to warn the patient that the health carer in question suffers from the infection.[99]

A problem that has arisen in Ireland, though the case has not been determined, concerns the claims of certain haemophiliacs (and their surviving families) whose statement of claim alleges that they contracted HIV/AIDS as a result of medical treatment with allegedly infected blood products.

Initially, a claim in the tort of negligence was taken by certain Irish haemophiliacs before the New York Courts.[100] The claim was referred back to the Irish courts as the 'forum conveniens'. The Irish Supreme Court[101] upheld the determination of the High Court, and held that the litigation should be prosecuted in Ireland, not in New York, which was a 'forum non conveniens' for the purpose of this action.[102]

TOBACCO

In the United States, although tobacco companies have been under legal fire for years, no plaintiff has ever recovered damages from a tobacco company. However, the momentum in tobacco litigation may be starting to shift, for two reasons. First, the Food and Drug Administration announced on 25 February 1994 that it was considering regulating cigarettes, because their nicotine content could make them 'drugs'. Second, an American Broadcasting Company news programme shortly after the FDA's announcement accused the tobacco companies of manipulating nicotine levels in order to addict smokers and keep them addicted.

Two massive class action law suits were filed within weeks of the FDA announcement, involving several of the best known plaintiff's lawyers in America. The group of law firms involved in this litigation has grown to forty, each of whom has agreed to add $100,000 to a litigation war chest.[103]

Furthermore, these plaintiffs may add racketeering charges to a class

99 In *Faya v. Almarez* [1993] 329 Md 435, a patient recovered for emotional distress without an accompanying physical injury when learning that a surgeon with AIDS failed to warn the patient.

100 Though the reasons for taking such a case in the US are not fully discovered in the judgments, it should be noted that in the US the concept of 'market share liability', may apply; not, as yet, in Ireland. General issues, such as the size of awards in tort claims the US as opposed to Ireland, may be of relevance here.

101 *John Doe & Ors v. Armour Pharmaceutical Co. Inc* [1994] ILRM 416; M. Cole & D. Tomkin, 'Doe v. Armour—Forum (non) Conveniens or political decision?' (1994) *Irish Law Times*, Vol. 12, No. 11, pp. 267-71.

102 In June 1994 the authors were informed that litigation is proceeding in Ireland.

103 See C. Maclachlan, 'Tobacco Foes Force Industry Showdown', *National Law Journal*, 2 May 1994, p. A.1

action against the tobacco companies, in light of newly unearthed documents showing that tobacco companies may have known for decades that nicotine is addictive. Specifically, Brown and Williamson Tobacco Corp, against whom a suit was filed in New Orleans on 29 March 1994, may, it is alleged, have known of the addictive nature of nicotine, although this allegation is denied.

Allegedly incriminating documents will be sought by the plaintiffs in discovery. These will decide whether suit should be amended to add charges under the Racketeer Influenced and Corrupt Organisations Act, which permits treble damages. RICO, as it is known, is a particularly powerful piece of legislation, and has been used extensively to fight organised crime. The tobacco industry already faces a federal racketeering suit in San Diego, seeking $9 billion (nine thousand million dollars) in damages over nicotine.[104] It is probably only a matter of time before the same issue falls to be decided before the Irish courts.

In Ireland there is very little control over tobacco. The principal legislation is to be found in the Tobacco (Health Promotion and Protection) Act 1988. This provides for the prohibition and restriction on the consumption of tobacco products in designated areas and facilities. It provides for restrictions on the sale of tobacco products to children under the age of sixteen. The Act also restricts the sale of cigarettes in packets of less than ten. A method of control of additives in tobacco products is provided for. The importation, manufacture and sale of oral smokeless tobacco products is prohibited. In addition the Act amends the law in relation to the control of advertising, sponsorship and promotion of tobacco products.

S. 2 of the Act empowers the Minister for Health to make regulations restricting or prohibiting the consumption of tobacco products in any facility, place or building in the State.

To date, the Minister has issued the Tobacco (Health Promotion and Protection) Regulations 1990, in exercise of the powers conferred on him by s. 2 of the 1988 Act. The effect of the Regulations is to prohibit and/or restrict the consumption of tobacco in various designated areas and facilities. Such designated areas are listed in Part 1 of the First Schedule to the Regulations, and include: public areas in all buildings owned by or in the occupation of the State or a body established by or under an Act of the Oireachtas, any part of a primary or secondary school (except in facilities which are specifically provided for staff who smoke), in the buildings of third level educational institutions (except in licensed premises in such institutions, specific facilities provided for staff or students who smoke or

---

104 See C. Maclachlan, 'Plaintiffs See Civil RICO Suit Tobacco Documents', *National Law Journal*, 23 May 1994, p. A1.

in the smoking areas of restaurants) canteens, cafes and snack bars and licensed premises in which food is stored or prepared for human consumption, waiting rooms in bus and railway stations, indoor spectator and games areas in sports centres, the auditoria of cinemas, theatres or halls which are built for the purpose of or adapted for the holding of concerts for public entertainment, art galleries and museums which belong to the State other than staff rooms or the smoking area of restaurants, cafes, canteens and snack bars therein, and public libraries (other than staff-rooms or restaurants, canteens cafes and snack bars therein).

The designated facilities in which the consumption of tobacco products is prohibited are outlined in Part 11 of the Second Schedule to the Regulations. These include: public buses, Dublin Area Rapid Transport (DART) trains, privately owned transport vehicles used by the public which have a seating capacity for eight persons or more and which are engaged in the transport of persons for financial reward.

S. 2 of the 1988 Act makes it an offence for any person to contravene the provisions of such regulations. Such offence is punishable by a fine not exceeding one hundred pounds on summary conviction. In addition, the owner, manager or person in charge of such designated area or facility who neglects or refuses to abide by the regulations shall be guilty of an offence and shall be liable on summary conviction to a fine not exceeding five hundred pounds or to imprisonment for a term not exceeding six months or both.

S. 3 of the 1988 Act provides that those who sell any tobacco product to a person under the age of sixteen years or to any one acting on behalf of someone under sixteen shall be guilty of an offence and shall be liable on summary conviction to a fine not exceeding five hundred pounds.

S. 4 provides that any person who sells cigarettes otherwise than in packets of ten or more shall be guilty of an offence and shall be liable on summary conviction to a fine not exceeding five hundred pounds.

In addition, s. 5 of the Act gives the Minister for Health power to determine what additives are used in tobacco products and to prohibit specific additives. S. 6 bans the importation, manufacture or sale of oral smokeless tobacco products.[105]

The Tobacco Products (Control of Advertising Sponsorship and Sales Promotion) Regulations 1991 control the promotion of tobacco products by means of advertising, sponsorship and certain other promotional activities. The Regulations implement EC Council Directive 89/622/EEC on the

---

105   Defined as 'any product or substance, made wholly or partly from tobacco, which is intended for use, unlit, by being placed in the mouth and kept there for a period, or by being placed in the mouth and sucked or chewed'.

approximation of the laws, regulations and administrative provisions of the member states concerning the labelling of tobacco products. The effect of the Regulations is to restrict the media which may be used for tobacco advertising to newspapers, magazines, duty free zones by means of permanent signs on packages of tobacco products, and internally in premises which are points of retail sale of tobacco products; to limit the content of advertisements of tobacco products; to require that advertisements and packages of tobacco products display in rotation a number of health warnings; to require the tar and nicotine content of cigarettes to be displayed on packages; to provide for the curtailment of expenditure on advertising of tobacco products and sponsorship by tobacco companies, to limit the form which advertising associated with sponsored events may take, and to prohibit the use of coupons, gifts, cut-price offers and sales promotions in relation to tobacco products.[106]

106. For a general comment on the efficacy of these regulations see D. Thomas, 'The Doctor's Role in Cutting Down Smoking Related Deaths', *Irish Medical Times* (1994) Vol. 28, No. 5 (4 February), p. 29.

APPENDICES

APPENDIX A: IRELAND'S LEGAL SYSTEM

Ireland is an independent, sovereign, democratic, bicameral republic whose head of state is the president (An tUachtarán). The head of government is the Prime Minister (An Taoiseach). Parliament (An tOireachtas) is divided into an upper house and a lower house (Seanad and Dáil), both situated in Dublin. The Oireachtas is given the 'sole and exclusive power of making laws for the state'.[1]

The Oireachtas There are sixty members of the Seanad,[2] of which eleven are non-elected; these are appointed by the Taoiseach. Six senators are elected by the graduates of the National University of Ireland and of the University of Dublin.[3] The remaining 43 senators are not elected by a vote of the people;[4] the electors are drawn from five panels representing the following interests: cultural and educational; agricultural; labour; industrial and commercial and public administrative.

Such a system adheres to a broadly corporatist model of the state.[5]

There are 166 members of the Dáil. These members are known as Teachtaí Dála (TDs). TDs are elected in general elections, occurring at least every five years, in which citizens aged eighteen years and over are eligible to vote.[6] The method of voting is proportional representation by single transferable vote.

1 Article 15(2).
2 Article 18(1).
3 Article 18(4).
4 Article 18.7 and the Senate Electoral (Panel Members) Acts 1937-1954.
5 The inspiration for this Article (Article 18.7.1) lay in the 1931 papal encyclical, *Quadragesimo Anno*. This encyclical was issued to commemorate the 40th Anniversary of Pope Leo XIII's encyclical, *Rerum Novarum*, which dealt with social and economic questions. *Rerum Novarum* was the Roman Catholic church's attempt to deal with a rapidly modernising world. The Church sought to win back its previous position of power by providing solutions to the socio-economic problems of the time. It called for the establishment of Roman Catholic political parties and Roman Catholic Trade Unions for a minimum wage. It wanted to provide an alternative to socialism and win back followers. *Quad-ragesimo Anno* reasserted the Church's opposition to communism and socialism. While being an anti-totalitarian document, it contained references to vocationalism, i.e. co-operation between employers and workers, which bore a striking resemblance to the Fascist type corporatism of the time. De Valera was attracted by the idea of vocationalism, and in the constitutional context, this is reflected in the election of members of the Senate from Vocational Panels.

6 See the Electoral Act 1992, and the Presidential Elections Acts 1937-1986, the European Assembly Acts 1977-1986, the Referendum Acts 1942-1992, the Seanad Electoral (University Members) Acts 1937-1973, the Seanad Electoral (Panel Members) Acts 1947-1972, the Local Elections Acts 1963-1991 the Electoral Acts 1923-63 and the Prevention of Electoral Abuses Act 1923.

Constitution of Ireland 1939 The primary source of Irish law is the Irish Constitution 1937, which establishes the basic structures of the state, according specific function to the President, the Oireachtas and the courts. In addition, the Constitution contains a number of important provisions guaranteeing basic protection for fundamental human rights. These rights may be enforced through court action, and many important constitutional actions have been brought before the courts particularly since the 1960s. This era saw the development of the articulation of a modern jurisprudence of personal rights, some of which impinge on the area of medical law.[7]

Bills Bills passed by the Dáil and the Seanad require the signature of the President for their enactment into law.[8] The President has the power to refer certain bills to the Supreme Court[9] (except money bills, or bills expressed to be containing a proposal to amend the Constitution, or bills in the opinion of Government necessitated by considerations of public emergency). The Supreme Court then adjudicates on the constitutionality of the referred bill. In addition, the President may, if petitioned by at least a majority of the Seanad, and a third of the Dáil, refer bills (other than those containing a proposed amendment to the Constitution) or may decline to sign a bill until its contents are first put before the people in referendum.[10]

Legislation may be divided into (a) Acts of the Old English Parliament (pre-1707); (b) Acts of the Old Irish Parliament (1782-1800); (c) Acts of the British parliament (1707-1800); (d) Acts of the Parliament of Great Britain and Ireland (1801-1922); (e) Acts of the Parliament of the Irish Free State (1922-1937), and, (f) Acts of the Oireachtas (post-1937).

Function of the courts The courts interpret and apply statutes. As is the case in the jurisdiction of England and Wales, and in other common law jurisdictions, the courts are bound by certain recognized methods and rules of statutory interpretation, which are not fixed, but alter and evolve. For a further account of statutory interpretation in Ireland, see the sources discussed in Byrne[11] and O'Malley.[12] In interpreting statutes, Irish courts adhere to the concept of presumption of constitutionality, that is, any statute enacted after 1937 is presumed to be constitutional, because it is presumed that Parliament intended to uphold the Constitution. If a statute can be interpreted in two ways, one of which is constitutional, then the constitutional one is followed.

The Supreme Court The Supreme Court has supreme jurisdiction in cases relating to the constitutionality of legislation. The Supreme Court is the Court of Final Appeal. Of course, this statement must be read in the light of the supremacy

---

7 See generally B. Chubb, *The Politics of The Irish Constitution* (IPA, Dublin, 1991), pp. 60-78.
8 Article 13.3.1.
9 Article 26.
10 Article 27.
11 R. Byrne, *Cases and Comment on Irish Commercial Law and Legal Technique*, 2nd ed. (The Round Hall Press, Dublin, 1988).
12 T. O'Malley, *The Round Hall Guide to the Sources of Law* (The Round Hall Press, Dublin, 1993).

of the law of the EU, and to Ireland's other legal obligations under treaty law. Thus, in the case of the law of the EU, Article 29.4 of the Constitution provides that:

> [n]o provision of this Constitution invalidates laws enacted, acts done or measures adopted by the State which are necessitated by the obligations of membership of the European Union of the Communities, or prevents laws enacted, acts done or measures adopted by the European Union or by the Communities, or by institutions thereof, or by bodies competent under the Treaties establishing the communities, from having force of law in the State.[13]

The President of the Supreme Court is the Chief Justice of Ireland.

The High Court   The Constitution provides that the High Court is invested with full original jurisdiction in and power to determine all matters and questions whether of law or fact civil or criminal.[14] The High Court is said to possess 'inherent' powers which do not have to be conferred on it by legislation, because such powers are conferred on it by the Constitution.

The High Court's function of judicial review of legislation and administrative decisions is an important one. This empowers the High Court to review the validity of any act or administrative decision.

Inferior courts   Courts of limited jurisdiction are the Circuit and District courts. Judges are appointed from among the senior members of the legal profession, and are guaranteed independence in the exercise of their functions.

Precedent   The doctrine of Precedent (*stare decisis*) therefore applies, which makes the decisions of higher courts binding on those of lower status. However the Supreme Court may, in certain circumstances, depart from its previous decisions. In the case of *State (Quinn) v. Ryan*[15] the Supreme Court first stated that it must have the liberty to alter its decisions. The decision in this case applies in Constitutional actions only. In the case of *Attorney General and Minister for Defence v. Ryan's Car Hire*[16] the Supreme Court stated that Stare Decisis may be departed from for 'compelling' reasons. This rationale applies in cases of a non-constitutional nature. There are two lines of thought as to what a compelling reason is.[17] The first is that the court can refuse to follow previous decisions if such decisions are not suited to contemporary social conditions. The second view is that a compelling reason only exists if a previous decision is clearly erroneous. Where, as is frequently the case, decisions of courts of other jurisdictions are cited in argument in Irish courts, such courts may elect to follow – or to depart – from them, depending on what seems most appropriate.

13 Art 34.4, as discussed in *Meagher v. Minister for Agriculture and Food, Ireland, and the Attorney General*, Supreme Court, unreported, 18 November 1993, No. 127/93. See also s. 1 of the Courts (Establishment and Constitution) Act 1961 and s. 7(1) of the Courts (Supplemental Provisions) Act 1961.

14 Article 34(3)(1). See also s. 2 of the Courts (Establishment & Constitution) Act 1961.

15 [1965] IR 70.

16 [1965] IR 642.

17 For a discussion on this aspect of the law see R. Byrne & J.P. McCutcheon, *The Irish Legal System*, 2nd ed. (Butterworth, Dublin, 1989), p. 121.

In the context of medical law, where no major specific legislative differences exist between Ireland and England or Scotland, Irish courts have adopted the reasoning set out in many of these decisions. However, in questions of abortion, for example, where the Irish Constitution contains a specific provision guaranteeing the right to life of the unborn, there is no question of Irish courts accepting without substantial qualification, the decisions of courts of other jurisdictions.

An influential source of law has been the decisions of the House of Lords, Court of Appeal and High Court of the UK, and the superior courts of record of the United States and of Canada, particularly so in recent times. Again, as has been explained above, these decisions, though not constituting binding precedent, are persuasive.

The determinations of industrial tribunals, such as those constituted under the Unfair Dismissals Act 1977, give assistance to the understanding of the workings of statutorily-imposed duties, and though such determinations are not of binding force, they form a valuable corpus of interpretation.

APPENDIX B: THE IRISH HEALTH SERVICES: HISTORICAL OVERVIEW

The origins of the Irish system of health care lie in private charitable institutions. In the Middle Ages such institutions as leper houses were established under the auspices of religious orders of monks and nuns. The voluntary hospitals of today are the successors of the medical charities of the eighteenth and nineteenth centuries, founded by philanthropic lay persons and religious orders of nursing sisters. In the early nineteenth century, hospitals such as St Vincent's in Dublin (1835) and the Mercy in Cork (1857) were founded by Roman Catholics, whose religious convictions tramnslated into the ethos of the institution. Likewise, in 1839, the Adelaide Hospital was established by the Protestant community, with which it is still identified. (However, all institutions provide now provide service to the community at large, employing medical and other staff without any question of religious affiliation.)

In the public sector, the Irish parliament had sanctioned the building of infirmaries for the relief of the poor in the eighteenth century. The Irish Poor Law of 1838 led to the development of one hundred and sixty three workhouses. The Poor Law required the workhouses to provide an infirmary and medical officer for the use of the poor. These institutions were funded by the Poor Rate, a levy on property. The infirmaries in these institutions were to become the basis for the county, district and geriatric hospitals of today. The dispensary service was established in 1851. Under this system, general practitioners received a salary for treating the poor. In addition, such practitioners treated private patients who paid for the doctor's services. The dispensary system remained substantially intact until its replacement by the General Medical Service (GMS) in 1972. Though major changes were introduced, the dispensary doctor service still exists, and in 1993 a total of 274 dispensing doctors were working in Ireland, providing services to approximately 100,000 patients, according to figures from the GMS (Payments) Board. The South Eastern Health Board has the greatest number of dispensing doctors, with 54, followed by the Western Health Board, with 48, and the North

Western Health Board, 43. There are just two dispensing doctors in the Eastern Health Board whose remit covers Dublin.[1]

The psychiatric services have their origin in the eighteenth century with the establishment of St Patrick's in 1757, the first private mental hospital in Ireland, and one of the first purpose-built mental hospitals in the world. The first publicly funded institution which took in mentally-ill patients was the Dublin House of Industry, from which developed the House of Industry Hospitals – the Richmond, Whitworth and Hardwicke and the Richmond Lunatic Asylum. Such asylums focused more on the detention of patients for their own protection and for the protection of society. In 1945 the Mental Treatment Act provided for temporary and voluntary admissions and for the establishment of out-patient clinics. The development of the private-public dichotomy occurred also in the voluntary hospital sector. Private hospitals began to be constructed near the public hospitals. The private patients were charged for treatment. Thus class origin became a basis for medical treatment in addition to one's medical condition. In 1909, a Minority Report of the Royal Commission on the Poor Law concluded that 'the function of preventing and treating disease among destitute persons cannot in practice, be distinguished from the prevention and treatment of disease in the other persons'.[2]

The public/private mix   The particular history of the Irish health care system has led to a unique combination of public and private provision of health care services.

There are three distinct types of hospitals categorised in terms of funding and management:

(a) *The Health Board hospitals*   Under Part III of the Health Act 1970, the responsibility for the provision and maintenance of hospitals, sanatoriums, homes, laboratories, clinics or health care centres lies with the Health Boards. The Health Boards set up by this Act replaced the old local government system. They regulate the administration of the health care system on a regional basis. The membership of the Health Boards is made up of in part of public representatives (members of county councils in the boards' functional areas) who form a majority of the membership. The other places are filled by elected representatives of the main health professions and a small number of members appointed by the Minister. These hospitals are managed by the Health Board and funding is sought from the allocation of funds granted to each Health Board by the Department of Health.

The group of hospitals administered by the Health Boards is made up of regional hospitals, county hospitals, district hospitals, fever hospitals and orthopaedic hospitals. They are financed by the Health Board budgets. The regional hospitals have specialised units not found in most county hospitals and are well staffed with consultants. The average county hospital provides general medical and surgical care and maternity services. The district hospitals are small hospitals with facilities for medical care and minor surgery and in some cases for obstetrics. They are staffed by general practitioners. In 1991, *Health Statistics* itemised nine regional hospitals,

1   Source: *Irish Medical News* (1993), Vol. 10, No. 28 (19 July), p. 11.
2   Quoted in W.P. Tormey, 'Two-Speed Public and Private Medical Practitioners in the Republic of Ireland', *Administration*, Vol. 40, No. 4 (Winter, 1992-3), 371 at p. 372.

most being teaching hospitals.[3] The County hospitals originally were staffed by one Consultant physician, one Consultant surgeon and were historically under-resourced. However, Hensey[4] notes the increase in numbers treated and in the numbers of additional consultant staff appointed. The district hospitals were smaller than County hospitals, with correspondingly reduced facilities for medical care, minor surgery, and in some cases, for obstetrics. These are staffed by General practitioners. Hensey notes that many of these hospitals have become long-stay institutions for chronic conditions. There are four fever hospitals, one each in Dublin, Cork, Galway and Killarney and three orthopaedic hospitals in Counties Limerick, Meath, Kilkenny.

The Hospitals Board (Comhairle na nOspidéal) was established under s. 41 of the Health Act 1970. Its first function is to advises the Minister for Health with respect to the work of hospitals in the context of general medical care. Secondly, its statutory executive role regulates the numbers and types of Consultant appointments in hospitals taking patients under the Health Acts and specifying qualifications for the appointments of Consultants.

The Hospitals Board consists of 27 members, of whom at least 14 must be registered medical practitioners, engaged in a Consultant capacity in the provision of hospital services. The other appointees come from either the Department of Health, the voluntary hospitals and the Health Boards. Sub-committees of the Board have been set up for enquiries that need more detail. Through the use of these sub-committees the Board is able to get through more work that otherwise would have been too time consuming. This time and resource efficiency leads to increased productivity and output.

(b) *The Public Voluntary hospitals*   The Irish voluntary hospital movement had its origins in the early decades of the eighteenth century. Philanthropic individuals, moved by the conditions of the sick poor, voluntarily took on themselves the task of establishing and running hospitals and raising money for them. The development of the Irish voluntary hospital was almost entirely confined to the city areas, particularly to Dublin. Many of the voluntary hospitals still exist, although they have now been joined by the Health Board hospitals. These hospitals are almost wholly subsidised by the Department of Health. Some of these bodies were set up by statute, others were set up as companies under the Companies Acts and many of the more recently constituted bodies have been set up by Ministerial Order under the Health (Corporate Bodies) Act 1961, which empowers the Minister to set up corporate bodies to administer a component of the health service.

The voluntary public hospitals may be divided into four categories – general teaching hospitals, general non-teaching hospitals, cottage hospitals and special hospitals.

It should be noted that the voluntary hospital sector received £30,000,000 from the VHI in respect of treatment of private patients in the financial year ending 1993.[5]

3   Planning Unit, Department of Health, *Health Statistics* (Stationery Office, Dublin, 1992).
4   B. Hensey, *The Health Services of Ireland*, 4th ed. (IPA, Dublin, 1988, repr. 1990), p. 118.
5   *Irish Medical Times* (1994), Vol. 28, No. 1, p. 7 (7 January).

(c) *Private hospitals* Most of the private general hospitals are managed by religious orders. They are financed by charges made on patients which in the majority of cases are made by the Voluntary Health Insurance Board's schemes. Some contributions towards their costs are met by the Health Boards. Eight of the seventeen private hospitals are in Dublin.

Within the last ten years, private hospitals with or without consultant clinics attached, owned by groups of consultants or run and managed by entrepreneurs have been established in Cork and Dublin.

(d) *Nursing homes* The Health (Nursing Homes) Act 1990, which came into force in September 1993, provides that nursing homes must be registered with the local Health Board.[6] The Health Board may refuse or terminate registration. Under the Act the Minister for Health is given power to make regulations to ensure proper standards in nursing homes.

S. 2 of the Act defines a 'nursing home' as 'an institution for the care and maintenance of more than two dependent persons'. For the purposes of the Act a 'dependent person' is defined as 'a person who requires assistance with the activities of daily living such as dressing, eating, walking, washing and bathing' as a result of physical infirmity, injury, defect or disease or mental infirmity.

S. 4 of the Act requires each Health Board to establish and maintain a register of nursing homes. Those who wish to set up such nursing homes must apply to the Health Board for registration. A Health Board may refuse such application if the home does not comply with the regulations under s. 6 of the Act, if the applicant or registered proprietor of the home or the person in charge of it has been convicted of an offence under the Act or under the Health (Homes for Incapacitated Persons) Act 1964 or of any other offence that may render such person unfit to operate a nursing home.

The Health Board may attach conditions to a registration. An appeal lies against the Health Board's decision in relation to such conditions. Section 5(£1) allows an applicant to appeal these conditions to the District Court. In addition it provides for an appeal to the District Court in respect of a refusal by the Health Board to register the home. Such appeal must be brought within 21 days from notification of the Health Board's decision.

S. 6 requires the making by the Minister for Health of regulations in relation to the standards to be observed in nursing homes. Such regulations may relate to such areas as the numbers and qualifications of staff, design, ventilation, washing and sanitary facilities, food provided for dependent persons, records, insurance, inspection of the premises. A person who refuses/fails to comply with such regulations shall be guilty of an offence. Section 6(4) allows the Circuit Court to disqualify a person convicted of an offence under s. 6 from managing a nursing home.

S. 9 allows a Health Board to manage a home if it is of the opinion that such home is being run in contravention of the regulations under s. 6.

S. 10 allows the Health Board to board out a person in a private dwelling, with that person's consent. Section 10 relates to persons who require a lesser degree of

6   For a survey of some of the financial and other aspects of the new legislation see *Irish Medical Times* (1993), Vol. 27, No. 44 (29 October), pp. 14-15.

care than 'dependent persons' as defined in the Act and whose interests can be served by living with another person in that person's private dwelling.

S. 11 provides that a person guilty of an offence under the Act shall be liable on summary conviction to a fine not exceeding £1,000 or to imprisonment for not more than three months or both. On conviction or indictment of an offence under s. 3 (operating an unregistered home), a person guilty of an offence shall be liable to a fine not exceeding £50,000 or to imprisonment for a term not exceeding two years or both.

APPENDIX C: GENERAL HISTORY OF THE MEDICAL PROFESSION IN IRELAND

The profession, since its earliest phase, has been divided internally between physicians and surgeons. Originally, those who wished to become physicians first took a university arts course and then pursued further studies in medicine. On completion of these studies, the student obtained a licence to practise from the university. Due to the fact that the medieval university was under the influence of the Church, there was a close connection between the medical profession and the Church. As students of the university, medical students in the medieval period were made clerks within the Church. Due to the political exigencies of the time, many physicians took orders in order to gain advancement in their chosen profession as promotion was gauged in terms of ranking within the ecclesiastical hierarchy.

However, surgery was not studied in the medieval university. As a result the medieval surgeon was not a university graduate and was looked upon differently from the physician. Surgeons in their early incarnation exemplify the oligarchic patronage model discussed earlier as their status in society was often attributed to their being accorded the patronage of royalty. Thus, as Carr-Saunders and Wilson[1] have noted: 'some of them, however, attained a high status, and when Henry V went to France, on the campaign which led to Agincourt, he took with him, as physician, Nicolas Colnet, and as surgeon Thomas Morstede, for each of whom were provided an equivalent guard and equal pay. In London these outstanding surgeons obtained ordinances and were recognized as constituting a separate mystery in 1353'.[2]

The surgeons were not to enjoy such high status for all of their history. In the fifteenth century, the guild of surgeons in England came to an arrangement with the guild of barbers and formed the guild of Barber-Surgeons in 1540. The barbers had obtained a charter in 1461 and carried out similar activities to the surgeons including healing and curing wounds and pulling teeth. However, in social terms they were not highly regarded due to the presence among their numbers of untrained individuals who inflicted severe injury on many a hapless patient. As a result of the amalgamation of the two guilds, surgery was regarded more as a trade than as a profession.

The Royal Colleges of Physicians, on the other hand, was granted a charter by

1   A.M. Carr-Saunders & P.A. Wilson, *The Professions*, 2nd impr. (Frank Cass & Co., London, 1964).
2   Ibid., pp. 68-9.

Henry VIII in 1518. Subsequently, an Act of 1522, provided that it was 'expedient and necessary to provide that no person . . . be suffered to exercise and practise physic but only those persons that be profound, sad and discreet, groundedly learned, and deeply studied in physic'.[3]

In addition to physicians and surgeons, there also existed the apothecaries. The apothecaries had their origins in the grocers guild. The grocers were awarded a charter in 1428. In 1616, the apothecaries obtained a charter of their own whereby only they were entitled to dispense drugs. The apothecaries and the Royal College of Physicians often came into conflict over their respective functions. The physicians saw the apothecaries as usurping the functions traditionally carried out by the physicians' profession. In 1703, this led to the House of Lords making a ruling on the issue in the case of *Rose v. Royal College of Physicians* ;[4] it was held that the function of the apothecary included directing and ordering the remedies to be employed in the treatment of disease and were not confined to merely dispensing medicines. The Society thenceforward took on the role of a lesser form of physician.

Meanwhile, the fortunes of the surgeons were beginning to witness an upturn. An Act of 1745 provided for the dissolution of the union between the surgeons and the barbers. This led to the founding of the Company of Surgeons. The Company of Surgeons lost its charter in 1796. However, a new charter was obtained in 1800 leading to the incorporation of the Royal College of Surgeons in London.

Nonetheless, the situation was far from satisfactory. The profession was internally divided, with the physicians occupying the superior position in the internal ranking. In addition there was a preponderance of licensing authorities in the United Kingdom. According to one estimate,[5] there existed eighteen separate licensing authorities in the United Kingdom in 1800. Thus, reform was urgently needed in order to establish a clearly defined and cohesive profession. As a result of calls for reform a number of select committees on the medical profession were established in the first half of the nineteenth century. The *Report of the Select Committee on Medical Education* was published in 1834. This led to various unsuccessful attempts at introducing legislation on the issue. In 1847 the *Report of the Select Committee on Medical Registration* appeared leading to the introduction of further bills on the subject of medical reform. It was not until 1858 that one of these bills proved successful, leading to the introduction of the Medical Act of 1858. The Act was a compromise solution. Instead of dissolving the disparate licensing bodies, and creating a single licensing authority, it created a controlling authority which would govern the existing licensing authorities. The Act provided for the establishment of the General Council of Medical Education and Registration of the United Kingdom. It also provided for the establishment of a register of medical practitioners. This allowed for a certain amount of control over entry to the profession and also allowed for the removal of practitioners for 'infamous conduct in any professional Respect' or on the grounds of having been convicted of a felony or misdemeanour, crime or offence.[7] However, the Act did provide the basis for a central registration, education and disciplinary body for the medical profession.

3   14 & 15 Hen. VIII, c.5.

4   (1703) 5 Bro Parl Cas 553. See A.M. Carr-Saunders & P.A. Wilson, op. cit., p. 73.

5   Ibid., p. 77.

6   Medical Practitioners Act 1858, 21 & 22 Vict. c.90, clause XXIX.

7   Id.

The organisation of the medical profession in Ireland

Training Medical education in Ireland has followed a pattern broadly similar to that in the United Kingdom and in Western Europe. Historically, there was a distinction between the education and training of physicians and of surgeons. The physicians have had a university training scheme in Ireland since the seventeenth century. On the other hand the practice of surgery started as an offshoot of the trade of barbers and until the modern medical instruction system commenced, their training was by practice. Today the historical differences are meaningless, at least in terms of practice.

Physicians Prior to the nineteenth century, the story of medical education in Ireland is a complex one. We do not deal with this topic here, interested readers are referred to specialist works.[8]

It appears as if the most important training of physicians was conducted by the Royal College of Physicians, and Trinity College Dublin.[9] Though Fleetwood notes that about 1627, it appears as if Trinity were empowered to give courses leading to medical degrees,[10] it is really with John Stearne (1624-69) that formal medical education was implemented by Trinity.[11] It is apparent that Stearne founded the 'President and Fraternity of Physicians' in 1654, and that this body was the precursor of the Royal College of Physicians. This body was initially sited at Trinity Hall, owned by Trinity College, and then given to Stearne, on the understanding that he would incorporate the President and Fraternity of Physicians, and presumably, regulate medical education. In 1667 Charles II granted the first charter of incorporation to 'The President & Fellows of the College of Physicians'. Stearne was nominated as president for life. After his death, presidents were to be elected by the Provost, Fellows and Scholars of Trinity, subject to the approval of the viceroy. From about 1670, the College of Physicians appears to have conducted systematic work, and maintained a relationship with Trinity College Dublin, interrupted from time to time by various academic quarrels.[12]

Medical education in Trinity College appears to have been placed on a more formal footing in the early seventeen-hundreds, and in 1711, a building was opened which was the precursor of the School of Physic. At this stage, Trinity College was, as it still is, the sole constituent college of the University of Dublin; it currently provides undergraduate and postgraduate medical education.

In the nineteenth century, in the wake of political reform and the enfranchisement of the native Catholic population by the English authorities, a school of medicine was established as part of the Royal University of Ireland. This body was succeeded by the National University of Ireland, incorporated by Act of Parliament in 1908, and its constituent colleges at University College Dublin and University College Cork and University College Galway currently provide undergraduate and postgraduate medical programmes.

With the passing of the Apothecaries Act 1815, the Society of Apothecaries in

---

8   See J.F. Fleetwood, *The History of*   10   Ibid., p. 32.
    Medicine in Ireland (Skellig Press, Dub-   11   Ibid., p. 33.
    lin, 1983), and reference therein.   12   Ibid., p. 39.
9   Fleetwood, op. cit., ch. 5.

England was empowered to license after examination all apothecaries in England and Wales. In Ireland similar rules obtained; an Irish foundation known as the Apothecaries Hall conducted lectures, directed an apprenticeship scheme and authorised a form of clinical training broadly similar to the medical education for undergraduates which was available through universities. Though this body ceased training doctors thirty years ago, it is not uncommon to find reference to practitioners who qualified through it. In fact the foundation still exists, though its main connection with the profession is funding an annual prize.

The Royal College of Physicians of Ireland was founded as a Fraternity of Physicians in 1654. In 1667, it received a charter from Charles II, though its current name dates from 1890. The original charter was supplemented in 1692. This body was entitled from 1692 to give a licence to practise medicine in Dublin and within seven miles around, and had the power to fine unlicensed practitioners. Originally the first Fellows were limited to fourteen in number who had to be members of the Established Church and graduates of the Universities of Oxford, Cambridge or Dublin.

This body administers an examination with the Royal College of Surgeons in Ireland (known as the Irish Conjoint) by which undergraduates who pass these exams after taking an undergraduate programme in the Royal College of Surgeons may acquire degrees. The Royal College of Physicians in Ireland also administers a two-part post graduate professional examination for admission to membership, which equates with the membership of the English Royal College and is regarded as a qualification exam. for any post as consultant physician. The Fellows are no longer limited to the original fourteen, nor do the other former criteria for fellowship obtain. In fact there are approximately 150 Fellows today selected from the members on grounds of merit or distinction as clinicians or researchers. Today the College conducts a wide-ranging postgraduate professional teaching and research programme, and its examinations are taken in certain centres in Asia. The College also conducts training and examination for a number of Diplomas in particular specialties.

Surgeons The Royal College of Surgeons in Ireland had its origins in a fraternity or guild of barbers which is thought to have existed as far back as the fifteenth century and which was accorded a charter in 1577. The union between barbers and surgeons was finally broken by the establishment of the College in more or less its present form by charter of George III in 1784. The College now has a thriving undergraduate and postgraduate school of medicine which, in addition to administering the courses and examinations for the undergraduate conjoint examination, also conducts and holds examinations in higher surgical qualifications. Most of the undergraduate students come from abroad to study.

Undergraduate education There are currently five undergraduate medical schools in Ireland, and the 1994 intake is approximately three hundred and twenty school leavers.[13] The Royal College of Surgeons (affiliated to the National University of Ireland and to the Royal College of Physicians in Ireland) issues undergraduate qualifications conferred by the National University of Ireland, and postgraduate qualifications conferred either jointly with the Royal College of Physicians, under

13 *Irish Medical Times* (1994), Vol. 28, No. 34, p. 1.

the aegis of its affiliation with the National University of Ireland, or in some circumstances, alone; Dublin University (Trinity College), and the University Colleges in Dublin, Cork and Galway. Apart from the College of Surgeons, these medical schools are dependent mainly on state finance and EU grants.[14] The Higher Education Authority is statutorily entrusted with the grant of state finance.

Under the Medical Practitioners Act 1978 the Medical Council is specifically responsible through its education and training committee for ensuring the suitability of the undergraduate education provided within the state, the facilities for the 'intern year' and the standards of postgraduate education. S. 35 of the 1978 Act states that it shall be the duty of the Council from time to time to satisfy itself '(a) as to the suitability of the medical education and training provided by any body in the state recognised by the Council for such purposes, (b) as to the standards of theoretical and practical knowledge required for primary qualifications, (c) as to the clinical training and experience required for the granting of a certificate of experience.

The Act provides a sanction. Only those holding qualifications recognised by the Council entitle any person to be entered in the Register of doctors. Thus a graduate of a non-approved institution can not acquire a licence to practise medicine. In this way, the Medical Council has overall control of the structure of medical education, since it can withdraw or accord recognition. The Council is of course conscious of the necessity of maintaining academic freedom and the autonomy of each medical school.

Each medical school has a broadly similar curriculum and regime: five years pre-clinical and clinical education and a year spent as an intern acquiring further experience. Within this broad pattern the curriculum in each medical school may vary in certain details. The process of evolution of the undergraduate curriculum may be noted by referring to the discussion of medical education in Ch. 4 of *The Report of the Working Party on the General Medical Service*,[15] but further elaboration is outside the scope of this work.

In 1987 the Medical Council carried out an exploratory survey of the five medical schools for which it had statutory responsibility and it has produced a short ten page statement on some aspects of medical education.

At the moment, admission to the medical schools other than the College of Surgeons, is by the results of the Leaving Certificate examination, which enables the universities through a central admissions body to award places on a points system. Entrance to the College of Surgeons is by direct application.

Postgraduate education Although once a doctor has obtained a degree from a recognised body, and has undergone the compulsory year of residence, and is placed on the Register, that doctor is entitled legally to practise medicine without any

---

14 A total of 349 Irish students were offered places in the five medical schools in the academic year 1992-1993. 309 of these places were to University College Dublin, Trinity College Dublin, University College Cork and University College Galway. 241 of these offers were made to students who expressed medicine as their first choice. There were 6392 applicants for these places. The Royal College of Surgeons had an intake of 160 of which 40 were Irish students.

15 Government Publications Office, Dublin, 1984 (Pl. 2531).

restriction, in fact, postgraduate educational or research qualifications are needed to ensure eligibility to one or other specialism, and to general practice.

Under the Medical Practitioners Act, the Council is bound to maintain a general register and also a register of medical specialists. In order to be registered in the latter register it is necessary to acquire specialist qualifications and experience in one of the recognised areas. In 1989 these included the following:

Anaesthetics, Cardiology, Child and Adolescent Psychiatry, Clinical Pharmacology and Therapeutics, General Surgery, Neurological Surgery, Ophthalmology, Orthopaedic Surgery, Otolaryngology, Paediatric Surgery, Plastic Surgery, Microbiology, Morbid Anatomy and Histopathology, Occupational Medicine, Paediatrics, Radiotherapy, Communicable Diseases, Community Medicine, Dermatology, Endocrinology and Diabetes Mellitus, Gastroenterology, General (Internal) Medicine, General Practice, Geriatrics, Thoracic Surgery, Urology, Haematology, Psychiatry, Diagnostic Radiology, Respiratory Medicine, Rheumatology, Tropical Medicine, Venereology, Obstetrics and Gynaecology, Chemical Pathology, Clinical Immunology, Nephrology, Neurology.

The qualifications that are recognised are of two sorts, first University degrees and diplomas such as MD, MCh, and secondly higher professional qualification such as Membership of the Royal College of Physicians, Fellowship of the Royal College of Surgeons and the like.

Under s. 35 of the Medical Practitioners Act 1978, the Medical Council has a duty to satisfy itself as to the suitability of undergraduate medical education and training provided by recognised medical schools, and as to the standard of theoretical and practical knowledge required at the examinations for primary qualification. It must also satisfy itself as to the clinical training and experience required for the granting of a certificate of experience, and the adequacy and suitability of postgraduate education and training. In all cases the council must see that the minimum standards specified in the relevant EC/EU Directives are satisfied.

Title III Article 23 of Council Directive 93/16/EEC of 5 April 1993 specifies that during the period of the doctor's training, the doctor must have acquired:

(a) adequate knowledge of the sciences on which medicine is based and a good understanding of the scientific methods including the principles of measuring biological functions, the evaluation of scientifically established facts and the analysis of data,

(b) sufficient understanding of the structure, functions and behaviour of healthy and sick persons, as well as reactions between the state of health and physical and social surroundings of the human being;

(c) adequate knowledge of clinical discipline and practices providing him with a coherent picture of mental and physical diseases, of medicine from the points of view of prophylaxis, diagnosis and therapy and of human reproduction.

(d) suitable clinical experience in hospitals under appropriate supervision.

A complete period of medical training of this kind shall comprise at least a six-year course or five thousand five hundred hours of theoretical and practical instruction given in a university or under the supervision of a university.

APPENDIX D: OTHER HEALTH CARE PROVIDERS

Traditionally, the doctor has been regarded as the principal health carer in Ireland. In demotic usage, the term 'doctor' covers surgeons, anaesthetists, physicians, specialists, and indeed dentists, but seldom, if ever, nurses, midwives, social workers, or radiographers. It thus is taken to refer to the whole range of 'registered medical practitioners', and it is in this sense that we use the term.

We here review briefly those other professional people who are involved in health care, either alone, or as members of a team.

Pharmacists The practice of pharmacy is regulated by the Pharmacy Acts. These Acts comprise of a series of measures commencing with the Pharmacy Act (Ireland) 1875, and include amendments contained in the Misuse of Drugs Act 1977. Regulations made by the Council of the Pharmaceutical Society of Ireland require the approval of the Minister for Health to become effective.

No person may practise pharmacy unless he is a registered pharmaceutical chemist, a registered dispensing chemist and druggist, or a registered medical practitioner who, before the commencement of the Act, began a course of study to be gone through for the purpose of obtaining a qualifying diploma for pharmacy, or a corresponding qualification awarded outside the State.

The Pharmacy Act 1962 provides that it is an offence to take or use the name or title of pharmaceutical chemist, dispensing chemist and druggist, registered druggist or to use any title implying that he is a registered pharmacist, unless he is in fact registered. It is also illegal to use the description of pharmacy, medical stores, drug stores, drug hall, medical supply stores or chemist in connection with any business involved in the retail of drugs or poisons, if the person involved in the selling, dispensing or compounding of Drugs or poisons possesses the requisite qualification.

The Pharmaceutical Society of Ireland was established in 1875, to regulate the qualification of pharmaceutical chemist. Under s. 4(1) of the Pharmacy Act 1962, the Council of the Society of Pharmacists is empowered to provide or make provision for the courses of training and examinations to be taken by candidates for registration on the Register of Pharmacists. The Council may determine the manner in which the conditions under which training shall be provided. The Council can regulate the criteria for accepting lecturers, teachers and examiners, for the conditions of admission to the examinations and for the granting of certificates to persons taking the courses and passing the examinations.

In order to practise as a pharmacist in Ireland, one has to be registered on the Register of Pharmaceutical Chemists. A student who has passed the final examination for the degree of Bachelor of Science (Pharmacy) must devote one year to practical training, under the direct personal supervision of a pharmacist as his sole pupil, in either a community pharmacy, a pharmaceutical department of a hospital, a pharmaceutical science department in a university or a manufacturing pharmaceutical establishment. Every person who is examined and certified by the examiners to be qualified to act as a pharmaceutical chemist is entitled to be registered as a pharmaceutical chemist.

Apart from the statutory duties, pharmacists are subject to a separate standard of professional behaviour, or code of ethics, as endorsed by themselves. Whereas the State through its various agencies will enforce legislation, it is considered to be a matter for the profession itself to ensure compliance with its own ethical code. The Pharmaceutical Society of Ireland has issued many statements of guidance over the years on a wide range of topics, but current legislation does not confer on the Society any authority for dealing with errant pharmacists whose professional behaviour falls below an acceptable standard. Applications to the Fitness to Practice Committee under the Medical Practitioners Act does not apply to pharmacy. Weedle and Cahill[1] comment that it is desirable for this lacuna to be filled by new pharmaceutical legislation. To be truly effective, a written code of ethics would need to be formally approved by the entire membership and updated periodically.

In Ireland, attempts to separate the practice of pharmacy from medicine began early in the seventeenth century.[2] Prior to this, it would appear as if medicine and surgery was practised at different levels. First, there were the recognized physicians and surgeons (such as O'Glacan and O'Connor, whose careers are described by Fleetwood) who had university qualifications.[3] Second, there were 'Surgeons and Physicians General to the Army in Ireland', who were responsible for the health of the armies in Ireland.[4] Third, there were some physicians and surgeons who dealt with the public, both in Dublin and in the provinces.[5] However, most ordinary people would have been treated by barber surgeons and apothecaries. In 1692, the Royal College of Physicians were issued with a Charter which entitled them to examine all who wished to become apothecaries' apprentices. In 1695, the Corporation of Barber Surgeons and Apothecaries, who proposed to object to the Royal College of Physicians' attempt to have the Charter ratified, counter-petitioned, claiming, amongst other things that any restriction on the administration of internal medicines would impinge on the accepted practices of surgeons and apothecaries, thus depriving the poor 'who could afford only the services of an apothecary or surgeon instead of the more expensive physician'.[6] From this it may be inferred that the poor dealt mainly with apothecaries, the third category of 'health care provider' at that time. Weedle & Cahill note that '[t]he College of Physicians did not concede to the apothecaries the right to practise medicine, but, because of lack of power, were not able to control them'.[7]

In 1741 it was proposed[8] that a separate category of trained persons should be created to make and sell medicines and to compound and dispense prescriptions and also that apothecaries should not be entitled to prescribe for the sick, except in cases of emergency, and suggested restrictions on the sale of potent substances. This proposal did not result in an immediate change in the law.

Although the Apothecaries Act, 1791 provided for the regulation of the profession of pharmacy,[9] it was not until the Pharmacy Act (Ireland) 1875, that the

1   P.B. Weedle & M.J. Cahill, *Medicines and Pharmacy Law in Ireland* (Kenlis Publications, Dublin, 1991).
2   Weedle & Cahill, op. cit., p. 15.
3   J. Fleetwood, *The History of Medicine in Ireland*, op. cit.
4   Ibid., p. 53.
5   Ibid., p. 55-7.
6   Ibid., p. 82-3.

7   See Weedle & Cahill, op. cit., p. 15.
8   Weedle & Cahill, op. cit., p. 15.
9   'In April 1838, the College of Surgeons charged the apothecaries as a whole with neglect of their business. Their main charges were that apothecaries had become medical practitioners instead of compounders: that shops in charge of unqualified persons 'and even women';

considerable separation between pharmacy and medicine was achieved. In the interim period, there were various suggestions that the division between what we would now call pharmacy and medicine was not clear-cut.[10]

The 1875 Act established the Pharmaceutical Society of Ireland and provided for a Council to manage the affairs of the Society. As of June 1994, a new Pharmacy Bill is in preparation.

Dentists The practice of dentistry is regulated by the Dentists Act 1985. This Act provides for the establishment of the Dental Council (An Chomhairle Fiacloireachta) which provides for the registration and control of persons engaged in the practice of dentistry.

The Dental Council's functions *vis-à-vis* dentists and dentistry are similar to those of the Medical Council relating to medical practitioners.

The general concern of the Dental Council is to promote high standards of professional education and professional conduct among dentists. The Council is empowered by the Act to regulate its own procedure.

The Council consists of nineteen members. Two persons are nominated by University College Cork and University College Dublin, one by the Royal College of Surgeons, seven by election by fully registered dentists, two by the Medical Council, one by the Minister for Education, and four by the Minister of Health. Of the latter category, at least two shall not be registered dentists and shall, in the interests of the Minister represent the interests of the general public as consumers of dental services.

Part III of the Act provides for the registration of dentists. S. 28(1) provides that where the Council is satisfied that a person intends to be in the State temporarily for the purpose of employment in the practice of dentistry and such person holds the requisite qualification, the Council can register that person temporarily for a period of time determined by the Council not exceeding five years.

The Council has established the Register of Dental Specialists. Every person who is on this Register is entitled to practice as a dentist in Ireland. It is an offence for a person who is not a registered dentist to use the title of a registered dentist. The Act prohibits the practising of dentistry by anyone who is not a registered dentist. This prohibition does not apply to registered medical practitioners, the performance of dental work by an auxiliary dental worker or the practice of dentistry under the supervision of a registered dentist by a student of dentistry or a student of medicine or any person who is working under the supervision of a registered dentist as part of a course of instruction in order to qualify for membership of a class of auxiliary dental worker recognised by the Council.

S. 52(1) provides that a body corporate is prohibited from engaging in the practice of dentistry. The practice of dentistry by Health Boards, hospitals, dental schools or two or more registered dentists in partnership are excluded from this prohibition.

The Dental Council or any person can apply to the Fitness to Practise Committee

---

that their Medical School was an illegal one and that they had successfully prosecuted surgeons who had dispensed medicines'. Fleetwood, op. cit., p. 91-92.

10 B. Hensey, *The Health Services of Ireland*, op. cit., pp. 84-6.

for an inquiry into the fitness of a registered dentist to practise dentistry on the grounds of (a) alleged professional misconduct, or (b) alleged unfitness to engage in such practice by reason of mental or physical disability.

The procedure followed by the Fitness to Practise Committee in case of such a reference is the same as that when a reference is made concerning a medical practitioner. The Dental Council has the same powers as the Medical Council to determine whether, in the case of a guilty verdict by the Fitness to Practise Committee, the name of the person should be erased from the register or alternatively whether the name should be retained on the register but with conditions attached.

The dental services in Ireland are arranged by the Health Boards under s. 55 and s. 56 of the Health Act 1953. It is largely involved in combating the effects of existing dental decay but it is regarded as important that there should be as much concentration as possible on prevention.[11] The instruction of children in good habits of dental care and oral hygiene is, therefore, a major aim of the service. Dental health campaigns, which are conducted by the Dental Health Education Committee of the Irish Dental Association, complement the activities of Health Boards in this field.

Nurses   The statutory controlling body for the nursing profession is an Bord Altranais (the Nursing Board). An Bord Altranais provides for the registration, control and education of nurses and for other matters relating to nurses and the practice of nursing.

The present board was set up by the Nurses Act 1985. It has 29 members, seventeen of whom are elected by the profession and the other twelve are appointed by the Minister for Health (at least three of the latter group must be doctors, others are representative of management and education and two are representative of the interest of the general public). The board is financed mainly by examination, registration and retention fees payable by nurses.In *Fennessy & Ors v. Minister for Health and An Bord Altranais*,[12] two main questions arose for decision. The first was whether nurses registered under the Nurses Act 1950 could be obliged to pay further fees, having been given a receipt on their initial registration for the initial consolidated retention fee. The nurses argued that this entitled them as a matter of contract to remain on the register without time limits. It was held that there was no contractual right not to be charged further fees, and also that if the 1950 Act was amended, the nurses would have to pay such further and other sums as might be prescribed. The second question was whether the newly constituted Bord Altranais was entitled to levy an annual retention fee. In this instance it was held that under the new act, there had been a procedural flaw in the way in which the Register of Nurses had been set up and the fees fixed for registration thereon.

The main functions of the board relate to:

— the maintenance of a register of nurses;

— undergraduate training and examinations (the board itself does not provide undergraduate training but does maintain a close control on it. The board does conduct examinations itself).

---

11 [1991] 2 IR 361.
12 *C.K. v. An Bord Altranais* [1990] 2 IR 396.

— postgraduate training, which it provides itself in some instances (in particular for public health nursing);

— professional misconduct and fitness to practice;

— the operation of EC/EU directives relating to nursing.

The board has, in relation to the training of nurses and midwives, powers more direct and detailed than those which the Medical Council has for doctors. The detailed syllabus for training is laid down by the Board and the training hospitals must be approved by the board and must comply with its conditions for recognition. These conditions include provisions as to the size of the hospital, the teaching staff and the accommodation and facilities available to the student nurses.

Registration as a nurse entitles one to use the title of registered nurse and it is an offence for anyone who is not registered to sue that title or to give the impression that she or he is registered. There is, however, no prohibition on anyone practising nursing. This is not so in midwifery. Attendance on women in childbirth is restricted by law, except where urgency makes this impracticable, to registered midwives and medical practitioners (and to bona fide students). Midwives practising their profession are supervised in their work by the Health Boards.

In January 1988, the Nursing Board issued a Code of Professional Conduct for each nurse and midwife, the purpose of which is to provide a framework to assist the nurse to make professional decisions, to carry out his responsibilities, and to promote high standards of professional conduct. The code has no binding legal effect, but merely provides guidelines for the behaviour of nurses. Specific issues are considered when they arise or may be the subject of interpretative statements to be issued from time to time by An Bord.

Where nurses fail to meet the requirements laid down in the Guidelines, they can be held by the Fitness to Practise Committee to be guilty of professional misconduct. In such a case An Bord can either erase the person's name from the register or can consider retaining the name on the register on certain conditions. Appropriate action can also be taken if the Fitness to Practise Committee hold the person unfit to engage in the practice of nursing because of physical or mental disability.[13]

Patterns of health and disease have changed considerably over the years demanding concomitant changes in the health care services. Such changes are characterised by a distinct move away from the hospital as the exclusive source, custodian and provider of health care, thus creating new and broader definitions of health care. The trend towards community care and the pattern of shorter duration of hospital stay will require a move from the historical predominance of hospital based nursing practice. This will mean the reorientation of many traditions in nursing including educational preparation and the role and function of hospital nurses, community nurses and public health nurses.

Midwives   The practice of midwifery is governed by the Nurses Act 1985, the Midwives Act 1902, the Midwives Act 1918, the Midwives Act 1944, the Nurses Act 1950 (which established An Bord Altranais (The Nursing Board)), and the

---

13   An Bord Altranais, *Guidelines for Midwives* (An Bord Altranais, Dublin, 1990).

Nurses Act 1961. The Nursing Authority stipulates that the training of midwives must be of the duration of two years. This is in accordance with EC Directive 80/155/EEC of 1980 specifying that each member state should recognise the diplomas, certificates and other evidence of formal qualifications in midwifery of other member states which comply with the conditions of the regulation.

S. 57(2) of the Nurses Act 1985 provides that it is the duty of a Health Board in whose functional area a midwife is practising or proposes to practise, to exercise general supervision and control over such a midwife.

An Bord Altranais (the Nursing Board) lays down guidelines for midwives in relation to professional practice.[14] The guidelines require that the standard of practice in the delivery of midwifery care be that which is acceptable in the context of current knowledge and clinical knowledge and clinical developments. The Guidelines emphasise that in all circumstances, the safety and welfare of the mother and her baby must be of primary importance. One of the general requirements of entitlement to practise as a midwife is that the midwife lives within reasonable distance of the patient/client. The midwife or Health Board shall arrange a midwife or a registered medical practitioner to act as substitute for a midwife when one is needed. In an emergency or where the midwife detects a deviation from normal in the health of the mother and/or baby, the midwife must call to her assistance a registered medical practitioner.

A practising midwife is required to enter in a personal register all records of observations and treatment of each of her patients during pregnancy, labour and the postnatal period, in accordance with agreed Health Board format. A midwife must provide every reasonable facility for inspection of methods of practice, records, equipment, such part of her residence as may be used for professional purposes.

APPENDIX E: DOCTORS AND INTERNATIONAL AGREEMENTS

The European Union   Article 29.4.3 of the Constitution of Ireland 1937, enacted after Referendum, permitted Ireland to join the EEC. The European Communities Act 1972 as amended by the Single European Act 1992 has provided for the integration of our law with law of the European Union. The effect of this is to provide that EU law has 'the paramount force and effect of constitutional provisions': *Doyle v. An Taoiseach.*[1] From this it can be seen that EU law is one of the determining features of the Irish medical law picture. Article 129 of the Maastricht Treaty provides that the Community shall 'contribute toward ensuring a high level of human health protection by encouraging co-operation between the Member States, and if necessary, lending support to their action. Community action shall be directed towards the prevention of diseases, in particular the major health scourges, including drug addiction, by promoting research into their causes and their transmission, as well as health information and education'.

1   [1986] ILRM 693.

The European Commission has set out its proposals for a *Framework for Action in the Field of Public Health* under Article 129.[2]

Ireland's membership of the European Union has implications for the medical profession. Ireland is a member of the European Union of Medical Specialists (UEMS) which examines standards and duration of training. Founded in 1958, its role is to represent hospital consultants and medical specialists throughout Europe. The Irish Medical Organization (IMO) is the representative body for Irish consultants on the UEMS. The objective of the UEMS include the promotion of the highest standards of medical care, solidarity between member states (including the free movement of doctors) and the exchange of medical expertise.

The Advisory Committee on Medical Training was set up by the EC in 1975 to advise the European Commission on matters related to Medical Training. Specifically, its function was to ensure a comparably demanding standard of medical training in the community. It is made up of members of the medical profession, the universities, and the statutory/regulatory bodies.

The Standing Committee of Doctors (Comité Permanent: CP) was established in 1959. This is an independent organisation and the umbrella body representing all doctors in Europe. Each of the twelve members states are members as of right. Ireland is represented by the IMO.

Policy statements and recommendations are conveyed by the standing committee to the European Commission. The presidency of the CP is held by one of the twelve member states of the EU on a rotation basis and the term of office is for three years.

The CP meets at least three times each year. At present there are four main sub-committees of the CP, which meet to up-date, amend or finalize documents being studied by them. The sub-committees are (1) professional training, continuing medical education and medical audit committee, (2) preventative medicine and environment committee, (3) medical ethics and code committee and (4) health care and social security, health economics and the pharmaceutical industry Committee.[3]

Ireland's membership of the EU has resulted in mutual entitlement of member state citizens to reciprocal access to social services. So where a person is covered by a social security system of any EU country, and needs essential medical care, while in Ireland, the Irish health authorities have an obligation to provide it. The cost is later reimbursed by the patient's home social security system. This results in immediate aid and treatment of the ill visitor, the cost of which is paid later.

As is the case in other EU jurisdictions, governmental intervention which aims to cut down the prescribed drugs bill by, for example, insisting on the prescription of generic drugs where medically appropriate, initially gave rise to questions about the medical ethical problems involved. However, in general, where the decisions have been doctor initiated or doctor approved, there has been little opposition on medical ethical grounds.[4]

The European Convention on Human Rights   Ireland is a signatory of the *European Convention on Human Rights and Fundamental Freedoms* of 4 February

2   *Sharing a healthier future* (Department of Health, Dublin, 1994, Pn. 0658), p. 73.
3   C. Twomey, 'The Single European Act – Implications for Irish Medicine, *Irish Medical News* (1993), Vol. 10, No. 6 (15 February), p. 10.
4   *Irish Medical Times* (1991), Vol. 25, No. 35 (30 August), p. 9.

1950. This Convention certainly impinges on domestic law, but to what extent and in what manner is a moot point. Article 29.6 of the Irish Constitution states that: '[n]o international agreement shall be part of domestic law of the State save as may be determined by the Oireachtas'. Thus the rights guaranteed by the Convention are not part of Irish law. This is an example of the dualist approach to international law, whereby a state is not bound internally by the terms of any treaty unless it is expressly made a part of its domestic law. The Supreme Court expressed a view in relation to the connection between the Convention and Irish law in the case of *In re Ó Laighléis*[5] where it was stated that:

> [t]he Oireachtas has not determined that the *Convention on Human Rights and Fundamental Freedoms* is to be part of the domestic law of the State, and accordingly this Court cannot give effect to the Convention if it will be contrary to domestic law or purports to grant rights or impose obligations additional to those of domestic law. . . . The Court accordingly cannot accept the idea that the primacy of domestic legislation is displaced by the State becoming a party to the *Convention for the Protection of Human Rights and Fundamental Freedoms.*[6]

In the case of *Desmond and Dedeir v. Glackin, Minister For Industry and Commerce, Ireland & Attorney General,*[7] O'Hanlon J stated that as Ireland had ratified the European Convention, it was legitimate to assume that public policy in this country accorded with the Convention. While the Convention itself is not a code of principles which is enforceable in Irish courts, he added, this does not prevent a judgment of the European Court of Human Rights in relation to the interpretation of the Convention from having persuasive effect in Irish courts. Another effect of Ireland's accession to the Treaty may be inferred from the case of *Norris v. Ireland*[8] in which the Republic's law criminalising consensual adult homosexual acts was held to contravene the Convention. As a result, Ireland introduced the Criminal Law (Sexual Offences) Act 1993.

5 [1960] IR 93.
6 Ibid. at pp. 124-5.
7 *Irish Times Law Reports*, 17 February 1992.
8 (1989) 13 EHHR 186; [1988] Judgment of 26 October 1988 (Plenary Court) (Series A, No. 142). For a review of some of the issues in this case, see D. Tomkin, 'Homosexuality and The Law' in D.M. Clarke, *Morality and the Law* (RTE/Mercier, Cork & Dublin, 1982).

INDEX